THE PHILOSOPHY OF THE SIXTEENTH AND SEVENTEENTH CENTURIES

READINGS IN THE HISTORY OF PHILOSOPHY

SERIES EDITORS:

PAUL EDWARDS, Brooklyn College
RICHARD H. POPKIN, University of California, San Diego

The Volumes and Their Editors:

GREEK PHILOSOPHY: THALES TO ARISTOTLE
Reginald E. Allen

GREEK AND ROMAN PHILOSOPHY AFTER ARISTOTLE
Jason L. Saunders

MEDIEVAL PHILOSOPHY:
ST. AUGUSTINE TO OCKHAM
Father Allan B. Wolter

THE PHILOSOPHY OF THE SIXTEENTH AND
SEVENTEENTH CENTURIES
Richard H. Popkin

EIGHTEENTH-CENTURY PHILOSOPHY
Lewis White Beck

NINETEENTH-CENTURY PHILOSOPHY:
HEGEL TO NIETZSCHE

TWENTIETH-CENTURY PHILOSOPHY:
THE SPECULATIVE TRADITION
Peter Koestenbaum

TWENTIETH-CENTURY PHILOSOPHY:
THE ANALYTIC TRADITION
Morris Weitz

The Philosophy of the Sixteenth and Seventeenth Centuries

Edited and with an Introduction by

Richard H. Popkin

THE FREE PRESS
A Division of Macmillan Publishing Co., Inc.
New York

PHILOSOPHERS DEPICTED ON THE COVER ARE,
READING CLOCKWISE SPINOZA, ERASMUS, MONTAIGNE, DESCARTES.

Printed in the United States of America

Collier Macmillan Canada, Inc.

Library of Congress Catalog Card Number: 66-10365

printing number

15 16 17 18 19 20

To Julie, Jerry, Maggi, and Susie

ACKNOWLEDGMENTS

I wish to thank several publishers for their kindly allowing me to use the following selections in this volume: Allen & Unwin Ltd., for permission to reprint portions of Nicolas Malebranche, *Dialogues on Metaphysics and on Religion,* trans. Morris Ginsberg (London and New York, 1923); selections from Pierre Bayle: *The Historical and Critical Dictionary,* translated by Richard H. Popkin, copyright © 1965 by Richard H. Popkin, reprinted by permission of the publishers, The Bobbs-Merrill Company, Inc.; selections from *Discoveries and Opinions of Galileo* by Stillman Drake. Copyright © 1957 by Stillman Drake. Reprinted by permission of Doubleday & Company, Inc.; Encyclopaedia Britannica, Inc., for permission to reprint portions of Johannes Kepler, *The Harmonies of the World,* trans. Charles Glenn Wallis ("Great Books of the Western World," Vol. XVI; Chicago, 1959); The Macmillan Company for permission to reprint Pierre Gassendi, selections from *Dissertations in the Form of Paradoxes Against the Aristotelians* (New York, in press); Routledge and Kegan Paul, Ltd., for permission to reprint portions of Gottfried Wilhelm von Leibniz, *Theodicy,* trans. Austin Farrar (London, 1951); Selections from Leibniz, *Selections,* edited by Philip P. Wiener, reprinted with the permission of Charles Scribner's Sons. Copyright 1951, Charles Scribner's Sons.

I also wish to thank Professor Leroy E. Loemker for permission to reprint his translation of Leibniz's letter to Foucher, originally published in Leibniz, *Philosophical Papers and Letters,* Vol. I (Chicago, 1956).

I should also like to thank Misses Betty Duimstra and Paula Hocks, Messrs. James Madill and Thomas Gelinske, all of the University of California, San Diego, for their help in the preparation of the manuscript, and I wish to thank Mr. Hoke Simpson for helping in the preparation of the index.

And, last, but by no means least, I should like to thank my family for their patience, fortitude, and assistance.

CONTENTS

THE PHILOSOPHY OF THE SIXTEENTH AND SEVENTEENTH CENTURIES

INTRODUCTION

During the sixteenth century, the very foundations and structure of the medieval intellectual world of western Europe were shaken and to a large degree destroyed. Some of the forces producing this tremendous intellectual change also brought with them new ingredients from which thinkers living through the Reformation, the Renaissance, and the Counter Reformation would produce a new world view. The period encompassed in this volume covers what has been called "the making of the modern mind." This, of course, does not mean that, prior to around 1500, western Europe was totally of one intellectual pattern and thereafter totally of another. The revolutionary change, swept on by the dynamic outburst of humanistic scholarship, religious fervor, national and secular interests, radical scientific discoveries, and hitherto unbelievable feats of exploration and expansion, had its roots in various medieval views, and these views continued to be expressed in various forms well into the seventeenth century, although often modified by the enormous innovations in thought and understanding going on throughout the learned world.

The sixteenth century was ushered in by a series of waves of discovery and rediscovery about the nature of our cosmos and the nature of our cultural heritage. Perhaps the most striking of these were the voyages of exploration emanating from Portugal and Spain. The Christian kings, after the reconquest of Spain, preserved and extended the geographical and astronomical learning that had been accumulated by Jewish and Moslem thinkers during the heyday of Moorish domination. Alfonso the Wise had Jewish and Moslem scholars work out the Alfonsine Tables of astronomy, which remained the summit of man's knowledge of astronomy until replaced by Johannes Kepler's Rudolphine Tables. Early in the fifteenth century, Prince Henry the Navigator (of Portugal) established his institute for geographical and navigational research at Cape St. Vincent and brought the most learned cartographers, mathematicians, and astronomers from all over Iberia to apply their wisdom to expanding man's knowledge of the surface of the earth. This high degree of technical skill, together with the rich economic resources of Portugal, led rapidly to a series of amazing discoveries, such as that of the lands along the African coast and the Azores; it inspired the quest for a sea passage to India that culminated in Bartholomeu Dias' rounding the Cape of Good Hope, Vasco da Gama's arrival in India, and, finally, Ferdinand Magellan's circumnavigation of the globe. Of course, the voyages that startled and forever changed man's picture of his world were those initiated by Christopher Columbus in 1492. Columbus, the mysterious figure of the Age of Discovery (even to this day, it remains somewhat of a mystery whether he was Spanish or Italian and whether the motive for his voyages was theological, economic, or what), set sail westward just as the Moors, with the fall of Granada, lost all political strength in Spain and just as the large, ancient, and influential Jewish community of Spain was driven from its ancestral land. The order for Columbus' voyage was issued from the Alhambra Palace, recently captured from the Moors, and the voyage began the day following the expulsion of the Jews. Columbus returned with fantastic news and findings but with a complete misunderstanding of where he had been. Until his dying day, he still saw his Indies as part of *the* Indies and his accomplishments as part of a theological drama leading to the establishment of the Messianic Age. (See, for instance, his *Book of Prophecies,* written to convince Queen Isabella of the need for a fourth voyage.)

The intellectual impact of these discoveries was not just the effect of the immense wealth gathered by the Spaniards in Mexico and Peru or by the Portuguese in India, Africa, and Brazil; nor was it the effect of the now preposterous division of the world between Spain and Portugal. The greatest consequence of the discoveries was the radical new interpretation of what had been discovered, made famous by Amerigo Vespucci—the notion of the New World. Vespucci, raised in Florence, the center of Italian humanism, and involved through his family in many of the artistic, literary, and philosophical changes then being wrought, was the first to realize the import of what had been found. Having none of Columbus' theological preconceptions nor his views about the passage to India and having a more humanistic background than the great early Portuguese and Spanish explorers, he quickly saw that all previous pictures of the world were false, that previous science and philosophy could not be relied on, and that the newly discovered lands to the west were new in a most radical sense —they had none of the moral and religious traditions and foibles of Christian Europe. The inhabitants of the new lands were people living according to nature and living, in some ways, a better life than that of the "civilized" Europeans. Vespucci's letter of 1503 so excited the European imagination and so affected everyone's conception of the world that the New World quickly became known as "America" rather than "Columbia," in recognition of the fact that the understanding and interpretation of what had been discovered was accomplished by Vespucci.

If a new world had been revealed by the explorers that showed that previous comprehension of the nature of our earth was wrong and that a world existed outside of Judeo-Christian history (later attempts were made to put it inside this history, culminating in the thesis of the seventeenth-century Amsterdam rabbi, Menasseh ben Israel, that the Indians were the Lost Tribes of Israel), other shocking "new" worlds—or newly rediscovered worlds—appeared on the scene. The humanists rediscovered the ancient world, with its riches of literatures, philosophies, and theologies and its wealth of insights with which to replace the sterile ones of Scholastic thought.

Desiderius Erasmus, although neither the greatest scholar nor the most original mind of the period, soon became the dean of all humanists and the most influential figure of his age. Among his many, many achievements, his edition of the Greek text of the New Testament and his work on the Church Fathers revealed in most shocking fashion the new perspectives that could be opened up by abandoning the entire Scholastic way of understanding and replacing it by pious humanistic study. Following up the documentary studies of the Italian humanist, Lorenzo Valla, Erasmus showed that the crucial line in the Vulgate edition of the Gospel according to St. John justifying the doctrine of the Trinity was not in the oldest known Greek manuscript and was not cited by the early Greek Church Fathers. Further, Erasmus showed that the Christianity of the early Church was far removed in spirit, if not in doctrine, from the highly sophisticated, highly organized, and immensely wealthy and powerful Church of his day. Rather than draw the inferences that his scholarship and that of others seemed to entail about the incorrectness of the views of the Church of Rome *circa* 1500, Erasmus ridiculed the whole intellectual and moral world built up to support Christendom. His inordinately popular and influential work, *In Praise of Folly,* written in a witty and engaging Latin in contrast to the dry Scholastic tract style, was like *The Emperor's New Clothes.*

The intellectual world of Christendom, from this new perspective, suddenly appeared grotesque and ridiculous—so ridiculous, in fact, that it would be hard for anyone to take it seriously thereafter. Erasmus had not undermined the Scholastic world by disproving its tenets. He had made it appear so silly that to this day, it is his picture of Scholasticism that we have in mind when we imagine bizarre intellectuals debating such questions as, "How many angels can stand on the head of a pin?"

Erasmus proposed to replace this farcical enterprise with "pious study," the spirit of early, unintellectualized Christianity, and patient, careful, critical, humanistic study of the Greek, Hebrew, and Latin past. Erasmus was not a philosopher or theologian, but actually a very learned, wise, witty anti-intellectual who saw the whole world of theorizing as sterile and empty. His attitude led future generations of intellectuals to fiercely devote themselves to scholarship and to radical innovations in theology (that he, cautious to the end, would not endorse). Although, as the saying goes, "Erasmus laid the egg that Luther hatched," Erasmus himself seems to have hoped for a revitalized simple Christianity within the Catholic Church rather than a genuine revolution against it and an attempt to replace it with another kind of Christian movement.

The success of Erasmus both inspired and popularized the humanistic rediscovery of the past. Scholars, especially at first in Italy, reveled in the rediscovery of "the glory that was Greece and the grandeur that was Rome." They learned Greek; they made Latin a real language again; they searched for manuscripts; and they edited and re-edited the classics, shorn of any Scholastic interpretations. Plato, Plotinus, and Aristotle rose again as genuine Greek thinkers, not as materials for Christian theological debates. Stoicism, Epicureanism, and Skepticism, heretofore not known outside of the Islamic world, re-entered Europe as exciting, inspiring ways of dealing with man's knowledge of the cosmos. Classical mathematical and scientific works, hardly known in medieval Europe (although known to Jewish and Moslem thinkers in Spain and Baghdad) were rediscovered, and the enormous achievements of the Greek mathematicians, especially Archimedes, once more appeared on the center of the intellectual stage to inspire Nicolaus Copernicus and Galileo Galilei.

Along with avid work on Greek and Latin sources, there was an equally eager quest into the so-called "Oriental languages"—Hebrew, Arabic, Syriac, Aramaic, and so forth. The combination of humanist zeal to recapture the premedieval past and the entry into Europe—because of Spanish Christian persecutions—of a large number of Hebrew and Arabic scholars led to a rapid exploration in depth of Semitic literature. Pico della Mirandola, in Florence, had six Hebrew teachers so that he could look into this humanistic dimension. Johann von Reuchlin (1455-1522), in Germany, prepared the first Hebrew grammar. Bomberg, in Venice, established his great Hebrew press and published the Bible, the Talmud, and other crucial Hebrew sources. Reuchlin and Agrippa von Nettesheim publicized the importance of cabala, that enormous treasury of Jewish esoteric, mystical-mathematical lore developed in Spain in the thirteenth century, which proposed that the secret key to the universe was to be found in a magical comprehension of the shapes, frequencies, and symbolism of the Hebrew letters. Scholars, mainly in Italy, put out new editions of the Arabic and Jewish medieval thinkers, such as Averroës and Maimonides.

Universities were challenged to teach and study the riches available in Greek, Hebrew, Arabic, and Latin. Such new avant-garde institutions as Louvain in Belgium quickly established professorships of Greek and Hebrew, and, gradually, all of the others had to follow suit and recognize the humanistic dimension of man's knowledge. Figures like Peter Ramus in Paris forced the reconsideration of the entire curriculum. Under the aegis of Cardinal Ximines in Spain and the flourishing university at Alcala, Greek and Hebrew scholars edited the Polyglot Bible, giving the text, established by the most careful study, in many ancient languages.

The Erasmian spirit turned humanistic scholarship into a crucial discovery of a "new world," that of the wisdom of the ages by-passed or ignored by the Scholastics. The Erasmian spirit also quickly inspired and encouraged another revolutionary spirit—religious reform. Very early in the sixteenth century, Erasmus became the hero of the liberal, humanistic theological movement in Spain, and he was invited to accept a professorship at Alcala (which, he told a friend, he was refusing because Spain had too many Jews). The Spanish theologians, mainly forced converts from Islam and Judaism, admired the spiritual rather than doctrinal interpretation Erasmus gave of Christianity and the anti-Trinitarian implications of his thought. In 1524, the Inquisition succeeded in condemning Spanish Erasmianism and forcing its adherents either underground or abroad. Some, like Juan de Valdes, fled to Italy and spawned various left-wing movements of the Reformation; others, like Miguel Servetus, fought against orthodox Christianity and finally perished as enemies of both Catholicism and Protestantism. The last remnant of Spanish Erasmianism flourished as the Socinian (Unitarian) movement in Poland and Roumania.

Erasmus' critique of the opulence, corruption, and humanistic illiteracy of the Church of Rome quickly gained adherents both within the hierarchy of Catholicism and in the opposition movements. Figures like Cardinal Reginald Pole pressed for reform from within, in recognition that Christianity could be based only on faith, not on Scholastic reason. Rebels, like Martin Luther, moved rapidly from pressing for institutional reform to pressing for complete overthrow of the Church of Rome.

Throughout the Middle Ages, radical reform movements had risen and been destroyed–the Bogomils in the Balkans, the Albigensians in southern France, the Flagellants in central Europe, the Wycliffe movement in England, and others. The Hussites had raised a basic challenge in Bohemia during the fifteenth century. But it was Luther's success in gaining powerful political support and a vast popular following in Germany rather than his innovations or theories, that produced the complete shattering of European Christendom. Even before Luther, the Church of Rome had never succeeded in being the monolithic controller of Europe, contrary to the picture we are usually given, since all through the Middle Ages it had had to struggle against non-Christian religions–Judaism, Mohammedanism, the remnants of paganism, and waves of popular heretical forces. But the Church had managed to hold a world together until Luther survived the making of his heretical utterances at Leipzig and at the Diet of Worms. Thereafter, Europe was rent asunder by the religious rebellions not only of Luther, but also of John Calvin, Huldreich Zwingli, and others, thus ending the ideal of a unified Christendom.

Luther initiated this great upheaval by a simple challenge about certain Church practices, in particular those concerning the sale of indulgences. The zeal of some local authorities quickly pushed him from the position of complainer to that of rebel. Luther had tried to keep his complaints within the framework of institutional Catholicism, but he was pressed by the theologian, Johann Eck, at the Leipzig disputation, until he announced that, even if his views were contrary to those of Popes and Councils, he and heretics like Huss could be right and the Church wrong. From Leipzig onward, Luther moved further and further away from accepting the Church's criterion of religious knowledge and truth towards a subjective criterion of conscience and private interpretation of Scripture.

The massive popular response to his rebel's cry as well as (and, probably, more importantly) the imminent danger of the conquest of Europe by the Ottoman Turks, saved Luther's life and unleashed the

Reformation. In Germany, Switzerland, southern France, the Lowlands, and England, a vast wave of anti-Roman enthusiasm set off varying forms of Reformation. But, when Charles V had to decide between crushing Luther or stopping the Turks at Vienna, he, rightly or wrongly, decided that the Turks were the greater menace. When the emperor had saved Vienna and turned back to Luther, it was already too late. The religious wars in France, Germany, Holland, and other places could only determine where each world would be, but could no longer re-establish the domination of the Church of Rome.

The Counter Reformation, the powerful reform movement within Catholicism that revitalized the Church and made it able to survive the rebellion, was partly a continuation of certain late medieval trends and partly a new and often mystical movement; it was inspired by fervent Spanish religious figures like Ignatius Loyola and Teresa of Avila. The militancy, zealousness, and total obedience of Loyola and his army of Jesuits breathed new life into a seriously wounded Catholicism, led it through the Council of Trent to define the key principles on which it would stand, converted millions in Asia and the New World, and built up troops of intellectuals to oppose the heretics, new and old. The mysticism of Santa Teresa and of San Juan de la Cruz, although originally strongly opposed by the Inquisition, restored Catholicism as living and dynamic a religion, as were the popular movements of the Reformation.

A further effect of some of these tidal waves of discovery, rediscovery, and religious change that were sweeping Europe was the beginnings of new scientific activity, breaking with medieval Aristotelianism and the Arabic theories that had dominated the scene. Magical and alchemic theories became the rage. Cabalism tempted many to look for the secret key to the universe. Doctor Faust types appeared everywhere. In the midst of this outburst of a new kind of experimentation and theorizing, certain developments occurred that we can now see as the road to the scientific revolution. Servetus and Vesalius, in medicine, made world-shaking discoveries through anatomical dissections that showed the unreliability of centuries of medical theory and practice. The strange Renaissance figure, Paracelcus, rejected the whole tradition of drug chemistry and, with his strange potions, began a new era. Copernicus, looking into the classics, found the heliocentric theory that was to revolutionize our whole way of thinking about the universe. And Kepler, from the wealth of bizarre Renaissance theories of numerology, Pythagoreanism, cabalism, and the like, and the enormous observational data collected by Tycho Brahe and himself, presented the most revolutionary insight of all: that the book of nature is written in mathematical characters by God, the Great Geometer, and, thus, that the key to it all could only be found by discovering the mathematical laws of the cosmos. Kepler's three laws of planetary motion destroyed the previously accepted Ptolemaic-Aristotelian earth-centered cosmos and replaced it with a sun-centered one, minus all metaphysical degrees of perfection, place, and motion. Kepler's world of planets moving in elliptical orbits with alterations of velocity and describable only in mathematical terms had lost all of the perfections and purposes of the former cosmos. Kepler eliminated the notion that the heavenly bodies moved in circular and constant paths. Such kinds of motion had previously been assumed to be perfect of their kind. According to Kepler the paths of the planets could be described in mathematical formulas without regarding these movements as being directed towards some goal. Galileo, aided by such new instruments as the telescope, was able to go further and destroy all illusions about the spherical perfection of the moon (since he could see the mountains on it) and the superperfection of the sun (since he could observe the sunspots), and he could show, by a series of thought experiments, that Aristotelian physics was useless in explaining the types of motions going on in the universe. Instead, a mathematical physics, in the style of Archimedes, could yield laws of terrestrial motion, like that of freely falling bodies, and of motion on an inclined plane, as well as a Copernican system of planetary motions.

The understanding of the cosmos from Columbus to Galileo had undergone a radical transformation, and man's beliefs about himself, his past, his present, and his place in the universe were all completely shaken or changed. This period of dynamic alteration in all directions that we call the Renaissance and the Reformation was also one of continuous attempts to understand the universe anew. Marsilio Ficino and Giovanni Pico della Mirandola in Florence, overwhelmed by Platonism, Neoplatonism, cabalism and the like, made one attempt. Aristotelians like Pietro Pompanazzi and Giacomo Zabarella in Padua made another. Still other thinkers, using the wealth of late ancient theories, tried to develop new conceptions of nature as a dynamic living organism full of secret powers. The new theologians, both Protestant and Catholic, looked everywhere for cosmologies and philosophies to replace Scholasticism and to serve as bases or interpretations of Christianity in their changing world. In such a ferment—with the intellectual world losing its established footing on all sides and with competing claims and beliefs on all sides—the revival of ancient Greek skepticism was an attempt to focus the problems, pose a universal "skeptical crisis," and force men like Francis Bacon and René Descartes to look for new foundations for the entire intellectual world.

In the midst of the crisis of belief produced by the shock waves of geographical, humanistic, medical, astronomical, and mathematical discoveries and the divergent claims about religious knowledge, the major texts of Greek skeptical thought—the writings of Sextus Empiricus—were rediscovered and published. They appeared in Latin translations in 1562 and 1569 and immediately reinforced certain skeptical, anti-intellectual, and fideistic tendencies of the sixteenth century, those of writers who questioned the merits of any of the new theories and instead insisted that ultimate knowledge cannot be gained except by faith. The editor of the 1569 edition of Sextus, Gentian Hervet, a leader of the Counter Reformation in France and secretary to the Cardinal of Lorraine, saw immediately that all this new skeptical argumentation could be turned against the Calvinists, by challenging their claims about religious knowledge, and could be used in favor of Catholicism, by showing that nothing could be known by rational means and that only by retaining one's traditional beliefs through faith alone could one remain secure. Various Jesuits in France—from Juan Maldonado, the first Jesuit professor at Paris, to François Veron, a teacher at La Flèche during Descartes' days there—used the newly rediscovered skeptical arguments to fashion a "machine of war" against the Protestants, undermining their claims about religious knowledge and insisting religion be based on faith rather than on any philosophical contentions.

The form of the "new skepticism" that was to affect the whole future of philosophy was the presentation of it by Michel de Montaigne and his distant cousin, Francisco Sanchez, professor of philosophy and medicine at Toulouse. They were both raised in the ferment of the refugee Iberian intellectuals at Bordeaux and Toulouse; both were aware of the range of new discoveries and theories of their era, and both were greatly affected by studying the skeptical arguments in the writings of Sextus Empiricus. In 1576, each wrote his version of the "new skepticism," Montaigne, "The Apology for Raimond Sebond" and Sanchez, *Quod nihil scitur (Why Nothing Can Be Known)*. The latter is much more didactic and systematically applies the skeptical arguments about knowledge to Aristotelianism. Sanchez argued at the end that, since nothing could be known about the absolute nature of reality, one should abandon that hopeless quest, accept religion on faith, and study the world of appearance item by item. Sanchez influenced the more theoretical spirits and was read until Leibniz' days.

The more popular version of the problem was Montaigne's. His long, rambling essay, "The Apology," used the materials in Sextus to erode every level of rational belief and certainty. Montaigne stressed the vast variety of conflicting opinion on all subjects about the ancients and amongst his contemporaries. Man's means for dealing with this, his senses and his reason, also yielded conflicting results. Man's senses and his reason, Montaigne showed, are both unreliable measures of the world about him. Sensory data varies with differing conditions, and rational conclusions depend on premises that are open to question; we seem to be able to find no criterion for judging when we can trust either our data or our best rational conclusions. The experts, including the great scientists of Montaigne's time, Copernicus and Philippus Paracelsus, all offer divergent and incompatible theories. The best we can do is follow the sage advice of the ancient Pyrrhonian skeptics–suspend judgment on all matters that go beyond the appearances of things and live morally by following nature and custom. To this, Montaigne added a note of Christian skepticism–purge oneself of all human opinions and accept completely the faith God gives us. This, Montaigne claimed, would keep one within Catholicism, since, to make a change, would require reasons that would always be dubious.

The skeptical fideism of Montaigne and its more didactic presentation by his disciple, the priest Pierre Charron (in *De la sagesse* [*On Wisdom*], 1603), swept the intellectual world of the day. His work and that of Charron was quickly translated into English, was read everywhere, and became the prevailing view of the avant-garde intellectuals of the early seventeenth century. In France, the court circle included a host of followers of Montaigne, Sanchez, and Charron, who coupled their philosophical skepticism with Machiavellian politics and, often, with an active interest in the "new science."

Pierre Gassendi, a priest who was a leading experimental scientist, was one such skeptic. In his early work, Gassendi turned the arsenal of Sextus and his new followers against Aristotelianism. From the beginning, Gassendi insisted that he was not trying to destroy either religion or science, but was trying to protect them both from the effects of bad reasoning. Religion should be accepted on faith, while science should be the constructive consequence of recognizing that, in a basic metaphysical sense, nothing can be known. After one has seen this, then one can examine experience, organize it, and use it to predict the future course of events. This science, without any metaphysical foundation, could, as Gassendi's friend and ally, Marin Mersenne, claimed, provide the "guide for life" in this vale of tears in which we cannot know the real natures of things. In the course of his career, Gassendi developed a revised form of Epicurean atomism as the middle way between complete skepticism and dogmatism (the contention that something can actually be known). Gassendi's atomism always presented as a hypothetical way of interpreting scientific findings, organizing them, and predicting future events. For Gassendi, atomism was not a theory about the nature of reality, but only an interpretive model for the world of appearances that enabled one to utilize the "new science" without having to resolve the skeptical crisis. Each time a new dogmatist appeared on the scene to offer *the way* to discover the true nature of reality, Gassendi fought back with all of his skeptical weapons. He challenged the magicians, the numerologists, the cabalists, and the Rosicrucians, as well as Francis Bacon, Herbert of Cherbury, and Descartes. The constructive skepticism of Gassendi (and of Mersenne as well) provided a pragmatic and positivistic interpretation of the "new science" that was to outlast the drama of the seventeenth-century metaphysicians and would flower again in new form in the world of Newtonian science.

The skeptical crisis of the late sixteenth and early seventeenth centuries inspired "the quest for certainty." Unwilling to accept either the complete doubt of Montaigne or the mitigated doubt of Sanchez, Gassendi, or Mersenne, new visionaries appeared on the scene to propose new ways of finding the truth that would overcome all doubt. They insisted that, if only the right methods were employed, then one could find a secure road to certain knowledge of the real world.

One of the first to make such a proposal was Francis Bacon, combining certain elements of Renaissance naturalism with his radical methodological program. Until the present, Bacon insisted, man had sought for truth by various means—the senses, reason, philosophical and theological theorizing—but had failed to see that such attempts were doomed by the very nature of the case unless new methods could be found for overcoming the innate obstacles that stood in man's way. The innate obstacles, which he called the four Idols, were the natural distortions in knowing the real nature of things due to (1) the weaknesses of human nature, (2) individual idiosyncrasies, (3) preconceptions of various theories, and (4) the problems of communication among men. Some of these could be alleviated by the use of aids or instruments—for example, eyeglasses could correct human or individual distortions. Others were endemic to the human condition. What can be done is to recognize that all knowledge is built on sense information, that the senses are in need of whatever assistance can be obtained, and that a new method is needed. Bacon's new method is a complicated and careful inductive procedure that seeks to establish the causes of phenomena by finding unique factors present when the phenomena occur and absent when they do not. The Baconian procedures—involving the compilation of practically endless tables of common instances, controlled experiments, and the like—are supposed to lead to fairly certain knowledge of the causes or forms of things. (As Bacon indicated in his plan of the *Novum Organum,* the complete enterprise would just about require compiling a natural history of the universe.) Knowledge is power, Bacon insisted, and with knowledge man not only can understand, but also he can do and can change the world. Minimal as Bacon's personal scientific achievements may have been (he died from an illness contracted while stuffing snow into a chicken during one of his experiments), he envisaged the potential of scientific knowledge and, he inspired those who would try to use it for the betterment of man's lot and not just for passive understanding.

The Continental thinkers, like Gassendi, Mersenne, and Descartes, sneered at Bacon's new method for solving the skeptical crisis. His admissions about the ineradicable nature of some features of the Idols and his reliance on sensory, inductive procedures left his results open to question and would thus reinforce the doubts of the skeptics without ever arriving at true and certain knowledge. Mersenne called Bacon "the ape of the Pyrrhonists" and attacked him for both doubting too much and claiming too much. If a firm, sure way to truth were to be found, it would require a much more radical method than Baconian induction and use of instruments.

The man who proposed this more radical method was René Descartes, one of the great mathematical geniuses of the scientific revolution. After achieving fame as a mathematician, Descartes visited Paris in the winter of 1628-1629 and attended a soirée at the home of the Papal Nuncio. An alchemist was speaking on the low state of human knowledge, the current doubts about everything, and the need for a new method. Everyone there except Descartes apparently approved of the alchemist's skepticism and his empirical, probabilistic, pragmatic proposals. Descartes rose in opposition and insisted that a method was needed that would insure complete certainty; he insisted that, without such a method, the most probable truths might turn out to be unreliable, false, or dubious. He then proceeded to give the audience a living lesson in complete skepticism by showing them that, on the standards they were willing to accept, the propositions they considered most certain could be cast in doubt. After this performance, Cardinal Bérulle, the founder of the very pious Augustinian institution, the Oratory, encouraged Descartes to work out his method in such a way that it would overcome all doubt. Descartes retired to Holland (where his career had earlier begun) and proceeded to do so.

The autobiographical sections of his *Discourse on Method* indicate that, in 1629, he worked out his method of doubt, of radical skepticism, doubting every proposition that, under some conceivable state of affairs, could be false. Sensory information was cast aside, since the senses are sometimes unreliable and could, perhaps, be unreliable even when they seem most trustworthy. Our whole sensory world might be the result of madness or might even be a dream. Our scientific knowledge, no matter how sound it appeared to be, might be just organized dream analysis, unrelated to any real world that might exist. (In a letter discussing Galileo, Descartes criticized the great scientist for having a good method for solving scientific problems but not having any foundation for it that would establish that these results were actually true of the real world.) Then, by pressing his method of doubt, Descartes went on to show that even mathematical propositions could be doubted, since we often make logical mistakes and cannot be sure in any given instance we haven't made one. If elementary truths, such as "two plus three equals five" and "a square has four sides," look impervious to this sort of doubting, Descartes then went on to the final stage of his method, introducing a more radical reason for doubting than previous skeptics like Sextus and Montaigne had ever offered—the demon hypothesis. Suppose there is some demonic force that wants to lead us astray and make us think that something is absolutely certain when it is actually false. Then, can we be sure of anything, no matter how indubitable it looks to us? Can we be sure there is a world, that there are other people, or even that we ourselves exist?

At this point, when all appears to be lost, Descartes claims that he has resolved the skeptical crisis. By carrying doubting to its extreme, beyond what any previous skeptics had been willing or able to do, an indubitable, unshakeable truth reveals itself. If I try to doubt that I exist, I am aware that I am thinking and that I do thereby exist. The famous *cogito, ergo sum* (I think, therefore I am) becomes the first truth that no skeptical hypothesis, even that of the demon, can make dubious. If I try to doubt it, I, by that very act, am forced to realize its truth. My act of doubting shows me that I both think and must exist. Descartes insisted (contrary to the interpretations of Hobbes, Gassendi, and other critics) that the *cogito* was not a form of syllogistic reasoning with the hidden unproved premise, "Whatever thinks, exists," but was a realization or an intuition that conquered complete doubt. It rested on nothing. It was encountered by doubting, not proven by doubting. Once encountered, its indubitability presumably overwhelmed the doubter. And its full force could only be realized by the extreme process of the method of doubt.

Having found one truth that no skeptical doubt could shake, Descartes rapidly went on to build up his new dogmatic edifice that would *now* establish the whole realm of truths about the universe. By inspecting his one truth, Descartes found his criterion for all truths—"that whatever is clearly and distinctly conceived is true." With this criterion, he then found the fundamental premises for establishing that God exists; that God is the cause of everything, including me and my ideas; that He is no deceiver (and, hence, there is no demon to worry about); that, since He makes me think that mathematical truths are certain, they are certain; and that there is a real physical universe corresponding to my clear and distinct ideas of it (that is, my mathematical ones).

The Cartesian cosmos has three basic elements: God, the Creator and Conserver of everything; mind, whose essence is thinking; and body or matter, whose essence is extension. Our minds can gain certain knowledge about the world through our clear and distinct mathematical ideas (although not through our unclear and indistinct sensory ones). Since the essence of the material world is extension, it is through mathematical physics that the entire natural cosmos can and should be understood. The vision of Kepler and the success of Galileo are justified by Cartesian metaphysics.

This tremendous achievement, establishing an unshakeable foundation for the sciences and a resolution of the skeptical crisis, formed the pattern of philosophizing throughout the next century. But the Cartesian "way of ideas" and its metaphysical distinction between mind and matter posed problems for all ensuing theorists. Had Descartes really established much, if anything, that was absolutely certain? Had he, perhaps, unleashed such doubts that nothing, not even the overwhelming force of the *cogito,* could overcome them? Perhaps, this mind that knows it exists knows only this, and all else is a pipe dream corresponding to nothing. When Gassendi proposed such a possibility (which Descartes called "the objection of objections"), Descartes, the father of modern philosophy, retorted that to take this seriously would be to shut the door on reason. But maybe the very method of doubt would make us do this. Could we really know about the material world from our private (perhaps, certain) world of ideas? If mind and matter are so radically different, can mind know matter, and can they affect each other? The so-called mind-body problem posed by Descartes' dualistic metaphysics was to haunt all later seventeenth-century metaphysicians. Descartes' own solution, that somehow they interact in the pineal gland, was quickly found to be unsatisfactory, and Descartes himself said that this was one of those matters best understood by thinking least about it.

Descartes had proudly proclaimed himself to be the first man to conquer skepticism and the one who had offered a new philosophy to account for the new world revealed by science. Immediately, objections were posed from all sides. The set of seven objections gathered together by Mersenne and appended to the *Meditations* in 1641 indicated the range of criticism—from Catholic complaints that Descartes was unorthodox and maybe even heretical, to criticisms by Hobbes, Gassendi, Mersenne, and Antoine Arnauld that he really hadn't proven very much and that there were holes and inconsistencies in his system. He might have found the type of system needed to interpret and justify the "new science," the world seen as a mathematical machine, but a more consistent or more plausible version would be needed if the "new philosophy," was really to be secured against skepticism and vindicated against alternative possibilities. Thomas Hobbes offered one possibility, Baruch Spinoza another, Nicolas Malebranche yet another, and Gottfried Wilhelm von Leibniz the final one of the great seventeenth-century metaphysical systems.

Hobbes, a close friend of Gassendi and Mersenne, proposed a kind of materialism in which mental events could be explained and interpreted as physical motions of extended bodies. Descartes had seen the entire cosmos except mind as part of a mathematical machine and, thereby, saw biology as a branch of physics. Hobbes, by construing mind as an effect of physical motions, saw that all mental processes could be understood in terms of physics and that all human and social behavior could also be thus explained, if one could discover the physical processes that moved men to think and act. The Hobbesian method was that of setting down definitions of key mental and human concepts in terms of motions of physical entities. Then, the mind could be portrayed as a kind of computer that went through a quasi-mechanical process called "ratiocination," shuffling the definitions, combining them, and thereby making judgments. The Hobbesian vision of a world whose constituents were just God who produced it and physical bodies in motion, causing as an effect the mental and social behavior of man, involved the possibility of a physical science of psychology, ethics, and sociology. The mechanization and mathematization of nature started by Kepler and Galileo and justified by Descartes could be extended to human nature as well.

The ultimate truth of such a system bothered Hobbes far less than it did Descartes. Hobbes defined "truth," as a human concept within his system, as the correct consequence of names or definitions. "Right reasoning" consisted of proper reckoning of the consequences of definitions. If people disagreed about who was reasoning correctly, some outside arbiter (the political sovereign) would have to decide this as a social matter. If people disagreed about what system of definitions to use, again it would be a social problem to be decided by the sovereign for maintenance of peace. The only check, ultimately, on Hobbes' own system of definitions–besides the fact that his views were not acceptable in English society and hence led to his being in exile a good deal of the time, was that of seeing if they squared with one's experience and made it possible to account for one's experience. Within his system, Hobbes was happy to admit that there could be no absolute, but only conditional knowledge–that is, for example, if such and such is the definition of x and something else the definition of y, then x and y are different. Hobbes was willing to make ratiocination our way of comprehending the material world (including man, his thoughts, and his behavior), but he was not willing to make grandiose claims about the absolute certitude of the results.

Spinoza, however, following out certain implications of Descartes and certain rationalistic tendencies amongst the Jewish thinkers of his day, was willing to make human reason the sole, certain, and complete judge of the cosmos and to portray such a cosmos as an eternal set of psychophysical laws having no supernatural source and being part of no religious history. Spinoza's total rationalism seems to have emerged, first, from certain religious controversies in the Spanish-Portuguese Jewish community of Amsterdam. Most of the members had been born and raised as Catholics in Spain, Portugal, France, or Italy, and had practiced Judaism secretly before they reached refuge in Holland. Their intellectual training was in large measure Christian. In Amsterdam, they kept up their Iberian cultural heritage and applied their intellectual training to the study of Judaism. Some found that the religion practiced in Amsterdam was incompatible with their own rational considerations on the matter. First, Uriel da Costa, originally a Portuguese priest, from about 1620 to 1640, carried on a rebellious campaign (with dire results for himself, ending in his suicide) charging that all historical religions are man-made inventions. In the 1650's, a Spanish doctor, Juan de Prado, was excommunicated from the community for contending that the law of reason takes precedence over the law of Moses. Spinoza, a younger ally of Prado, was also excommunicated apparently for going even farther and challenging Judaism and all other historical religions as kinds of superstition, and directly attacking the Bible as a or the source of revealed truth. Others, like the French thinker, Isaac La Peyrère (Pereira) questioned whether the Bible dealt with all human history or just Judeo-Christian history. La Peyrère, a friend of Gassendi's, shocked the mid-seventeenth-century world with his thesis that there were men before Adam and that the Mexicans, the Eskimos, the Chinese, and so forth, had developed historically independent of Biblical events.

Spinoza's *Tractatus,* apparently a reworking of his original answer to the synagogue after his expulsion, analyzed the Bible on strictly rationalistic criteria, with extremely critical results. Then, employing both the Spanish Scholastic and Judaic theories he had been taught and some of the Cartesian views, Spinoza began working out his picture of the universe solely in terms of rationally acceptable premises. If reason and reason alone is the judge of truth, Spinoza found that traditional religion only made sense as the effect of disturbed human psyches. The universe that man could comprehend was logically ordered, consisting of one and only one substance, God or Nature, whose knowable attributes are thought and extension. Everything we are aware of is a mode of this one substance and is to be understood in terms of its logical relation to God or Nature. Spinoza found Cartesian dualism totally unacceptable, since, from the very definition of substance, there could be only one substance, and that one is God or Nature. Mind and matter, since they are created and are dependent on God or Nature, cannot be considered as separate substances, but only as ways of comprehending God or Nature.

Spinoza's vision of the world seen from the aspect of eternity was pantheistic (everything is an aspect of God, and God is everything), describable in two different but compatible ways: as a mathematically related series of physical events or as a logically ordered series of ideas. These are two ways of expressing and understanding the same universe.

There is no mind-body problem, since the mental and the physical are two equivalent aspects of the same thing, God or Nature. The world, understood rationally, is a set of necessary relationships, logical or mathematical, that account for why everything occurs as it does. No supernatural forces or revealed data are needed, and the alleged supernatural and revealed data of Judeo-Christianity can themselves be understood rationally as the effects of psychological and sociological forces. By pressing the logic of some aspects of the Cartesian theory, Spinoza revealed what the cosmos would look like if reason, especially as rational science, were the sole means for comprehending it. Its entire historical-religious dimension would vanish, and the world would be only a purposeless complex of necessarily acting forces. This is why Pierre Bayle said of Spinoza that he was the first to reduce atheism to a system and was thereby the first to portray what the world of modern science, shorn of all Judeo-Christian roots and aspects, would look like.

Although Spinoza made no effort to propagate or disseminate his views, preferring the quiet life of the truth-seeker to engaging in controversy, his theories were known widely, even before the posthumous publication of his *Ethics,* and were considered extremely shocking and dangerous. Others tried to show that a metaphysical system could be developed that encompassed the results of modern science without challenging all of the foundations of traditional belief as well.

Father Nicolas Malebranche, a scholar in the Oratory of Cardinal Bérulle, presented one possibility, perhaps the logical result of Cartesianism. Starting with his *Recherche de la verité* (*The Search after Truth*), written in 1674, Malebranche presented the theory that man knows (by divine illumination) only ideas that are located in the mind of God and that they constitute an uncreated world of intelligible extension. Besides this knowledge, essentially that of pure mathematics, which is eternal and necessary, man also has feelings, that is, sensory experiences. None of these tell him anything about a real physical world. Malebranche insisted that there can be no demonstration that there even is a physical world, since God is not required to create it. The only guarantee we have that there is such a world is the opening lines of Genesis in which it is revealed that God did in fact create heaven and earth. In the world that we are aware of, the experienced world, we can find no necessary connections between events, but only sequences. Our understanding of the cosmos consists in comprehending the world of intelligible extension and describing the world of experience. The explanation of what is going on is entirely in terms of God. He is the sole causal agent and creator of whatever exists. He creates the physical world (revealed to us by faith) and the experienced world felt by us. Since He operates by the most economical and general laws, He patterns His creations after the ideal world of intelligible extension. Hence, we can apply our mathematical understanding to the physical world. In relating this physical world to our experienced one, we can never find any necessary connections. What is going on is that, on the occasion of the occurrence of an event in one order, God causes an event in the other. Thus, there is no causal connection between the mathematically describable events of a vibrating string and the sound heard by human beings. But, on the occasion of one of these events, God makes the other occur, according to His general laws. As Leibniz described it, Malebranche's world was like two totally separate clocks, kept in harmony by the constant intervention of the clock-maker.

Malebranche's occasionalism and his theory that "we see all things in God," which were to have great influence on Berkeley and Hume in the next century, represented in some ways the end of the Cartesian attempt to gain certainty about all aspects of the universe. The visible world, in Malebranche's account, cannot be known, but only described. The existence of the physical world can only be known by faith. The explanation of all physical and experimental events is, "God so wills." The world that we can understand through divine illumination is that of pure mathematics, and the world has no rationally discoverable, necessary connection with any other. The study of the experienced world has been made unintelligible in any rationalistic sense and can only be carried on descriptively. (To this degree, whether intended or not, Malebranche was extremely influential in separating empirical scientific study from metaphysics, by developing a theory in which one could not be explained by the other.)

Malebranche's theory, contrary to Spinoza's, portrayed the world as essentially a continuous, divine drama. It resolved the Cartesian mind-body problem by completely denying any connection at all between the two realms (and paved the way for Berkeley's immaterialism by making the material world essentially unnecessary and unknowable). But it left a picture of the world that seemed to his contemporaries, like Locke and Leibniz, entirely incredible and entirely miraculous, although it claimed to be one of the most rationalistic analyses ever offered. The Cartesian dream, of explaining everything through clear and distinct ideas, seemed to have culminated in making everything a divine mystery.

Leibniz made the last great effort of the seventeenth century to develop a rational metaphysics that would explain everything. He was the universal genius of the century, knowing just about every field and every development and himself making enormous original contributions in physics, mathematics, law, logic, linguistics, history, and more (all the while holding down a full-time job as a court functionary in Germany). In the 1670's and 1680's, while critically scrutinizing the various metaphysical theories of the seventeenth century, Leibniz began formulating his own solution to all the problems. Methodologically, he sought a universal, mathematical language in which all problems could be stated and in which solutions worked out by calculation from definitions and first principles—for example, his law of sufficient reason, that nothing happens without a reason.

Leibniz contended that to avoid the difficulties and strange results of seventeenth-century theorizing, a new basic concept was needed. Cartesian matter was inactive and extended and could not explain why anything happens. God had to be brought in as the constant source of action. Why not, instead, make activity the basic unit and extension one of its forms? So, the theory of monads, active centers of force, was proposed. Everything was a monad or collections of monads. All the activities of monads had to have a reason; the reason had to be found in their definitions. Hence, each monad had to be a self-contained, active universe whose complete definition included all of the propositions that could ever be true of that monad. If everything that happened to a monad was true by its own definition, then no monad could influence another (since that would require affecting its fixed definition), and each was essentially "windowless." If each monad could be understood only in its own terms and if every property of each monad was true by definition, then why does the world look as if one object influences or affects another? This, Leibniz explained, was due to the pre-established harmony. God established a world of the greatest number of compossible monads (that is, ones that would not contradict one another). Each mirrored the universe in its own individual way (that is, its definition included its relations to all of the others). Since the existing ones in this world (the best of all possible worlds, according to Leibniz) were all independent and compatible, it was their pre-established harmony that accounted for their apparent but illusory interconnection. In his clock analogy, Leibniz contended, it is as if the different clocks keep the same time, not because of constant intervention of the clock-maker (Malebranche's view), or that they are all the same clock (Spinoza's view), or that they are somehow connected (Descartes' view), but that they are made perfectly in the first place.

Leibniz's theory of active force centers, monads, appeared, as Bertrand Russell has said, to offer a marvelously consistent and yet completely incredible explanation of everything. Leibniz, in his controversies with Malebranche, Arnauld, Bayle, Locke, Clarke, and others, sought to show that other theories were full of difficulties and that his could not be disproven. Even in the *Theodicy,* written against Bayle to show that this *is* the best of all possible worlds, Leibniz insisted that all problems could be solved within his system. But, as Bayle had argued in the article in his *Dictionary* on "Rorarius," although Leibniz' theory might be the most ingenious and original of the period, it led to totally unbelievable results. If this was what a completely consistent metaphysical system looked like, then, unfortunately, one had better abandon the enterprise entirely.

Throughout the seventeenth century, the skeptics fought back against each stage of the attempt to find a new metaphysical foundation for the new world of science and belief. Gassendi had attacked Descartes. Bishop Pierre-Daniel Huet and Simon Foucher had attacked Descartes, Malebranche, and Leibniz. Pascal, at first one of the greatest scientists and mathematicians of them all, rejected the whole enterprise and insisted that faith, and faith alone, could provide any worthwhile answers to any serious questions. The *coup de grâce* was given by the last skeptic of the century, Pierre Bayle. He, unlike the others, was originally a Calvinist, then a convert to Catholicism, and then a reconvert to Protestantism. A refugee in Holland for the last twenty-five years of his life, he proclaimed that he was a Protestant in the full sense of the term—that he was opposed to everything that was said and everything that was done.

An advocate of complete toleration of belief and an enemy of all sorts of superstition, he culminated his career with the monumental *Historical and Critical Dictionary* (1697, 2nd ed. 1702), an enormous compendium of arguments against all sorts of theories in philosophy, theology, science, and so forth. The *Dictionary* was allegedly a biographical one, giving the lives of persons great, obscure, fictional, and so on. The heart of it, however, was the digressive footnotes in which theory after theory was dissected, criticized, and refuted, and the whole world of seventeenth-century thought torn asunder. In the longest article in the *Dictionary* he attacked Spinoza. In another ("Rorarius"), he attacked his friend Leibniz. The theories of Descartes, Hobbes, Locke, Malebranche, Newton, Aristotle, Plato, and anyone else were examined, dissected, and found to be "big with contradiction and absurdity." A whole series of problems—for example, the problem of evil, the nature of mind or matter, the problem of the relation of mind and matter, and the like—could not be successfully solved by any rational system. Over and over again, Bayle insisted, as he dissolved one theory after another, what this showed was the hopeless inadequacy of reason to make sense of the world. Reason should be abandoned for faith. And the faith Bayle portrayed was blind, unintelligible, and amoral.

Bayle's *Dictionary* was a *summa,* in the medieval sense, of man's attempt to understand his radically changed and changing cosmos. Unfortunately, every attempt had failed and made the cosmos more unintelligible. The heroic attempts to put all the pieces together after the outbursts of the Renaissance, the Reformation, and the Counter Reformation had failed. The new Columbuses—the seventeenth-century metaphysicians—had sought unshakable, indubitable havens of certainty that could guarantee that it all made sense and all fitted harmoniously together. Bayle shattered all illusions on this score and bequeathed the problems anew to the Age of the Enlightenment to try other means of comprehending what had happened and what we actually know about the universe. Bayle provided what Voltaire called "the arsenal of the Enlightenment." But, as the two who followed him most closely, Hume and Voltaire, saw, for all of the Enlightenment's enthusiastic belief that man had finally comprehended the universe, essentially all was still in doubt. The drama of seventeenth-century metaphysics had not only reinforced skepticism about man's natural and rational knowledge of the cosmos, but had also shaken his ability to accept any traditional faith as well. The legacies of Spinoza and Bayle were to stay with mankind through our own day, no matter how heroic or horrendous the attempts to understand anew our cosmos (as unfolded by the latest scientific findings) and ourselves (as revealed by the latest psychological, psychiatric, and sociological theories). The intellectual revolutions of the sixteenth century and the brave attempts of the seventeenth century to establish new and certain ways of understanding the cosmos were to leave a legacy of yet unsolved problems, while undermining man's previous ways of dealing with them.

I

VESPUCCI

AMERIGO VESPUCCI (1454-1512), a Florentine, educated in the new humanistic atmosphere, started out in a diplomatic career, traveling to Paris and elsewhere. He moved to Seville in 1492 and became involved in affairs connected with the voyages of exploration, including those of Columbus. Vespucci's first voyage was apparently in 1497, to the Gulf of Mexico. In 1499-1500, he voyaged to Brazil and Venezuela; in 1501-1502, to Africa and the South American coast; and, in 1503-1504 to Brazil to start the first settlement there. In 1508, he was appointed Pilot Major of Spain. His letter of 1503 on the New World, addressed to Lorenzo di Pier Francesco de Medici, quickly became the best known and most exciting account of the new discoveries and was widely read throughout Europe. In 1507, as a result of the letter, a new introduction to geography, published in Saint-Dié, France, gave the name "America" to the New World. Vespucci's letter, more than those of Columbus or other early explorers, indicates the revolutionary significance of the newly discovered lands for the intellectual world of the time.

Mundus Novis
Letter on the New World

1503

¶ AMERICO VESPUCCI OFFERS HIS BEST COMPLIMENTS TO LORENZO PIETRO DI MEDICI

On a former occasion I wrote to you at some length concerning my return from those new regions which we found and explored with the fleet, at the cost, and by the command of this Most Serene King of Portugal. And these we may rightly call a new world.

Because our ancestors had no knowledge of them, and it will be a matter wholly new to all those who hear about them. For this transcends the view held by our ancients, inasmuch as most of them hold that there is no continent to the south beyond the equator, but only the sea which they named the Atlantic; and if some of them did aver that a continent there was, they denied with abundant argument that it was a habitable land. But that this their opinion is false and utterly opposed to the truth, this my last voyage has made manifest; for in those southern parts I have found a continent more densely peopled and abounding in animals than our Europe or Asia or Africa, and, in addition, a climate milder and more delightful than in any other region known to us, as you shall learn in the following account wherein we shall set succinctly down only capital matters and the things more worthy of comment and memory seen or heard by me in this new world, as will appear below.

On the fourteenth of the month of May, one thousand five hundred and one we set sail from Lisbon under fair sailing conditions, in compliance with the commands of the aforementioned king, with these ships for the purpose of seeking new regions toward the south; and for twenty months we continuously pursued this southern course. The route of this voyage is as follows: Our course was set for the Fortunate Isles, once so called, but which are now termed the Grand Canary

Islands; these are in the third climate and on the border of the inhabited west. Thence by sea we skirted the whole African coast and part of Ethiopia as far as the Ethiopic Promontory, so called by Ptolemy, which we now call Cape Verde and the Ethiopians Beseghice. And that region, Mandingha, lies within the torrid zone fourteen degrees north of the equator; it is inhabited by tribes and nations of blacks. Having there recovered our strength and taken on all that our voyage required, we weighed anchor and made sail. And directing our course over the vast ocean toward the Antarctic we for a time bent westward, owing to the wind called Vulturnus; and from the day when we set sail from the said promontory we cruised for the space of two months and three days, before any land appeared to us. But what we suffered on that vast expanse of sea, what perils of shipwreck, what discomforts of the body we endured, with what anxiety of mind we toiled, this I leave to the judgment of those who out of rich experience have well learned what it is to seek the uncertain and to attempt discoveries even though ignorant. And that in a word I may briefly narrate all, you must know that of the sixty-seven days of our sailing we had forty-four of constant rain, thunder and lightning—so dark that never did we see sun by day or fair sky by night. By reason of this such fear invaded us that we soon abandoned almost all hope of life. But during these tempests of sea and sky, so numerous and so violent, the Most High was pleased to display before us a continent, new lands, and an unknown world. At sight of these things we were filled with as much joy as anyone can imagine usually falls to those who have gained refuge from varied calamity and hostile fortune. It was on the seventh day of August, one thousand five hundred and one that we anchored off the shores of those parts, thanking our God with formal ceremonial and with the celebration of a choral mass. We knew that land to be a continent and not an island both because it stretches forth in the form of a very long and unbending coast, and because it is replete with infinite inhabitants. For in it we found innumerable tribes and peoples and species of all manner of wild beasts which are found in our lands and many others never seen by us concerning which it would take long to tell in detail. God's mercy shone upon us much when we landed at that spot, for there had come a shortage of fire-wood and water; and in a few days we might have ended our lives at sea. To Him the honor, glory, and thanksgiving.

We adopted the plan of following the coast of this continent toward the east and never losing sight of it. We sailed along until at length we reached a bend where the shore made a turn to the south; and from that point where we first touched land to that corner it was about three hundred leagues, in which sailing distance we frequently landed and had friendly relations with those people, as you will hear below. I had forgotten to write you that from the promontory of Cape Verde to the nearest part of that continent is about seven hundred leagues, although I should estimate that we sailed more than eighteen hundred, partly through ignorance of the route and the ship-master's want of knowledge, partly owing to tempests and winds which kept us from the proper course and compelled us to put about frequently. Because, if my companions had not heeded me, who had knowledge of cosmography, there would have been no ship-master, nay not the leader of our expedition himself, who would have known where we were within five hundred leagues. For we were wandering and uncertain in our course, and only the instruments for taking the altitudes of the heavenly bodies showed us our true course precisely; and these were the quadrant and the astrolabe, which all men have come to know. For this reason they subsequently made me the object of great honor; for I showed them that though a man without practical experience, yet through the teaching of the marine chart for navigators I was more skilled than all the ship-masters of the whole world. For these have no knowledge except of those waters to which they often sailed. Now, where the said corner of land showed us southern trend of the coast we agreed to sail beyond it and inquire what there might be in those parts. So we sailed along the coast about six hundred leagues, and often landed and mingled and associated with the natives of those regions, and by them we were received in brotherly fashion; and we would dwell with them too, for fifteen or twenty days continuously, maintaining amicable and hospitable relations, as you shall learn below. Part of this new continent lies in the torrid zone beyond the equator toward the Antarctic pole, for it begins eight degrees beyond the equator. We sailed along this coast until we passed the tropic of Capricorn and found the Antarctic pole fifty degrees higher than that horizon. We advanced to within seventeen and a half degrees of the Antarctic circle, and what I there have seen and learned concerning the nature of those races, their manners, their tractability and the fertility of the soil, the salubrity of the climate, the position of the heavenly bodies in the sky, and especially concerning the fixed stars of the eighth sphere, never seen or studied by our ancestors, these things I shall relate in order.

First then as to the people. We found in those parts such a multitude of people as nobody could enumerate (as we read in the Apocalypse), a race I say gentle and amenable. All of both sexes go about naked, covering no part of their bodies; and just as they spring from their mothers' wombs so they go until death. They have indeed large square-built bodies, well formed and proportioned, and in color verging upon reddish. This I think has come to them, because, going about naked, they are colored by the sun. They have, too, hair plentiful and black. In their gait and when playing their games they are agile and dignified. They are comely, too, of countenance which they nevertheless themselves destroy; for they bore their cheeks, lips, noses and ears. Nor think those holes small or that they have one only. For some I have seen having in a single face seven borings any one of which was capable of holding a plum. They stop up these holes of theirs with blue stones, bits of marble, very beautiful crystals of alabaster, very white bones, and other things artificially prepared according to their customs. But if you could see a thing so unwonted and monstrous, that is to say a man having in his cheeks and lips alone seven stones some of which are a span and a half in length, you would not be without wonder. For I frequently observed and discovered that seven such stones weighed sixteen ounces aside from the fact that in their ears, each perforated with three holes, they have other stones dangling on rings; and this usage applies to the men alone. For women do not bore their faces, but their ears only. They have another custom, very shameful and beyond all human belief. For their women, being very lustful, cause the private parts of their husbands to swell up to such a huge size that they appear deformed and disgusting; and this is accomplished by a certain device of theirs, the biting of certain poisonous animals. And in consequence of this many lose their organs which break through lack of attention, and they remain eunuchs. They have no cloth either of wool, linen or cotton, since they need it not; neither do they have goods of their own, but all things are held in common. They live together without king, without government, and each is his own master. They marry as many wives as they please; and son cohabits with mother, brother with sister, male cousin with female, and any man with the first woman he meets. They dissolve their marriages as often as they please, and observe no sort of law with respect to them. Beyond the fact that they have no church, no religion and are not idolaters, what more can I say? They live according to nature, and may be called Epicureans rather than Stoics. There are no merchants among their number, nor is there barter. The nations wage war upon one another without art or order. The elders by means of certain harangues of theirs bend the youths to their will and inflame them to wars in which they cruelly kill one another, and those whom they bring home captives from war they preserve, not to spare their lives, but that they may be slain for food; for they eat one another, the victors the vanquished, and among other kinds of meat human flesh is a common article of diet with them. Nay be the more assured of this fact because the father has already been seen to eat children and wife, and I knew a man whom I also spoke to who was reputed to have eaten more than three hundred human bodies. And I likewise remained twenty-seven days in a certain city where I saw salted human flesh suspended from beams between the houses, just as with us it is the custom to hang pork. I say further: they themselves wonder why we do not eat our enemies and do not use as food their flesh which they say is most savory. Their weapons are bows and arrows, and when they advance to war they cover no part of their bodies for the sake of protection, so like beasts are they in this matter. We endeavored to the extent of our power to dissuade them and persuade them to desist from these depraved customs, and they did promise us that they would leave off. The women as I have said go about naked and are very libidinous; yet they have bodies which are tolerably beautiful and cleanly. Nor are they so unsightly as one perchance might imagine; for, inasmuch as they are plump, their ugliness is the less apparent, which indeed is for the most part concealed by the excellence of their bodily structure. It was to us a matter of astonishment that none was to be seen among them who had a flabby breast, and those who had borne children were not to be distinguished from virgins by the shape and shrinking of the womb; and in the other parts of the body similar things were seen of which in the interest of modesty I make no mention. When they had the opportunity of copulating with Christians, urged by excessive lust, they defiled and prostituted themselves. They live one hundred and fifty years, and rarely fall ill, and if they do fall victims to any disease, they cure themselves with certain roots and herbs. These are the most noteworthy things I know about them. The climate there was very temperate and good, and as I was able to learn from their accounts, there was never there any pest or epidemic caused by corruption of the air; and unless they die a violent death they live long. This I take to be because the south winds are ever blowing there, and especially that which we call Eurus, which is the same to them as the Aquilo is to us. They are zealous in the art of fishing, and that sea is replete and abounding in every kind of fish. They are not hunters. This I deem to be because there are there many sorts of wild animals, and especially lions and bears and innumerable serpents and other horrid and ugly beasts, and also because forests and trees of huge size there extend far and wide; and they dare not, naked and without covering and arms, expose themselves to such hazards. The land in those parts is very fertile and pleasing, abounding in numerous hills and mountains, boundless valleys and mighty rivers, watered by refreshing springs, and filled with broad, dense and well-nigh impenetrable forests full of every sort of wild animal. Trees grow to immense size without cultivation. Many of these yield fruits delectable to the taste and beneficial to the human body; some indeed do not, and no fruits there are like those of ours. Innumerable species of herbs and roots grow there too, of which they make bread and excellent food. They have, too, many seeds altogether unlike these of ours. They have there no metals of any description except gold, of which those regions have a great plenty, although to be sure we have brought none thence on this our first voyage. This the natives called to our attention, who averred that in the districts remote from the coast there is a great abundance of gold, and by them it is in no respect esteemed or valued. They are rich in pearls as I wrote you before. If I were to seek to recount in detail what things are there and to write concerning the numerous species of animals and the great number of them, it would be a matter all too prolix and vast. And I truly believe that our Pliny did not touch upon a thousandth part of the species of parrots and other birds and the animals, too, which exist in those same regions so diverse as to form and color; because Policleitus, the master of painting in all its perfection would have fallen short in depicting them. There all trees are fragrant and they emit each and all gum, oil, or some sort of sap. If the properties of these were known to us, I doubt not but that they would be salutary to the human body. And surely if the terrestrial paradise be in any part of this earth, I esteem that it is not far distant from those parts. Its situation, as I have related, lies toward the south in such a temperate climate that icy winters and fiery summers alike are never there experienced. . . .

I observed many other very beautiful stars, the movements of which I have diligently noted down and have described beautiful with diagrams in a certain little book of mine treating of this my voyage. But at present this Most Serene King has it, which I hope he will restore to me. In that hemisphere I saw things incompatible with the opinions of philosophers. A white rainbow was twice seen about midnight, not only by me but by all the sailors. Likewise we have frequently seen the new moon on that day when it was in conjunction with the sun. Every night in that part of the sky innumerable vapors and glowing meteors fly about. I said a little while ago respecting that hemisphere that it really cannot properly be spoken of as a complete hemisphere comparing it to ours, yet since it approaches such a form, such may we be permitted to call it. . . .

These have been the more noteworthy things which I have seen in this my last voyage which I call my third chapter. For two other chapters consisted of two other voyages which I made to the west by command of the most Serene King of the Spains, during which I noted down the marvellous works wrought by that sublime creator of all things, our God. I kept a diary of noteworthy things that if sometime I am granted leisure I may bring together these singular and wonderful things and write a cosmographical or geographical work so that I may live with posterity and that the immense work of almighty God, partly unknown to the ancients, but known to us, may be understood. Accordingly I pray the most merciful God to prolong the days of my life that with His good favour and the salvation of my soul I may carry out in the best possible manner this my will. . . .

Jocundus, the translator, is turning this epistle from the Italian into the Latin tongue, that Latinists may know how many wonderful things are daily being discovered, and that the audacity of those who seek to scrutinize heaven and sovereignty and to know more than it is licit to know may be held in check inasmuch as ever since that remote time when the world began the vastness of the earth and what therein is contained has been unknown.

II

ERASMUS

Desiderius Erasmus (1469-1536) was born in Rotterdam, the illegitimate son of a priest. He was educated in the school of the Brethren of the Common Life and became a priest. He was a secretary to the Bishop of Cambrai and then a student at the University of Paris, where he studied Greek. In 1499, he went to England and became friendly with the humanists Thomas More and John Colet, who encouraged him to work on the Greek text of the New Testament. From 1500 onwards, he published a series of very popular literary works—the *Enchiridion militis Christiani*, the *Adagia*, and the *Colloquia*—that made him famous all over Europe. He traveled widely, living at various times in England, Italy, Belgium, and Switzerland. *In Praise of Folly* was written in 1509, and his critical edition of the Greek New Testament was published in 1516. He was renowned as the leading classical and humanist scholar of his day and as an advocate of Church reform. He refused at first to either support or condemn Luther but finally, in 1524, attacked him on the question of free will. Erasmus remained a Catholic throughout the rest of his life, pleading for tolerance and the spirit of Christianity against fanatics on all sides. The translation that follows is by Leonard Dean.

In Praise of Folly

The notion that happiness comes from a knowledge of things as they really are is wrong. Happiness resides in opinion. Human affairs are so obscure and various that nothing can be clearly known. This was the sound conclusion of the Academics, who were the least surly of the philosophers. At least if something can be truly known, it is rarely anything that adds to the pleasure of life. Anyway, man's mind is much more taken with appearances than with reality. This can be easily and surely tested by going to church. When anything serious is being said, the congregation dozes or squirms. But if the ranter—I mean the reverend—begins some old wives' tale, as often happens, everyone wakes up and strains to hear. You will also see more devotion being paid to such fabulous and poetic saints as George, Christopher, or Barbara than to Peter or Paul or even Christ Himself. But these examples belong elsewhere. . . .

After the lawyers come the philosophers, who are reverenced for their beards and the fur on their gowns. They announce that they alone are wise, and that the rest of men are only passing shadows. Their folly is a pleasant one. They frame countless worlds, and measure the sun, moon, stars, and spheres as with thumb and line. They unhesitatingly explain the causes of lightning, winds, eclipses, and other inexplicable things. One would think that they had access to the secrets of nature, who is the maker of all things, or that they had just come from a council of the gods. Actually, nature laughs uproariously at them all the time. The fact that they can never explain why they constantly disagree with each other is sufficient proof that they do not know the truth about anything. They know nothing at all, yet profess to know everything. They are ignorant even of themselves, and are often too absent-minded or near-sighted to see the ditch or stone in front of them. At the same time, they assert that they can see ideas, universals, pure forms, original matter, and essences—things so shadowy that I doubt if Lynceus could perceive them. They show their scorn of the layman whenever they produce their triangles, quadrangles, circles, and other mathematical forms, lay one on another or entangle them into a labyrinth, then maneuver letters as if in battle formation, and presently reverse the arrangement. It is all designed to fool the uninitiated. Among these philosophers are some who predict future events by consulting the stars, and others who promise even greater wonders. And these fortunate fellows find people to believe them.

Perhaps it would be wise to pass over the theologians in silence. That short-tempered and supercilious crew is as unpleasant to deal with as Lake Camarina or *Anagyris foetida*. They may attack me with an army of six hundred syllogisms; and if I do not recant, they will proclaim me a heretic. With this thunderbolt they terrify the people they don't like. They are extremely reluctant to acknowledge my benefits to them, which are nevertheless considerable. Their opinion of themselves is so great that they behave as if they were already in heaven; they look down pityingly on other men as so many worms. A wall of imposing definitions, conclusions, corollaries, and explicit and implicit propositions protects them. They have so many hideouts that even Vulcan could not catch them with his net. They escape through distinctions, and cut knots as easily as with a double-bitted axe from Tenedos. They are full of big words and newly-invented terms.

They explain (to suit themselves) the most difficult mysteries: how the world was created and set in order; through what channels original sin has passed to successive generations; by what means, in what form, and for how long the perfect Christ was in the womb of the Virgin; and how accidents subsist in the Eucharist without their subject. But these are nothing. Here are questions worthy of these great and reputedly illuminated theologians. If they encounter these questions they will have to extend themselves. Was divine generation at a particular instant? Are there several sonships in Christ? Is this a possible proposition: God the Father hates the Son? Could God have assumed the form of a woman, a devil, an ass, a gourd, a stone? If so, how could the gourd have preached, performed miracles, and been crucified? What would Peter have consecrated if he had administered the sacrament when Christ's body hung on the Cross? And was Christ at that moment a man? After the resurrection will it be forbidden to eat and drink? (They are providing now against hunger and thirst!) These subtleties are countless, and include even more refined propositions dealing with instants of time, opinions, relations, accidents, quiddities, entities, which no one can discern unless, like Lynceus, he can see in blackest darkness things that are not there.

There are in addition those moral maxims, or rather, contradictions, that make the so-called Stoic paradoxes seem like child's play. For example: it is less of a sin to cut the throats of a thousand men than to stitch a poor man's shoe on Sunday; it is better to commit the whole world to destruction than to tell a single lie, even a white one. These subtlest of subtleties are made more subtle by the methods of the scholastic philosophers. It is easier to escape from a maze than from the tangles of Realists, Nominalists, Thomists, Albertists, Occamists, and Scotists, to name the chief ones only. There is so much erudition and obscurity in the various schools that I imagine the apostles themselves would need some other spiritual assistance if they were to argue these topics with modern theologians.

Paul could exhibit faith, but when he said, "Faith is the substance of things hoped for, the evidence of things not seen," he did not define it scholastically. Although he exemplified charity supremely well, he analyzed and defined it with little logical subtlety in his first epistle to the Corinthians, Chapter Thirteen. No doubt the apostles consecrated the Eucharist devoutly; but suppose you had examined them about the *terminus ad quo* and the *terminus ad quem,* or about transubstantiation: in what way the body is in many places at once; the difference between the body of Christ in heaven, on the Cross, and in the sacrament; and the point at which transubstantiation takes place, considering the fact that the prayer effecting it is a distinct quantity in time. I rather doubt if they would have answered you as acutely as the Scotists do. The apostles knew the mother of Jesus, but who among them has demonstrated philosophically how she was kept free from the sin of Adam, as our theologians have done? Peter received the keys, and from Him who did not entrust them to an unworthy person; yet I suspect that he never understood—since he never became very sophisticated—how a person may have the key to wisdom without first having wisdom himself. The apostles baptized many, although they were never taught the formal, material, efficient, and final causes of baptism, nor do they observe that it has a delible and an indelible character. They certainly worshipped, but spiritually, following only the Gospel: "God is a spirit, and they that worship Him must worship Him in spirit and in truth." It does not appear to have been revealed to them that one should worship a charcoal picture on the wall as if it were Christ Himself—that is, if it has two fingers extended, the hair unshorn, and three rays in the halo behind the head. After all, who could comprehend these things if he had not devoted thirty-six years to the physics and metaphysics of Aristotle and the Scotists?

Similarly, the apostles teach grace, and yet they never distinguished between the grace that is freely given and the grace that makes one deserving. They urge good works without defining work, work worked, and work working. They always preach charity; yet they do not separate innate from acquired charity, nor explain whether charity is an accident or a substance, created or uncreated. They detest sin, but I'll stake my life that they could not define scientifically what we call sin, unless they happened to be guided by the spirit of the Scotists.

I will never believe that Paul, whose erudition was typical, would have so often condemned questions, arguments, genealogies, and what he called "strife of words," if he had been a really expert controversialist. Certainly, the debates of that time were primitive and rude, especially when compared with the more than Chrysippean subtleties of our Doctors. At the same time, these doctors are exceptionally modest: whenever they encounter something of the apostles that was written perchance in a somewhat careless or a little less than scholarly manner, they do not damn it utterly but, instead, give it a generous interpretation. This is done, of course, out of honor to the antiquity of the work and to the fame of the apostles. After all, it would be unfair to require modern scholarship from the apostles, since they had no instruction in it from their Master. If a similar error appears in Chrysostom, Basil, or Jerome, however, our scholars unhesitatingly label it, "Not accepted."

The apostles confuted the pagan philosophers and the Jews, who are the stubbornest of all, but they did so by miracles and the examples of their lives, rather than by syllogisms—a method proper to people who had not enough wit to get through a single *quodlibet* of Scotus. Nowadays, what heathen or heretic does not give in at once to our finespun subtleties? None, unless he is so stupid that he cannot understand them, or so impudent that he scorns them, or so familiar with such tricks that he can hold his own. Then, it is like matching two magicians, or two men with equally charmed swords. The result is to reweave the web of Penelope. I think the Christians would be wise to replace their heavy foot soldiers, who have had rather uneven success against the Turks and Saracens, with noisy Scotists, stubborn Occamists, invincible Albertists, and all the other sophists. They would see, I am sure, a jolly fight and a remarkable victory. Who is so calm that the keenness of these fighters would not excite him? Who so dull that such sharp points would not spur him on? Who so sharp-sighted that they would not blind him?

You may feel that I am almost joking. As a matter of fact some of the more humane divines are themselves nauseated by theological disputation. There are those who condemn as a kind of sacrilege and extreme impiety this tendency to speak with unclean lips about sacred things, which are to be worshipped rather than analyzed, to dispute with the profane methods of the heathens, to define with pride, and to defile the majesty of divine theology with pedantic and wordy language. Nevertheless, the others are so pleased with themselves and so absorbed with their smooth chatter, that they have no time to open a gospel or the epistles of Paul. They are convinced that when they are engaged in their scholastic busywork they are really, Atlas-like, supporting with syllogistic props the universal church, which otherwise would fall in ruins. They delight in altering and reforming the Holy Scriptures as if they were so much wax. It pleases them to insist that their own conclusions, which are subscribed to by a few other schoolmen, are superior to the laws of Solon and more authoritative than papal decrees. They censor whatever does not square with their implied or expressed dogmas, which they pronounce oracularly: "This proposition is scandalous. That one lacks reverence. This is heretical. That is false." Not baptism and the gospel, not Paul, Peter, Jerome, and Augustine, not even the Aristotelian Thomas himself can make a Christian, apparently, without the approving nod of these learned doctors.

III

LUTHER

MARTIN LUTHER (1483-1546) was born at Eisleben, Germany. He became an Augustinian friar and devoted himself to studying the Scriptures and the writings of the Church Fathers. He became a teacher at the Universities at Wittenberg and later Erfurt. In 1517, he began his attack on the sale of indulgences by posting his ninety-five theses on the door of the castle church at Wittenberg. In 1519, he debated Dr. Johann Eck at Leipzig and began advancing his revolutionary views. Shortly thereafter, he wrote the *Address to the German Nobility, The Liberty of the Christian Man,* and the Babylonic *Captivity of the Church,* all attacking the Catholic Church. He was excommunicated and called before the Emperor, Charles V, at the Diet of Worms in 1521, where he refused to recant. The German princes protected him, allowing him to lead the Reformation and form his own church. Thereafter, he translated the Bible into German; opposed the Peasants' Revolt (1524-1525); got married; argued with Erasmus and other Reformers; along with Melancthon, formulated the principles of Lutheranism.

Address to the Nobility

INTRODUCTION

To his most Serene and Mighty Imperial Majesty and to the Christian Nobility of the German Nation.

Dr. Martinus Luther

The grace and might of God be with you, Most Serene Majesty, most gracious, well-beloved gentlemen!

It is not out of mere arrogance and perversity that I, an individual poor man, have taken upon me to address your lordships. The distress and misery that oppress all the Christian estates, more especially in Germany, have led not only myself, but every one else, to cry aloud and to ask for help, and have now forced me too to cry out and to ask if God would give His Spirit to any one to reach a hand to His wretched people. Councils have often put forward some remedy, but it has adroitly been frustrated, and the evils have become worse, through the cunning of certain men. Their malice and wickedness I will now, by the help of God, expose, so that, being known, they may henceforth cease to be so obstructive and injurious. God has given us a young and noble sovereign, and by this has roused great hopes in many hearts; now it is right that we too should do what we can, and make good use of time and grace.

The first thing that we must do is to consider the matter with great earnestness, and, whatever we attempt, not to trust in our own strength and wisdom alone, even if the power of all the world were ours; for God will not endure that a good work should be begun trusting to our own strength and wisdom. He destroys it; it is all useless, as we read in Psalm xxxiii., "There is no king saved by the multitude of a host; a mighty man is not delivered by much strength." And I fear it is for that reason that those beloved princes the Emperors Frederick, the First and the Second, and many other German emperors were, in former times, so piteously spurned and oppressed by the popes, though they were feared by all the world. Perchance they trusted rather in their own strength than in God; therefore they could not but fall; and how would the sanguinary tyrant Julius II. have risen so high in our own days but that, I fear, France, Germany, and Venice trusted to themselves? The children of Benjamin slew forty-two thousand Israelites, for this reason: that these trusted to their own strength (Judges xx., etc.).

That such a thing may not happen to us and to our noble Emperor Charles, we must remember that in this matter we wrestle not against flesh and blood, but against the rulers of the darkness of this world (Eph. vi. 12), who may fill the world with war and bloodshed, but cannot themselves be overcome thereby. We must renounce all confidence in our natural strength, and take the matter in hand with humble trust in God; we must seek God's help with earnest prayer, and have nothing before our eyes but the misery and wretchedness of Christendom, irrespective of what punishment the wicked may deserve. If we do not act thus, we may begin the game with great pomp; but when we are well in it, the spirits of evil will make such confusion that the whole world will be immersed in blood, and yet nothing be done. Therefore let us act in the fear of God and prudently. The greater the might of the foe, the greater is the misfortune, if we do not act in the fear of God and with humility. If popes and Romanists have hitherto, with the devil's help, thrown kings into confusion, they may still do so, if we attempt things with our own strength and skill, without God's help.

THE THREE WALLS OF THE ROMANISTS

The Romanists have, with great adroitness, drawn three walls round themselves, with which they have hitherto protected themselves, so that no one could reform them, whereby all Christendom has fallen terribly.

Firstly, if pressed by the temporal power, they have affirmed and maintained that the temporal power has no jurisdiction over them, but, on the contrary, that the spiritual power is above the temporal.

Secondly, if it were proposed to admonish them with the Scriptures, they objected that no one may interpret the Scriptures but the Pope.

Thirdly, if they are threatened with a council, they pretend that no one may call a council but the Pope.

Thus they have secretly stolen our three rods, so that they may be unpunished, and entrenched themselves behind these three walls, to act with all the wickedness and malice, which we now witness. And whenever they have been compelled to call a council, they have made it of no avail by binding the princes beforehand with an oath to leave them as they were, and to give moreover to the Pope full power over the procedure of the council, so that it is all one whether we have many councils or no councils, in addition to which they deceive us with false pretences and tricks. So grievously do they tremble for their skin before a true, free council; and thus they have overawed kings and princes, that these believe they would be offending God, if they were not to obey them in all such knavish, deceitful artifices.

Now may God help us, and give us one of those trumpets that overthrew the walls of Jericho, so that we may blow down these walls of straw and paper, and that we may set free our Christian rods for the chastisement of sin, and expose the craft and deceit of the devil, so that we may amend ourselves by punishment and again obtain God's favour. . . .

¶ (*b*) The Second Wall

That no one may interpret the Scriptures but the Pope

The second wall is even more tottering and weak: that they alone pretend to be considered masters of the Scriptures; although they learn nothing of them all their life. They assume authority, and juggle before us with impudent words, saying that the Pope cannot err in matters of faith, whether he be evil or good, albeit they cannot prove it by a single letter. That is why the canon law contains so many heretical and unchristian, nay unnatural, laws; but of these we need not speak now. For whereas they imagine the Holy Ghost never leaves them, however unlearned and wicked they may be, they grow bold enough to decree whatever they like. But were this true, where were the need and use of the Holy Scriptures? Let us burn them, and content ourselves with the unlearned gentlemen at Rome, in whom the Holy Ghost dwells, who, however, can dwell in pious souls only. If I had not read it, I could never have believed that the devil should have put forth such follies at Rome and find a following.

But not to fight them with our own words, we will quote the Scriptures. St. Paul says, "If anything be revealed to another that sitteth by, let the first hold his peace" (I Cor. xiv. 30). What would be the use of this commandment, if we were to believe him alone that teaches or has the highest seat? Christ Himself says, "And they shall be all taught of God" (St. John xi. 45). Thus it may come to pass that the Pope and his followers are wicked and not true Christians, and not being taught by God, have no true understanding, whereas a common man may have true understanding. Why should we then not follow him? Has not the Pope often erred? Who could help Christianity, in case the Pope errs, if we do not rather believe another who has the Scriptures for him?

Therefore it is a wickedly devised fable—and they cannot quote a single letter to confirm it—that it is for the Pope alone to interpret the Scriptures or to confirm the interpretation of them. They have assumed the authority of their own selves. And though they say that this authority was given to St. Peter when the keys were given to him, it is plain enough that the keys were not given to St. Peter alone, but to the whole community. Besides, the keys were not ordained for doctrine or authority, but for sin, to bind or loose; and what they claim besides this from the keys is mere invention. But what Christ said to St. Peter: "I have prayed for thee that thy faith fail not" (St. Luke xxii. 32), cannot relate to the Pope, inasmuch as the greater part of the Popes have been without faith, as they are themselves forced to acknowledge; nor did Christ pray for Peter alone, but for all the Apostles and all Christians, as He says, "Neither pray I for these alone, but for them also which shall believe on Me through their word" (St. John xvii.). Is not this plain enough?

Only consider the matter. They must needs acknowledge that there are pious Christians among us that have the true faith, spirit, understanding, word, and mind of Christ: why then should we reject their word and understanding, and follow a pope who has neither understanding nor spirit? Surely this were to deny our whole faith and the Christian Church. Moreover, if the article of our faith is right, "I believe in the holy Christian Church," the Pope cannot alone be right; else we must say, "I believe in the Pope of Rome," and reduce the Christian Church to one man, which is a devilish and damnable heresy. Besides that, we are all priests, as I have said, and have all one faith, one Gospel, one Sacrament; how then should we not have the power of discerning and judging what is right or wrong in matters of faith? What becomes of St. Paul's words, "But he that is spiritual judgeth all things, yet he himself is judged of no man" (1 Cor. ii. 15), and also, "we having the same spirit of faith"? (2 Cor. iv. 13). Why then should we not perceive as well as an unbelieving pope what agrees or disagrees with our faith?

By these and many other texts we should gain courage and freedom, and should not let the spirit of liberty (as St. Paul has it) be frightened away by the inventions of the popes; we should boldly judge what they do and what they leave undone by our own believing understanding of the Scriptures, and force them to follow the better understanding, and not their own. Did not Abraham in old days have to obey his Sarah, who was in stricter bondage to him than we are to any one on earth? Thus, too, Balaam's ass was wiser than the prophet. If God spoke by an ass against a prophet, why should He not speak by a pious man against the Pope? Besides, St. Paul withstood St. Peter as being in error (Gal. ii.). Therefore it behooves every Christian to aid the faith by understanding and defending it and by condemning all errors. . . .

25. The universities also require a good, sound reformation. I must say this, let it vex whom it may. The fact is that whatever the papacy has ordered or instituted is only designed for the propagation of sin and error. What are the universities, as at present ordered, but, as the book of Maccabees says, "schools of 'Greek fashion' and 'heathenish manners' " (2 Macc. iv. 12, 13), full of dissolute living, where very little is taught of the Holy Scriptures and of the Christian faith, and the blind heathen teacher, Aristotle, rules even further than Christ? Now, my advice would be that the books of Aristotle, the *Physics,* the *Metaphysics, Of the Soul, Ethics,* which have hitherto been considered the best, be altogether abolished, with all others that profess to treat of nature, though nothing can be learned from them, either of natural or of spiritual things. Besides, no one has been able to understand his meaning, and much time has been wasted and many noble souls vexed with much useless labour, study, and expense. I venture to say that any potter has more knowledge of natural things than is to be found in these books. My heart is grieved to see how many of the best Christians this accursed, proud, knavish heathen has fooled and led astray with his false words. God sent him as a plague for our sins.

Does not the wretched man in his best book, *Of the Soul,* teach that the soul dies with the body, though many have tried to save him with vain words, as if we had not the Holy Scriptures to teach us fully of all things of which Aristotle had not the slightest perception? Yet this dead heathen has conquered, and has hindered and almost suppressed the books of the living God; so that, when I see all this misery I cannot but think that the evil spirit has introduced this study.

Then there is the *Ethics,* which is accounted one of the best, though no book is more directly contrary to God's will and the Christian virtues. Oh that such books could be kept out of the reach of all

Christians! Let no one object that I say too much, or speak without knowledge. My friend, I know of what I speak. I know Aristotle as well as you or men like you. I have read him with more understanding than St. Thomas or Scotus, which I may say without arrogance, and can prove if need be. It matters not that so many great minds have exercised themselves in these matters for many hundred years. Such objections do not affect me as they might have done once, since it is plain as day that many more errors have existed for many hundred years in the world and the universities.

I would, however, gladly consent that Aristotle's books of Logic, Rhetoric, and Poetry, should be retained, or they might be usefully studied in a condensed form, to practise young people in speaking and preaching; but the notes and comments should be abolished, and, just as Cicero's Rhetoric is read without note or comment, Aristotle's Logic should be read without such long commentaries. But now neither speaking nor preaching is taught out of them, and they are used only for disputation and toilsomeness. Besides this, there are languages–Latin, Greek, and Hebrew–the mathematics, history; which I recommend to men of higher understanding: and other matters, which will come of themselves, if they seriously strive after reform. And truly it is an important matter, for it concerns the teaching and training of Christian youths and of our noble people, in whom Christianity still abides. Therefore I think that pope and emperor could have no better task than the reformation of the universities, just as there is nothing more devilishly mischievous than an unreformed university.

Physicians I would leave to reform their own faculty; lawyers and theologians I take under my charge, and say firstly that it would be right to abolish the canon law entirely, from beginning to end, more especially the decretals. We are taught quite sufficiently in the Bible how we ought to act; all this study only prevents the study of the Scriptures, and for the most part it is tainted with covetousness and pride. And even though there were some good in it, it should nevertheless be destroyed, for the Pope having the canon law *in scrinio pectoris,*[1] all further study is useless and deceitful. At the present time the canon law is not to be found in the books, but in the whims of the Pope and his sycophants. You may have settled a matter in the best possible way according to the canon law, but the Pope has his *scrinium pectoris,* to which all law must bow in all the world. Now this *scrinium* is oftentimes directed by some knave and the devil himself, whilst it

1. In the shrine of his heart.

boasts that it is directed by the Holy Ghost. This is the way they treat Christ's poor people, imposing many laws and keeping none, forcing others to keep them or to free themselves by money. . . .

Our worthy theologians have saved themselves much trouble and labour by leaving the Bible alone and only reading the Sentences.[2] I should have thought that young theologians might begin by studying the Sentences, and that doctors should study the Bible. Now they invert this: the Bible is the first thing they study; this ceases with the Bachelor's degree; the Sentences are the last, and these they keep forever with the Doctor's degree, and this, too, under such sacred obligation that one that is not a priest may read the Bible, but a priest must read the Sentences; so that, as far as I can see, a married man might be a doctor in the Bible, but not in the Sentences. How should we prosper so long as we act so perversely, and degrade the Bible, the holy word of God? Besides this, the Pope orders with many stringent words that his laws be read and used in schools and courts; while the law of the Gospel is but little considered. The result is that in schools and courts the Gospel lies dusty underneath the benches, so that the Pope's mischievous laws may alone be in force.

Since then we hold the name and title of teachers of the Holy Scriptures, we should verily be forced to act according to our title, and to teach the Holy Scriptures and nothing else. Although, indeed, it is a proud, presumptuous title for a man to proclaim himself teacher of the Scriptures, still it could be suffered, if the works confirmed the title. But as it is, under the rule of the Sentences, we find among theologians more human and heathenish fallacies than true holy knowledge of the Scriptures. What then are we to do? I know not, except to pray humbly to God to give us Doctors of Theology. Doctors of Arts, of Medicine, of Law, of the Sentences, may be made by popes, emperors, and the universities; but of this we may be certain: a Doctor of the Holy Scriptures can be made by none but the Holy Ghost, as Christ says, "They shall all be taught of God" (John vi. 45). Now the Holy Ghost does not consider red caps or brown, or any other pomp, nor whether we are young or old, layman or priest, monk or secular, virgin or married; nay, He once spoke by an ass against the prophet that rode on it. Would to God we were worthy of having such

2. Luther refers here to the "Sentences" of Petrus Lombardus, the so-called *magister sententiarum,* which formed the basis of all dogmatic interpretation from about the middle of the twelfth century down to the Reformation.

doctors given us, be they laymen or priests, married or unmarried! But now they try to force the Holy Ghost to enter into popes, bishops, or doctors, though there is no sign to show that He is in them.

We must also lessen the number of theological books, and choose the best, for it is not the number of books that makes the learned man, nor much reading, but good books often read, however few, makes a man learned in the Scriptures and pious. Even the Fathers should only be read for a short time as an introduction to the Scriptures. As it is we read nothing else, and never get from them into the Scriptures, as if one should be gazing at the signposts and never follow the road. These good Fathers wished to lead us into the Scriptures by their writings, whereas we lead ourselves out by them, though the Scriptures are our vineyard, in which we should all work and exercise ourselves.

IV

COPERNICUS

Nicolaus Copernicus (Niklas Koppernigk, 1473-1543) was a German priest born in Torun, Poland. He attended the University at Cracow and then went to Italy, studying Canon Law, astronomy, and then medicine. Around 1506, he started his duties as a canon of Frauenberg Cathedral. There, he did some astronomical observations and began working on his heliocentric theory of astronomy, probably as early as 1510. Although he had not yet published his revolutionary views, his theory became widely known. A young German mathematician, George Joachim Rheticus, visited Copernicus in 1539 and, in 1540, published the first brief statement of the theory. The good reception of this work led Copernicus finally to permit publication of his *De revolutionibus orbium coelestium* by Rheticus and a Lutheran clergyman, Andraes Osiander. The work, dedicated to Pope Paul III (and with a spurious preface by Osiander claiming the theory was only offered as a hypothesis), was printed just as the author was dying, and the first copy was placed in his hands at the last moments of his life.

The Revolutions of the Heavenly Bodies

Dedication

TO POPE PAUL III

I can easily conceive, most Holy Father, that as soon as some people learn that in this book which I have written concerning the revolutions of the heavenly bodies, I ascribe certain motions to the Earth, they will cry out at once that I and my theory should be rejected. For I am not so much in love with my conclusions as not to weigh what others will think about them, and although I know that the meditations of a philosopher are far removed from the judgment of the laity, because his endeavor is to seek out the truth in all things, so far as this is permitted by God to the human reason, I still believe that one must avoid theories altogether foreign to orthodoxy. Accordingly, when I considered in my own mind how absurd a performance it must seem to those who know that the judgment of many centuries has approved the view that the Earth remains fixed as center in the midst of the heavens, if I should, on the contrary, assert that the Earth moves; I was for a long time at a loss to know whether I should publish the commentaries which I have written in proof of its motion, or whether it were not better to follow the example of the Pythagoreans and of some others, who were accustomed to transmit the secrets of Philosophy not in writing but orally, and only to their relatives and friends, as the letter from Lysis to Hipparchus bears witness. They did this, it seems to me, not as some think, because of a certain selfish reluctance to give their views to the world, but in order that the noblest truths, worked out by the careful study of great men, should not be despised by those who are vexed at the idea of taking great pains with any forms of literature except such as would be profitable, or by those who, if they are driven to the study of Philosophy for its own sake by the admonitions and the example of others, nevertheless, on account of their stupidity, hold a place among philosophers similar to that of drones among bees. Therefore, when I considered this carefully, the contempt which I had to fear because of the novelty and apparent absurdity of my view, nearly induced me to abandon utterly the work I had begun.

My friends, however, in spite of long delay and even resistance on my part, withheld me from this decision. First among these was Nicolaus Schonberg, Cardinal of Capua, distinguished in all branches of learning. Next to him comes my very dear friend, Tidemann Giese, Bishop of Culm, a most earnest student, as he is, of sacred and, indeed, of all good learning. The latter has often urged me, at times even spurring me on with reproaches, to publish and at last bring to the light the book which had lain in my study not nine years merely, but already going on four times nine. Not a few other very eminent and scholarly men made the same request, urging that I should no longer through fear refuse to give out my work for the common benefit of students of Mathematics. They said I should find that the more absurd most men now thought this theory of mine concerning the motion of the Earth, the more admiration and gratitude it would command after they saw in the publication of my commentaries the mist of absurdity cleared away by most transparent proofs. So, influenced by these advisors and this hope, I have at length allowed my friends to publish the work, as they had long besought me to do.

But perhaps Your Holiness will not so much wonder that I have ventured to publish these studies of mine, after having taken such pains in elaborating them that I have not hesitated to commit to writing my views of the motion of the Earth, as you will be curious to hear how it occurred to me to venture, contrary to the accepted view of mathematicians, and well-nigh contrary to common sense, to form a conception of any terrestrial motion whatsoever. Therefore I would not have it unknown to Your Holiness, that the only thing which induced me to look for another way of reckoning the movements of the heavenly bodies was that I knew that mathematicians by no means agree in their investigations thereof. For, in the first place, they are so much in doubt concerning the motion of the sun and the moon, that they can not even demonstrate and prove by observation the constant length of a complete year; and in the second place, in determining the motions both of these and of the five other planets, they fail to employ consistently one set of first principles and hypotheses, but use methods of proof based only upon the apparent revolutions and motions. For some employ concentric circles only; others, eccentric circles and epicycles; and even by these means they do not completely attain the desired end. For, although those who have depended upon concentric circles have shown that certain diverse motions can be deduced from these, yet they have not succeeded thereby in laying down any sure principle, corresponding indisputably to the phenomena. These, on the other hand, who have devised systems of eccentric circles, although they seem in great part to have solved the apparent movements by calculations which by these eccentrics are made to fit, have nevertheless introduced many things which seem to contradict the first principles of the uniformity of motion. Nor have they been able to discover or calculate from these the main point, which is the shape of the world and the fixed symmetry of its parts; but their procedure has been as if someone were to collect hands, feet, a head, and other members from various places, all very fine in themselves, but not proportionate to one body, and no single one corresponding in its turn to the others, so that a monster rather than a man would be formed from them. Thus in their process of demonstration which they term a "method," they are found to have omitted something essential, or to have included something foreign and not pertaining to the matter in hand. This certainly would never have happened to them if they had followed fixed principles; for if the hypotheses they assumed were not false, all that resulted therefrom would be verified indubitably. Those things which I am saying now may be obscure, yet they will be made clearer in their proper place.

Therefore, having turned over in my mind for a long time this uncertainty of the traditional mathematical methods of calculating the motions of the celestial bodies, I began to grow disgusted that no more consistent scheme of the movements of the mechanism of the universe, set up for our benefit by that best and most law abiding Architect of all things, was agreed upon by philosophers who otherwise investigate so carefully the most minute details of this world. Wherefore I undertook the task of rereading the books of all the philosophers I could get access to, to see whether any one ever was of the opinion that the motions of the celestial bodies were other than those postulated by the men who taught mathematics in the schools. And I found first, indeed, in Cicero, that Nicetas perceived that the Earth moved; and afterward in Plutarch I found that some others were of this opinion, whose words I have seen fit to quote here, that they may be accessible to all:—

"Some maintain that the Earth is stationary, but Philolaus the Pythagorean says that it revolves in a circle about the fire of the ecliptic, like the sun and moon. Heraklides of Pontus and Ekphantus the Pythagorean make the Earth move, not changing its position, however, confined in its falling and rising around its own center in the manner of a wheel."

Taking this as a starting point, I began to consider the mobility of the Earth; and although the idea seemed absurd, yet because I knew that the liberty had been granted to others before me to postulate all sorts of little circles for explaining the phenomena of the stars, I thought I also might easily be permitted to try whether by postulating some motion of the Earth, more reliable conclusions could be reached regarding the revolution of the heavenly bodies, than those of my predecessors.

And so, after postulating movements, which, farther on in the book, I ascribe to the Earth, I have found by many and long observations that if the movements of the other planets are assumed for the circular motion of the Earth and are substituted for the revolution of each star, not only do their phenomena follow logically therefrom, but the relative positions and magnitudes both of the stars and all their orbits, and of the heavens themselves, become so closely related that in none of its parts can anything be changed without causing confusion in the other parts and in the whole universe. Therefore, in the course of the work I have followed this plan: I describe in the first book all the positions of the orbits together with the movements which I ascribe to the Earth, in order that this book might contain, as it were, the general scheme of the universe. Thereafter in the remaining books, I set forth the motions of the other stars and of all their orbits together with the movement of the Earth, in order that one may see from this to what extent the movements and appearances of the other stars and their orbits can be saved, if they are transferred to the movement of the Earth. Nor do I doubt that ingenious and learned mathematicians will sustain me, if they are willing to recognize and weigh, not superficially, but with that thoroughness which Philosophy demands above all things, those matters which have been adduced by me in this work to demonstrate these theories. In order, however, that both the learned and the unlearned equally may see that I do not avoid anyone's judgment, I have preferred to dedicate these lucubrations of mine to Your Holiness rather than to any other, because, even in this remote center of the world where I live, you are considered to be the most eminent man in dignity of rank and in love of all learning and even of mathematics, so that by your authority and judgment you can easily suppress the bites of slanderers, albeit the proverb hath it that there is no remedy for the bite of a sycophant. If perchance there shall be idle talkers, who, though they are ignorant of all mathematical sciences, nevertheless assume the right to pass judgment on these things, and if they should dare to criticise and attack this theory of mine because of some passage of scripture which they have falsely distorted for their own purpose, I care not at all; I will even despise their judgment as foolish. For it is not unknown that Lactantius, otherwise a famous writer but a poor mathematician, speaks most childishly of the shape of the Earth when he makes fun of those who said that the Earth has the form of a sphere. It should not seem strange then to zealous students, if some such people shall ridicule us also. Mathematics are written for mathematicians, to whom, if my opinion does not deceive me, our labors will seem to contribute something to the ecclesiastical state whose chief office Your Holiness now occupies; for when not so very long ago, under Leo X, in the Lateran Council the question of revising the ecclesiastical calendar was discussed, it then remained unsettled, simply because the length of the years and months, and the motions of the sun and moon were held to have been not yet sufficiently determined. Since that time, I have given my attention to observing these more accurately, urged on by a very distinguished man, Paul, Bishop of Fossombrone, who at that time had charge of the matter. But what I may have accomplished herein I leave to the judgment of Your Holiness in particular, and to that of all other learned mathematicians; and lest I seem to Your Holiness to promise more regarding the usefulness of the work than I can perform, I now pass to the work itself.

V

KEPLER

Johannes Kepler (1571-1630), born in the Duchy of Württemberg, came from a very poor, noble family. He went to the University of Tübingen, where he studied astronomy and theology. In 1594, he was appointed to the chair of astronomy at Graz. He published his first work on astronomy in 1596, which brought him into contact with Tycho Brahe and Galileo. In 1600, he went to Prague to serve as Brahe's assistant, and, a year later, Kepler became his successor as imperial mathematician. Using Brahe's and his own observations, he published a series of works culminating in his *New Aetiological Astronomy* (1609), in which he formulated his famous laws of planetary motion, and in his *Rudolphine Tables* of astronomy (1627). After many misfortunes, he became mathematician to Upper Austria at Linz, in 1613, and there wrote his *Harmonies of the World* (1619), dedicated to James I of England, and his *Epitome of Astronomy* (1618-1621). The following selections are from the former work, translation by Charles Glenn Wallace.

The Harmonies of the World

PROEM

[268] As regards that which I prophesied two and twenty years ago (especially that the five regular solids are found between the celestial spheres), as regards that of which I was firmly persuaded in my own mind before I had seen Ptolemy's *Harmonies,* as regards that which I promised my friends in the title of this fifth book before I was sure of the thing itself, that which, sixteen years ago, in a published statement, I insisted must be investigated, for the sake of which I spent the best part of my life in astronomical speculations, visited Tycho Brahe, [269] and took up residence at Prague: finally, as God the Best and Greatest, Who had inspired my mind and aroused my great desire, prolonged my life and strength of mind and furnished the other means through the liberality of the two Emperors and the nobles of this province of Austria-on-the-Anisana: after I had discharged my astronomical duties as much as sufficed, finally, I say, I brought it to light and found it to be truer than I had even hoped, and I discovered among the celestial movements the full nature of harmony, in its due measure, together with all its parts unfolded in Book III—not in that mode wherein I had conceived it in my mind (this is not last in my joy) but in a very different mode which is also very excellent and very perfect. There took place in this intervening time, wherein the very laborious reconstruction of the movements held me in suspense, an extraordinary augmentation of my desire and incentive for the job, a reading of the *Harmonies* of Ptolemy, which had been sent to me in manuscript by John George Herward, Chancellor of Bavaria, a very distinguished man and of a nature to advance philosophy and every type of learning. There, beyond my expectations and with the greatest wonder, I found approximately the whole third book given over to the same consideration of celestial harmony, fifteen hundred years ago. But indeed astronomy was far from being of age as yet; and Ptolemy, in an unfortunate attempt, could make others subject

to despair, as being one who, like Scipio in Cicero, seemed to have recited a pleasant Pythagorean dream rather than to have aided philosophy. But both the crudeness of the ancient philosophy and this exact agreement in our meditations, down to the last hair, over an interval of fifteen centuries, greatly strengthened me in getting on with the job. For what need is there of many men? The very nature of things, in order to reveal herself to mankind, was at work in the different interpreters of different ages, and was the finger of God—to use the Hebrew expression; and here, in the minds of two men, who had wholly given themselves up to the contemplation of nature, there was the same conception as to the configuration of the world, although neither had been the other's guide in taking this route. But now since the first light eight months ago, since broad day three months ago, and since the sun of my wonderful speculation has shone fully a very few days ago: nothing holds me back. I am free to give myself up to the sacred madness, I am free to taunt mortals with the frank confession that I am stealing the golden vessels of the Egyptians, in order to build of them a temple for my God, far from the territory of Egypt. If you pardon me, I shall rejoice; if you are enraged, I shall bear up. The die is cast, and I am writing the book—whether to be read by my contemporaries or by posterity matter not. Let it await its reader for a hundred years, if God Himself has been ready for His contemplator for six thousand years. . . .

Firstly [I], therefore, let my readers grasp that today it is absolutely certain among all astronomers that all the planets revolve around the sun, with the exception of the moon, which alone has the Earth as its centre: the magnitude of the moon's sphere or orbit is not great enough for it to be delineated in this diagram in a just ratio to the rest. Therefore, to the other five planets, a sixth, the Earth, is added, which traces a sixth circle around the sun, whether by its own proper movement with the sun at rest, or motionless itself and with the whole planetary system revolving.

Secondly [II]: It is also certain that all the planets are eccentric, i.e., they change their distances from the sun, in such fashion that in one part of the circle they become farthest away from the sun, [276] and in the opposite part they come nearest to the sun. . . .

Fourthly [IV]: As regards the ratio of the planetary orbits, the ratio between two neighbouring planetary orbits is always of such a magnitude that it is easily apparent that each and every one of them approaches the single ratio of the spheres of one of the five regular solids, namely, that of the sphere circumscribing to the sphere inscribed in the figure. Nevertheless it is not wholly equal, as I once dared to promise concerning the final perfection of astronomy. For, after completing the demonstration of the intervals from Brahe's observations, I discovered the following: if the angles of the cube [277] are applied to the inmost circle of Saturn, the centres of the planes are approximately tangent to the middle circle of Jupiter; and if the angles of the tetrahedron are placed against the inmost circle of Jupiter, the centres of the planes of the tetrahedron are approximately tangent to the outmost circle of Mars; thus if the angles of the octahedron are placed against any circle of Venus (for the total interval between the three has been very much reduced), the centres of the planes of the octahedron penetrate and descend deeply within the outmost circle of Mercury, but nonetheless do not reach as far as the middle circle of Mercury; and finally, closest of all to the ratios of the dodecahedral and icosahedral spheres—which ratios are equal to one another—are the ratios or intervals between the circles of Mars and the Earth, and the Earth and Venus; and those intervals are similarly equal, if we compute from the inmost circle of Mars to the middle circle of the Earth, but from the middle circle of the Earth to the middle circle of Venus. For the middle distance of the Earth is a mean proportional between the least distance of Mars and the middle distance of Venus. However, these two ratios between the planetary circles are still greater than the ratios of those two pairs of spheres in the figures, in such fashion that the centres of the dodecahedral planes are not tangent to the outmost circle of the Earth, and the centres of the icosahedral planes are not tangent to the outmost circle of Venus; nor, however, can this gap be filled by the semidiameter of the lunar sphere, by adding it, on the upper side, to the greatest distance of the Earth and subtracting it, on the lower, from the least distance of the same. But I find a certain other ratio of figures —namely, if I take the augmented dodecahedron, to which I have given the name of echinus (as being fashioned from twelve quinquangular stars and thereby very close to the five regular solids), if I take it, I say, and place its twelve points in the inmost circle of Mars, then the sides of the pentagons, which are the bases of the single rays or points, touch the middle circle of Venus. In short: the cube and the octahedron, which are consorts, do not penetrate their planetary spheres at all; the dodecahedron and the icosahedron, which are consorts, do not wholly reach to theirs; the tetrahedron exactly touches both: in the first case there is falling short; in the second, excess; and in the third, equality, with respect to the planetary intervals.

Wherefore it is clear that the very ratios of the planetary intervals from the sun have not been taken from the regular solids alone. For the Creator, who is the very source of geometry and, as Plato wrote, "practices eternal geometry," does not stray from his own archetype. And indeed that very thing could be inferred from the fact that all the planets change their intervals throughout fixed periods of time, in such fashion that each has two marked intervals from the sun, a greatest and a least; and a fourfold comparison of the intervals from the sun is possible between two planets: the comparison can be made between either the greatest, or the least, or the contrary intervals most remote from one another, or the contrary intervals nearest together. In this way the comparisons made two by two between neighbouring planets are twenty in number, although on the contrary there are only five regular solids. But it is consonant that if the Creator had any concern for the ratio of the spheres in general, He would also have had concern for the ratio which exists between the varying intervals of the single planets specifically and that the concern is the same in both cases and the one is bound up with the other If we ponder that, we will comprehend that for setting up the diameters and eccentricities conjointly, there is need of more principles, outside of the five regular solids. . . .

The Genesis of the Eccentricities in the Single Planets from the Procurement of the Consonances between their Movements

Accordingly, since we see that the universal harmonies of all six planets cannot take place by chance, especially in the case of the extreme movements, all of which we see concur in the universal harmonies—except two, which concur in harmonies closest to the universal—and since much less can it happen by chance that all the pitches of the system of the octave (as set up in Book III) by means of harmonic divisions are designated by the extreme planetary movements, but least of all that the very subtle business of the distinction of the celestial consonances into two modes, the major and minor, should be the outcome of chance, without the special attention of the Artisan: accordingly it follows that the Creator, the source of all wisdom, the everlasting approver of order, the eternal and superexistent geyser of geometry and harmony, it follows, I say, that He, the Artisan of the celestial movements Himself, should have conjoined to the five regular solids the harmonic ratios arising from the regular plane figures, and out of both classes should have formed one most perfect archetype of the heavens: in order that in this archetype, as through the five regular solids the shapes of the spheres shine through on which the six planets are carried, so too through the consonances, which are generated from the plane figures, and deduced from them in Book III, the measures of the eccentricities in the single planets might be determined so as to proportion the movements of the planetary bodies; and in order that there should be one tempering together of the ratios and the consonances, and that the greater ratios of the spheres should yield somewhat to the lesser ratios of the eccentricities necessary for procuring the consonances, and conversely those in especial of the harmonic ratios which had a greater kinship with each solid figure should be adjusted to the planets—in so far as that could be effected by means of consonances. And in order that, finally, in that way both the ratios of the spheres and the eccentricities of the single planets might be born of the archetype simultaneously, while from the amplitude of the spheres and the bulk of the bodies the periodic times of the single planets might result.

[301] While I struggle to bring forth this process into the light of human intellect by means of the elementary form customary with geometers, may the Author of the heavens be favourable, the Father of intellects, the Bestower of mortal senses, Himself immortal and superblessed, and may He prevent the darkness of our mind from bringing forth in this work anything unworthy of His Majesty, and may He effect that we, the imitators of God by the help of the Holy Ghost, should rival the perfection of His works in sanctity of life, for which He chose His church throughout the Earth and, by the blood of His Son, cleansed it from sins, and that we should keep at a distance all the discords of enmity, all contentions, rivalries, anger, quarrels, dissensions, sects, envy, provocations, and irritations arising through mocking speech and the other works of the flesh; and that along with myself, all who possess the spirit of Christ will not only desire but will also strive by deeds to express and make sure their calling, by spurning all crooked morals of all kinds which have been veiled and painted over with the cloak of zeal or of the love of truth or of singular erudition or modesty over against contentious teachers, or with any other showy garment. Holy Father, keep us safe in the concord of our love for one another, that we may be one, just as Thou art one with Thy Son, Our Lord, and with the Holy Ghost, and just as through the sweetest bonds of harmonies Thou hast made all Thy works one; and that from the bringing of Thy people into concord the body of Thy Church may be built up in the Earth, as Thou didst erect the heavens themselves out of harmonies.

VI

GALILEO

Galileo Galilei (1564-1642) was born in Pisa. Originally a medical student, he changed to mathematics and was professor of that subject at Pisa from 1588-1591 and, later, at Padua from 1592-1610. He became court mathematician and astronomer to the Duke of Tuscany at Florence. His various discoveries in physics, astronomy, and mathematics attracted great attention. Using the telescope he had made, he found much data against the Ptolemaic and Aristotelian theories and in support of Copernicus. In 1616, he promised the Church not to teach or defend the Copernican theory. His publication (originally inspired by his friend, Pope Urban VIII) of the *Dialogue on the Two World Systems* in 1632 led to his arrest and public recantation. Thereafter, he lived in forced retirement, visited by scientific dignitaries from all over the world. In 1636, he wrote his last great work, the *Dialogues Concerning Two New Sciences,* laying the foundation for modern physics. The following selections are from his earlier works, *Letters on Sunspots* (1613), *Letter to the Grand Duchess Christina* (1615), and *The Assayer* (1623), in which he tried to justify his radical scientific views, which were under attack as heresies. The translation is by Stillman Drake.

Letters on Sunspots

. . . Now, in order that we may harvest some fruit from the unexpected marvels that have remained hidden until this age of ours, it will be well if in the future we once again lend ear to those wise philosophers whose opinion of the celestial substance differed from Aristotle's. He himself would not have departed so far from their view if his knowledge had included our present sensory evidence, since he not only admitted manifest experience among the ways of forming conclusions about physical problems, but even gave it first place. So when he argued the immutability of the heavens from the fact that no alteration had been seen in them during all the ages, it may be believed that had his eyes shown him what is now evident to us, he would have adopted the very opinion to which we are led by these remarkable discoveries. I should even think that in making the celestial material alterable, I contradict the doctrine of Aristotle much less than do those people who still want to keep the sky inalterable; for I am sure that he never took its inalterability to be as certain as the fact that all human reasoning must be placed second to direct experience. Hence they will philosophize better who give assent to propositions that depend upon manifest observations, than they who persist in opinions repugnant to the senses and supported only by probable reasons. . . .

But in my opinion we need not entirely give up contemplating things just because they are very remote from us, unless we have indeed determined that it is best to defer every act of reflection in favor of other occupations. For in our speculating we either seek to penetrate the true and internal essence of natural substances, or content ourselves with a knowledge of some of their properties. The former I hold to be as impossible an undertaking with regard to the closest elemental substances as with more remote celestial things. The substances composing the earth and the moon seem to me to be equally unknown, as do those of our elemental clouds and of sunspots. I do not see that in comprehending substances near at hand we have any advantage except copious detail; all the things among which men wander remain equally unknown, and we pass by things both near and far with very little or no real acquisition of knowledge. When I ask what the substance of clouds may be and am told that it is a moist vapor, I shall wish to know in turn what vapor is. Peradventure I shall be told that it is water, which when attenuated by heat is resolved into vapor. Equally curious about what water is, I shall then seek to find that out, ultimately learning that it is this fluid body which runs in our rivers and which we constantly handle. But this final information about water is no more intimate than what I knew about clouds in the first place; it is merely closer at hand and dependent upon more of the senses. In the same way I know no more about the true essences of earth or fire than about those of the moon or sun, for that knowledge is withheld from us, and is not to be understood until we reach the state of blessedness.

But if what we wish to fix in our minds is the apprehension of some properties of things, then it seems to me that we need not despair of our ability to acquire this respecting distant bodies just as well as those close at hand—and perhaps in some cases even more precisely in the former than in the latter. Who does not understand the periods and movements of the planets better than those of the waters of our various oceans? Was not the spherical shape of the moon discovered long before that of the earth, and much more easily? Is it not still argued whether the earth rests motionless or goes wandering, whereas we know positively the movements of many stars? Hence I should infer that although it may be vain to seek to determine the true substance of the sunspots, still it does not follow that we cannot know some properties of them, such as their location, motion, shape, size, opacity, mutability, generation, and dissolution. These in turn may become the means by which we shall be able to philosophize better about other and more controversial qualities of natural substances. And finally by elevating us to the ultimate end of our labors, which is the love of the divine Artificer, this will keep us steadfast in the hope that we shall learn every other truth in Him, the source of all light and verity. . . .

Letter to the Grand Duchess Christina

The reason produced for condemning the opinion that the earth moves and the sun stands still is that in many places in the Bible one may read that the sun moves and the earth stands still. Since the Bible cannot err, it follows as a necessary consequence that anyone takes an erroneous and heretical position who maintains that the sun is inherently motionless and the earth movable.

With regard to this argument, I think in the first place that it is very pious to say and prudent to affirm that the holy Bible can never speak untruth—whenever its true meaning is understood. But I believe nobody will deny that it is often very abstruse, and may say things which are quite different from what its bare words signify. Hence in expounding the Bible if one were always to confine oneself to the unadorned grammatical meaning, one might fall into error. Not only contradictions and propositions far from true might thus be made to appear in the Bible, but even grave heresies and follies. Thus it would be necessary to assign to God feet, hands, and eyes, as well as corporeal and human affections, such as anger, repentance, hatred, and sometimes even the forgetting of things past and ignorance of those to come. These propositions uttered by the Holy Ghost were set down in that manner by the sacred scribes in order to accommodate them to the capacities of the common people, who are rude and unlearned. For the sake of those who deserve to be separated from the herd, it is necessary that wise expositors should produce the true senses of such passages, together with the special reasons for which they were set down in these words. This doctrine is so widespread and so definite with all theologians that it would be superfluous to adduce evidence for it.

Hence I think that I may reasonably conclude that whenever the Bible has occasion to speak of any physical conclusion (especially those which are very abstruse and hard to understand), the rule has been observed of avoiding confusion in the minds of the common people which would render them contumacious toward the higher mysteries. Now the Bible, merely to condescend to popular capacity, has not hesitated to obscure some very important pronouncements, attributing to God himself some qualities extremely remote from (and even contrary to) His essence. Who, then, would positively declare that this principle has been set aside, and the Bible has confined itself rigorously to the bare and restricted sense of its words, when speaking but casually of the earth, of water, of the sun, or of any other created thing? Especially in view of the fact that these things in no way concern the primary purpose of the sacred writings, which is the service of God and the salvation of souls—matters infinitely beyond the comprehension of the common people.

This being granted, I think that in discussions of physical problems we ought to begin not from the authority of scriptural passages, but from sense-experiences and necessary demonstrations; for the holy Bible and the phenomena of nature proceed alike from the divine Word, the former as the dictate of the Holy Ghost and the latter as the observant executrix of God's commands. It is necessary for the Bible, in order to be accommodated to the understanding of every man, to speak many things which appear to differ from the absolute truth so far as the bare meaning of the words is concerned. But Nature, on the other hand, is inexorable and immutable; she never transgresses the laws imposed upon her, or cares a whit whether her abstruse reasons and methods of operation are understandable to men. For that reason it appears that nothing physical which sense-experience sets before our eyes, or which necessary demonstrations prove to us, ought to be called in question (much less condemned) upon the testimony of biblical passages which may have some different meaning beneath their words. For the Bible is not chained in every expression to conditions as strict as those which govern all physical effects; nor is God any less excellently revealed in Nature's actions than in the sacred statements of the Bible. Perhaps this is what Tertullian meant by these words:

"We conclude that God is known first through Nature, and then again, more particularly, by doctrine; by Nature in His works, and by doctrine in His revealed word."[1]

From this I do not mean to infer that we need not have an extraordinary esteem for the passages of holy Scripture. On the contrary, having arrived at any certainties in physics, we ought to utilize these as the most appropriate aids in the true exposition of the Bible and in the investigation of those meanings which are necessarily contained therein, for these must be concordant with demonstrated truths. I should judge that the authority of the Bible was designed to persuade men of those articles and propositions which, surpassing all human reasoning, could not be made credible by science, or by any other means than through the very mouth of the Holy Spirit.

Yet even in those propositions which are not matters of faith, this authority ought to be preferred over that of all human writings which are supported only by bare assertions or probable arguments, and not set forth in a demonstrative way. This I hold to be necessary and

1. *Adversus Marcionem,* ii, 18.

proper to the same extent that divine wisdom surpasses all human judgment and conjecture.

But I do not feel obliged to believe that that same God who has endowed us with senses, reason, and intellect has intended to forgo their use and by some other means to give us knowledge which we can attain by them. He would not require us to deny sense and reason in physical matters which are set before our eyes and minds by direct experience or necessary demonstrations. This must be especially true in those sciences of which but the faintest trace (and that consisting of conclusions) is to be found in the Bible. Of astronomy, for instance, so little is found that none of the planets except Venus are so much as mentioned, and this only once or twice uder the name of "Lucifer." If the sacred scribes had had any intention of teaching people certain arrangements and motions of the heavenly bodies, or had they wished us to derive such knowledge from the Bible, then in my opinion they would not have spoken of these matters so sparingly in comparison with the infinite number of admirable conclusions which are demonstrated in that science. Far from pretending to teach us the constitution and motions of the heavens and the stars, with their shapes, magnitudes, and distances, the authors of the Bible intentionally forbore to speak of these things, though all were quite well known to them. . . .

From these things it follows as a necessary consequence that, since the Holy Ghost did not intend to teach us whether heaven moves or stands still, whether its shape is spherical or like a discus or extended in a plane, nor whether the earth is located at its center or off to one side, then so much the less was it intended to settle for us any other conclusion of the same kind. And the motion or rest of the earth and the sun is so closely linked with the things just named, that without a determination of the one, neither side can be taken in the other matters. Now if the Holy Spirit has purposely neglected to teach us propositions of this sort as irrelevant to the highest goal (that is, to our salvation), how can anyone affirm that it is obligatory to take sides on them, and that one belief is required by faith, while the other side is erroneous? Can an opinion be heretical and yet have no concern with the salvation of souls? Can the Holy Ghost be asserted not to have intended teaching us something that does concern our salvation? I would say here something that was heard from an ecclesiastic of the most eminent degree: "That the intention of the Holy Ghost is to teach us how one goes to heaven, not how heaven goes." . . .

The Assayer

A Letter to the Illustrious and Very Reverend Don Virginio Cesarini[1]

I have never understood, Your Excellency, why it is that every one of the studies I have published in order to please or to serve other people has aroused in some men a certain perverse urge to detract, steal, or deprecate that modicum of merit which I thought I had earned, if not for my work, at least for its intention. In my *Starry Messenger* there were revealed many new and marvelous discoveries in the heavens that should have gratified all lovers of true science; yet scarcely had it been printed when men sprang up everywhere who envied the praises belonging to the discoveries there revealed. Some, merely to contradict what I had said, did not scruple to cast doubt upon things they had seen with their own eyes again and again.

My lord the Grand Duke Cosimo II, of glorious memory, once ordered me to write down my opinions about the causes of things floating or sinking in water, and in order to comply with that command I put on paper everything I could think of beyond the teachings of Archimedes, which perhaps is as much as may truly be said on this subject. Immediately the entire press was filled with attacks against my *Discourse*. My opinions were contradicted without the least regard for the fact that what I had set forth was supported and proved by geometrical demonstrations; and such is the strength of men's passion that they failed to notice how the contradiction of geometry is a bald denial of truth.

How many men attacked my *Letters on Sunspots*, and under what disguises! The material contained therein ought to have opened to the mind's eye much room for admirable speculation; instead it met with scorn and derision. Many people disbelieved it or failed to appreciate it. Others, not wanting to agree with my ideas, advanced ridiculous and impossible opinions against me; and some, overwhelmed and convinced by my arguments, attempted to rob me of that glory which was mine, pretending not to have seen my writings and trying to represent themselves as the original discoverers of these impressive marvels. . . .

---

1. Cesarini (1595-1624) was a brilliant man of letters at whose house in Rome Galileo had often debated in favor of Copernicus during his ill-starred visit in 1615-1616. He had served as confidential secretary to Pope Gregory XV and was appointed chamberlain by Urban VIII in 1623.

In Sarsi I seem to discern the firm belief that in philosophizing one must support oneself upon the opinion of some celebrated author, as if our minds ought to remain completely sterile and barren unless wedded to the reasoning of some other person. Possibly he thinks that philosophy is a book of fiction by some writer, like the *Iliad* or *Orlando Furioso,* productions in which the least important thing is whether what is written there is true. Well, Sarsi, that is not how matters stand. Philosophy is written in this grand book, the universe, which stands continually open to our gaze. But the book cannot be understood unless one first learns to comprehend the language and read the letters in which it is composed. It is written in the language of mathematics, and its characters are triangles, circles, and other geometric figures without which it is humanly impossible to understand a single word of it; without these, one wanders about in a dark labryinth. . . .

It now remains for me to tell Your Excellency, as I promised, some thoughts of mine about the proposition "motion is the cause of heat," and to show in what sense this may be true. But first I must consider what it is that we call heat, as I suspect that people in general have a concept of this which is very remote from the truth. For they believe that heat is a real phenomenon, or property, or quality, which actually resides in the material by which we feel ourselves warmed. Now I say that whenever I conceive any material or corporeal substance, I immediately feel the need to think of it as bounded, and as having this or that shape; as being large or small in relation to other things, and in some specific place at any given time; as being in motion or at rest; as touching or not touching some other body; and as being one in number, or few, or many. From these conditions I cannot separate such a substance by any stretch of my imagination. But that it must be white or red, bitter or sweet, noisy or silent, and of sweet or foul odor, my mind does not feel compelled to bring in as necessary accompaniments. Without the senses as our guides, reason or imagination unaided would probably never arrive at qualities like these. Hence I think that tastes, odors, colors, and so on are no more than mere names so far as the object in which we place them is concerned, and that they reside only in the consciousness. Hence if the living creature were removed, all these qualities would be wiped away and annihilated. But since we have imposed upon them special names, distinct from those of the other and real qualities mentioned previously, we wish to believe that they really exist as actually different from those.

I may be able to make my notion clearer by means of some examples. I move my hand first over a marble statue and then over a living man. As to the effect flowing from my hand, this is the same with regard to both objects and my hand; it consists of the primary phenomena of motion and touch, for which we have no further names. But the live body which receives these operations feels different sensations according to the various places touched. When touched upon the soles of the feet, for example, or under the knee or armpit, it feels in addition to the common sensation of touch a sensation on which we have imposed a special name, "tickling." This sensation belongs to us and not to the hand. Anyone would make a serious error if he said that the hand, in addition to the properties of moving and touching, possessed another faculty of "tickling," as if tickling were a phenomenon that resided in the hand that tickled. A piece of paper or a feather drawn lightly over any part of our bodies performs intrinsically the same operations of moving and touching, but by touching the eye, the nose, or the upper lip it excites in us an almost intolerable titillation, even though elsewhere it is scarcely felt. This titillation belongs entirely to us and not to the feather; if the live and sensitive body were removed it would remain no more than a mere word. I believe that no more solid an existence belongs to many qualities which we have come to attribute to physical bodies—tastes, odors, colors, and many more.

A body which is solid and, so to speak, quite material, when moved in contact with any part of my person produces in me the sensation we call touch. This, though it exists over my entire body, seems to reside principally in the palms of the hands and in the finger tips, by whose means we sense the most minute differences in texture that are not easily distinguished by other parts of our bodies. Some of these sensations are more pleasant to us than others. . . . The sense of touch is more material than the other senses; and, as it arises from the solidity of matter, it seems to be related to the earthly element.

Perhaps the origin of two other senses lies in the fact that there are bodies which constantly dissolve into minute particles, some of which are heavier than air and descend, while others are lighter and rise up. The former may strike upon a certain part of our bodies that is much more sensitive than the skin, which does not feel the invasion of such subtle matter. This is the upper surface of the tongue; here the tiny particles are received, and mixing with and penetrating its moisture, they give rise to tastes, which are sweet or unsavory according to the various shapes, numbers, and speeds of the particles. And those minute particles which rise up may enter by our nostrils and strike upon some small protuberances which are the instrument of smelling; here likewise their touch and passage is received to our like or dislike according as they have this or that shape, are fast or slow, and are numerous or few. The tongue and nasal passages are providently arranged for these things, as the one extends from below to receive descending particles, and the other is adapted to those which ascend. Perhaps the excitation of tastes may be given a certain analogy to fluids, which descend through air, and odors to fires, which ascend.

Then there remains the air itself, an element available for sounds, which come to us indifferently from below, above, and all sides—for we reside in the air and its movements displace it equally in all directions. The location of the ear is most fittingly accommodated to all positions in space. Sounds are made and heard by us when the air—without any special property of "sonority" or "transonority"—is ruffled by a rapid tremor into very minute waves and moves certain cartilages of a tympanum in our ear. External means capable of thus ruffling the air are very numerous, but for the most part they may be reduced to the trembling of some body which pushes the air and disturbs it. Waves are propagated very rapidly in this way, and high tones are produced by frequent waves and low tones by sparse ones.

To excite in us tastes, odors, and sounds I believe that nothing is required in external bodies except shapes, numbers, and slow or rapid movements. I think that if ears, tongues, and noses were removed, shapes and numbers and motions would remain, but not odors or tastes or sounds. The latter, I believe, are nothing more than names when separated from living beings, just as tickling and titillation are nothing but names in the absence of such things as noses and armpits. And as these four senses are related to the four elements, so I believe that vision, the sense eminent above all others in the proportion of the finite to the infinite, the temporal to the instantaneous, the quantitative to the indivisible, the illuminated to the obscure—that vision, I say, is related to light itself. But of this sensation and the things pertaining to it I pretend to understand but little; and since even a long time would not suffice to explain that trifle, or even to hint at an explanation, I pass this over in silence.

Having shown that many sensations which are supposed to be qualities residing in external objects have no real existence save in us, and outside ourselves are mere names, I now say that I am inclined to believe heat to be of this character. Those materials which produce heat in us and make us feel warmth, which are known by the general name of "fire," would then be a multitude of minute particles having certain shapes and moving with certain velocities. Meeting with our bodies, they penetrate by means of their extreme subtlety, and their touch as felt by us when they pass through our substance is the sensation we call "heat." This is pleasant or unpleasant according to the greater or smaller speed of these particles as they go pricking and penetrating; pleasant when this assists our necessary transpiration, and obnoxious when it causes too great a separation and dissolution of our substance. The operation of fire by means of its particles is merely that in moving it penetrates all bodies, causing their speedy or slow dissolution in proportion to the number and velocity of the fire-corpuscles and the density or tenuity of the bodies. Many materials are such that in their decomposition the greater part of them passes over into additional tiny corpuscles, and this dissolution continues so long as these continue to meet with further matter capable of being so resolved. I do not believe that in addition to shape, number, motion, penetration, and touch there is any other quality in fire corresponding to "heat"; this belongs so intimately to us that when the live body is taken away, heat becomes no more than a simple name. . . .

VII

MONTAIGNE

MICHEL DE MONTAIGNE (1533-1592) was born near Bordeaux of a Catholic father and a Spanish Jewish mother. He was educated at the Collège de Guyenne and, possibly, at the University of Toulouse. He held various political posts, including that of Mayor of Bordeaux and was a friend of various leaders of the Reformation and Counter Reformation in France, including Henri of Navarre (later Henri IV). He translated the rationalistic theological treatise of Raimond Sebond because his father wished him to. The "Apology for Raimond Sebond" (from which these selections are taken) was written around 1576, during Montaigne's "skeptical crisis," caused in part by his reading of the Greek skeptic, Sextus Empiricus. The "Apology" was first published as part of the *Essais,* Montaigne's various rambling discussions on all sorts of topics, in 1580. (The complete set of the *Essais* appeared in 1588.) The "Apology" quickly became the best known statement of skepticism in the European intellectual world. The translation is by Donald M. Frame.

The Apology for Raimond Sebond

. . . Now it is nevertheless a great consolation to the Christian to see our frail mortal tools so properly suited to our holy and divine faith, that when they are used on subjects that are by their nature frail and mortal, they are no more completely and powerfully appropriate. Let us see then if man has within his power other reasons more powerful than those of Sebond, or indeed if it is in him to arrive at any certainty by argument and reason. . . .

What does truth preach to us when she exhorts us to flee worldly philosophy, when she so often inculcates in us that our wisdom is but folly before God; that of all vanities the vainest is man; that the man who is presumptuous of his knowledge does not yet know what knowledge is; and that man, who is nothing, if he thinks he is something, seduces and deceives himself? . . .

Let us then consider for the moment man alone, without outside assistance, armed solely with his own weapons, and deprived of divine grace and knowledge, which is his whole honor, his strength, and the foundation of his being. Let us see how much presence he has in this fine array. Let him help me to understand, by the force of his reason, on what foundations he has built these great advantages that he thinks he has over other creatures. Who has persuaded him that the admirable motion of the celestial vault, the eternal light of those torches rolling so proudly above his head, the fearful movements of that infinite sea, were established and have lasted so many centuries for his convenience and his service? Is it possible to imagine anything so ridiculous as that this miserable and puny creature, who is not even master of himself, exposed to the attacks of all things, should call himself master and emperor of the universe, the least part of which it is not in his power to know, much less to command? . . .

Presumption is our natural and original malady. The most vulnerable and frail of all creatures is man, and at the same time the most arrogant. He feels and sees himself lodged here, amid the mire and dung of the world, nailed and riveted to the worst, the deadest, and the most stagnant part of the universe, on the lowest story of the house and the farthest from the vault of heaven, with the animals of the worst condition of the three, and in his imagination he goes planting himself above the circle of the moon, and bringing the sky down beneath his feet. It is by the vanity of this same imagination that he equals himself to God, attributes to himself divine characteristics, picks himself out and separates himself from the horde of other creatures, carves out their shares to his fellows and companions the animals, and distributes among them such portions of faculties and powers as he sees fit. How does he know, by the force of his intelligence, the secret internal stirrings of animals? By what comparison between them and us does he infer the stupidity that he attributes to them?

When I play with my cat, who knows if I am not a pastime to her more than she is to me? . . .

But even if knowledge would actually do what they say, blunt and lessen the keenness of the misfortunes that pursue us, what does it do but what ignorance does much more purely and more evidently? The philosopher Pyrrho, incurring the peril of a great storm at sea, offered those who were with him nothing better to imitate than the assurance of a pig that was travelling with them, and that was looking at this tempest without fear. Philosophy, at the end of her precepts, sends us back to the examples of an athlete or a muleteer, in whom we ordinarily see much less feeling of death, pain, and other discomforts, and more firmness than knowledge ever supplied to any man who had not been born and prepared for it on his own by natural habit. . . .

What they tell us of the Brazilians, that they died only of old age, which is attributed to the serenity and tranquillity of their air, I attribute rather to the tranquillity and serenity of their souls, unburdened with any tense or unpleasant passion or thought or occupation, as people who spent their life in admirable simplicity and ignorance, without letters, without law, without king, without religion of any kind. . . .

The participation that we have in the knowledge of truth, whatever it may be, has not been acquired by our own powers. God has taught us that clearly enough by the witnesses that he has chosen from the common people, simple and ignorant, to instruct us in his admirable secrets. Our faith is not of our own acquiring, it is a pure present of another's liberality. It is not by reasoning or by our understanding that we have received our religion; it is by external authority and command. The weakness of our judgment helps us more in this than its strength, and our blindness more than our clear-sightedness. It is by the mediation of our ignorance more than of our knowledge that we are learned with that divine learning. It is no wonder if our natural and earthly powers cannot conceive that supernatural and heavenly knowledge; let us bring to it nothing of our own but obedience and submission. For, as it is written, "I will destroy the wisdom of the wise, and will bring to nothing the understanding of the prudent. Where is the wise? where is the scribe? where is the disputer of this world? hath not God made foolish the wisdom of this world? For after that the world by wisdom knew not God, it pleased God by the foolishness of preaching to save them that believe" [I Corinthians].

Yet must I see at last whether it is in the power of man to find what he seeks, and whether that quest that he has been making for so many centuries has enriched him with any new power and any solid truth.

I think he will confess to me, if he speaks in all conscience, that all the profit he has gained from so long a pursuit is to have learned to acknowledge his weakness. The ignorance that was naturally in us we have by long study confirmed and verified. . . .

Ignorance that knows itself, that judges itself and condemns itself, is not complete ignorance: to be that, it must be ignorant of itself. So to be sure of nothing, to answer for nothing. . . .

. . . They do not fear contradiction in their discussion. When they say that heavy things go down, they would be very sorry to have anyone take their word for it; and they seek to be contradicted, so as to create doubt and suspension of judgment, which is their goal. They advance their propositions only to combat those they think we believe in. . . .

. . . Is it not better to remain in suspense than to entangle yourself in the many errors that the human fancy has produced? Is it not better to suspend your conviction than to get mixed up in these seditious and quarrelsome divisions?

What am I to choose? What you like, provided you choose! There is a stupid answer, to which nevertheless all dogmatism seems to come, by which we are not allowed not to know what we do not know.

Take the most famous theory, it will never be so sure but that in order to defend it you will have to attack and combat hundreds of contrary theories. Is it not better to keep out of this melee? . . .

The Pyrrhonians have kept themselves a wonderful advantage in combat, having rid themselves of the need to cover up. It does not matter to them that they are struck, provided they strike; and they do their work with everything. If they win, your proposition is lame; if you win, theirs is. If they lose, they confirm ignorance; if you lose, you confirm it. . . . They use their reason to inquire and debate, but not to conclude and choose. Whoever will imagine a perpetual confession of ignorance, a judgment without leaning or inclination, on any occasion whatever, he has a conception of Pyrrhonism. . . .

There is nothing in man's invention that has so much verisimilitude and usefulness. It presents man naked and empty, acknowledging his natural weakness, fit to receive from above some outside power; stripped of human knowledge, and all the more apt to lodge divine knowledge in himself, annihilating his judgment to make more room for faith; neither disbelieving nor setting up any doctrine against the common observances; humble, obedient, teachable, zealous; a sworn enemy of heresy, and consequently free from the vain and irreligious opinions introduced by the false sects. He is a blank tablet prepared to take from the finger of God such forms as he shall be pleased to engrave on it. . . .

I can see why the Pyrrhonian philosophers cannot express their general conception in any manner of speaking; for they would need a new language. Ours is wholly formed of affirmative propositions, which to them are utterly repugnant; so that when they say "I doubt," immediately you have them by the throat to make them admit that at least they know and are sure of this fact, that they doubt. Thus they have been constrained to take refuge in this comparison from medicine, without which their attitude would be inexplicable: when they declare "I do not know" or "I doubt," they say that this proposition carries itself away with the rest, no more nor less than rhubarb, which expels evil humors and carries itself off with them.

This idea is more firmly grasped in the form of interrogation: "What do I know?"—the words I bear as a motto, inscribed over a pair of scales. . . .

It is very easy, upon accepted foundations, to build what you please; for according to the law and ordering of this beginning, the rest of the parts of the building are easily done, without contradictions. By this path we find our reason well founded, and we argue with great ease. For our masters occupy and win beforehand as much room in our belief as they need in order to conclude afterward whatever they wish, in the manner of the geometricians with their axioms; the consent and approval that we lend them giving them the wherewithal to drag us left or right, and to spin us around at their will. Whoever is believed in his presuppositions, he is our master and our God. . . . For each science has its presupposed principles, by which human judgment is bridled on all sides. If you happen to crash this barrier in which lies the principal error, immediately they have this maxim in their mouth, that there is no arguing against people who deny first principles.

Now there cannot be first principles for men, unless the Divinity has revealed them; all the rest–beginning, middle, and end–is nothing but dreams and smoke. To those who fight by presupposition, we must presuppose the opposite of the same axiom we are disputing about. For every human presupposition and every enunciation has as much authority as another, unless reason shows the difference between them. Thus they must all be put in the scales, and first of all the general ones, and those which tyrannize over us. The impression of certainty is a certain token of folly and extreme uncertainty . . .

That things do not lodge in us in their own form and essence, or make their entry into us by their own power and authority, we see clearly enough. Because, if that were so, we should receive them in the same way: wine would be the same in the mouth of a sick man as in the mouth of a healthy man; he who has chapped or numb fingers would find the same hardness in the wood or iron he handles as does another. Thus external objects surrender to our mercy; they dwell in us as we please.

Now if for our part we received anything without alteration, if the human grip was capable and firm enough to grasp the truth by our own means; these means being common to all men, this truth would be bandied from hand to hand, from one man to another; and at least there would be one thing in the world, out of all there are, that would be believed by all men with universal consent. But this fact, that no proposition can be seen which is not debated and controverted among us, or which may not be, well shows that our natural judgment does not grasp very clearly what it grasps. For my judgment cannot make my companion's judgment accept it; which is a sign that I have grasped it by some other means than by a natural power that is in me and in all men.

Let us leave aside that infinite confusion of opinions that is seen among the philosophers themselves, and that perpetual and universal debate over the knowledge of things. For this is a very true presupposition: that men are in agreement about nothing. I mean even the most gifted and ablest scholars, not even that the sky is over our head. For those who doubt everything also doubt that; and those who deny that we can understand anything say that we have not understood that the sky is over our head; and these two views are incomparably the strongest in number.

Besides this infinite diversity and division, it is easy to see by the confusion that our judgment gives to our own selves, and the uncertainty that each man feels within himself, that it has a very insecure seat. How diversely we judge things! How many times we change our notions! What I hold today and what I believe, I hold and believe it with all my belief; all my tools and all my springs of action grip this opinion and sponsor it for me in every way they can. I could not embrace or preserve any truth with more strength than this one. I belong to it entirely, I belong to it truly. But has it not happened to me, not once, but a hundred times, a thousand times, and every day, to have embraced with these same instruments, in this same condition, something else that I have since judged false? . . .

Now from the knowledge of this mobility of mine I have accidentally engendered in myself a certain constancy of opinions, and have scarcely altered my original and natural ones. For whatever appearance of truth there may be in novelty, I do not change easily, for fear of losing in the change. And since I am not capable of choosing, I accept other people's choice and stay in the position where God put me. Otherwise I could not keep myself from rolling about incessantly. Thus I have, by the grace of God, kept myself intact, without agitation or disturbance of conscience, in the ancient beliefs of our religion, in the midst of so many sects and divisions that our century has produced.

The writings of the ancients, I mean the good writings, full and solid, tempt me and move me almost wherever they please; the one I am listening to always seems to me the strongest; I find each one right in his turn, although they contradict each other. . . .

The sky and the stars have been moving for three thousand years; everybody had so believed, until it occurred to Cleanthes of Samos, or (according to Theophrastus) to Nicetas of Syracuse, to maintain that it was the earth that moved, through the oblique circle of the Zodiac; turning about its axis; and in our day Copernicus has grounded this doctrine so well that he uses it very systematically for all astronomical deductions. What are we to get out of that, unless that we should not bother which of the two is so? And who knows whether a third opinion, a thousand years from now, will not overthrow the preceding two? . . .

Thus when some new doctrine is offered to us, we have great occasion to distrust it, and to consider that before it was produced its opposite was in vogue; and, as it was overthrown by this one, there may arise in the future a third invention that will likewise smash the second. Before the principles which Aristotle introduced were in credit, other principles satisfied human reason, as his satisfy us at this moment. What letters-patent have these, what special privilege, that the course of our invention stops at them, and that to them belongs possession of our belief for all time to come? They are no more exempt from being thrown out than were their predecessors. . . .

How long is it that medicine has been in the world? They say that a newcomer, whom they call Paracelsus, is changing and overthrowing the whole order of the ancient rules, and maintaining that up to this moment it has been good for nothing but killing men. I think he will easily prove that; but as for putting my life to the test of his new experience, I think that would not be great wisdom.

We must not believe every man, says the maxim, because any man may say anything.

A man of that profession of novelties and of reforms in physics was saying to me not long ago that all the ancients had evidently been mistaken about the nature and movements of the winds, which fact he would make so palpable that I could touch it, if I would hear him out. After I had taken some patience to listen to his arguments, which were full of likelihood: "What?" I said to him. "Then did those who navigated under the laws of Theophrastus go west when they headed east? Did they go sideways, or backward?" "That was luck," he replied; "at all events they miscalculated." I then replied to him that I would rather follow facts than reason. . . .

Ptolemy, who was a great man, had established the limits of our world; all the ancient philosophers thought they had its measure, except for a few remote islands that might escape their knowledge. It would have been Pyrrhonizing, a thousand years ago, to cast in doubt the science of cosmography, and the opinions that were accepted about it by one and all; it was heresy to admit the existence of the Antipodes. Behold in our century an infinite extent of terra firma, not an island or one particular country, but a portion nearly equal in size to the one we know, which has just been discovered. The geographers of the present time do not fail to assure us that now all is discovered and all is seen,

> For what we have at hand always seems best of all.
>
> —LUCRETIUS

The question is, if Ptolemy was once mistaken on the grounds of his reason, whether it would not be stupid for me now to trust to what these people say about it; and whether it is not more likely that this great body that we call the world is something quite different from what we judge. . . .

This subject has brought me to the consideration of the senses, in which lies the greatest foundation and proof of our ignorance. All that is known, is doubtless known through the faculty of the knower; for since judgment comes from the operation of him who judges, it stands to reason that he performs this operation by his means and will, not by the constraint of others, as would happen if we knew things through the power and according to the law of their own essence.

Now all knowledge makes its way into us through the senses; they are our masters: . . . Knowledge begins through them and is resolved into them.

After all, we would know no more than a stone, if we did not know that there is sound, smell, light, taste, measure, weight, softness, hardness, roughness, color, smoothness, breadth, depth. These are the base and the principles of the whole edifice of our knowledge. And according to some, knowledge is nothing else but sensation. Whoever can force me to contradict the senses has me by the throat; he could not make me retreat any further. The senses are the beginning and the end of human knowledge: . . .

Attribute to them as little as you can, still you must grant them this, that by way of them and by their mediation proceeds all our instruction. . . .

The first consideration that I offer on the subject of the senses is that I have my doubts whether man is provided with all the senses of nature. I see many animals that live a complete and perfect life, some without sight, others without hearing; who knows whether we too do not still lack one, two, three, or many other senses? For if any one is lacking, our reason cannot discover its absence. It is the privilege of the senses to be the extreme limit of our perception. There is nothing beyond them that can help us to discover them; no, nor can one sense discover the other: . . .

It is impossible to make a man who was born blind conceive that he does not see; impossible to make him desire sight and regret its absence. Wherefore we should take no assurance from the fact that our soul is content and satisfied with those senses we have, seeing that it has no means of feeling its malady and imperfection therein, if any there be. . . .

. . . The properties that we call occult in many things, as that of the magnet to attract iron—is it not likely that there are sensory faculties in nature suitable to judge them and perceive them, and that the lack of such faculties causes our ignorance of the true essence of such things? Perhaps it is some particular sense that reveals to cocks the hours of morning and midnight, and moves them to crow; . . .

. . . We have formed a truth by the consultation and concurrence of our five senses; but perhaps we needed the agreement of eight or ten senses, and their contribution, to perceive it certainly and in its essence. . . .

As for the error and uncertainty of the operation of the senses, each man can furnish himself with as many examples as he pleases, so ordinary are the mistakes and deceptions that they offer us. At the echo in a valley, the sound of a trumpet seems to come from in front of us, when it comes from a league behind . . .

. . . For that the senses are many a time masters of reason, and constrain it to receive impressions that it knows and judges to be false, is seen at every turn. . . .

Put a philosopher in a cage of thin wire in large meshes, and hang it from the top of the towers of Notre Dame of Paris: he will see by evident reason that it is impossible for him to fall, and yet (unless he is used to the trade of the steeplejacks) he cannot keep the sight of this extreme height from terrifying and paralyzing him. . . .

This same deception that the senses convey to our understanding they receive in their turn. Our souls at times take a like revenge; they compete in lying and deceiving each other. What we see and hear when stirred with anger, we do not hear as it is: . . . The object that we love seems to us more beautiful than it is—

> Thus women oft we see, ugly and bent,
> Receive men's love, and honors eminent
> —LUCRETIUS

—and uglier the one that we loathe. To a man vexed and afflicted the brightness of the day seems darkened and gloomy. Our senses are not only altered, but often completely stupefied by the passions of the soul. . . .

Those who have compared our life to a dream were perhaps more right than they thought. . . .

Sleeping we are awake, and waking asleep. I do not see so clearly in sleep; but my wakefulness I never find pure and cloudless enough. Moreover sleep in its depth sometimes puts dreams to sleep. But our wakefulness is never so awake as to purge and properly dissipate reveries, which are the dreams of the waking, and worse than dreams.

Since our reason and our soul accept the fancies and opinions which arise in it while sleeping, and authorize the actions of our dreams with the same approbation as they do those of the day, why do we not consider the possibility that our thinking, our acting, may be another sort of dreaming, and our waking another kind of sleep?

If the senses are our first judges, it is not ours alone that must be consulted, for in this faculty the animals have as much right as we have, or more. It is certain that some have hearing keener than man's, others sight, others smell, others touch or taste. Democritus said that the gods and the animals had much more perfect sensitive faculties than man. . . .

Those who have jaundice see all things as yellowish and paler than we do: . . . Those who have that malady that the doctors call hyposphagma, which is a suffusion of blood under the skin, see everything as red and bloody. These humors which thus change the operations of our sight, how do we know but that they predominate in animals and are the ordinary thing with them? For we see some that have yellow eyes like our sufferers from jaundice, others that have them red and bloodshot. It is probable that to them the color of objects appears different than to us. Which of the two is the true judgment? . . .

To judge the action of the senses, then, we should first of all be in agreement with the animals, and second, among ourselves. Which we are not in the least; and we get into disputes at every turn because one man hears, sees, or tastes something differently from someone else; and we dispute about the diversity of the images that the senses bring us as much as about anything else. By the ordinary rule of nature, a child hears, sees, and tastes otherwise than a man of thirty, and he otherwise than a sexagenarian.

The senses are in some people more obscure and dim, in others more open and acute. We receive things in one way and another, according to what we are and what they seem to us. Now since our seeming is so uncertain and controversial, it is no longer a miracle if we are told that we can admit that snow appears white to us, but that we cannot be responsible for proving that it is so of its essence and in truth; and, with this starting point shaken, all the knowledge in the world necessarily goes by the board. . . .

Moreover, since the accidents of illnesses, madness, or sleep make things appear to us otherwise than they appear to healthy people, wise men, and waking people, is it not likely that our normal state and our natural disposition can also assign to things an essence corresponding to our condition, and accommodate them to us, as our disordered states do? And that our health is as capable of giving them its own appearance as sickness? Why should the temperate man not have some vision of things related to himself, like the intemperate man, and likewise imprint his own character on them? . . .

Now, since our condition accommodates things to itself and transforms them according to itself, we no longer know what things are in truth; for nothing comes to us except falsified and altered by our senses. When the compass, the square, and the ruler are off, all the proportions drawn from them, all the buildings erected by their measure, are also necessarily imperfect and defective. The uncertainty of our senses makes everything they produce uncertain: . . . Furthermore, who shall be fit to judge these differences? As we say in disputes about religion that we need a judge not attached to either party, free from preference and passion, which is impossible among Christians, so it is in this. For if he is old, he cannot judge the sense perception of old age, being himself a party in this dispute; if he is young, likewise; healthy, likewise; likewise sick, asleep, or awake. We would need someone exempt from all these qualities, so that with an unprejudiced judgment he might judge of these propositions as of things indifferent to him; and by that score we would need a judge that never was.

To judge the appearances that we receive of objects, we would need a judicatory instrument; to verify this instrument, we need a demonstration; to verify the demonstration, an instrument: there we are in a circle.

Since the senses cannot decide our dispute, being themselves full of uncertainty, it must be reason that does so. No reason can be established without another reason: there we go retreating back to infinity.

Our conception is not itself applied to foreign objects, but is conceived through the mediation of the senses; and the senses do not comprehend the foreign object, but only their own impressions. And thus the conception and semblance we form is not of the object, but only of the impression and effect made on the sense; which impression and the object are different things. Wherefore whoever judges by appearances judges by something other than the object.

And as for saying that the impressions of the senses convey to the soul the quality of the foreign objects by resemblance, how can the soul and understanding make sure of this resemblance, having of itself no communication with foreign objects? Just as a man who does not know Socrates, seeing his portrait, cannot say that it resembles him.

Now if anyone should want to judge by appearances anyway, to judge by all appearances is impossible, for they clash with one another by their contradictions and discrepancies, as we see by experience. Shall some selected appearances rule the others? We shall have to verify this selection by another selection, the second by a third; and thus it will never be finished.

Finally, there is no existence that is constant, either of our being or of that of objects. And we, and our judgment, and all mortal things go on flowing and rolling unceasingly. Thus nothing certain can be established about one thing by another, both the judging and the judged being in continual change and motion.

We have no communication with being, because every human nature is always midway between birth and death, offering only a dim semblance and shadow of itself, and an uncertain and feeble opinion. And if by chance you fix your thought on trying to grasp its essence, it will be neither more nor less than if someone tried to grasp water: for the more he squeezes and presses what by its nature flows all over, the more he will lose what he was trying to hold and grasp. Thus, all things being subject to pass from one change to another, reason, seeking a real stability in them, is baffled, being unable to apprehend anything stable and permanent; because everything is either coming into being and not yet fully existent, or beginning to die before it is born. . . .

. . . Nor can man raise himself above himself and humanity; for he can see only with his own eyes, and seize only with his own grasp.

He will rise, if God by exception lends him a hand; he will rise by abandoning and renouncing his own means, and letting himself be raised and uplifted by purely celestial means.

It is for our Christian faith, not for his Stoical virtue, to aspire to that divine and miraculous metamorphosis.

VIII

BACON

FRANCIS BACON (BARON VERULAM, Viscount St. Albans, 1560-1626) was educated at Trinity College, Cambridge, later studied law, and, in 1584, was elected to Parliament. He became an important civil servant and rose to be Solicitor-General (1607), Attorney-General (1613), and Lord Chancellor (1618). In the struggles between Parliament and the Crown, Bacon was usually on the King's side. In 1621, he was convicted of taking bribes, was briefly imprisoned, and his political career ended. While active in Parliament and the government, he wrote most of his major works: the *Essays* (1597). *The Advancement of Learning* (1603), *The New Atlantis* (1617) and the *Novum Organum* and *The Great Instauration* (*Instauratio Magna,* 1620). In his last years, in disgrace, he continued writing scientific and philosophical works and died as a result of bronchitis, contracted while performing an experiment involving stuffing snow into a chicken.

The Great Instauration

PROOEMIUM

FRANCIS OF VERULAM

Reasoned thus with himself,
and judged it to be for the interest of the present and future generations that they should be made acquainted with his thoughts

Being convinced that the human intellect makes its own difficulties, not using the true helps which are at man's disposal soberly and judiciously; whence follows manifold ignorance of things, and by reason of that ignorance mischiefs innumerable; he thought all trial should be made, whether that commerce between the mind of man and the nature of things, which is more precious than anything on earth, or at least than anything that is of the earth, might by any means be restored to its perfect and original condition, or if that may not be, yet reduced to a better condition than that in which it now is. Now that the errors which have hitherto prevailed, and which will prevail forever, should (if the mind be left to go its own way), either by the natural force of the understanding or by help of the aids and instruments of logic, one by one correct themselves, was a thing not to be hoped for: because the primary notions of things which the mind readily and passively imbibes, stores up, and accumulates (and it is from them that all the rest flow) are false, confused, and overhastily abstracted from the facts; nor are the secondary and subsequent notions less arbitrary and inconstant: whence it follows that the entire fabric of human reason which we employ in the inquisition of nature, is badly put together and built up, and like some magnificent structure without any foundation. For while men are occupied in admiring and applauding the false powers of the mind, they pass by and throw away those true powers, which, if it be supplied with the proper aids and can itself be content to wait upon nature instead of vainly affecting to overrule her, are within its reach. There was but one course left, therefore,—to try the whole thing anew upon a better plan, and to commence a total reconstruction of sciences, arts, and all human knowledge, raised upon the proper foundations. And this, though in the project and undertaking it may seem a thing infinite and beyond the powers of man, yet when it comes to be dealt with it will be found sound and sober, more so than what has been done hitherto. For of this there is some issue; whereas in what is now done in the matter of science there is only a whirling round about, and perpetual agitation, ending where it began. . . .

. . . Not that I would be understood to mean that nothing whatever has been done in so many ages by so great labors. We have no reason to be ashamed of the discoveries which have been made, and no doubt the ancients proved themselves in everything that turns on wit and abstract mediation, wonderful men. But as in former ages when men sailed only by observation of the stars, they could indeed coast along the shores of the old continent or cross a few small and mediterranean seas; but before the ocean could be traversed and the new world discovered, the use of the mariner's needle, as a more faithful and certain guide, had to be found out: in like manner the discoveries which have been hitherto made in the arts and sciences are such as might be made by practice, meditation, observation, argumentation—for they lay near to the senses, and immediately beneath common notions; but before we can reach the remoter and more hidden parts of nature, it is necessary that a more perfect use and application of the human mind and intellect be introduced. . . .

I have not sought (I say) nor do I seek either to force or ensnare men's judgments; but I lead them to things themselves and the concordance of things, that they may see for themselves what they have, what they can dispute, what they can add and contribute to the common stock. And for myself, if in anything I have been either too credulous or too little awake and attentive, or if I have fallen off by the way and left the inquiry incomplete, nevertheless I so present these things naked and open, that my errors can be marked and set aside before the mass of knowledge be further infected by them; and it will be easy also for others to continue and carry on my labors. And by these means I suppose that I have established for ever a true and lawful marriage between the empirical and the rational faculty, the unkind and ill-starred divorce and separation of which has thrown into confusion all the affairs of the human family.

Wherefore, seeing that these things do not depend upon myself, at the outset of the work I most humbly and fervently pray to God the Father, God the Son, and God the Holy Ghost, that remembering the sorrows of mankind and the pilgrimage of this our life wherein we wear out days few and evil, They will vouchsafe through my hands to endow the human family with new mercies. This likewise I humbly pray, that things human may not interfere with things divine, and that from the opening of the ways of sense and the increase of natural light there may arise in our minds no incredulity or darkness with regard to the divine mysteries; but rather that the understanding being thereby purified and purged of fancies and vanity, and yet not the less subject and entirely submissive to the divine oracles, may give to faith that which is faith's. Lastly, that knowledge being now discharged of that venom which the serpent infused into it, and which makes the mind of man to swell, we may not be wise above measure and sobriety, but cultivate truth in charity.

And now having said my prayers, I turn to men; to whom I have certain salutary admonitions to offer and certain fair requests to make. My first admonition (which was also my prayer) is that men confine the sense within the limits of duty in respect of things divine: for the sense is like the sun, which reveals the face of earth, but seals and shuts up the face of heaven. My next, that in flying from this evil they fall not into the opposite error, which they will surely do if they think that the inquisition of nature is in any part interdicted or forbidden. For it was not that pure and uncorrupted natural knowledge whereby Adam gave names to the creatures according to their propriety, which gave occasion to the fall. It was the ambitious and proud desire of moral knowledge to judge of good and evil, to the end that man may revolt from God and give laws to himself, which was the form and manner of the temptation. Whereas of the sciences which regard nature, the divine philosopher declares that "it is the glory of God to conceal a thing, but it is the glory of the King to find a thing out." Even as though the divine nature took pleasure in the innocent and kindly sport of children playing a hide and seek, and vouchsafed of his kindness and goodness to admit the human spirit for his playfellow at that game. Lastly, I would address one general admonition to all: that they consider what are the true ends of knowledge, and that they seek it not either for pleasure of the mind, or for contention, or for superiority to others, or for profit, or fame, or power, or any of these inferior things; but for the benefit and use of life; and that they perfect and govern it in charity. . . .

¶ The Plan of the Work

The work is in six Parts:—

I. The Divisions of the Sciences.

II. The New Organon; or, Directions concerning the Interpretation of Nature.

III. The Phenomena of the Universe; or, a Natural and Experimental History for the Foundation of Philosophy.

IV. The Ladder of the Intellect.

V. The Forerunners; or, Anticipations of the New Philosophy.

VI. The New Philosophy; or, Active Science.

. . . Now what the sciences stand in need of is a form of induction which shall analyze experience and take it to pieces, and by a due process of exclusion and rejection lead to an inevitable conclusion. And if that ordinary mode of judgment practiced by the logicians was so laborious, and found exercise for such great wits, how much more labor must we be prepared to bestow upon this other, which is extracted not merely out of the depths of the mind, but out of the very bowels of nature.

The sense fails in two ways. Sometimes it gives no information, sometimes it gives false information. For first, there are very many things which escape the sense, even when best disposed and no way obstructed; by reason either of the subtlety of the whole body, or the minuteness of the parts, or distance of place, or slowness or else swiftness of motion, or familiarity of the object, or other causes. And again when the sense does apprehend a thing its apprehension is not much to be relied upon. For the testimony and information of the sense has reference always to man, not to the universe; and it is a great error to assert that the sense is the measure of things.

To meet these difficulties, I have sought on all sides diligently and faithfully to provide helps for the sense—substitutes to supply its failures, rectifications to correct its errors; and this I endeavor to accomplish not so much by instruments as by experiments. For the subtlety of experiments is far greater than that of the sense itself, even when assisted by exquisite instruments; such experiments, I mean, as are skillfully and artificially devised for the express purpose of determining the point in question. To the immediate and proper perception of the sense therefore I do not give much weight; but I contrive that the office of the sense shall be only to judge of the experiment, and that the experiment itself shall judge of the thing. And thus I conceive that I perform the office of a true priest of the sense (from which all knowledge in nature must be sought, unless men mean to go mad) and a not unskilled interpreter of its oracles; and that while others only profess to uphold and cultivate the sense, I do so in fact. Such then are the provisions I make for finding the genuine light of nature and kindling and bringing it to bear. And they would be sufficient of themselves, if the human intellect were even, and like a fair sheet of paper with no writing on it. But since the minds of men are strangely possessed and beset, so that there is no true and even surface left to reflect the genuine rays of things, it is necessary to seek a remedy for this also.

Now the idols, or phantoms, by which the mind is occupied are either adventitious or innate. The adventitious come into the mind from without; namely, either from the doctrines and sects of philosophers, or from perverse rules of demonstration. But the innate are inherent in the very nature of the intellect, which is far more prone to error than the sense is. For let men please themselves as they will in admiring and almost adoring the human mind, this is certain: that as an uneven mirror distorts the rays of objects according to its own figure and section, so the mind, when it receives impressions of objects through the sense, cannot be trusted to report them truly, but in forming its notions mixes up its own nature with the nature of things.

And as the first two kinds of idols are hard to eradicate, so idols of this last kind cannot be eradicated at all. All that can be done is to point them out, so that this insidious action of the mind may be marked and reproved (else as fast as old errors are destroyed new ones will spring up out of the ill complexion of the mind itself, and so we shall have but a change of errors, and not a clearance); and to lay it down once for all as a fixed and established maxim, that the intellect is not qualified to judge except by means of induction, and induction in its legitimate form. This doctrine then of the expurgation of the intellect to qualify it for dealing with truth, is comprised in three refutations: the refutation of the Philosophies, the refutation of the Demonstrations, and the refutation of the Natural Human Reason. The explanation of which things, and of the true relation between the nature of things and the nature of the mind, is as the strewing and decoration of the bridal chamber of the Mind and the Universe, the Divine Goodness assisting; out of which marriage let us hope (and be this the prayer of the bridal song) there may spring helps to man, and a line and race of inventions that may in some degree subdue and overcome the necessities and miseries of humanity. This is the second part of the work.

The sixth part of my work (to which the rest is subservient and ministrant) discloses and sets forth that philosophy which by the legitimate, chaste, and severe course of inquiry which I have explained and provided is at length developed and established. The completion however of this last part is a thing both above my strength and beyond my hopes. I have made a beginning of the work—a beginning, as I hope, not unimportant:—the fortune of the human race will give the issue; —such an issue, it may be, as in the present condition of things and men's minds cannot easily be conceived or imagined. For the matter in hand is no mere felicity of speculation, but the real business and fortunes of the human race, and all power of operation. For man is but the servant and interpreter of nature: what he does and what he knows is only what he has observed of nature's order in fact or in thought; beyond this he knows nothing and can do nothing. For the chain of causes cannot by any force be loosed or broken, nor can nature be commanded except by being obeyed. And so those twin objects, human knowledge and human power, do really meet in one; and it is from ignorance of causes that operation fails.

THE SECOND PART OF THE WORK,

which is called

THE NEW ORGANON;

or,

TRUE DIRECTIONS

concerning

THE INTERPRETATION OF NATURE

¶ Preface

Those who have taken upon them to lay down the law of nature as a thing already searched out and understood, whether they have spoken in simple assurance or professional affectation, have therein done philosophy and the sciences great injury. For as they have been successful in inducing belief, so they have been effective in quenching and stopping inquiry; and have done more harm by spoiling and putting an end to other men's efforts than good by their own. Those on the other hand who have taken a contrary course, and asserted that absolutely nothing can be known—whether it were from hatred of the ancient sophists, or from uncertainty and fluctuation of mind, or even from a kind of fulness of learning, that they fell upon this opinion,—have certainly advanced reasons for it that are not to be despised; but yet they have neither started from true principles nor rested in the just conclusion, zeal and affectation having carried them much too far. The more ancient of the Greeks (whose writings are lost) took up with better judgment a position between these two extremes,—between the presumption of pronouncing on everything, and the despair of comprehending anything; and though frequently and bitterly complaining of the difficulty of inquiry and the obscurity of things, and like impatient horses champing the bit, they did not the less follow up their object and engage with nature; thinking (it seems) that this very question—viz., whether or no anything can be known—was to be settled not by arguing, but by trying. And yet they too, trusting entirely to the force of their understanding, applied no rule, but made everything turn upon hard thinking and perpetual working and exercise of the mind.

Now my method, though hard to practice, is easy to explain; and it is this. I propose to establish progressive stages of certainty. The evidence of the sense, helped and guarded by a certain process of correction, I retain. But the mental operation which follows the act of sense I for the most part reject; and instead of it, I open and lay out a new and certain path for the mind to proceed in, starting directly from the simple sensuous perception. The necessity of this was felt no doubt by those who attributed so much importance to logic; showing thereby that they were in search of helps for the understanding, and had no confidence in the native and spontaneous process of the mind. But this remedy comes too late to do any good, when the mind is already, through the daily intercourse and conversation of life, occupied with unsound doctrines and beset on all sides by vain imaginations. And therefore that art of logic, coming (as I said) too late to the rescue, and no way able to set matters right again, has had the effect of fixing errors rather than disclosing truth. There remains but one course for the recovery of a sound and healthy condition,—namely, that the entire work of the understanding be commenced afresh, and the mind itself be from the very outset not left to take its own course, but guided at every step; and the business be done as if by machinery. . . .

APHORISMS
concerning
THE INTERPRETATION OF NATURE
and
THE KINGDOM OF MAN

¶ Aphorism

i

Man, being the servant and interpreter of nature, can do and understand so much and so much only as he has observed in fact or in thought of the course of nature: beyond this he neither knows anything nor can do anything.

ii

Neither the naked hand nor the understanding left to itself can effect much. It is by instruments and helps that the work is done, which are as much wanted for the understanding as for the hand. And as the instruments of the hand either give motion or guide it, so the instruments of the mind supply either suggestions for the understanding or cautions.

iii

Human knowledge and human power meet in one; for where the cause is not known the effect cannot be produced. Nature to be commanded must be obeyed; and that which in contemplation is as the cause is in operation as the rule.

iv

Towards the effecting of works, all that man can do is to put together or put asunder natural bodies. The rest is done by nature working within.

v

The study of nature with a view to works is engaged in by the mechanic, the mathematician, the physician, the alchemist, and the magician; but by all (as things now are) with slight endeavor and scanty success. . . .

ix

The cause and root of nearly all evils in the sciences is this—that while we falsely admire and extol the powers of the human mind we neglect to seek for its true helps. . . .

xviii

The discoveries which have hitherto been made in the sciences are such as lie close to vulgar notions, scarcely beneath the surface. In order to penetrate into the inner and further recesses of nature, it is necessary that both notions and axioms be derived from things by a more sure and guarded way; and that a method of intellectual operation be introduced altogether better and more certain.

xix

There are and can be only two ways of searching into and discovering truth. The one flies from the senses and particulars to the most general axioms, and from these principles, the truth of which it takes for settled and immovable, proceeds to judgment and to the discovery of middle axioms. And this way is now in fashion. The other derives axioms from the senses and particulars, rising by a gradual and unbroken ascent, so that it arrives at the most general axioms last of all. This is the true way, but as yet untried. . . .

xxii

Both ways set out from the senses and particulars, and rest in the highest generalities; but the difference between them is infinite. For the one just glances at experiment and particulars in passing, the other dwells duly and orderly among them. The one, again, begins at once by establishing certain abstract and useless generalities, the other rises by gradual steps to that which is prior and better known in the order of nature. . . .

xxxi

It is idle to expect any great advancement in science from the superinducing and engrafting of new things upon old. We must begin anew from the very foundations, unless we would revolve forever in a circle with mean and contemptible progress. . . .

xxxvii

The doctrine of those who have denied that certainty could be attained at all, has some agreement with my way of proceeding at the first setting out; but they end in being infinitely separated and opposed. For the holders of that doctrine assert simply that nothing can be known; I also assert that not much can be known in nature by the way which is now in use. But then they go on to destroy the authority of the senses and understanding; whereas I proceed to devise and supply helps for the same.

xxxviii

The idols and false notions which are now in possession of the human understanding, and have taken deep root therein, not only so beset men's minds that truth can hardly find entrance, but even after entrance obtained, they will again in the very instauration of the sciences meet and trouble us, unless men being forewarned of the danger fortify themselves as far as may be against their assaults.

xxxix

There are four classes of idols which beset men's minds. To these for distinction's sake I have assigned names,—calling the first class *Idols of the Tribe;* the second, *Idols of the Cave;* the third, *Idols of the Marketplace;* the fourth, *Idols of the Theater.*

xl

The formation of ideas and axioms by true induction is no doubt the proper remedy to be applied for the keeping off and clearing away of idols. To point them out, however, is of great use, for the doctrine of idols is to the interpretation of nature what the doctrine of the refutation of sophisms is to common logic.

xli

The Idols of the Tribe have their foundation in human nature itself, and in the tribe or race of men. For it is a false assertion that the sense of man is the measure of things. On the contrary, all perceptions, as well of the sense as of the mind, are according to the measure of the individual and not according to the measure of the universe. And the human understanding is like a false mirror, which, receiving rays irregularly, distorts and discolors the nature of things by mingling its own nature with it.

xlii

The Idols of the Cave are the idols of the individual man. For everyone (besides the errors common to human nature in general) has a cave or den of his own, which refracts and discolors the light of nature; owing either to his own proper and peculiar nature or to his education and conversation with others; or to the reading of books, and the authority of those whom he esteems and admires; or to the differences of impressions, accordingly as they take place in a mind preoccupied and predisposed or in a mind indifferent and settled; or the like. So that the spirit of man (according as it is meted out to different individuals) is in fact a thing variable and full of perturbation, and governed as it were by chance. . . .

xliii

There are also idols formed by the intercourse and association of men with each other, which I call Idols of the Market-place, on account of the commerce and consort of men there. For it is by discourse that men associate; and words are imposed according to the apprehension of the vulgar. And therefore the ill and unfit choice of words wonderfully obstructs the understanding. Nor do the definitions or explanations wherewith in some things learned men are wont to guard and defend themselves, by any means set the matter right. But words plainly force and overrule the understanding, and throw all into confusion, and lead men away into numberless empty controversies and idle fancies.

xliv

Lastly, there are idols which have immigrated into men's minds from the various dogmas of philosophies, and also from wrong laws of demonstration. These I call Idols of the Theater; because in my judgment all the received systems are but so many stage-plays, representing worlds of their own creation after an unreal and scenic fashion. Nor is it only of the systems now in vogue, or only of the ancient sects and philosophies, that I speak: for many more plays of the same kind may yet be composed and in like artificial manner set forth; seeing that errors the most widely different have nevertheless causes for the most part alike. Neither again do I mean this only of entire systems, but also of many principles and axioms in science, which by tradition, credulity, and negligence have come to be received. . . .

l

But by far the greatest hindrance and aberration of the human understanding proceeds from the dullness, incompetency, and deceptions of the senses; in that things which strike the sense outweigh things which do not immediately strike it, though they be more important. Hence it is that speculation commonly ceases where sight ceases, insomuch that of things invisible there is little or no observation. Hence all the working of the spirits inclosed in tangible bodies lies hid and unobserved of men. So also all the more subtle changes of form in the parts of coarser substances (which they commonly call alteration, though it is in truth local motion through exceedingly small spaces) is in like manner unobserved. And yet unless these two things just mentioned be searched out and brought to light, nothing great can be achieved in nature, as far as the production of works is concerned. So again the essential nature of our common air, and of all bodies less dense than air (which are very many), is almost unknown. For the sense by itself is a thing infirm and erring; neither can instruments for enlarging or sharpening the senses do much: but all the truer kind of interpretation of nature is effected by instances and experiments fit and apposite; wherein the sense decides touching the experiment only, and the experiment touching the point in nature and the thing itself. . . .

liii

The *Idols of the Cave* take their rise in the peculiar constitution, mental or bodily, of each individual; and also in education, habit, and accident. Of this kind there is a great number and variety; but I will instance those the pointing out of which contains the most important caution, and which have most effect in disturbing the clearness of the understanding.

liv

Men become attached to certain particular sciences and speculations, either because they fancy themselves the authors and inventors thereof, or because they have bestowed the greatest pains upon them and become most habituated to them. But men of this kind, if they betake themselves to philosophy and contemplations of a general character, distort and color them in obedience to their former fancies; a thing especially to be noticed in Aristotle, who made his natural philosophy a mere bondservant to his logic, thereby rendering it contentious and well-nigh useless. The race of chemists again out of a few experiments of the furnace have built up a fantastic philosophy, framed with reference to a few things; and Gilbert also, after he had employed himself most laboriously in the study and observation of the lodestone, proceeded at once to construct an entire system in accordance with his favorite subject. . . .

lviii

Let such then be our provision and contemplative prudence for keeping off and dislodging the Idols of the Cave, which grow for the most part either out of the predominance of a favorite subject, or out of an excessive tendency to compare or to distinguish, or out of partiality for particular ages, or out of the largeness or minuteness of the objects contemplated. And generally let every student of nature take this as a rule, —that whatever his mind seizes and dwells upon with peculiar satisfaction is to be held in suspicion, and that so much the more care is to be taken in dealing with such questions to keep the understanding even and clear.

lix

But the *Idols of the Market-place* are the most troublesome of all: idols which have crept into the understanding through the alliances of words and names. For men believe that their reason governs words; but it is also true that words react on the understanding; and this it is that has rendered philosophy and the sciences sophistical and inactive. Now words, being commonly framed and applied according to the capacity of the vulgar, follow those lines of division which are most obvious to the vulgar understanding. And whenever an understanding of greater acuteness or a more diligent observation would alter those lines to suit the true divisions of nature, words stand in the way and resist the change. Whence it comes to pass that the high and formal discussions of learned men end oftentimes in disputes about words and names; with which (according to the use and wisdom of the mathematicians) it would be more prudent to begin, and so by means of definitions reduce them to order. Yet even definitions cannot cure this evil in dealing with natural and material things; since the definitions themselves consist of words, and those words beget others: so that it is necessary to recur to individual instances, and those in due series and order. . . .

lx

The idols imposed by words on the understanding are of two kinds. They are either names of things which do not exist (for as there are things left unnamed through lack of observation, so likewise are there names which result from fantastic suppositions and to which nothing in reality corresponds), or they are names of things which exist, but yet confused and ill-defined, and hastily and irregularly derived from realities. Of the former kind are Fortune, the Prime Mover, Planetary Orbits, Elements of Fire, and like fictions which owe their origin to false and idle theories. And this class of idols is more easily expelled, because to get rid of them it is only necessary that all theories should be steadily rejected and dismissed as obsolete.

But the other class, which springs out of a faulty and unskillful abstraction, is intricate and deeply rooted. Let us take for example such a word as *humid,* and see how far the several things which the word is used to signify agree with each other; and we shall find the word *humid* to be nothing else than a mark loosely and confusedly applied to denote a variety of actions which will not bear to be reduced to any constant meaning. . . .

lxi

But the *Idols of the Theater* are not innate, nor do they steal into the understanding secretly, but are plainly impressed and received into the mind from the play-books of philosophical systems and the perverted rules of demonstration. To attempt refutations in this case would be merely inconsistent with what I have already said: for since we agree neither upon principles nor upon demonstrations there is no place for argument. And this is so far well, inasmuch as it leaves the honor of the ancients untouched. For they are no wise disparaged—the question between them and me being only as to the way. For as the saying is, the lame man who keeps the right road outstrips the runner who takes a wrong one. Nay it is obvious that when a man runs the wrong way, the more active and swift he is the further he will go astray. . . .

lxii

Idols of the Theater, or of Systems, are many, and there can be and perhaps will be yet many more. . . .

In general however there is taken for the material of philosophy either a great deal out of a few things, or a very little out of many things; so that on both sides philosophy is based on too narrow a foundation of experiment and natural history, and decides on the authority of too few cases. For the rational school of philosophers snatches from experience a variety of common instances, neither duly ascertained nor diligently examined and weighed, and leaves all the rest to meditation and agitation of wit.

There is also another class of philosophers, who having bestowed much diligent and careful labor on a few experiments, have thence made bold to educe and construct systems; wresting all other facts in a strange fashion to conformity therewith.

And there is yet a third class, consisting of those who out of faith and veneration mix their philosophy with theology and traditions; among whom the vanity of some has gone so far aside as to seek the origin of science among spirits and genii. So that this parent stock of errors—this false philosophy—is of three kinds; the *sophistical,* the *empirical,* and the *superstitious.* . . .

lxiv

But the empirical school of philosophy gives birth to dogmas more deformed and monstrous than the sophistical or rational school. For it has its foundations not in the light of common notions (which, though it be a faint and superficial light, is yet in a manner universal, and has reference to many things) but in the narrowness and darkness of a few experiments. To those therefore who are daily busied with these experiments, and have infected their imagination with them, such a philosophy seems probable and all but certain; to all men else incredible and vain. Of this there is a notable instance in the alchemists and their dogmas; though it is hardly to be found elsewhere in these times, except perhaps in the philosophy of Gilbert. Nevertheless with regard to philosophies of this kind there is one caution not to be omitted; for I foresee that if ever men are roused by my admonitions to betake themselves seriously to experiment and bid farewell to sophistical doctrines, then indeed through the premature hurry of the understanding to leap or fly to universals and principles of things, great danger may be apprehended from philosophies of this kind; against which evil we ought even now to prepare.

lxv

But the corruption of philosophy by superstition and an admixture of theology is far more widely spread, and does the greatest harm, whether to entire systems or to their parts. For the human understanding is obnoxious to the influence of the imagination no less than to the influence of common notions. For the contentious and sophistical kind of philosophy ensnares the understanding; but this kind, being fanciful and tumid and half poetical, misleads it more by flattery. For there is in man an ambition of the understanding, no less than of the will, especially in high and lofty spirits.

Of this kind we have among the Greeks a striking example in Pythagoras, though he united with it a coarser and more cumbrous superstition; another in Plato and his school, more dangerous and subtle. It shows itself likewise in parts of other philosophies, in the introduction of abstract forms and final causes and first causes, with the omission in most cases of causes intermediate, and the like. Upon this point the greatest caution should be used. For nothing is so mischievous as the apotheosis of error; and it is a very plague of the understanding for vanity to become the object of veneration. Yet in this vanity some of the moderns have with extreme levity indulged so far as to attempt to found a system of natural philosophy on the first chapters of Genesis, on the book of Job, and other parts of the sacred writings; seeking for the dead among the living: which also makes the inhibition and repression of it the more important, because from this unwholesome mixture of things human and divine there arises not only a fantastic philosophy but also an heretical religion. Very meet it is therefore that we be sober-minded, and give to faith that only which is faith's. . . .

lxvii

A caution must also be given to the understanding against the intemperance which systems of philosophy manifest in giving or withholding assent; because intemperance of this kind seems to establish idols and in some sort to perpetuate them, leaving no way open to reach and dislodge them.

This excess is of two kinds: the first being manifest in those who are ready in deciding; and render sciences dogmatic and magisterial; the other in those who deny that we can know anything, and so introduce a wandering kind of inquiry that leads to nothing; of which kinds the former subdues, the later weakens the understanding. For the philosophy of Aristotle, after having by hostile confutations destroyed all the rest (as the Ottomans serve their brothers), has laid down the law on all points: which done, he proceeds himself to raise new questions of his own suggestion, and dispose of them likewise; so that nothing may remain that is not certain and decided,–a practice which holds and is in use among his successors.

The school of Plato, on the other hand, introduced *Acatalepsia,* at first in jest and irony, and in disdain of the older sophists, Protagoras, Hippias, and the rest, who were of nothing else so much ashamed as of seeming to doubt about anything. But the New Academy made a dogma of it, and held it as a tenet. And though theirs is a fairer seeming way than arbitrary decisions; since they say that they by no means destroy all investigation, like Pyrrho and his Refrainers, but allow of some things to be followed as probable, though of none to be maintained as true; yet still when the human mind has once despaired of finding truth, its interest in all things grows fainter; and the result is that men turn aside to pleasant disputations and discourses and roam as it were from object to object, rather than keep on a course of severe inquisition. But, as I said at the beginning and am ever urging, the human senses and understanding, weak as they are, are not to be deprived of their authority, but to be supplied with helps.

lxviii

So much concerning the several classes of idols, and their equipage: all of which must be renounced and put away with a fixed and solemn determination, and the understanding thoroughly freed and cleansed;

the entrance into the kingdom of man, founded on the sciences, being not much other than the entrance into the kingdom of heaven, whereinto none may enter except as a little child.

lxix

But vicious demonstrations are as the strongholds and defenses of idols; and those we have in logic do little else than make the world the bond-slave of human thought, and human thought the bond-slave of words. Demonstrations truly are in effect the philosophies themselves and the sciences. For such as *they* are, well or ill established, such are the systems of philosophy and the contemplations which follow. Now in the whole of the process which leads from the sense and objects to axioms and conclusions, the demonstrations which we use are deceptive and incompetent. This process consists of four parts, and has as many faults. In the first place, the impressions of the sense itself are faulty; for the sense both fails us and deceives us. But its shortcomings are to be supplied, and its deceptions to be corrected. Secondly, notions are ill drawn from the impressions of the senses, and are indefinite and confused, whereas they should be definite and distinctly bounded. Thirdly, the induction is amiss which infers the principles of sciences by simple enumeration, and does not, as it ought, employ exclusions and solutions (or separations) of nature. Lastly, that method of discovery and proof according to which the most general principles are first established, and then intermediate axioms are tried and proved by them, is the parent of error and the curse of all science. Of these things however, which now I do but touch upon, I will speak more largely, when, having performed these expiations and purgings of the mind, I come to set forth the true way for the interpretation of nature.

lxx

But the best demonstration by far is experience, if it go not beyond the actual experiment. For if it be transferred to other cases which are deemed similar, unless such transfer be made by a just and orderly process, it is a fallacious thing. But the manner of making experiments which men now use is blind and stupid. And therefore, wandering and straying as they do with no settled course, and taking counsel only from things as they fall out, they fetch a wide circuit and meet with many matters, but make little progress; and sometimes are full of hope, sometimes are distracted; and always find that there is something beyond to be sought. For it generally happens that men make their trials carelessly, and as it were in play; slightly varying experiments already known, and, if the thing does not answer, growing weary and abandoning the attempt. And even if they apply themselves to experiments more seriously and earnestly and laboriously, still they spend their labor in working out some one experiment, as Gilbert with the magnet, and the chemists with gold, —a course of proceeding not less unskillful in the design than small in the attempt. For no one successfully investigates the nature of a thing in the thing itself; the inquiry must be enlarged, so as to become more general.

And even when they seek to educe some science or theory from their experiments, they nevertheless almost always turn aside with overhasty and unseasonable eagerness to practice; not only for the sake of the uses and fruits of the practice, but from impatience to obtain in the shape of some new work an assurance for themselves that it is worth their while to go on; and also to show themselves off to the world, and so raise the credit of the business in which they are engaged. . . .

lxxxi

Again there is another great and powerful cause why the sciences have made but little progress; which is this. It is not possible to run a course aright when the goal itself has not been rightly placed. Now the true and lawful goal of the sciences is none other than this: that human life be endowed with new discoveries and powers. But of this the great majority have no feeling, but are merely hireling and professorial; except when it occasionally happens that some workman of acuter wit and covetous of honor applies himself to a new invention; which he mostly does at the expense of his fortunes. But in general, so far are men from proposing to themselves to augment the mass of arts and sciences, that from the mass already at hand they neither take nor look for anything more than what they may turn to use in their lectures, or to gain, or to reputation, or to some similar advantage. And if any one out of all the multitude court science with honest affection and for her own sake, yet even with him the object will be found to be rather the variety of contemplations and doctrines than the severe and rigid search after truth. And if by chance there be one who seeks after truth in earnest, yet even he will propose to himself such a kind of truth as shall yield satisfaction to the mind and understanding in rendering causes for things long since discovered, and not the truth which shall lead to new assurance of works and new light of axioms. If then the end of the sciences has not yet been well placed, it is not strange that men have erred as to the means. . . .

lxxxix

Neither is it to be forgotten that in every age natural philosophy has had a troublesome adversary and hard to deal with; namely, superstition, and the blind and immoderate zeal of religion. For we see among the Greeks that those who first proposed to men's then uninitiated ears the natural causes for thunder and for storms, were thereupon found guilty of impiety. Nor was much more forbearance shown by some of the ancient fathers of the Christian church to those who on most convincing grounds (such as no one in his senses would now think of contradicting) maintained that the earth was round, and of consequence asserted the existence of the antipodes.

Moreover, as things now are, to discourse of nature is made harder and more perilous by the summaries and systems of the schoolmen; who having reduced theology into regular order as well as they were able, and fashioned it into the shape of an art, ended in incorporating the contentious and thorny philosophy of Aristotle, more than was fit, with the body of religion.

To the same result, though in a different way, tend the speculations of those who have taken upon them to deduce the truth of the Christian religion from the principles of philosophers, and to confirm it by their authority; pompously solemnizing this union of the sense and faith as a lawful marriage, and entertaining men's minds with a pleasing variety of matter, but all the while disparaging things divine by mingling them with things human. Now in such mixtures of theology with philosophy only the received doctrines of philosophy are included; while new ones, albeit changes for the better, are all but expelled and exterminated.

Lastly, you will find that by the simpleness of certain divines, access to any philosophy, however pure, is well nigh closed. Some are weakly afraid lest a deeper search into nature should transgress the permitted limits of sober-mindedness; wrongfully wresting and transferring what is said in holy writ against those who pry into sacred mysteries, to the hidden things of nature, which are barred by no prohibition. . . . But if the matter be truly considered, natural philosophy is after the word of God at once the surest medicine against superstition, and the most approved nourishment for faith, and therefore she is rightly given to religion as her most faithful handmaid, since the one displays the will of God, the other his power. For he did not err who said "Ye err in that ye know not the Scriptures and the power of God," thus coupling and blending in an indissoluble bond information concerning his will and meditation concerning his power. Meanwhile it is not surprising if the growth of natural philosophy is checked, when religion, the thing which has most power over men's minds, has by the simpleness and incautious zeal of certain persons been drawn to take part against her. . . .

xcii

But by far the greatest obstacle to the progress of science and to the undertaking of new tasks and provinces therein, is found in this—that men despair and think things impossible. For wise and serious men are wont in these matters to be altogether distrustful; considering with themselves the obscurity of nature, the shortness of life, the deceitfulness of the senses, the weakness of the judgment, the difficulty of experiment and the like; and so supposing that in the revolution of time and of the ages of the world the sciences have their ebbs and flows; that at one season they grow and flourish, at another wither and decay, yet in such sort that when they have reached a certain point and condition they can advance no further. If therefore any one believes or promises more, they think this comes of an ungoverned and unripened mind, and that such attempts have prosperous beginnings, become difficult as they go on, and end in confusion. Now since these are thoughts which naturally present themselves to grave men and of great judgment, we must take good heed that we be not led away by our love for a most fair and excellent object to relax or diminish the severity of our judgment; we must observe diligently what encouragement dawns upon us and from what quarter; and, putting aside the lighter breeze of hope, we must thoroughly sift and examine those which promise greater steadiness and constancy. Nay, and we must take state-prudence too into our counsels, whose rule is to distrust, and to take the less favorable view of human affairs. I am now therefore to speak touching *hope;* especially as I am not a dealer in promises, and wish neither to force nor to ensnare men's judgments, but to lead them by the hand with their good will. And though the strongest means of inspiring hope will be to bring men to particulars; especially to particulars digested and arranged in my Tables of Discovery (the subject partly of the second, but much more of the fourth part of my *Instauration*), since this is not merely the promise of the thing but the thing itself: nevertheless that everything may be done with gentleness, I will proceed with my plan of preparing men's minds; of which preparation to give hope is no unimportant part. For without it the rest tends rather to make men sad (by giving them a worse and meaner opinion of things as they are than they have now, and making them more fully to feel and know the unhappiness of their own condition) than to induce any alacrity or to whet their industry in making trial. And therefore it is fit that I publish and set forth those conjectures of mine which make hope in this matter reasonable: just as Columbus did, before that wonderful voyage of his across the Atlantic, when he gave the reasons for his conviction that new lands and continents might be discovered besides those which were known before; which reasons, though rejected at first, were afterwards made good by experience, and were the causes and beginnings of great events. . . .

xcv

Those who have handled sciences have been either men of experiment or men of dogmas. The men of experiment are like the ant; they only collect and use: the reasoners resemble spiders, who make cobwebs out of their own substance. But the bee takes a middle course, it gathers its material from the flowers of the garden and of the field, but transforms and digests it by a power of its own. Not unlike this is the true business of philosophy: for it neither relies solely or chiefly on the powers of the mind, nor does it take the matter which it gathers from natural history and mechanical experiments and lay it up in the memory whole, as it finds it; but lays it up in the understanding altered and digested. Therefore from a closer and purer league between these two faculties, the experimental and the rational, (such as has never yet been made) much may be hoped. . . .

xcviii

Now for grounds of experience—since to experience we must come—we have as yet had either none or very weak ones; no search has been made to collect a store of particular observations sufficient either in number, or in kind, or in certainty, to inform the understanding, or in any way adequate. On the contrary, men of learning, but easy withal and idle, have taken for the construction or for the confirmation of their philosophy certain rumors and vague fames or airs of experience, and allowed to these the weight of lawful evidence. And just as if some kingdom or state were to direct its counsels and affairs, not by letters and reports from ambassadors and trustworthy messengers, but by the gossip of the streets; such exactly is the system of management introduced into philosophy with relation to experience. Nothing duly investigated, nothing verified, nothing counted, weighed, or measured, is to be found in natural history: and what in observation is loose and vague, is in information deceptive and treacherous. And if anyone thinks that this is a strange thing to say, and something like an unjust complaint, seeing that Aristotle, himself so great a man, and supported by the wealth of so great a king, has composed so accurate a history of animals; and that others with greater diligence, though less pretense, have made many additions; while others, again, have compiled copious histories and descriptions of metals, plants, and fossils; it seems that he does not rightly apprehend what it is that we are now about. For a natural history which is composed for its own sake is not like one that is collected to supply the understanding with information for the building up of philosophy. They differ in many ways, but especially in this; that the former contains the variety of natural species only, and not experiments of the mechanical arts. For even as in the business of life a man's disposition and the secret workings of his mind and affections are better discovered when he is in trouble than at other times; so likewise the secrets of nature reveal themselves more readily under the vexations of art than when they go their own way. Good hopes may therefore be conceived of natural philosophy, when natural history, which is the basis and foundation of it, has been drawn up on a better plan; but not till then. . . .

cii

Moreover, since there is so great a number and army of particulars, and that army so scattered and dispersed as to distract and confound the understanding, little is to be hoped for from the skirmishings and slight attacks and desultory movements of the intellect, unless all the particulars which pertain to the subject of inquiry shall, by means of Tables of Discovery, apt, well arranged, and as it were animate, be drawn up and marshaled; and the mind be set to work upon the helps duly prepared and digested which these tables supply. . . .

civ

The understanding must not however be allowed to jump and fly from particulars to remote axioms and of almost the highest generality (such as the first principles, as they are called, of arts and things), and taking stand upon them as truths that cannot be shaken, proceed to prove and frame the middle axioms by reference to them: which has been the practice hitherto; the understanding being not only carried that way by a natural impulse, but also by the use of syllogistic demonstration trained and inured to it. But then, and then only, may we hope well of the sciences, when in a just scale of ascent, and by successive steps not interrupted or broken, we rise from particulars to lesser axioms; and then to middle axioms, one above the other; and last of all to the most general. For the lowest axioms differ but slightly from bare experience, while the highest and most general (which we now have) are notional and abstract and without solidity. But the middle are the true and solid and living axioms, on which depend the affairs and fortunes of men; and above them again, last of all, those which are indeed the most general, —such I mean as are not abstract, but of which those intermediate axioms are really limitations.

The understanding must not therefore be supplied with wings, but rather hung with weights, to keep it from leaping and flying. Now this has never yet been done; when it is done, we may entertain better hopes of the sciences.

cv

In establishing axioms, another form of induction must be devised than has hitherto been employed; and it must be used for proving and discovering not first principles (as they are called) only, but also the lesser axioms, and the middle, and indeed all. For the induction which proceeds by simple enumeration is childish; its conclusions are precarious, and exposed to peril from a contradictory instance; and it generally decides on too small a number of facts, and on those only which are at hand. But the induction which is to be available for the discovery and demonstration of sciences and arts, must analyze nature by proper rejections and exclusions; and then, after a sufficient number of negatives, come to a conclusion on the affirmative instances: which has not yet been done or even attempted, save only by Plato, who does indeed employ this form of induction to a certain extent for the purpose of discussing definitions and ideas. But in order to furnish this induction or demonstration well and duly for its work, very many things are to be provided which no mortal has yet thought of; insomuch that greater labor will have to be spent in it than has hitherto been spent on the syllogism. And this induction must be used not only to discover axioms, but also in the formation of notions. And it is in this induction that our chief hope lies. . . .

cxxvi

It will also be thought that by forbidding men to pronounce and to set down principles as established until they have duly arrived through the intermediate steps at the highest generalities, I maintain a sort of suspension of the judgment, and bring it to what the Greeks call *Acatalepsia,*—a denial of the capacity of the mind to comprehend truth. But in reality that which I meditate and propound is not *Acatalepsia,* but *Eucatalepsia;* not denial of the capacity to understand, but provision for understanding truly; for I do not take away authority from the senses, but supply them with helps; I do not slight the understanding, but govern it. And better surely it is that we should know all we need to know, and yet think our knowledge imperfect, than that we should think our knowledge perfect, and yet not know anything we need to know. . . .

SECOND BOOK OF APHORISMS

¶ APHORISM

ii

. . . In what an ill condition human knowledge is at the present time, is apparent even from the commonly received maxims. It is a correct position that "true knowledge is knowledge by causes." And causes again are not improperly distributed into four kinds: the material, the formal, the efficient, and the final. But of these the final cause rather corrupts than advances the sciences, except such as have to do with human action. The discovery of the formal is despaired of. The efficient and the material (as they are investigated and received, that is, as remote causes, without reference to the latent process leading to the form) are but slight and superficial, and contribute little, if anything, to true and active science. Nor have I forgotten that in a former passage I noted and corrected as an error of the human mind the opinion that forms give existence. For though in nature nothing really exists beside individual bodies, performing pure individual acts according to a fixed law, yet in philosophy this very law, and the investigation, discovery, and explanation of it, is the foundation as well of knowledge as of operation. And it is this law, with its clauses, that I mean when I speak of *forms;* a name which I the rather adopt because it has grown into use and become familiar. . . .

x

Having thus set up the mark of knowledge, we must go on to precepts, and that in the most direct and obvious order. Now my directions for the interpretation of nature embrace two generic divisions: the one how to educe and form axioms from experience; the other how to deduce and derive new experiments from axioms. The former again is divided into three ministrations: a ministration to the sense, a ministration to the memory, and a ministration to the mind or reason.

For first of all we must prepare a *Natural and Experimental History*, sufficient and good; and this is the foundation of all; for we are not to imagine or suppose, but to discover, what nature does or may be made to do.

But natural and experimental history is so various and diffuse, that it confounds and distracts the understanding, unless it be ranged and presented to view in a suitable order. We must therefore form *Tables and Arrangements of Instances*, in such a method and order that the understanding may be able to deal with them.

And even when this is done, still the understanding, if left to itself and its own spontaneous movements, is incompetent and unfit to form axioms, unless it be directed and guarded. Therefore in the third place we must use *Induction*, true and legitimate induction, which is the very key of interpretation. But of this, which is the last, I must speak first, and then go back to the other ministrations.

xi

The investigation of Forms proceeds thus: a nature being given, we must first of all have a muster or presentation before the understanding of all known instances which agree in the same nature, though in substances the most unlike. And such collection must be made in the manner of a history, without premature speculation, or any great amount of subtlety. . . .

xii

Secondly, we must make a presentation to the understanding of instances in which the given nature is wanting; because the Form, as stated above, ought no less to be absent when the given nature is absent, than present when it is present. But to note all these would be endless.

The negatives should therefore be subjoined to the affirmatives, and the absence of the given nature inquired of in those subjects only that are most akin to the others in which it is present and forthcoming. This I call the *Table of Deviation, or of Absence in Proximity*. . . .

xiii

Thirdly, we must make a presentation to the understanding of instances in which the nature under inquiry is found in different degrees, more or less; which must be done by making a comparison either of its increase and decrease in the same subject, or of its amount in different subjects, as compared one with another. For since the Form of a thing is the very thing itself, and the thing differs from the form no otherwise than as the apparent differs from the real, or the external from the internal, or the thing in reference to man from the thing in reference to the universe; it necessarily follows that no nature can be taken as the true form, unless it always decrease when the nature in question decreases, and in like manner always increase when the nature in question increases. This Table therefore I call the *Table of Degrees* or the *Table of Comparison*. . . .

xv

The work and office of these three tables I call the Presentation of Instances to the Understanding. Which presentation having been made, Induction itself must be set at work; for the problem is, upon a review of the instances, all and each, to find such a nature as is always present or absent with the given nature, and always increases and decreases with it; and which is, as I have said, a particular case of a more general nature. Now if the mind attempt this affirmatively from the first, as when left to itself it is always wont to do, the result will be fancies and guesses and notions ill defined and axioms that must be mended every day; unless like the schoolmen we have a mind to fight for what is false; though doubtless these will be better or worse according to the faculties and strength of the understanding which is at work. To God, truly, the Giver and Architect of Forms, and it may be to the angels and higher intelligences, it belongs to have an affirmative knowledge of Forms immediately, and from the first contemplation. But this assuredly is more than man can do, to whom it is granted only to proceed at first by negatives, and at last to end in affirmatives, after exclusion has been exhausted. . . .

lii

So much then for the Dignities or Prerogatives of Instances. It must be remembered however that in this Organum of mine I am handling logic, not philosophy. But since my logic aims to teach and instruct the understanding, not that it may with the slender tendrils of the mind snatch at and lay hold of abstract notions (as the common logic does), but that it may in very truth dissect nature, and discover the virtues and actions of bodies, with their laws as determined in matter; so that this science flows not merely from the nature of the mind, but also from the nature of things; no wonder that it is everywhere sprinkled and illustrated with speculations and experiments in nature, as examples of the art I teach. . . . But now I must proceed to the supports and rectifications of Induction, and then to concretes, and Latent Processes, and Latent Configurations, and the rest, as set forth in order in the twenty-first Aphorism; that at length (like an honest and faithful guardian) I may hand over to men their fortunes, now their understanding is emancipated and come as it were of age; whence there cannot but follow an improvement in man's estate, and an enlargement of his power over nature. For man by the fall fell at the same time from his state of innocency and from his dominion over creation. Both of these losses however can even in this life be in some part repaired; the former by religion and faith, the later by arts and sciences. For creation was not by the curse made altogether and for ever a rebel, but in virtue of that charter "In the sweat of thy face shalt thou eat bread," it is now by various labors (not certainly by disputations or idle magical ceremonies, but by various labors) at length and in some measure subdued to the supplying of man with bread; that is, to the uses of human life.

IX

GASSENDI

Pierre Gassendi (1592-1655) was born in Provence, studied at Digne, and was lecturing there when he was sixteen. Later, he became a professor at Aix, canon of Grenoble, provost of the Cathedral of Digne, and finally Professor of Mathematics in Paris in 1645. Gassendi early gained his reputation as a scientist and as a skeptical opponent of Aristotelianism. His first work, the *Exercitationes paradoxicae adversus Aristoteleos* (*Dissertations in the Form of Paradoxes against the Aristotelians,* 1624), caused a great stir, and only the first book was published in his lifetime. (The selections below are from Book II, published first in 1658.) He next devoted himself to attacking Renaissance naturalism, alchemy, Rosicrucians, and the like, in concert with his friend Mersenne. Then, he revived Epicureanism as a hypothetical system for encompassing the results of the "new science." His mitigated skepticism and hypothetical Epicureanism (modified to avoid conflict with Christianity) rivaled Descartes' views throughout most of the seventeenth century. This translation is by R. H. Popkin, with the assistance of Betty Duimstra.

Dissertations in the Form of Paradoxes Against the Aristotelians

SIXTH DISSERTATION

That there is no science, and especially no Aristotelian science.

ART. 1. *There cannot be a science of the sort that Aristotle sets forth.*

One should not be astonished if, from the outset, every science does not seem to have to be equally attacked by us. First of all it is possible to claim that knowledge of the Mysteries of the orthodox Faith ought to be called Science, or that it can be so called. . . . Next it could be allowed that a kind of knowledge, that is experimental and related to the appearances of things, should be called Science, seeing that I am said to know that, this actual moment, I am sitting rather than standing, that it is daytime rather than night, that I am fasting rather than eating, at home and not in the public square. Similarly I know that honey appears sweet to me rather than bitter, fire hot rather than cold, snow white rather than black, the sun shining rather than hidden. Therefore, in order that no one seek here to arouse ill-will against us because we would refuse to acknowledge things so clear and so well-known, and that we would dispute against them, we have consequently the obligation to point out that such a science is not in any way the one that we are here combatting. And besides it can be understood that [such a science] is not under consideration. If you will maintain consistently that Science is a certain and evident knowledge of something, obtained by means of necessary causes or demonstration, then this knowledge, experimental or relating to appearances, does not deserve the name "Science." But, however, when we wish to apply it only to your Aristotelian science, and then, departing from scholastic usage, lowering yourself to ordinary usage, and confusing one science with another, you suddenly object, "What? If there is no science, then do we not know that fire is hot, that the sun shines at noon, and similar things?"

Because of this, we have had to state precisely what kind of science is being attacked here. Therefore, to make completely clear the difference between these two and the nature of our view, here is an example. When I am questioned about something like the sweetness of honey, I reply that honey actually appears sweet to me every time this sweetness is experienced by my tongue and felt by my palate. If next you should ask me if I know that honey appears sweet to me, or that I experience the sweetness of honey in tasting it, I will reply affirmatively, and will agree that there is a science of this kind and about these sorts of things. But if now you ask me this: do you know if honey is naturally and really sweet in itself, it is this that I contend I do not know, for I am not aware of the necessary cause nor the demonstration in virtue of which it has to be thus. Instead there are moreover a host of reasons for suspecting that honey by nature is not rather sweet than bitter, whatever may be the way it seems to me, according to my disposition or in relation to me. Such then is the type of Science that we intend to combat, and in such a way that after having overthrown the demonstration that constitutes, it is believed, its best support, we will go on to show more particularly that it is impossible for us to know, that is to say, to acquire certain and evident knowledge, and to affirm surely and infallibly that something is by nature and in itself, and as a result of basic, necessary and infallible causes, constituted in a certain way. . . .

ART. 6. *It can only be known how a thing appears to one or another.*

. . . It remains for us only to answer objections that are usually scornfully made. First of all, we shall not spend much time resolving that difficulty that they take for their Achilles, presenting it proudly about in this form. *Either you actually know that there is no science, or you actually do not know this. If you do not know this, what temerity to assert it! But if you know this, then this itself shows there is a science: of what is not known;* and consequently this proposition itself, *that nothing is known,* or that there is no science, is false. Now the answer is simple after what has been stated earlier; first we are not of those who wish to condemn the ordinary and usual way of speaking which says that we know all sorts of things, as in the examples cited at the outset. This is why we have said that we maintain the science that can be considered as that of experience or appearances. Thus, and in accordance with that, in a few words, we answer that we are sure that nothing is known (in Aristotle's sense), and therefore there is something of which there is a science [or "of which we have knowledge"]; but we do not possess however an Aristotelian science of this, and it follows still less that [this science] whose existence we have admitted is Aristotelian, since in effect in examining all the bases of a science of this type, we have seen that they have no solidity. . . . You will say that this science by which we know that we know nothing in Aristotle's sense, is either certain and evident, and consequently is arrived at by means of necessary causes and demonstration, or is not. In the first case, it will be an Aristotelian science; in the second, it will not be a science, but rather an opinion. However the science in question is not indubitably absolutely certain or evident, and does not issue from causes or an extended demonstration of the Aristotelian variety. But just the same it does not lack an adequate certitude, and an evidence approaching probability, in that it rests on conjectures and reason sufficiently apparent and capable of stopping the mind from adhering to the proposition: "There is an Aristotelian science." Call this then "opinion" or any other name you wish. It matters not, for we say indifferently (or, alternatively) that we have such an opinion, or that we know such a thing, as the ordinary way of speaking allows, and if one wishes to be careful about this, science and opinion can be considered as synonymous; for one can speak of a certain science and a certain opinion, and even of a poor science and a weak opinion, in such a way that this entire distinction is hardly but a Scholastic affair [quibble].—You will return to the attack. When it is the case that so many people claim that they know something in an absolutely certain and evident way, and by necessary causes, is it not rash for someone who is unaware of this certitude, evidence and necessity to oppose them? But why would this not be rather a sign of a lively love of truth in such a person, who just as he does not wish to be deceived himself, cannot also suffer that others take error for truth? And it is the case that some too hastily take numerous affirmations as plainly evident and correctly demonstrated, and as a result believe themselves right in stating that they themselves know these with certainty. But why should he who, in examining and weighing everything carefully, sees that these people, as a result of prejudices, are deceived by an appearance of truth; be judged rash for refusing to assent right away as they do, and for also warning them to examine everything more carefully. And indeed it often happens that one recants for something formerly accepted as absolutely indubitable. . . . I add here only that fine and just answer of Pyrrho, that Diogenes Laertius and then Sextus Empiricus tell us of, namely that the proposition by which we affirm that nothing is known is of such a nature that in destroying others it also destroys itself, and that in eliminating all science of other matters, it also eliminates the science of itself, in the manner by which a purge, he says, expels the defective humors from the body, and expels itself with them.

ART. 7. *The Pyrrhonians are not unjust towards Nature when they declare that nothing can be known.*

It is objected that the Pyrrhonians greatly oppose Nature, since all men desire by nature to know [i.e., to have science], as Aristotle states, and as experience proves. For nature would not have vainly inspired such a desire, if men could not obtain any knowledge. Now what confirms this is, on the one hand, that there are various means of knowing, like the intellect, and demonstration; on the other hand, there are things that can be known, namely all those that happen naturally. It is thus that in no case does Nature permit a diminution of science. This is further confirmed by the fact that it would be unjust to make useless the efforts of so many excellent philosophers who, up to now, have had so assiduous a zeal for science. Nature seems to have designed them so that through them science is established in a world in which ignorance, which is the opposite of science, triumphs. For further confirmation, the words of Aristotle that follow the enumeration of opinions that we have given earlier can be added. For, he says, what results from this is completely absurd. If those who have seen the truth as much as is possible (and these are the people who search for it and love it with full ardor) had such opinions themselves, and accepted such a view about truth, would not those who are just beginning the study of philosophy have their souls discouraged? To search for the truth would then be nothing other than chasing birds in flight. Lastly, this could be further confirmed by the fact that it would be absurd that physics, metaphysics, jurisprudence and other sciences were only empty names, and especially mathematics itself, thanks to which nobody who is not mad can deny that we have a most certain and evident knowledge of many things, so many of the mathematical demonstrations being luminous and convincing. We can however reply to all of this in a few words.

First it does not seem that these people do any injury to Nature who, as they take nothing from her, at the same time do not bestow on her anything that is not just (for it seems to be as wrong to say of her something that is not so, as not to say what is so), and who consequently recognize that Nature has given all men the desire to know, but not however to know all matters or means. Insofar as men seek to know as much as possible about things, both by experience and by what appears to them, it is true that it is as a result of a natural tendency that they desire to know this. But, when they further wish to know the inner nature of things and their necessary causes, then this is a type of science which belongs to the angelic or even Divine nature and not to simple humanity, so that such a desire can no longer be considered as coming from nature. Similarly it is true that all men desire immortality. But who would think that this desire is inspired by Nature when she has instead established as a law that it is appointed unto all men once to die? That is why, in spite of the desire of all men never to die, nonetheless from the fact that no one has attained immortality, that we conclude that such a desire is not natural; and in the same way, since no one has penetrated to the inner nature of the slightest thing, we can conclude that it is not a natural desire which leads the seekers on.—Next, and in keeping with this, it can be asserted that the conditions of science exist, but, however, of an experimental science, and I may add, based on appearances. In effect, our intellect only has science or knowledge through examining various appearances. We can show what is in several ways, by pointing a finger, by teaching through discourse, by some other such means. But nevertheless our mind does not know anything in the manner depicted by Aristotle, and hence there is no such thing as an Aristotelian demonstration. It can be stated also that there are many things that can be known, but not however those that can be known by such an Aristotelian science: only by an experimental science or one following appearances. If you claim that mind is capable, from what occurs in experience, or what appears to the senses, of deducing other more hidden matters, I will reply that nonetheless one cannot proceed further by reasoning than to things that must be again submitted to experience or of which it must be possible to set forth some sensible appearance. All that we are denying, in sum, is that one can penetrate to the intimate nature of things. This can be applied with equal reason to the work of the greatest philosophers and it is not necessary to judge that their efforts have been useless on the basis that they have not yielded an Aristotelian science as yet, since they have furnished us with another truer and more useful one, namely an experimental science [based on] the appearance of things. This is why we should have the highest regard for these great men, since they wish to transmit to us from hand to hand, and according to proper method and order, their observations based on experience, learning and reasoning. For how far would our contemporary philosophers be advanced, I ask, if they were not carried on the shoulders of so many giants? It is thus that we are far from denying that they have been chosen to chase away ignorance, since the science of which we speak is too opposed to ignorance. On the other hand, ignorance as conceived by our adversaries is not any more a human defect than is the fact that we do not possess one hundred fingers on our hands; for in the same way that Nature does not owe man the presence of so many fingers, it also does not owe him, it seems, knowledge of the bases of things. Therefore it can be seen how unjustified Aristotle's reproach is: for there is no reason for those who want to philosophize to fall into despair on the pretext that they see great philosophers declare that nothing can be known; I mean, nothing concerning the inner nature of things, since it is on this point that they acknowledge their ignorance; but nonetheless they are recognized as extremely learned, because of the things that it is possible to know, nothing is hidden from them, so that someone has been able to say justly that their ignorance was very learned, in that sense that it is evidently not an ordinary merit to raise oneself up to seeing as ignorance what others believe to be science, and seeing sincerely that one is ignorant of what really is not known.

ART. 8. *Although the existence of various sciences ought to be admitted.*

Though something still can be added about the existence of various sciences, this will produce hardly any difficulty if we examine those that remain. For neither physics in its entirety can, as we have said, pronounce on what is internally and in itself the nature of the slightest thing, nor can metaphysics set forth anything but feeble conjectures, except for all that the orthodoxy of the Faith makes certain; nor does ethics offer itself with any unity, but it varies according to the diversity of nations and individuals and is subject to great changes; nor is jurisprudence anything but a complex collection of many laws which neither apply everywhere nor at all times; nor does medicine contain anything but the observation of numerous effects produced by various medicines taken at random, and the application of these same medicines or others like them to produce the same or analogous effects; and so with the others. Thus although while I can say that those are the sciences, it is evident nonetheless that they are not sciences of the Aristotelian type, if all things are considered rigorously—But the difficulty is much greater with regard to the mathematical sciences, because of the things which they put in the way. However, first there is no lack of Peripatetics to deny that mathematics is really a science.

Pereira sustains this well with subtility and elegance. . . . I have cited him at length, first as speaking as a Peripatetic, next because one cannot show more clearly that the mathematical discipline is not a science in the sense that Aristotle employs. —I add in the second place the mathematician, when he demonstrates an unknown proposition to you, does nothing more than he who, by placing a label on a box, or by opening it, makes you know what is inside. For in the same way that the latter only makes known what is contained within, for example, an antidote for poison, without the inscription or the action of opening making it the case that the antidote be there; the mathematician also simply shows you that this figure is of such a nature without his demonstration making it be such. Let us keep to the example proposed. You are told that the three angles of a triangle are equal to two right angles. You do not realize that it is so, just as you could not see that there was treacle in the box, no matter how you are assured of it. But you see it clearly when angles equal to the preceding ones are constructed, and which evidently are equivalent to two right angles. And, of course, you also see that the antidote is in the box when you have read the inscription or raised the lid; and I gladly admit that in the two cases a certain knowledge of the thing is born, in the sense of something that was not known formerly; but finally this knowledge is only that of the appearance of the thing and of what falls under our experience; and it is in effect only from that that we draw lessons about the way in which things appear to us, by experiencing them. This is to say that the equality of the three angles to two right angles is not apparent to you, because you cannot measure so exactly the respective value of each of these angles by looking at them, but as soon as the look cast on the other angles has come to the eyes' aid, then the fact is clearly apparent. What is all this but the appearance better considered of one and the same object? Indeed, in the same way that it was simple negligence not to open the box when you did not know whether the antidote was inside, it was also a simple insufficiency of your eyes which prevented you from seeing formerly in the triangle what you later see there. Thus the mathematician only makes you consider most attentively what at first you did not notice. From which it follows that the demonstration proposed to you, or the method which is employed, is not the cause of the thing's being what it is . . . , but simply makes you see that it is so. Hence this is not a science in Aristotle's sense, but rather one of those that we have judged ought to be retained. I conclude therefore that all that is certain and evident in mathematics relates to appearances, but in no way to absolute causes or inner natures. —I add however that through mathematics, I am able to assure myself, for example, that the Earth is actually spherical. This can be made apparent by means of the eclipses of the Moon, and the variable height of the Poles. But why the Earth is spherical, or what its absolute nature is, whether it is animate or not, and if it is, what its soul's nature is, what functions it has, or what properties it is provided with, why it remains immobile in its center, or, if it moves, what force puts it in motion; all things which can as well be asked of the Sun and of the other stars; and similarly on the subject of sound which music is occupied with; on the subject of visual rays on which optics is based, and so on; truly, as soon as we go beyond the limits of what appears and falls under the senses and experience in order to seek to attain the most profound things, mathematics as well as every other science remains blind. Let it not be said that this can be true of applied mathematics, but not of geometry or arithmetic, because these reveal the inner nature and actual properties of figures and numbers. For from the moment that figures and numbers are considered abstractly, as if they were nowhere; they are thus nothing. Let us say on this that in order that they be somewhere and something, they have to be considered as inherent properties of the things affected by them. But if this is so, the same difficulty reappears, for whatever may be your profound reflections about figures, you will however never know the inner nature of the thing which is figured, and the same must be said as well about number. –You will then say that geometry should only deal with chimerical objects, since it should only deal with figures in an abstract way and not the figures of such and such real objects. I reply however that it is false that it does not deal with the figures of such and such a concrete thing; in effect it does not deal with them in particular or in isolation; but it does deal with them all in general. Now everyone knows that all the species are contained in the genus. If then, for example, we demonstrate something about the triangle, it is not such or such triangle that we thus designate, but however we do bring in this one or that one in our thoughts, not actually in isolation, but in conjunction with all the others. And it is certain that if we did not establish conclusions on the basis of certain triangles given under a material appearance, we would only pursue vain chimeras, since it is impossible to find other triangles than those. But the difference between geometry and applied mathematics consists in that the latter deals with the particular feaures of the figures of certain things, while the former deals with the general figures of all things. Needless to say that a figure in itself does not seem to have reality; but the development of this point belongs to another subject.

Lastly, it is usually objected that the Pyrrhonians are in opposition to ordinary life and common sense. For, first of all, they cannot speak like the rest of men, among whom we frequently hear "science," "certainty," and such, spoken of. If they [the Pyrrhonians] used such terms, they could not do so without contradicting themselves, as in effect they do in affirming, for example, that with regard to all reasonings, ones of equal force can be opposed, or that all things are indefinite; and similarly when they deny that such a thing be thus rather than otherwise, or that it is necessary to adopt one opinion rather than another, etc. Indeed, let them affirm or deny, it is a fact that they always set something forth, and thus assert a dogmatic proposition, which is, however, contrary to their intention. Thus, they can not at all live like other men, who approach the fire because they find that it is hot, take food because they believe it requisite for appeasing their hunger, and necessary for maintaining life; who carry on affairs, direct the army, acquire wealth, avoid dangers, fight against fraud, worship God, honor their parents, defend their country, raise their children, help their friends, protect the innocent, and regulate their conduct in accordance with other duties which are involved in living, because they think that this is good, pious and lawful. But the Pyrrhonians, not believing that anything is hot rather than cold, good rather than bad, necessary rather than superfluous, and having consequently to hold everything as indifferent, if, at least, they want to be consistent with themselves, they will have to, then, if they are cold, not approach the fire rather than the snow, and the same in other similar cases; for otherwise they would have to admit that a thing is uniquely this rather than something else. . . .

I reply however that no conduct less contradicts ordinary life than that of the Pyrrhonians; for, as has been many times repeated, they do not at all suppress the appearances of things, in the pursuit of, and flight from which life consists. But, to say a word at first about the manner of expression, it is evident that it is necessary to continue to make use of the same words that usage has confirmed, and especially so when they are attributed to sensible appearances. Snow, for example, is called white because it seems so, fire hot because it appears so, and so on with the rest. These appellations consequently will be maintained by Pyrrho. Doubtless, if you should wish to stop there, he could say that snow is white by nature, fire hot by nature, but for himself, as he does not boast of knowing what snow and fire are by nature, he refuses to pronounce on this, believing that it is enough to say what that appears to him. Now what more is necessary for ordinary conversation? You say that wine is sweet, he also will say that wine is sweet, and both of you then say the same thing; but since you hint that wine is sweet by nature, he that it is so according to appearance, there is really a difference there, but not indeed in the manner of expression. It seems then completely established that Pyrrho is not deceived in what he pronounces about appearances; but as to the truth of what you think, it is this that we have shown dubious by preceding deductions. Which then should be preferred? But, you say, he sets forth a dogmatic affirmation. In truth, besides what concerns appearances, he sets forth absolutely nothing. . . .

X

DESCARTES

RENE DESCARTES (1596-1650), born in the Touraine and educated at the new Jesuit college at La Flèche, moved to Holland in 1618 where he became an officer in the Dutch army. During the campaigns of 1618-1621, he became a famous mathematician, discovering the principles of analytic geometry. After a visit to Paris in 1628, he retired to Holland to work out his philosophical system. It first appeared in his *Discourse on Method* (1637) and was more completely stated in his *Meditations on First Philosophy* (1641). Objections to his views, gathered by his friend Mersenne, led to his statement of his case in "geometrical" form. In 1644, he published his *Principles of Philosophy*. As a result of his growing reputation as the great new philosopher, he was invited to the court of Queen Christina of Sweden and, in 1649, he left Holland for Stockholm and died there the following year. This translation is by John Veitch.

Meditations on First Philosophy

In which the existence of God and the real distinction of mind and body, are demonstrated

To the Very Sage and Illustrious the Dean and Doctors of the Sacred Faculty of Theology of Paris

Gentlemen,

The motive which impels me to present this Treatise to you is so reasonable, and, when you shall learn its design, I am confident that you also will consider that there is ground so valid for your taking it under your protection, that I can in no way better recommend it to you than by briefly stating the end which I proposed to myself in it. I have always been of the opinion that the two questions respecting God and the Soul were the chief of those that ought to be determined by help of Philosophy rather than of Theology; for although to us, the faithful, it be sufficient to hold as matters of faith, that the human soul does not perish with the body, and that God exists, it yet assuredly seems impossible ever to persuade infidels of the reality of any religion, or almost even any moral virtue, unless, first of all, those two things be proved to them by natural reason. And since in this life there are frequently greater rewards held out to vice than to virtue, few would prefer the right to the useful, if they were restrained neither by the fear of God nor the expectation of another life . . . ; and although it is quite true that the existence of God is to be believed since it is taught in the sacred Scriptures, and that, on the other hand, the sacred Scriptures are to be believed because they come from God (for since faith is a gift of God, the same Being who bestows grace to enable us to believe other things, can likewise impart of it to enable us to believe his own existence), nevertheless, this cannot be submitted to infidels, who would consider that the reasoning proceeded in a circle. And, indeed, I have observed that you, with all the other theologians, not only affirmed the sufficiency of natural reason for the proof of the existence of God, but also, that it may be inferred from sacred Scripture, that the knowledge of God is much clearer than of many created things, and that it is really so easy of acquisition as to leave those who do not possess it blameworthy. This is manifest from these words of the Book of Wisdom, chap. xiii., where it is said, *Howbeit they are not to be excused; for if their understanding was so great that they could discern the world and the creatures, why did they not rather find out the Lord thereof?* And in Romans, chap. i., it is said that they are *without excuse;* and again, in the same place, by these words,—*That which may be known of God is manifest in them*—we seem to be admonished that all which can be known of God may be made manifest by reasons obtained from no other source than the inspection of our own minds. I have, therefore, thought that it would not be unbecoming in me to inquire how and by what way, without going out of ourselves, God may be more easily and certainly known than the things of the world.

And as regards the Soul, although many have judged that its nature could not be easily discovered, and some have even ventured to say that human reason led to the conclusion that it perished with the body, and that the contrary opinion could be held through faith alone; nevertheless, since the Lateran Council, held under Leo X. (in session viii.), condemns these, and expressly enjoins Christian philosophers to refute their arguments, and establish the truth according to their ability, I have ventured to attempt it in this work. Moreover, I am aware that most of the irreligious deny the existence of God, and the distinctness of the human soul from the body, for no other reason than because these points, as they allege, have never as yet been demonstrated. Now, although I am by no means of their opinion, but, on the contrary, hold that almost all the proofs which have been adduced on these questions by great men, possess, when rightly understood, the force of demonstrations, and that it is next to impossible to discover new, yet there is, I apprehend, no more useful service to be performed in Philosophy, than if some one were, once for all, carefully to seek out the best of these reasons, and expound them so accurately and clearly that, for the future, it might be manifest to all that they are real demonstrations. And finally, since many persons were greatly desirous of this, who knew that I had cultivated a certain Method of resolving all kinds of difficulties in the sciences, which is not indeed new (there being nothing older than truth), but of which they were aware I had made successful use in other instances, I judged it to be my duty to make trial of it also on the present matter.

Now the sum of what I have been able to accomplish on the subject is contained in this treatise. Not that I here essayed to collect all the diverse reasons which might be adduced as proofs on this subject, for this does not seem to be necessary, unless on matters where no one proof of adequate certainty is to be had; but I treated the first and chief alone in such a manner that I should venture now to propose them as demonstrations of the highest certainty and evidence. And I will also add that they are such as to lead me to think that there is no way open to the mind of man by which proofs superior to them can ever be discovered; for the importance of the subject, and the glory of God, to which all this relates, constrain me to speak here somewhat more freely of myself than I have been accustomed to do. Nevertheless, whatever certitude and evidence I may find in these demonstrations, I cannot therefore persuade myself that they are level to the comprehension of all. But just as in geometry there are many of the demonstrations of Archimedes, Apollonius, Pappus, and others, which, though received by all as highly evident and certain (because indeed they manifestly contain nothing which, considered by itself, it is not very easy to understand, and no consequents that are inaccurately related to their antecedents), are nevertheless understood by a very limited number, because they are somewhat long, and demand the whole attention of the reader: so in the same way, although I consider the demonstrations of which I here make use, to be equal or even superior to the geometrical in certitude and evidence, I am afraid, nevertheless, that they will not be adequately understood by many, as well because they also are somewhat long and involved, as chiefly because they require the mind to be entirely free from prejudice, and able with ease to detach itself from the commerce of the senses. And, to speak the truth, the ability for metaphysical studies is less general than for those of geometry. And, besides, there is still this difference that, as in geometry, all are persuaded that nothing is usually advanced of which there is not a certain demonstration, those but partially versed in it err more frequently in assenting to what is false, from a desire of seeming to understand it, than in denying what is true. In philosophy, on the other hand, where it is believed that all is doubtful, few sincerely give themselves to the search after truth, and by far the greater number seek the reputation of bold thinkers by audaciously impugning such truths as are of the greatest moment.

Hence it is that, whatever force my reasonings may possess, yet because they belong to philosophy, I do not expect they will have much effect on the minds of men, unless you extend to them your patronage and approval. But since your Faculty is held in so great esteem by all, and since the name of SORBONNE is of such authority, that not only in matters of faith, but even also in what regards human philosophy, has the judgment of no other society, after the Sacred Councils, received so great deference, it being the universal conviction that it is impossible elsewhere to find greater perspicacity and solidity, or greater wisdom and integrity in giving judgment, I doubt not,—if you but condescend to pay so much regard to this Treatise as to be willing, in the first place, to correct it (for, mindful not only of my humanity, but chiefly also of my ignorance, I do not affirm that it is free from errors); in the second place, to supply what is wanting in it, to perfect what is incomplete, and to give more ample illustration where it is demanded, or at least to indicate these defects to myself that I may endeavour to remedy them; and, finally, when the reasonings contained in it, by which the existence of God and the distinction of the human soul from the body are established, shall have been brought to such degree of perspicuity as to be esteemed exact demonstrations, of which I am assured they admit, if you condescend to accord them the authority of your approbation, and render a public testimony of their truth and certainty,—I doubt not, I say, but that henceforward all the errors which have ever been entertained on these questions will very soon be effaced from the minds of men. For truth itself will readily lead the remainder of the ingenious and the learned to subscribe to your judgment; and your authority will cause the atheists, who are in general sciolists rather than ingenious or learned, to lay aside the spirit of contradiction, and lead them, perhaps, to do battle in their own persons for reasonings which they find considered demonstrations by all men of genius, lest they should seem not to understand them; and, finally, the rest of mankind will readily trust to so many testimonies, and there will no longer be any one who will venture to doubt either the existence of God or the real distinction of mind and body. It is for you, in your singular wisdom, to judge of the importance of the establishment of such beliefs, [who are cognisant of the disorders which doubt of these truths produces].[1] But it would not here become me to commend at greater length the cause of God and of religion to you, who have always proved the strongest support of the Catholic Church.

1. The square brackets, here and throughout this section, are used to mark additions to the original of the revised French translation.

SYNOPSIS OF THE SIX FOLLOWING MEDITATIONS

In the First Meditation I expound the grounds on which we may doubt in general of all things, and especially of material objects, so long, at least, as we have no other foundations for the sciences than those we have hitherto possessed. Now, although the utility of a doubt so general may not be manifest at first sight, it is nevertheless of the greatest, since it delivers us from all prejudice, and affords the easiest pathway by which the mind may withdraw itself from the senses; and, finally, makes it impossible for us to doubt wherever we afterwards discover truth.

In the Second, the mind which, in the exercise of the freedom peculiar to itself, supposes that no object is, of the existence of which it has even the slightest doubt, finds that, meanwhile, it must itself exist. And this point is likewise of the highest moment, for the mind is thus enabled easily to distinguish what pertains to itself, that is, to the intellectual nature, from what is to be referred to the body. But since some, perhaps, will expect, at this stage of our progress, a statement of the reasons which establish the doctrine of the immortality of the soul, I think it proper here to make such aware, that it was my aim to write nothing of which I could not give exact demonstration, and that I therefore felt myself obliged to adopt an order similar to that in use among the geometers, viz., to premise all upon which the proposition in question depends, before coming to any conclusion respecting it. Now, the first and chief pre-requisite for the knowledge of the immortality of the soul is our being able to form the clearest possible conception of the soul itself, and such as shall be absolutely distinct from all our notions of body; and how this is to be accomplished is there shown. There is required, besides this, the assurance that all objects which we clearly and distinctly think are true (really exist) in that very mode in which we think them; and this could not be established previously to the Fourth Meditation. Farther, it is necessary, for the same purpose, that we possess a distinct conception of corporeal nature, which is given partly in the Second and partly in the Fifth and Sixth Meditations. And, finally, on these grounds, we are necessitated to conclude, that all those objects which are clearly and distinctly conceived to be diverse substances, as mind and body, are substances really reciprocally distinct; and this inference is made in the Sixth Meditation. The absolute distinction of mind and body is, besides, confirmed in this Second Meditation, by showing that we cannot conceive body unless as divisible; while, on the other hand, mind cannot be conceived unless as indivisible. For we are not able to conceive the half of a mind, as we can of any body, however small, so that the natures of these two substances are to be held, not only as diverse, but even in some measure as contraries. I have not, however, pursued this discussion further in the present treatise, as well for the reason that these considerations are sufficient to show that the destruction of the mind does not follow from the corruption of the body, and thus to afford to men the hope of a future life, as also because the premises from which it is competent for us to infer the immortality of the soul, involve an explication of the whole principles of Physics: in order to establish, in the first place, that generally all substances, that is, all things which can exist only in consequence of having been created by God, are in their own nature incorruptible, and can never cease to be, unless God himself, by refusing his concurrence to them, reduce them to nothing; and, in the second place, that body, taken generally, is a substance, and therefore can never perish, but that the human body, in as far as it differs from other bodies, is constituted only by a certain configuration of members, and by other accidents of this sort, while the human mind is not made up of accidents, but is a pure substance. For although all the accidents of the mind be changed—although, for example, it think certain things, will others, and perceive others, the mind itself does not vary with these changes; while, on the contrary, the human body is no longer the same if a change take place in the form of any of its parts: from which it follows that the body may, indeed, without difficulty perish, but that the mind is in its own nature immortal.

In the Third Meditation, I have unfolded at sufficient length, as appears to me, my chief argument for the existence of God. But yet, since I was there desirous to avoid the use of comparisons taken from material objects, that I might withdraw, as far as possible, the minds of my readers from the senses, numerous obscurities perhaps remain, which, however, will, I trust, be afterwards entirely removed in the Replies to the Objections: thus, among other things, it may be difficult to understand how the idea of a being absolutely perfect, which is found in our minds, possesses so much objective reality [i. e., participates by representation in so many degrees of being and perfection] that it must be held to arise from a cause absolutely perfect. This is illustrated in the Replies by the comparison of a highly perfect machine, the idea of which exists in the mind of some workman; for as the objective (i.e., representative) perfection of this idea must have some cause, viz., either the science of the workman, or of some other person from whom he has received the idea, in the same way the idea of God, which is found in us, demands God himself for its cause.

In the Fourth, it is shown that all which we clearly and distinctly perceive (apprehend) is true; and, at the same time, is explained wherein consists the nature of error; points that require to be known as well for confirming the preceding truths, as for the better understanding of those that are to follow. But, meanwhile, it must be observed, that I do not at all there treat of Sin, that is, of error committed in the pursuit of good and evil, but of that sort alone which arises in the determination of the true and the false. Nor do I refer to matters of faith, or to the conduct of life, but only to what regards speculative truths, and such as are known by means of the natural light alone.

In the Fifth, besides the illustration of corporeal nature, taken generically, a new demonstration is given of the existence of God, not free, perhaps, any more than the former, from certain difficulties, but of these the solution will be found in the Replies to the Objections. I further show, in what sense it is true that the certitude of geometrical demonstrations themselves is dependent on the knowledge of God.

Finally, in the Sixth, the act of the understanding is distinguished from that of the imagination; the marks of this distinction are described; the human mind is shown to be really distinct from the body, and, nevertheless, to be so closely conjoined therewith, as together to form, as it were, a unity. The whole of the errors which arise from the senses are brought under review, while the means of avoiding them are pointed out; and, finally, all the grounds are adduced from which the existence of material objects may be inferred; not, however, because I deemed them of great utility in establishing what they prove, viz., that there is in reality a world, that men are possessed of bodies, and the like, the truth of which no one of sound mind ever seriously doubted; but because, from a close consideration of them, it is perceived that they are neither so strong nor clear as the reasonings which conduct us to the knowledge of our mind and of God; so that the latter are, of all which come under human knowledge, the most certain and manifest—a conclusion which it was my single aim in these Meditations to establish; on which account I here omit mention of the various other questions which, in the course of the discussion, I had occasion likewise to consider.

MEDITATION I

¶ OF THE THINGS OF WHICH WE MAY DOUBT

Several years have now elapsed since I first became aware that I had accepted, even from my youth, many false opinions for true, and that consequently what I afterwards based on such principles was highly doubtful; and from that time I was convinced of the necessity of undertaking once in my life to rid myself of all the opinions I had adopted, and of commencing anew the work of building from the foundation, if I desired to establish a firm and abiding superstructure in the sciences. But as this enterprise appeared to me to be one of great magnitude, I waited until I had attained an age so mature as to leave me no hope that at any stage of life more advanced I should be better able to execute my design. On this account, I have delayed so long that I should henceforth consider I was doing wrong were I still to consume in deliberation any of the time that now remains for action. To-day, then, since I have opportunely freed my mind from all cares, [and am happily disturbed by no passions], and since I am in the secure possession of leisure in a peaceable retirement, I will at length apply myself earnestly and freely to the general overthrow of all my former opinions. But, to this end, it will not be necessary for me to show that the whole of these are false—a point, perhaps, which I shall never reach; but as even now my reason convinces me that I ought not the less carefully to withhold belief from what is not entirely certain and indubitable, than from what is manifestly false, it will be sufficient to justify the rejection of the whole if I shall find in each some ground for doubt. Nor for this purpose will it be necessary even to deal with each belief individually, which would be truly an endless labour; but, as the removal from below of the foundation necessarily involves the downfall of the whole edifice, I will at once approach the criticism of the principles on which all my former beliefs rested.

All that I have, up to this moment, accepted as possessed of the highest truth and certainty, I received either from or through the senses. I observed, however, that these sometimes misled us; and it is the part of prudence not to place absolute confidence in that by which we have even once been deceived.

But it may be said, perhaps, that, although the senses occasionally mislead us respecting minute objects, and such as are so far removed from us as to be beyond the reach of close observation, there are yet many other of their informations (presentations), of the truth of which it is manifestly impossible to doubt; as for example, that I am in this place, seated by the fire, clothed in a winter dressing-gown, that I hold in my hands this piece of paper, with other intimations of the same nature. But how could I deny that I possess these hands and this body, and withal escape being classed with persons in a state of insanity, whose brains are so disordered and clouded by dark bilious vapours as to cause them pertinaciously to assert that they are monarchs when they are in the greatest poverty; or clothed [in gold] and purple when destitute of any covering; or that their head is made of clay, their body of glass, or that they are gourds? I should certainly be not less insane than they, were I to regulate my procedure according to examples so extravagant.

Though this be true, I must nevertheless here consider that I am a man, and that, consequently, I am in the habit of sleeping, and representing to myself in dreams those same things, or even sometimes others less probable, which the insane think are presented to them in their waking moments. How often have I dreamt that I was in these familiar circumstances,—that I was dressed, and occupied this place by the fire, when I was lying undressed in bed? At the present moment, however, I certainly look upon this paper with eyes wide awake; the head which I now move is not asleep; I extend this hand consciously and with express purpose, and I perceive it; the occurrences in sleep are not so distinct as all this. But I cannot forget that, at other times, I have been deceived in sleep by similar illusions; and, attentively considering those cases, I perceive so clearly that there exist no certain marks by which the state of waking can ever be distinguished from sleep, that I feel greatly astonished; and in amazement I almost persuade myself that I am now dreaming.

Let us suppose, then, that we are dreaming, and that all these particulars—namely, the opening of the eyes, the motion of the head, the forth-putting of the hands—are merely illusions; and even that we really possess neither an entire body nor hands such as we see. Nevertheless, it must be admitted at least that the objects which appear to us in sleep are, as it were, painted representations which could not have been formed unless in the likeness of realities; and, therefore, that those general objects, at all events,—namely, eyes, a head, hands, and an entire body—are not simply imaginary, but really existent. For, in truth, painters themselves, even when they study to represent sirens and satyrs by forms the most fantastic and extraordinary, cannot bestow upon them natures absolutely new, but can only make a certain medley of the members of different animals; or if they chance to

sounds, and all external things, are nothing better than the illusions of dreams, by means of which this being has laid snares for my credulity; I will consider myself as without hands, eyes, flesh, blood, or any of the senses, and as falsely believing that I am possessed of these; I will continue resolutely fixed in this belief, and if indeed by this means it be not in my power to arrive at the knowledge of truth, I shall at least do what is in my power, viz., [suspend my judgment], and guard with settled purpose against giving my assent to what is false, and being imposed upon by this deceiver, whatever be his power and artifice.

But this undertaking is arduous, and a certain indolence insensibly leads me back to my ordinary course of life; and just as the captive, who, perchance, was enjoying in his dreams an imaginary liberty, when he begins to suspect that it is but a vision, dreads awakening, and conspires with the agreeable illusions that the deception may be prolonged; so I, of my own accord, fall back into the train of my former beliefs, and fear to arouse myself from my slumber, lest the time of laborious wakefulness that would succeed this quiet rest, in place of bringing any light of day, should prove inadequate to dispel the darkness that will arise from the difficulties that have now been raised.

MEDITATION II

¶ Of the Nature of the Human Mind; and That It Is More Easily Known Than the Body

The Meditation of yesterday has filled my mind with so many doubts, that it is no longer in my power to forget them. Nor do I see, meanwhile, any principle on which they can be resolved; and, just as if I had fallen all of a sudden into very deep water, I am so greatly disconcerted as to be unable either to plant my feet firmly on the bottom or sustain myself by swimming on the surface. I will, nevertheless, make an effort, and try anew the same path on which I had entered yesterday, that is, proceed by casting aside all that admits of the slightest doubt, not less than if I had discovered it to be absolutely false; and I will continue always in this track until I shall find something that is certain, or at least, if I can do nothing more, until I shall know with certainty that there is nothing certain. Archimedes, that he might transport the entire globe from the place it occupied to another, demanded only a point that was firm and immovable; so also, I shall be entitled to entertain the highest expectations, if I am fortunate enough to discover only one thing that is certain and indubitable.

I suppose, accordingly, that all the things which I see are false (fictitious); I believe that none of those objects which my fallacious memory represents ever existed; I suppose that I possess no senses; I believe that body, figure, extension, motion, and place are merely fictions of my mind. What is there, then, that can be esteemed true? Perhaps this only, that there is absolutely nothing certain.

But how do I know that there is not something different altogether from the objects I have now enumerated, of which it is impossible to entertain the slightest doubt? Is there not a God, or some being, by whatever name I may designate him, who causes these thoughts to arise in my mind? But why suppose such a being, for it may be I myself am capable of producing them? Am I, then, at least not something? But I before denied that I possessed senses or a body; I hesitate, however, for what follows from that? Am I so dependent on the body and the senses that without these I cannot exist? But I had the persuasion that there was absolutely nothing in the world, that there was no sky and no earth, neither minds nor bodies; was I not, therefore, at the same time, persuaded that I did not exist? Far from it; I assuredly existed, since I was persuaded. But there is I know not what being, who is possessed at once of the highest power and the deepest cunning, who is constantly employing all his ingenuity in deceiving me. Doubtless, then, I exist, since I am deceived; and, let him deceive me as he may, he can never bring it about that I am nothing, so long as I shall be conscious that I am something. So that it must, in fine, be maintained, all things being maturely and carefully considered, that this proposition I am, I exist, is necessarily true each time it is expressed by me, or conceived in my mind.

But I do not yet know with sufficient clearness what I am, though assured that I am; and hence, in the next place, I must take care, lest perchance I inconsiderately substitute some other object in room of what is properly myself, and thus wander from truth, even in that knowledge (cognition) which I hold to be of all others the most certain and evident. For this reason, I will now consider anew what I formerly believed myself to be, before I entered on the present train of thought; and of my previous opinion I will retrench all that can in the least be invalidated by the grounds of doubt I have adduced, in order that there may at length remain nothing but what is certain and indubitable. What then did I formerly think I was? Undoubtedly I judged that I was a man. But what is a man? Shall I say a rational animal? Assuredly not; for it would be necessary forthwith to inquire into what is meant by animal, and what by rational, and thus, from a single question, I should insensibly glide into others, and these more difficult than the first; nor do I now possess enough of leisure to warrant me in wasting my time amid subtleties of this sort. I prefer here to attend to the thoughts that sprung up of themselves in my mind, and were inspired by my own nature alone, when I applied myself to the consideration of what I was. In the first place, then, I thought that I possessed a countenance, hands, arms, and all the fabric of members that appears in a corpse, and which I called by the name of body. It further occurred to me that I was nourished, that I walked, perceived, and thought, and all those actions I referred to the soul; but what the soul itself was I either did not stay to consider, or, if I did, I imagined that it was something extremely rare and subtile, like wind, or flame, or ether, spread through my grosser parts. As regarded the body, I did not even doubt of its nature, but thought I distinctly knew it, and if I had wished to describe it according to the notions I then entertained, I should have explained myself in this manner: By body I understand all that can be terminated by a certain figure; that can be comprised in a certain place, and so fill a certain space as therefrom to exclude every other body; that can be perceived either by touch, sight, hearing, taste, or smell; that can be moved in different ways, not indeed of itself, but by something foreign to it by which it is touched [and from which it receives the impression]; for the power of self-motion, as likewise that of perceiving and thinking, I held as by no means pertaining to the nature of body; on the contrary, I was somewhat astonished to find such faculties existing in some bodies.

But [as to myself, what can I now say that I am], since I suppose there exists an extremely powerful, and, if I may so speak, malignant being, whose whole endeavours are directed towards deceiving me? Can I affirm that I possess any one of all those attributes of which I have lately spoken as belonging to the nature of body? After attentively considering them in my own mind, I find none of them that can properly be said to belong to myself. To recount them were idle and tedious. Let us pass, then, to the attributes of the soul. The first mentioned were the powers of nutrition and walking; but, if it be true that I have no body, it is true likewise that I am capable neither of walking nor of being nourished. Perception is another attribute of the soul; but perception too is impossible without the body: besides, I have frequently, during sleep, believed that I perceived objects which I afterwards observed I did not in reality perceive. Thinking is another attribute of the soul; and here I discover what properly belongs to myself. This alone is inseparable from me. I am—I exist: this is certain; but how often? As often as I think; for perhaps it would even happen, if I should wholly cease to think, that I should at the same time altogether cease to be. I now admit nothing that is not necessarily true: I am therefore, precisely speaking, only a thinking thing, that is, a mind, understanding, or reason,—terms whose signification was before unknown to me. I am, however, a real thing, and really existent; but what thing? The answer was, a thinking thing. The question now arises, am I aught besides? I will stimulate my imagination with a view to discover whether I am not still something more than a thinking being. Now it is plain I am not the assemblage of members called the human body; I am not a thin and penetrating air diffused through all these members, or wind, or flame, or vapour, or breath, or any of all the things I can imagine; for I supposed that all these were not, and, without changing the supposition, I find that I still feel assured of my existence.

But it is true, perhaps, that those very things which I suppose to be non-existent, because they are unknown to me, are not in truth different from myself whom I know. This is a point I cannot determine, and do not now enter into any dispute regarding it. I can only judge of things that are known to me: I am conscious that I exist, and I who know that I exist inquire into what I am. It is, however, perfectly certain that the knowledge of my existence, thus precisely taken, is not dependent on things, the existence of which is as yet unknown to me: and consequently it is not dependent on any of the things I can feign in imagination. Moreover, the phrase itself, I frame an image, reminds me of my error; for I should in truth frame one if I were to imagine myself to be anything, since to imagine is nothing more than to contemplate the figure or image of a corporeal thing; but I already know that I exist, and that it is possible at the same time that all those images, and in general all that relates to the nature of body, are merely dreams [or chimeras]. From this I discover that it is not more reasonable to say, I will excite my imagination that I may know more distinctly what I am, than to express myself as follows: I am now awake, and perceive something real, but because my perception is not sufficiently clear, I will of express purpose go to sleep that my dreams may represent to me the object of my perception with more truth and clearness. And, therefore, I know that nothing of all that I can embrace in imagination belongs to the knowledge which

I have of myself, and that there is need to recall with the utmost care the mind from this mode of thinking, that it may be able to know its own nature with perfect distinctness.

But what, then, am I? A thinking thing, it has been said. But what is a thinking thing? It is a thing that doubts, understands, [conceives], affirms, denies, wills, refuses, that imagines also, and perceives. Assuredly it is not little, if all these properties belong to my nature. But why should they not belong to it? Am I not that very being who now doubts of almost everything; who, for all that, understands and conceives certain things; who affirms one alone as true, and denies the others; who desires to know more of them, and does not wish to be deceived; who imagines many things, sometimes even despite his will; and is likewise percipient of many, as if through the medium of the senses. Is there nothing of all this as true as that I am, even although I should be always dreaming, and although he who gave me being employed all his ingenuity to deceive me? Is there also any one of these attributes that can be properly distinguished from my thought, or that can be said to be separate from myself? For it is of itself so evident that it is I who doubt, I who understand, and I who desire, that it is here unnecessary to add anything by way of rendering it more clear. And I am as certainly the same being who imagines; for, although it may be (as I before supposed) that nothing I imagine is true, still the power of imagination does not cease really to exist in me and to form part of my thought. In fine, I am the same being who perceives, that is, who apprehends certain objects as by the organs of sense, since, in truth, I see light, hear a noise, and feel heat. But it will be said that these presentations are false, and that I am dreaming. Let it be so. At all events it is certain that I seem to see light, hear a noise, and feel heat; this cannot be false, and this is what in me is properly called perceiving, which is nothing else than thinking. From this I begin to know what I am with somewhat greater clearness and distinctness than heretofore.

But, nevertheless, it still seems to me, and I cannot help believing, that corporeal things, whose images are formed by thought, [which fall under the senses], and are examined by the same, are known with much greater distinctness than that I know not what part of myself which is not imaginable; although, in truth, it may seem strange to say that I know and comprehend with greater distinctness things whose existence appears to me doubtful, that are unknown, and do not belong to me, than others of whose reality I am persuaded, that are known to me, and appertain to my proper nature: in a word, than myself. But

I see clearly what is the state of the case. My mind is apt to wander, and will not yet submit to be restrained within the limits of truth. Let us therefore leave the mind to itself once more, and, according to it every kind of liberty, [permit it to consider the objects that appear to it from without], in order that, having afterwards withdrawn it from these gently and opportunely, [and fixed it on the consideration of its being and the properties it finds in itself], it may then be the more easily controlled.

Let us now accordingly consider the objects that are commonly thought to be [the most easily, and likewise] the most distinctly known, viz., the bodies we touch and see; not, indeed, bodies in general, for these general notions are usually somewhat more confused, but one body in particular. Take, for example, this piece of wax; it is quite fresh, having been but recently taken from the bee-hive; it has not yet lost the sweetness of the honey it contained; it still retains somewhat of the odour of the flowers from which it was gathered; its colour, figure, size, are apparent (to the sight); it is hard, cold, easily handled; and sounds when struck upon with the finger. In fine, all that contributes to make a body as distinctly known as possible, is found in the one before us. But, while I am speaking, let it be placed near the fire—what remained of the taste exhales, the smell evaporates, the colour changes, its figure is destroyed, its size increases, it becomes liquid, it grows hot, it can hardly be handled, and, although struck upon, it emits no sound. Does the same wax still remain after this change? It must be admitted that it does remain; no one doubts it, or judges otherwise. What, then, was it I knew with so much distinctness in the piece of wax? Assuredly, it could be nothing of all that I observed by means of the senses, since all the things that fell under taste, smell, sight, touch, and hearing are changed, and yet the same wax remains. It was perhaps what I now think, viz., that this wax was neither the sweetness of honey, the pleasant odour of flowers, the whiteness, the figure, nor the sound, but only a body that a little before appeared to me conspicuous under these forms, and which is now perceived under others. But, to speak precisely, what is it that I imagine when I think of it in this way? Let it be attentively considered, and, retrenching all that does not belong to the wax, let us see what remains. There certainly remains nothing, except something extended, flexible, and movable. But what is meant by flexible and movable? Is it not that I imagine that the piece of wax, being round, is capable of becoming square, or of passing from a square into a triangular figure? Assuredly such is not the case, because I conceive that it admits of an infinity of similar changes; and I am, moreover, unable to compass this infinity by imagination, and consequently this conception which I have of the wax is not the product of the faculty of imagination. But what now is this extension? Is it not also unknown? for it becomes greater when the wax is melted, greater when it is boiled, and greater still when the heat increases; and I should not conceive [clearly and] according to truth, the wax as it is, if I did not suppose that the piece we are considering admitted even of a wider variety of extension than I ever imagined. I must, therefore, admit that I cannot even comprehend by imagination what the piece of wax is, and that it is the mind alone which perceives it. I speak of one piece in particular; for, as to wax in general, this is still more evident. But what is the piece of wax that can be perceived only by the [understanding or] mind? It is certainly the same which I see, touch, imagine; and, in fine, it is the same which, from the beginning, I believed it to be. But (and this it is of moment to observe) the perception of it is neither an act of sight, of touch, nor of imagination, and never was either of these, though it might formerly seem so, but is simply an intuition of the mind, which may be imperfect and confused, as it formerly was, or very clear and distinct, as it is at present, according as the attention is more or less directed to the elements which it contains, and of which it is composed.

But, meanwhile, I feel greatly astonished when I observe [the weakness of my mind, and] its proneness to error. For although, without at all giving expression to what I think, I consider all this in my own mind, words yet occasionally impede my progress, and I am almost led into error by the terms of ordinary language. We say, for example, that we see the same wax when it is before us, and not that we judge it to be the same from its retaining the same colour and figure: whence I should forthwith be disposed to conclude that the wax is known by the act of sight, and not by the intuition of the mind alone, were it not for the analogous instance of human beings passing on in the street below, as observed from a window. In this case I do not fail to say that I see the men themselves just as I say that I see the wax; and yet what do I see from the window beyond hats and cloaks that might cover artificial machines, whose motions might be determined by springs? But I judge that there are human beings from these appearances, and thus I comprehend, by the faculty of judgment alone which is in the mind, what I believed I saw with my eyes.

The man who makes it his aim to rise to knowledge superior to the common, ought to be ashamed to seek occasions of doubting from the vulgar forms of speech: instead, therefore, of doing this, I shall proceed with the matter in hand, and inquire whether I had a clearer and more perfect perception of the piece of wax when I first saw it, and when I thought I knew it by means of the external sense itself, or, at all events, by the common sense (*sensus communis*), as it is called, that is, by the imaginative faculty; or whether I rather apprehend it more clearly at present, after having examined with greater care, both what it is, and in what way it can be known. It would certainly be ridiculous to entertain any doubt on this point. For what, in that first perception, was there distinct? What did I perceive which any animal might not have perceived? But when I distinguish the wax from its exterior forms, and when, as if I had stripped it of its vestments, I consider it quite naked, it is certain, although some error may still be found in my judgment, that I cannot, nevertheless, thus apprehend it without possessing a human mind.

But, finally, what shall I say of the mind itself, that is, of myself? for as yet I do not admit that I am anything but mind. What, then! I who seem to possess so distinct an apprehension of the piece of wax, —do I not know myself, both with greater truth and certitude, and also much more distinctly and clearly? For if I judge that the wax exists because I see it, it assuredly follows, much more evidently, that I myself am or exist, for the same reason: for it is possible that what I see may not in truth be wax, and that I do not even possess eyes with which to see anything; but it cannot be that when I see, or, which comes to the same thing, when I think I see, I myself who think am nothing. So likewise, if I judge that the wax exists because I touch it, it will still also follow that I am; and if I determine that my imagination, or any other cause, whatever it be, persuades me of the existence of the wax, I will still draw the same conclusion. And what is here remarked of the piece of wax, is applicable to all the other things that are external to me. And further, if the [notion or] perception of wax appeared to me more precise and distinct, after that not only sight and touch, but many other causes besides, rendered it manifest to my apprehension, with how much greater distinctness must I now know myself, since all the reasons that contribute to the knowledge of the nature of wax, or of any body whatever, manifest still better the nature of my mind? And there are besides so many other things in the mind itself that contribute to the illustration of its nature, that those dependent on the body, to which I have here referred, scarcely merit to be taken into account.

But, in conclusion, I find I have insensibly reverted to the point I desired; for, since it is now manifest to me that bodies themselves are not properly perceived by the senses nor by the faculty of imagination, but by the intellect alone; and since they are not perceived because they are seen and touched, but only because they are understood [or rightly comprehended by thought], I readily discover that there is nothing more easily or clearly apprehended than my own mind. But because it is difficult to rid one's self so promptly of an opinion to which one has been long accustomed, it will be desirable to tarry for some time at this stage, that, by long continued meditation, I may more deeply impress upon my memory this new knowledge.

MEDITATION III

¶ Of God: That He Exists

I will now close my eyes, I will stop my ears, I will turn away my senses from their objects, I will even efface from my consciousness all the images of corporeal things; or at least, because this can hardly be accomplished, I will consider them as empty and false; and thus, holding converse only with myself, and closely examining my nature, I will endeavour to obtain by degrees a more intimate and familiar knowledge of myself. I am a thinking (conscious) thing, that is, a being who doubts, affirms, denies, knows a few objects, and is ignorant of many, —[who loves, hates], wills, refuses,—who imagines likewise, and perceives; for, as I before remarked, although the things which I perceive or imagine are perhaps nothing at all apart from me [and in themselves], I am nevertheless assured that those modes of consciousness which I call perceptions and imaginations, in as far only as they are modes of consciousness, exist in me. And in the little I have said I think I have summed up all that I really know, or at least all that up to this time I was aware I knew. Now, as I am endeavouring to extend my knowledge more widely, I will use circumspection, and consider with care whether I can still discover in myself anything further which I have not yet hitherto observed. I am certain that I am a thinking thing; but do I not therefore likewise know what is required to render me certain of a truth? In this first knowledge, doubtless, there is nothing that gives me assurance of its truth except the clear and distinct perception of what I affirm, which would not indeed be sufficient to give me the assurance that what I say is true, if it could ever happen that anything I thus clearly and distinctly perceived should prove false; and accordingly it seems to me that I may now take as a general rule, that all that is very clearly and distinctly apprehended (conceived) is true.[1]

Nevertheless I before received and admitted many things as wholly certain and manifest, which yet I afterwards found to be doubtful. What, then, were those? They were the earth, the sky, the stars, and all the other objects which I was in the habit of perceiving by the senses. But what was it that I clearly [and distinctly] perceived in them? Nothing more than that the ideas and the thoughts of those objects were presented to my mind. And even now I do not deny that these ideas are found in my mind. But there was yet another thing which I affirmed, and which, from having been accustomed to believe it, I thought I clearly perceived, although, in truth, I did not perceive it at all; I mean the existence of objects external to me, from which those ideas proceeded, and to which they had a perfect resemblance; and it was here I was mistaken, or if I judged correctly, this assuredly was not to be traced to any knowledge I possessed.

But when I considered any matter in arithmetic and geometry, that was very simple and easy, as, for example, that two and three added together make five, and things of this sort, did I not view them with at least sufficient clearness to warrant me in affirming their truth? Indeed, if I afterwards judged that we ought to doubt of these things, it was for no other reason than because it occurred to me that a God might perhaps have given me such a nature as that I should be deceived,

---

1. In the *Principles of Philosophy,* Descartes further discusses the idea of clear and distinct perception.

I. 45. *What constitutes a clear and distinct perception.*

There are even some people who, in their entire life, never perceive anything as they should in order to judge of it properly. For the knowledge upon which a certain and indubitable judgment can be based, ought to be not only clear, but also distinct. I term that clear which is present and manifest to an attentive mind: in the same way that we are said to see objects clearly when being present, they act strongly enough, and when our eyes are disposed to look at them. And distinct, that which is so precise and different from all other items, that it only contains in itself that which seems manifest *to him who considers it as he should.*

I. 46. *That something can be clear without being distinct, but not vice-versa.*

For example, when someone feels a violent pain, the knowledge he has of this pain is clear to him, but is not thereby always distinct, because he usually confounds it with the false/or obscure/judgment that he makes concerning the nature of what he thinks to be in the affected part which he believes to be like *the idea or* feeling of pain that is in his thought, although he perceives nothing clearly but the feeling *or confused thought which is in him.* Thus knowledge can be clear without being distinct, and can only be distinct if it be at the same time clear.

even respecting the matters that appeared to me the most evidently true. But as often as this preconceived opinion of the sovereign power of a God presents itself to my mind, I am constrained to admit that it is easy for him, if he wishes it, to cause me to err, even in matters where I think I possess the highest evidence; and, on the other hand, as often as I direct my attention to things which I think I apprehend with great clearness, I am so persuaded of their truth that I naturally break out into expressions such as these: Deceive me who may, no one will yet ever be able to bring it about that I am not, so long as I shall be conscious that I am, or at any future time cause it to be true that I have never been, it being now true that I am, or make two and three more or less than five, in supposing which, and other like absurdities, I discover a manifest contradiction.

And in truth, as I have no ground for believing that Deity is deceitful, and as, indeed, I have not even considered the reasons by which the existence of a Deity of any kind is established, the ground of doubt that rests only on this supposition is very slight, and, so to speak, metaphysical. But, that I may be able wholly to remove it, I must inquire whether there is a God, as soon as an opportunity of doing so shall present itself; and if I find that there is a God, I must examine likewise whether he can be a deceiver; for, without the knowledge of these two truths, I do not see that I can ever be certain of anything. And that I may be enabled to examine this without interrupting the order of meditation I have proposed to myself [which is, to pass by degrees from the notions that I shall find first in my mind to those I shall afterwards discover in it], it is necessary at this stage to divide all my thoughts into certain classes, and to consider in which of these classes truth and error are, strictly speaking, to be found.

Of my thoughts some are, as it were, images of things, and to these alone properly belongs the name *idea;* as when I think [represent to my mind] a man, a chimera, the sky, an angel, or God. Others, again, have certain other forms; as when I will, fear, affirm, or deny, I always, indeed, apprehend something as the object of my thought, but I also embrace in thought something more than the representation of the object; and of this class of thoughts some are called volitions or affections, and others judgments.

Now, with respect to ideas, if these are considered only in themselves, and are not referred to any object beyond them, they cannot, properly speaking, be false; for, whether I imagine a goat or a chimera, it is not less true that I imagine the one than the other. Nor need we fear that falsity may exist in the will or affections; for, although

I may desire objects that are wrong, and even that never existed, it is still true that I desire them. There thus only remain our judgments, in which we must take diligent heed that we be not deceived. But the chief and most ordinary error that arises in them consists in judging that the ideas which are in us are like or conformed to the things that are external to us; for assuredly, if we but considered the ideas themselves as certain modes of our thought (consciousness), without referring them to anything beyond, they would hardly afford any occasion of error.

But, among these ideas, some appear to me to be innate, others adventitious, and others to be made by myself (factitious); for, as I have the power of conceiving what is called a thing, or a truth, or a thought, it seems to me that I hold this power from no other source than my own nature; but if I now hear a noise, if I see the sun, or if I feel heat, I have all along judged that these sensations proceeded from certain objects existing out of myself; and, in fine, it appears to me that sirens, hippogryphs, and the like, are inventions of my own mind. But I may even perhaps come to be of opinion that all my ideas are of the class which I call adventitious, or that they are all innate, or that they are all factitious, for I have not yet clearly discovered their true origin; and what I have here principally to do is to consider, with reference to those that appear to come from certain objects without me, what grounds there are for thinking them like these objects.

The first of these grounds is that it seems to me I am so taught by nature; and the second that I am conscious that those ideas are not dependent on my will, and therefore not on myself, for they are frequently presented to me against my will,—as at present, whether I will or not, I feel heat; and I am thus persuaded that this sensation or idea of heat is produced in me by something different from myself, viz., by the heat of the fire by which I sit. And it is very reasonable to suppose that this object impresses me with its own likeness rather than any other thing.

But I must consider whether these reasons are sufficiently strong and convincing. When I speak of being taught by nature in this matter, I understand by the word nature only a certain spontaneous impetus that impels me to believe in a resemblance between ideas and their objects, and not a natural light that affords a knowledge of its truth. But these two things are widely different; for what the natural light shows to be true can be in no degree doubtful, as, for example, that I am because I doubt, and other truths of the like kind: inasmuch as I possess no other faculty whereby to distinguish truth from error, which can teach me the falsity of what the natural light declares to be true, and which is equally trustworthy; but with respect to [seemingly] natural impulses, I have observed, when the question related to the choice of right or wrong in action, that they frequently led me to take the worse part; nor do I see that I have any better ground for following them in what relates to truth and error. Then, with respect to the other reason, which is that because these ideas do not depend on my will, they must arise from objects existing without me, I do not find it more convincing than the former; for, just as those natural impulses, of which I have lately spoken, are found in me, notwithstanding that they are not always in harmony with my will, so likewise it may be that I possess some power not sufficiently known to myself capable of producing ideas without the aid of external objects, and, indeed, it has always hitherto appeared to me that they are formed during sleep, by some power of this nature, without the aid of aught external. And, in fine, although I should grant that they proceeded from those objects, it is not a necessary consequence that they must be like them. On the contrary, I have observed, in a number of instances, that there was a great difference between the object and its idea. Thus, for example, I find in my mind two wholly diverse ideas of the sun; the one, by which it appears to me extremely small, draws its origin from the senses, and should be placed in the class of adventitious ideas; the other, by which it seems to be many times larger than the whole earth, is taken up on astronomical grounds, that is, elicited from certain notions born with me, or is framed by myself in some other manner. These two ideas cannot certainly both resemble the same sun; and reason teaches me that the one which seems to have immediately emanated from it is the most unlike. And these things sufficiently prove that hitherto it has not been from a certain and deliberate judgment, but only from a sort of blind impulse, that I believed in the existence of certain things different from myself, which, by the organs of sense, or by whatever other means it might be, conveyed their ideas or images into my mind [and impressed it with their likenesses].

But there is still another way of inquiring whether, of the objects whose ideas are in my mind, there are any that exist out of me. If ideas are taken in so far only as they are certain modes of consciousness, I do not remark any difference or inequality among them, and all seem, in the same manner, to proceed from myself; but, considering them as images, of which one represents one thing and another a different, it is evident that a great diversity obtains among them. For, without doubt, those that represent substances are something more, and contain in themselves, so to speak, more objective reality [that is, participate by representation in higher degrees of being or perfection], than those that represent only modes or accidents; and again, the idea by which I conceive a God [sovereign], eternal, infinite, [immutable], all-knowing, all-powerful, and the creator of all things that are out of himself,—this, I say, has certainly in it more objective reality than those ideas by which finite substances are represented.

Now, it is manifest by the natural light that there must at least be as much reality in the efficient and total cause as in its effect; for whence can the effect draw its reality if not from its cause? and how could the cause communicate to it this reality unless it possessed it in itself? And hence it follows, not only that what is cannot be produced by what is not, but likewise that the more perfect,—in other words, that which contains in itself more reality,—cannot be the effect of the less perfect: and this is not only evidently true of those effects, whose reality is actual or formal, but likewise of ideas, whose reality is only considered as objective. Thus, for example, the stone that is not yet in existence, not only cannot now commence to be, unless it be produced by that which possesses in itself, formally or eminently, all that enters into its composition, [in other words, by that which contains in itself the same properties that are in the stone, or others superior to them]; and heat can only be produced in a subject that was before devoid of it, by a cause that is of an order [degree or kind], at least as perfect as heat; and so of the others. But further, even the idea of the heat, or of the stone, cannot exist in me unless it be put there by a cause that contains, at least, as much reality as I conceive existent in the heat or in the stone: for, although that cause may not transmit into my idea anything of its actual or formal reality, we ought not on this account to imagine that it is less real; but we ought to consider that, [as every idea is a work of the mind], its nature is such as of itself to demand no other formal reality than that which it borrows from our consciousness, of which it is but a mode, [that is, a manner or way of thinking]. But in order that an idea may contain this objective reality rather than that, it must doubtless derive it from some cause in which is found at least as much formal reality as the idea contains of objective; for, if we suppose that there is found in an idea anything which was not in its cause, it must of course derive this from nothing. But, however imperfect may be the mode of existence by which a thing is objectively [or by representation] in the understanding by its idea, we certainly cannot, for all that, allege that this mode of existence is nothing, nor, consequently, that the idea owes its origin to nothing. Nor must it be imagined that, since the reality which is considered in these ideas is only objective, the same reality need not be formally (actually) in the causes of these ideas, but only objectively: for, just as the mode of existing objectively belongs to ideas by their peculiar nature, so likewise the mode of existing formally appertains to the causes of these ideas (at least to the first and principal), by their peculiar nature. And although an idea may give rise to another idea, this regress cannot, nevertheless, be infinite; we must in the end reach a first idea, the cause of which is, as it were, the archetype in which all the reality [or perfection] that is found objectively [or by representation] in these ideas is contained formally [and in act]. I am thus clearly taught by the natural light that ideas exist in me as pictures or images, which may in truth readily fall short of the perfection of the objects from which they are taken, but can never contain anything greater or more perfect.

And in proportion to the time and care with which I examine all those matters, the conviction of their truth brightens and becomes distinct. But, to sum up, what conclusion shall I draw from it all? It is this;—if the objective reality [or perfection] of any one of my ideas be such as clearly to convince me, that this same reality exists in me neither formally nor eminently, as if, as follows from this, I myself cannot be the cause of it, it is a necessary consequence that I am not alone in the world, but that there is besides myself some other being who exists as the cause of that idea; while, on the contrary, if no such idea be found in my mind, I shall have no sufficient ground of assurance of the existence of any other being besides myself; for, after a most careful search, I have, up to this moment, been unable to discover any other ground.

But, among these my ideas, besides that which represents myself, respecting which there can be here no difficulty, there is one that represents a God; others that represent corporeal and inanimate things; others angels; others animals; and, finally, there are some that represent men like myself. But with respect to the ideas that represent other men, or animals, or angels, I can easily suppose that they were formed by the mingling and composition of the other ideas which I have of myself, of corporeal things, and of God, although there were, apart from myself, neither men, animals, nor angels. And with regard to the ideas of corporeal objects, I never discovered in them anything so great or excellent which I myself did not appear capable of originating; for, by considering these ideas closely and scrutinising them individually, in the same way that I yesterday examined the idea of wax, I find that there is but little in them that is clearly and distinctly perceived. As belonging to the class of things that are clearly apprehended, I recognise the following, viz., magnitude or extension in length, breadth, and depth; figure, which results from the termination of extension; situation, which bodies of diverse figures preserve with reference to each other; and motion or the change of situation; to which may be added substance, duration, and number. But with regard to light, colours, sounds, odours, tastes, heat, cold, and the other tactile qualities, they are thought with so much obscurity and confusion, that I cannot determine even whether they are true or false; in other words, whether or not the ideas I have of these qualities are in truth the ideas of real objects. For although I before remarked that it is only in judgments that formal falsity, or falsity properly so called, can be met with, there may nevertheless be found in ideas a certain material falsity, which arises when they represent what is nothing as if it were something. Thus, for example, the ideas I have of cold and heat are so far from being clear and distinct, that I am unable from them to discover whether cold is only the privation of heat, or heat the privation of cold; or whether they are not real qualities: and since, ideas being as it were images, there can be none that does not seem to us to represent some object, the idea which represents cold as something real and positive will not improperly be called false, if it be correct to say that cold is nothing but a privation of heat; and so in other cases. To ideas of this kind, indeed, it is not necessary that I should assign any author besides myself: for if they are false, that is, represent objects that are unreal, the natural light teaches me that they proceed from nothing; in other words, that they are in me only because something is wanting to the perfection of my nature; but if these ideas are true, yet because they exhibit to me so little reality that I cannot even distinguish the object represented from non-being, I do not see why I should not be the author of them.

With reference to those ideas of corporeal things that are clear and distinct, there are some which, as appears to me, might have been taken from the idea I have for myself, as those of substance, duration, number, and the like. For when I think that a stone is a substance, or a thing capable of existing of itself, and that I am likewise a substance, although I conceive that I am a thinking and non-extended thing, and that the stone, on the contrary, is extended and unconscious, there being thus the greatest diversity between the two concepts,—yet these two ideas seem to have this in common that they both represent substances. In the same way, when I think of myself as now existing, and recollect besides that I existed some time ago, and when I am conscious of various thoughts whose number I know, I then acquire the ideas of duration and number, which I can afterwards transfer to as many objects as I please. With respect to the other qualities that go to make up the ideas of corporeal objects, viz., extension, figure, situation, and motion, it is true that they are not formally in me, since I am merely a thinking being; but because they are only certain modes of substance, and because I myself am a substance, it seems possible that they may be contained in me eminently.

There only remains, therefore, the idea of God, in which I must consider whether there is anything that cannot be supposed to originate with myself. By the name God, I understand a substance infinite, [eternal, immutable], independent, all-knowing, all-powerful, and by which I myself, and every other thing that exists, if any such there be, were created. But these properties are so great and excellent, that the more attentively I consider them the less I feel persuaded that the idea I have of them owes its origin to myself alone. And thus it is absolutely necessary to conclude, from all that I have before said, that God exists: for though the idea of substance be in my mind owing to this, that I myself am a substance, I should not, however, have the idea of an infinite substance, seeing I am a finite being, unless it were given me by some substance in reality infinite.

And I must not imagine that I do not apprehend the infinite by a true idea, but only by the negation of the finite, in the same way that I comprehend repose and darkness by the negation of motion and light: since, on the contrary, I clearly perceive that there is more reality in the infinite substance than in the finite, and therefore that in some way I possess the perception (notion) of the infinite before that of the finite, that is, the perception of God before that of myself, for how could I know that I doubt, desire, or that something is wanting to me, and that I am not wholly perfect, if I possessed no idea of a being more perfect than myself, by comparison of which I knew the deficiencies of my nature?

And it cannot be said that this idea of God is perhaps materially false, and consequently that it may have arisen from nothing, [in other words, that it may exist in me from my imperfection], as I before said of the ideas of heat and cold, and the like: for, on the contrary, as this idea is very clear and distinct, and contains in itself more objective reality than any other, there can be no one of itself more true, or less open to the suspicion of falsity.

The idea, I say, of a being supremely perfect, and infinite, is in the highest degree true; for although, perhaps, we may imagine that such a being does not exist, we cannot, nevertheless, suppose that his idea represents nothing real, as I have already said of the idea of cold. It is likewise clear and distinct in the highest degree, since whatever the mind clearly and distinctly conceives as real or true, and as implying any perfection, is contained entire in this idea. And this is true, nevertheless, although I do not comprehend the infinite, and although there may be in God an infinity of things that I cannot comprehend, nor perhaps even compass by thought in any way; for it is of the nature of the infinite that it should not be comprehended by the finite; and it is enough that I rightly understand this, and judge that all which I clearly perceive, and in which I know there is some perfection, and perhaps also an infinity of properties of which I am ignorant, are formally or eminently in God, in order that the idea I have of him may become the most true, clear, and distinct of all the ideas in my mind.

But perhaps I am something more than I suppose myself to be, and it may be that all those perfections which I attribute to God, in some way exist potentially in me, although they do not yet show themselves, and are not reduced to act. Indeed, I am already conscious that my knowledge is being increased [and perfected] by degrees; and I see nothing to prevent it from thus gradually increasing to infinity, nor any reason why, after such increase and perfection, I should not be able thereby to acquire all the other perfections of the Divine nature; nor, in fine, why the power I possess of acquiring those perfections, if it really now exist in me, should not be sufficient to produce the ideas of them. Yet, on looking more closely into the matter, I discover that this cannot be; for, in the first place, although it were true that my knowledge daily acquired new degrees of perfection, and although there were potentially in my nature much that was not as yet actually in it, still all these excellences make not the slightest approach to the idea I have of the Deity, in whom there is no perfection merely potentially [but all actually] existent; for it is even an unmistakable token of imperfection in my knowledge, that it is augmented by degrees. Further, although my knowledge increase more and more, nevertheless I am not, therefore, induced to think that it will ever be actually infinite, since it can never reach that point beyond which it shall be incapable of further increase. But I conceive God as actually infinite, so that nothing can be added to his perfection. And, in fine, I readily perceive that the objective being of an idea cannot be produced by a being that is merely potentially existent, which, properly speaking, is nothing, but only by a being existing formally or actually.

And, truly, I see nothing in all that I have now said which it is not easy for any one, who shall carefully consider it, to discern by the natural light; but when I allow my attention in some degree to relax, the vision of my mind being obscured, and, as it were, blinded by the images of sensible objects, I do not readily remember the reason why the idea of a being more perfect than myself, must of necessity have proceeded from a being in reality more perfect. On this account I am here desirous to inquire further, whether I, who possess this idea of God, could exist supposing there were no God. And I ask, from whom could I, in that case, derive my existence? Perhaps from myself, or from my parents, or from some other causes less perfect than God; for anything more perfect, or even equal to God, cannot be thought or imagined. But if I [were independent of every other existence, and] were myself the author of my being, I should doubt of nothing, I should desire nothing, and, in fine, no perfection would be awanting to me; for I should have bestowed upon myself every perfection of which I possess the idea, and I should thus be God. And it must not be imagined that what is now wanting to me is perhaps of more difficult acquisition than that of which I am already possessed; for, on the contrary, it is quite manifest that it was a matter of much higher difficulty that I, a thinking being, should arise from nothing, than it would be for me to acquire the knowledge of many things of which I am ignorant, and which are merely the accidents of a thinking substance; and certainly, if I possessed of myself the greater perfection of which I have now spoken, [in other words, if I were the author of my own existence], I would not at least have denied to myself things that may be more easily obtained, [as that infinite variety of knowledge of which I am at present destitute]. I could not, indeed, have denied to myself any property which I perceive is contained in the idea of God, because there is none of these that seems to me to be more difficult to make or acquire; and if there were any that should happen to be more difficult to acquire, they would certainly appear so to me (supposing that I myself were the source of the other things I possess), because I should discover in them a limit to my power. And though I were to suppose that I always was as I now am, I should not, on this ground, escape the force of these reasonings, since it would not follow, even on this supposition, that no author of my existence needed to be sought after. For the whole time of my life may be divided into an infinity of parts, each of which is in no way dependent on any other; and, accordingly, because I was in existence a short time ago, it does not follow that I must now exist, unless in this moment some cause create me anew as it were,—that is, conserve me. In truth, it is perfectly clear and evident to all who will attentively consider the nature of duration, that the conservation of a substance, in each moment of its duration, requires the same power and act that would be necessary to create it, supposing it were not yet in existence; so that it is manifestly a dictate of the natural light that conservation and creation differ merely in respect of our mode of thinking [and not in reality]. All that is here required, therefore, is that I interrogate myself to discover whether I possess any power by means of which I can bring it about that I, who now am, shall exist a moment afterwards; for, since I am merely a thinking thing (or since, at least, the precise question, in the meantime, is only of that part of myself), if such a power resided in me, I should, without doubt, be conscious of it; but I am conscious of no such power, and thereby I manifestly know that I am dependent upon some being different from myself.

But perhaps the being upon whom I am dependent, is not God, and I have been produced either by my parents, or by some causes less perfect than Deity. This cannot be: for, as I before said, it is perfectly evident that there must at least be as much reality in the cause as in its effect; and accordingly, since I am a thinking thing, and possess in myself an idea of God, whatever in the end be the cause of my existence, it must of necessity be admitted that it is likewise a thinking being, and that it possess in itself the idea and all the perfections I attribute to Deity. Then it may again be inquired whether this cause owes its origin and existence to itself, or to some other cause. For if it be self-existent, it follows, from what I have before laid down, that this cause is God; for, since it possesses the perfection of self-existence, it must likewise, without doubt, have the power of actually possessing every perfection of which it has the idea,—in other words, all the perfections I conceive to belong to God. But if it owe its existence to another cause than itself, we demand again, for a similar reason, whether this second cause exists of itself or through some other, until, from stage to stage, we at length arrive at an ultimate cause, which will be God. And it is quite manifest that in this manner there can be no infinite regress of causes, seeing that the question raised respects not so much the cause which once produced me, as that by which I am at this present moment conserved.

Nor can it be supposed that several causes concurred in my production, and that from one I received the idea of one of the perfections I attribute to Deity, and from another the idea of some other, and thus that all those perfections are indeed found somewhere in the universe, but do not all exist together in a single being who is God; for, on the contrary, the unity, the simplicity or inseparability of all the properties of Deity, is one of the chief perfections I conceive him to possess; and the idea of this unity of all the perfections of Deity could certainly not be put into my mind by any cause from which I did not likewise receive the ideas of all the other perfections; for no power could enable me to embrace them in an inseparable unity, without at the same time giving me the knowledge of what they were [and of their existence in a particular mode].

Finally, with regard to my parents [from whom it appears I sprung], although all that I believed respecting them be true, it does not, nevertheless, follow that I am conserved by them, or even that I was produced by them, in so far as I am a thinking being. All that, at the most, they contributed to my origin was the giving of certain dispositions (modifications) to the matter in which I have hitherto judged that I or my mind, which is what alone I now consider to be myself, is enclosed; and thus there can here be no difficulty with respect to them, and it is absolutely necessary to conclude from this alone that I am, and possess the idea of a being absolutely perfect, that is, of God, that his existence is most clearly demonstrated.

There remains only the inquiry as to the way in which I received this idea from God; for I have not drawn it from the senses, nor is it even presented to me unexpectedly, as is usual with the ideas of sensible objects, when these are presented or appear to be presented to the external organs of the senses; it is not even a pure production or fiction of my mind, for it is not in my power to take from or add to it; and consequently there but remains the alternative that it is innate, in the same way as is the idea of myself. And, in truth, it is not to be wondered at that God, at my creation, implanted this idea in me, that it might serve, as it were, for the mark of the workman impressed on his work; and it is not also necessary that the mark should be something different from the work itself; but considering only that God is my creator, it is highly probable that he in some way fashioned me after his own image and likeness, and that I perceive this likeness, in which is contained the idea of God, by the same faculty by which I apprehend myself,—in other words, when I make myself the object of reflection, I not only find that I am an incomplete, [imperfect] and dependent being, and one who unceasingly aspires after something better and greater than he is; but, at the same time, I am assured likewise that he upon whom I am dependent possesses in himself all the goods after which I aspire, [and the ideas of which I find in my mind], and that not merely indefinitely and potentially, but infinitely and actually, and that he is thus God. And the whole force of the argument of which I have here availed myself to establish the existence of God, consists in this, that I perceive I could not possibly be of such a nature as I am, and yet have in my mind the idea of a God, if God did not in reality exist,—this same God, I say, whose idea is in my mind—that is, a being who possesses all those lofty perfections, of which the mind may have some slight conception, without, however, being able fully to comprehend them—and who is wholly superior to all defect, [and has nothing that marks imperfection]: whence it is sufficiently manifest that he cannot be a deceiver, since it is a dictate of the natural light that all fraud and deception spring from some defect.

But before I examine this with more attention, and pass on to the consideration of other truths that may be evolved out of it, I think it proper to remain here for some time in the contemplation of God himself—that I may ponder at leisure his marvellous attributes—and behold, admire, and adore the beauty of this light so unspeakably great, as far, at least, as the strength of my mind, which is to some degree dazzled by the sight, will permit. For just as we learn by faith that the supreme felicity of another life consists in the contemplation of the Divine majesty alone, so even now we learn from experience that a like meditation, though incomparably less perfect, is the source of the highest satisfaction of which we are susceptible in this life.

MEDITATION IV

¶ Of Truth and Error

I have been habituated these bygone days to detach my mind from the senses, and I have accurately observed that there is exceedingly little which is known with certainty respecting corporeal objects,—that we know much more of the human mind, and still more of God himself. I am thus able now without difficulty to abstract my mind from the contemplation of [sensible or] imaginable objects, and apply it to those which, as disengaged from all matter, are purely intelligible. And certainly the idea I have of the human mind in so far as it is a thinking thing, and not extended in length, breadth, and depth, and participating in none of the properties of body, is incomparably more distinct than the idea of any corporeal object; and when I consider that I doubt, in other words, that I am an incomplete and dependent being, the idea of a complete and independent being, that is to say of God, occurs to my mind with so much clearness and distinctness,—and from the fact alone that this idea is found in me, or that I who possess it exist, the conclusions that God exists, and that my own existence, each moment of its continuance, is absolutely dependent upon him, are so manifest,—as to lead me to believe it impossible that the human mind can know anything with more clearness and certitude. And now I seem to discover a path that will conduct us from the contemplation of the true God, in whom are contained all the treasures of science and wisdom, to the knowledge of the other things in the universe.

For, in the first place, I discover that it is impossible for him ever to deceive me, for in all fraud and deceit there is a certain imperfection: and although it may seem that the ability to deceive is a mark of subtlety or power, yet the will testifies without doubt of malice and weakness; and such, accordingly, cannot be found in God. In the next place, I am conscious that I possess a certain faculty of judging [or discerning truth from error], which I doubtless received from God, along with whatever else is mine; and since it is impossible that he should will to deceive me, it is likewise certain that he has not given me a faculty that will ever lead me into error, provided I use it aright.

And there would remain no doubt on this head, did it not seem to follow from this, that I can never therefore be deceived; for if all I possess be from God, and if he planted in me no faculty that is deceitful, it seems to follow that I can never fall into error. Accordingly, it is true that when I think only of God (when I look upon myself as coming from God, Fr.), and turn wholly to him, I discover [in myself] no cause of error or falsity: but immediately thereafter, recurring to myself, experience assures me that I am nevertheless subject to innumerable errors. When I come to inquire into the cause of these, I observe that there is not only present to my consciousness a real and positive idea of God, or of a being supremely perfect, but also, so to speak, a certain negative idea of nothing,—in other words, of that which is at an infinite distance from every sort of perfection, and that I am, as it were, a mean between God and nothing, or placed in such a way between absolute existence and non-existence, that there is in truth nothing in me to lead me into error, in so far as an absolute being is my creator; but that, on the other hand, as I thus likewise participate in some degree of nothing or of non-being, in other words, as I am not myself the supreme Being, and as I am wanting in many perfections, it is not surprising I should fall into error. And I hence discern that error, so far as error is not something real, which depends for its existence on God, but is simply defect; and therefore that, in order to fall into it, it is not necessary God should have given me a faculty expressly for this end, but that my being deceived arises from the circumstance that the power which God has given me of discerning truth from error is not infinite.

Nevertheless this is not yet quite satisfactory; for error is not a pure negation, [in other words, it is not the simple deficiency or want of some knowledge which is not due], but the privation or want of some knowledge which it would seem I ought to possess. But, on considering the nature of God, it seems impossible that he should have planted in his creature any faculty not perfect in its kind, that is, wanting in some perfection due to it: for if it be true, that in proportion to the skill of the maker the perfection of his work is greater, what thing can have been produced by the supreme Creator of the universe that is not absolutely perfect in all its parts? And assuredly there is no doubt that God could have created me such as that I should never be deceived; it is certain, likewise, that he always wills what is best; is it better, then, that I should be capable of being deceived than that I should not?

Considering this more attentively, the first thing that occurs to me is the reflection that I must not be surprised if I am not always capable of comprehending the reasons why God acts as he does; nor must I doubt of his existence because I find, perhaps, that there are several other things besides the present respecting which I understand neither why nor how they were created by him; for, knowing already that my nature is extremely weak and limited, and that the nature of God, on the other hand, is immense, incomprehensible, and infinite, I have no longer any difficulty in discerning that there is an infinity of things in his power whose causes transcend the grasp of my mind: and this consideration alone is sufficient to convince me, that the whole class of final causes is of no avail in physical [or natural] things; for it appears to me that I cannot, without exposing myself to the charge of temerity, seek to discover the [impenetrable] ends of Deity.

It further occurs to me that we must not consider only one creature apart from the others, if we wish to determine the perfection of the works of Deity, but generally all his creatures together; for the same object that might perhaps, with some show of reason, be deemed highly imperfect if it were alone in the world, may for all that be the most perfect possible, considered as forming part of the whole universe: and although, as it was my purpose to doubt of everything, I only as yet know with certainty my own existence and that of God, nevertheless, after having remarked the infinite power of Deity, I cannot deny that he may have produced many other objects, or at least that he is able to produce them, so that I may occupy a place in the relation of a part to the great whole of his creatures.

Whereupon, regarding myself more closely, and considering what my errors are (which alone testify to the existence of imperfection in me), I observe that these depend on the concurrence of two causes, viz., the faculty of cognition which I possess, and that of election or the power of free choice,—in other words, the understanding and the will. For by the understanding alone, I [neither affirm nor deny anything, but] merely apprehend the ideas regarding which I may form a judgment; nor is any error, properly so called, found in it thus accurately taken. And although there are perhaps innumerable objects in the world of which I have no idea in my understanding, it cannot, on that account, be said that I am deprived of those ideas [as of something that is due to my nature], but simply that I do not possess them, because, in truth, there is no ground to prove that Deity ought to have endowed me with a larger faculty of cognition than he has actually bestowed upon me; and however skilful a workman I suppose him to be, I have no reason, on that account, to think that it was obligatory on him to give to each of his works all the perfections he is able to bestow upon some. Nor, moreover, can I complain that God has not given me freedom of choice, or a will sufficiently ample and perfect, since, in truth, I am conscious of will so ample and extended as to be superior to all limits. And what appears to me here to be highly remarkable is that, of all the other properties I possess, there is none so great and perfect as that I do not clearly discern it could be still greater and more perfect. For, to take an example, if I consider the faculty of understanding which I possess, I find that it is of very small extent, and greatly limited, and at the same time I form the idea of another faculty of the same nature, much more ample and even infinite; and seeing that I can frame the idea of it, I discover, from this circumstance alone, that it pertains to the nature of God. In the same way, if I examine the faculty of memory or imagination, or any other faculty I possess, I find none that is not small and circumscribed, and in God immense [and infinite]. It is the faculty of will only, or freedom of choice, which I experience to be so great that I am unable to conceive the idea of another that shall be more ample and extended; so that it is chiefly my will which leads me to discern that I bear a certain image and similitude of Deity. For although the faculty of will is incomparably greater in God than in myself, as well in respect of the knowledge and power that are conjoined with it, and that render it stronger and more efficacious, as in respect of the object, since in him it extends to a greater number of things, it does not, nevertheless, appear to me greater, considered in itself formally and precisely: for the power of will consists only in this, that we are able to do or not to do the same thing (that is, to affirm or deny, to pursue or shun it), or rather in this alone, that in affirming or denying, pursuing or shunning, what is proposed to us by the understanding, we so act that we are not conscious of being determined to a particular action by any external force. For, to the possession of freedom, it is not necessary that I be alike indifferent towards each of two contraries; but, on the contrary, the more I am inclined towards the one, whether because I clearly know that in it there is the reason of truth and goodness, or because God thus internally disposes my thought, the more freely do I choose and embrace it; and assuredly divine grace and natural knowledge, very far from diminishing liberty, rather augment and fortify it. But the indifference of which I am conscious when I am not impelled to one side rather than to another for want of a reason, is the lowest grade of liberty, and manifests defect or negation of knowledge rather than perfection of will; for if I always clearly knew what was true and good, I should never have any difficulty in determining what judgment I ought to come to, and what choice I ought to make, and I should thus be entirely free without ever being indifferent.

From all this I discover, however, that neither the power of willing, which I have received from God, is of itself the source of my errors, for it is exceedingly ample and perfect in its kind; nor even the power of understanding, for as I conceive no object unless by means of the faculty that God bestowed upon me, all that I conceive is doubtless rightly conceived by me, and it is impossible for me to be deceived in it.

Whence, then, spring my errors? They arise from this cause alone, that I do not restrain the will, which is of much wider range than the understanding, within the same limits, but extend it even to things I do not understand, and as the will is of itself indifferent to such, it readily falls into error and sin by choosing the false in room of the true, and evil instead of good.

For example, when I lately considered whether aught really existed in the world, and found that because I considered this question, it very manifestly followed that I myself existed, I could not but judge that what I so clearly conceived was true, not that I was forced to this judgment by any external cause, but simply because great clearness of the understanding was succeeded by strong inclination in the will; and I believed this the more freely and spontaneously in proportion as I was less indifferent with respect to it. But now I not only know that I exist, in so far as I am a thinking being, but there is likewise presented to my mind a certain idea of corporeal nature; hence I am in doubt as to whether the thinking nature which is in me, or rather which I myself am, is different from that corporeal nature, or whether both are merely one and the same thing, and I here suppose that I am as yet ignorant of any reason that would determine me to adopt the one belief in preference to the other: whence it happens that it is a matter of perfect indifference to me which of the two suppositions I affirm or deny, or whether I form any judgment at all in the matter.

This indifference, moreover, extends not only to things of which the understanding has no knowledge at all, but in general also to all those which it does not discover with perfect clearness at the moment the will is deliberating upon them; for, however probable the conjectures may be that dispose me to form a judgment in a particular matter, the simple knowledge that these are merely conjectures, and not certain and indubitable reasons, is sufficient to lead me to form one that is directly the opposite. Of this I lately had abundant experience, when I laid aside as false all that I had before held for true, on the single ground that I could in some degree doubt of it. But if I abstain from judging of a thing when I do not conceive it with sufficient clearness and distinctness, it is plain that I act rightly, and am not deceived; but if I resolve to deny or affirm, I then do not make a right use of my free will; and if I affirm what is false, it is evident that I am deceived: moreover, even although I judge according to truth, I stumble upon it by chance, and do not therefore escape the imputation of a wrong use of my freedom; for it is a dictate of the natural light, that the knowledge of the understanding ought always to precede the determination of the will.

And it is this wrong use of the freedom of the will in which is found the privation that constitutes the form of error. Privation, I say, is found in the act, in so far as it proceeds from myself, but it does not exist in the faculty which I received from God, nor even in the act, in so far as it depends on him; for I have assuredly no reason to complain that God has not given me a greater power of intelligence or more perfect natural light than he has actually bestowed, since it is of the nature of a finite understanding not to comprehend many things, and of the nature of a created understanding to be finite; on the contrary, I have every reason to render thanks to God, who owed me nothing, for having given me all the perfections I possess, and I should be far from thinking that he has unjustly deprived me of, or kept back, the other perfections which he has not bestowed upon me.

I have no reason, moreover, to complain because he has given me a will more ample than my understanding, since, as the will consists only of a single element, and that indivisible, it would appear that this faculty is of such a nature that nothing could be taken from it [without destroying it]; and certainly, the more extensive it is, the more cause I have to thank the goodness of him who bestowed it upon me.

And, finally, I ought not also to complain that God concurs with me in forming the acts of this will, or the judgments in which I am deceived, because those acts are wholly true and good, in so far as they depend on God; and the ability to form them is a higher degree of perfection in my nature than the want of it would be. With regard to privation, in which alone consists the formal reason of error and sin, this does not require the concurrence of Deity, because it is not a thing [or existence], and if it be referred to God as to its cause, it ought not to be called privation, but negation, [according to the signification of these words in the schools]. For in truth it is no imperfection in Deity that he has accorded to me the power of giving or withholding my assent from certain things of which he has not put a clear and distinct knowledge in my understanding; but it is doubtless an imperfection in me that I do not use my freedom aright, and readily give my judgment on matters which I only obscurely and confusedly conceive.

I perceive, nevertheless, that it was easy for Deity so to have constituted me as that I should never be deceived, although I still remained free and possessed of a limited knowledge, viz., by implanting in my understanding a clear and distinct knowledge of all the objects respecting which I should ever have to deliberate; or simply by so deeply engraving on my memory the resolution to judge of nothing without previously possessing a clear and distinct conception of it, that I should never forget it. And I easily understand that, in so far as I consider myself as a single whole, without reference to any other being in the universe, I should have been much more perfect than I now am, had Deity created me superior to error; but I cannot therefore deny that it is not somehow a greater perfection in the universe, that certain of its parts are not exempt from defect, as others are, than if they were all perfectly alike.

And I have no right to complain because God, who placed me in the world, was not willing that I should sustain that character which of all others is the chief and most perfect; I have even good reason to remain satisfied on the ground that, if he has not given me the perfection of being superior to error by the first means I have pointed out above, which depends on a clear and evident knowledge of all the matters regarding which I can deliberate, he has at least left in my power the other means, which is, firmly to retain the resolution never to judge where the truth is not clearly known to me: for, although I am conscious of the weakness of not being able to keep my mind continually fixed on the same thought, I can nevertheless, by attentive and oft-repeated meditation, impress it so strongly on my memory that I shall never fail to recollect it as often as I require it, and I can acquire in this way the habitude of not erring; and since it is in being superior to error that the highest and chief perfection of man consists, I deem that I have not gained little by this day's meditation, in having discovered the source of error and falsity.

And certainly this can be no other than what I have now explained: for as often as I so restrain my will within the limits of my knowledge, that it forms no judgment except regarding objects which are clearly and distinctly represented to it by the understanding, I can never be deceived; because every clear and distinct conception is doubtless something, and as such cannot owe its origin to nothing, but must of necessity have God for its author—God, I say, who, as supremely perfect, cannot, without a contradiction, be the cause of any error; and consequently it is necessary to conclude that every such conception [or judgment] is true. Nor have I merely learned to-day what I must avoid to escape error, but also what I must do to arrive at the knowledge of truth; for I will assuredly reach truth if I only fix my attention sufficiently on all the things I conceive perfectly, and separate these from others which I conceive more confusedly and obscurely: to which for the future I shall give diligent heed.

MEDITATION V

¶ Of the Essence of Material Things; and again of God; that He exists

Several other questions remain for consideration respecting the attributes of God and my own nature or mind. I will, however, on some other occasion perhaps resume the investigation of these. Meanwhile, as I have discovered what must be done and what avoided to arrive at the knowledge of truth, what I have chiefly to do is to essay to emerge from the state of doubt in which I have for some time been, and to discover whether anything can be known with certainty regarding material objects. But before considering whether such objects as I conceive exist without me, I must examine their ideas in so far as these are to be found in my consciousness, and discover which of them are distinct and which confused.

In the first place, I distinctly imagine that quantity which the philosophers commonly call continuous, or the extension in length, breadth, and depth that is in this quantity, or rather in the object to which it is attributed. Further, I can enumerate in it many diverse parts, and attribute to each of these all sorts of sizes, figures, situations, and local motions; and, in fine, I can assign to each of these motions all degrees of duration. And I not only distinctly know these things when I thus consider them in general; but besides, by a little attention, I discover innumerable particulars respecting figures, numbers, motion, and the like, which are so evidently true, and so accordant with my nature, that when I now discover them I do not so much appear to learn anything new, as to call to remembrance what I before knew, or for the first time to remark what was before in my mind, but to which I had not hitherto directed my attention. And what I here find of most importance is, that I discover in my mind innumerable ideas of certain objects, which cannot be esteemed pure negations, although perhaps they possess no reality beyond my thought, and which are not framed by me though it may be in my power to think, or not to think them, but possess true and immutable natures of their own. As, for example, when I imagine a triangle, although there is not perhaps and never was in any place in the universe apart from my thought one such figure, it remains true nevertheless that this figure possesses a certain determinate nature, form, or essence, which is immutable and eternal, and not framed by me, nor in any degree dependent on my thought; as appears from the circumstance, that diverse properties of the triangle may be demonstrated, viz., that its three angles are equal to two right, that its greatest side is subtended by its greatest angle, and the like, which, whether I will or not, I now clearly discern to belong to it, although before I did not at all think of them, when, for the first time, I imagined a triangle, and which accordingly cannot be said to have been invented by me. Nor is it a valid objection to allege, that perhaps this idea of a triangle came into my mind by the medium of the senses, through my having seen bodies of a triangular figure;

for I am able to form in thought an innumerable variety of figures with regard to which it cannot be supposed that they were ever objects of sense, and I can nevertheless demonstrate diverse properties of their nature no less than of the triangle, all of which are assuredly true since I clearly conceive them: and they are therefore something, and not mere negations; for it is highly evident that all that is true is something, [truth being identical with existence]; and I have already fully shown the truth of the principle, that whatever is clearly and distinctly known is true. And although this had not been demonstrated, yet the nature of my mind is such as to compel me to assent to what I clearly conceive while I so conceive it; and I recollect that even when I still strongly adhered to the objects of sense, I reckoned among the number of the most certain truths those I clearly conceived relating to figures, numbers, and other matters that pertain to arithmetic and geometry, and in general to the pure mathematics.

But now if because I can draw from my thought the idea of an object, it follows that all I clearly and distinctly apprehend to pertain to this object, does in truth belong to it, may I not from this derive an argument for the existence of God? It is certain that I no less find the idea of a God in my consciousness, that is, the idea of a being supremely perfect, than that of any figure or number whatever: and I know with not less clearness and distinctness that an [actual and] eternal existence pertains to his nature than that all which is demonstrable of any figure or number really belongs to the nature of that figure or number; and, therefore, although all the conclusions of the preceding Meditations were false, the existence of God would pass with me for a truth at least as certain as I ever judged any truth of mathematics to be, although indeed such a doctrine may at first sight appear to contain more sophistry than truth. For, as I have been accustomed in every other matter to distinguish between existence and essence, I easily believe that the existence can be separated from the essence of God, and that thus God may be conceived as not actually existing. But, nevertheless, when I think of it more attentively, it appears that the existence can no more be separated from the essence of God, than the idea of a mountain from that of a valley, or the equality of its three angles to two right angles, from the essence of a [rectilineal] triangle; so that it is not less impossible to conceive a God, that is, a being supremely perfect, to whom existence is awanting, or who is devoid of a certain perfection, than to conceive a mountain without a valley.

But though, in truth, I cannot conceive a God unless as existing, any more than I can a mountain without a valley, yet, just as it does not follow that there is any mountain in the world merely because I conceive a mountain with a valley, so likewise, though I conceive God as existing, it does not seem to follow on that account that God exists; for my thought imposes no necessity on things; and as I may imagine a winged horse, though there be none such, so I could perhaps attribute existence to God, though no God existed. But the cases are not analogous, and a fallacy lurks under the semblance of this objection: for because I cannot conceive a mountain without a valley, it does not follow that there is any mountain or valley in existence, but simply that the mountain or valley, whether they do or do not exist, are inseparable from each other; whereas, on the other hand, because I cannot conceive God unless as existing, it follows that existence is inseparable from him, and therefore that he really exists: not that this is brought about by my thought, or that it imposes any necessity on things, but, on the contrary, the necessity which lies in the thing itself, that is, the necessity of the existence of God, determines me to think in this way: for it is not in my power to conceive a God without existence, that is, a being supremely perfect, and yet devoid of an absolute perfection, as I am free to imagine a horse with or without wings.

Nor must it be alleged here as an objection, that it is in truth necessary to admit that God exists, after having supposed him to possess all perfections, since existence is one of them, but that my original supposition was not necessary; just as it is not necessary to think that all quadrilateral figures can be inscribed in the circle, since, if I supposed this, I should be constrained to admit that the rhombus, being a figure of four sides, can be therein inscribed, which, however, is manifestly false. This objection is, I say, incompetent; for although it may not be necessary that I shall at any time entertain the notion of Deity, yet each time I happen to think of a first and sovereign being, and to draw, so to speak, the idea of him from the storehouse of the mind, I am necessitated to attribute to him all kinds of perfections, though I may not then enumerate them all, nor think of each of them in particular. And this necessity is sufficient, as soon as I discover that existence is a perfection, to cause me to infer the existence of this first and sovereign being: just as it is not necessary that I should ever imagine any triangle, but whenever I am desirous of considering a rectilineal figure composed of only three angles, it is absolutely necessary to attribute those properties to it from which it is correctly inferred that its three angles are not greater than two right angles, although perhaps I may not then advert to this relation in particular. But when

I consider what figures are capable of being inscribed in the circle, it is by no means necessary to hold that all quadrilateral figures are of this number; on the contrary, I cannot even imagine such to be the case, so long as I shall be unwilling to accept in thought aught that I do not clearly and distinctly conceive: and consequently there is a vast difference between false suppositions, as is the one in question, and the true ideas that were born with me, the first and chief of which is the idea of God. For indeed I discern on many grounds that this idea is not factitious, depending simply on my thought, but that it is the representation of a true and immutable nature: in the first place, because I can conceive no other being, except God, to whose essence existence [necessarily] pertains; in the second, because it is impossible to conceive two or more gods of this kind; and it being supposed that one such God exists, I clearly see that he must have existed from all eternity, and will exist to all eternity; and finally, because I apprehend many other properties in God, none of which I can either diminish or change.

But, indeed, whatever mode of probation I in the end adopt, it always returns to this, that it is only the things I clearly and distinctly conceive which have the power of completely persuading me. And although, of the objects I conceive in this manner, some, indeed, are obvious to every one, while others are only discovered after close and careful investigation; nevertheless, after they are once discovered, the latter are not esteemed less certain than the former. Thus, for example, to take the case of a right-angled triangle, although it is not so manifest at first that the square of the base is equal to the squares of the other two sides, as that the base is opposite to the greatest angle; nevertheless, after it is once apprehended, we are as firmly persuaded of the truth of the former as of the latter. And, with respect to God, if I were not pre-occupied by prejudices, and my thought beset on all sides by the continual presence of the images of sensible objects, I should know nothing sooner or more easily than the fact of his being. For is there any truth more clear than the existence of a Supreme Being, or of God, seeing it is to his essence alone that [necessary and eternal] existence pertains? And although the right conception of this truth has cost me much close thinking, nevertheless at present I feel not only as assured of it as of what I deem most certain, but I remark further that the certitude of all other truths is so absolutely dependent on it, that without this knowledge it is impossible ever to know anything perfectly.

For although I am of such a nature as to be unable, while I possess a very clear and distinct apprehension of a matter, to resist the conviction of its truth, yet because my constitution is also such as to incapacitate me from keeping my mind continually fixed on the same object, and as I frequently recollect a past judgment without at the same time being able to recall the grounds of it, it may happen meanwhile that other reasons are presented to me which would readily cause me to change my opinion, if I did not know that God existed; and thus I should possess no true and certain knowledge, but merely vague and vacillating opinions. Thus, for example, when I consider the nature of the [rectilineal] triangle, it most clearly appears to me, who have been instructed in the principles of geometry, that its three angles are equal to two right angles, and I find it impossible to believe otherwise, while I apply my mind to the demonstration; but as soon as I cease from attending to the process of proof, although I still remember that I had a clear comprehension of it, yet I may readily come to doubt of the truth demonstrated, if I do not know that there is a God: for I may persuade myself that I have been so constituted by nature as to be sometimes deceived, even in matters which I think I apprehend with the greatest evidence and certitude, especially when I recollect that I frequently considered many things to be true and certain which other reasons afterwards constrained me to reckon as wholly false.

But after I have discovered that God exists, seeing I also at the same time observed that all things depend on him, and that he is no deceiver, and thence inferred that all which I clearly and distinctly perceive is of necessity true: although I no longer attend to the grounds of a judgment, no opposite reason can be alleged sufficient to lead me to doubt of its truth, provided only I remember that I once possessed a clear and distinct comprehension of it. My knowledge of it thus becomes true and certain. And this same knowledge extends likewise to whatever I remember to have formerly demonstrated, as the truths of geometry and the like: for what can be alleged against them to lead me to doubt of them? Will it be that my nature is such that I may be frequently deceived? But I already know that I cannot be deceived in judgments of the grounds of which I possess a clear knowledge. Will it be that I formerly deemed things to be true and certain which I afterwards discovered to be false? But I had no clear and distinct knowledge of any of those things, and, being as yet ignorant of the rule by which I am assured of the truth of a judgment, I was led to give my assent to them on grounds which I afterwards discovered were less strong than at the time I imagined them to be. What further objection, then, is there? Will it be said that perhaps I am dreaming (an objection

I lately myself raised), or that all the thoughts of which I am now conscious have no more truth than the reveries of my dreams? But although, in truth, I should be dreaming, the rule still holds that all which is clearly presented to my intellect is indisputably true.

And thus I very clearly see that the certitude and truth of all science depends on the knowledge alone of the true God, insomuch that, before I knew him, I could have no perfect knowledge of any other thing. And now that I know him, I possess the means of acquiring a perfect knowledge respecting innumerable matters, as well relative to God himself and other intellectual objects as to corporeal nature, in so far as it is the object of pure mathematics [which do not consider whether it exists or not].

MEDITATION VI

¶ Of the Existence of Material Things; and of the Real Distinction between the Mind and the Body of Man

There now only remains the inquiry as to whether material things exist. With regard to this question, I at least know with certainty that such things may exist, in as far as they constitute the object of the pure mathematics, since, regarding them in this aspect, I can conceive them clearly and distinctly. For there can be no doubt that God possesses the power of producing all the objects I am able distinctly to conceive, and I never considered anything impossible to him, unless when I experienced a contradiction in the attempt to conceive it aright. Further, the faculty of imagination which I possess, and of which I am conscious that I make use when I apply myself to the consideration of material things, is sufficient to persuade me of their existence: for, when I attentively consider what imagination is, I find that it is simply a certain application of the cognitive faculty to a body which is immediately present to it, and which therefore exists.

And to render this quite clear, I remark, in the first place, the difference that subsists between imagination and pure intellection [or conception]. For example, when I imagine a triangle I not only conceive that it is a figure comprehended by three lines, but at the same time also I look upon these three lines as present by the power and internal application of my mind, and this is what I call imagining. But if I desire to think of a chiliogon, I indeed rightly conceive that it is a figure composed of a thousand sides, as easily as I conceive that a triangle is a figure composed of only three sides; but I cannot imagine the thousand sides of a chiliogon as I do the three sides of a triangle, nor, so to speak, view them as present [with the eyes of my mind]. And although, in accordance with the habit I have of always imagining something when I think of corporeal things, it may happen that, in conceiving a chiliogon, I confusedly represent some figure to myself, yet it is quite evident that this is not a chiliogon, since it in no wise differs from that which I would represent to myself, if I were to think of a myriogon, or any other figure of many sides; nor would this representation be of any use in discovering and unfolding the properties that constitute the difference between a chiliogon and other polygons. But if the question turns on a pentagon, it is quite true that I can conceive its figure, as well as that of a chiliogon, without the aid of imagination; but I can likewise imagine it by applying the attention of my mind to its five sides, and at the same time to the area which they contain. Thus I observe that a special effort of mind is necessary to the act of imagination, which is not required to conceiving or understanding; and this special exertion of mind clearly shows the difference between imagination and pure intellection. I remark, besides, that this power of imagination which I possess, in as far as it differs from the power of conceiving, is in no way necessary to my [nature or] essence, that is, to the essence of my mind; for although I did not possess it, I should still remain the same that I now am, from which it seems we may conclude that it depends on something different from the mind. And I easily understand that, if some body exists, with which my mind is so conjoined and united as to be able, as it were, to consider it when it chooses, it may thus imagine corporeal objects; so that this mode of thinking differs from pure intellection only in this respect, that the mind in conceiving turns in some way upon itself, and considers some one of the ideas it possesses within itself; but in imagining it turns towards the body, and contemplates in it some object conformed to the idea which it either of itself conceived or apprehended by sense. I easily understand, I say, that imagination may be thus formed, if it is true that there are bodies; and because I find no other obvious mode of explaining it, I thence, with probability, conjecture that they exist, but only with probability; and although I carefully examine all things, nevertheless I do not find that, from the distinct idea of corporeal nature I have in my imagination, I can necessarily infer the existence of any body.

But I am accustomed to imagine many other objects besides that corporeal nature which is the object of the pure mathematics, as, for example, colours, sounds, tastes, pain, and the like, although with less distinctness; and, inasmuch as I perceive these objects much better by the senses, through the medium of which and of memory, they seem to have reached the imagination, I believe that, in order the more advantageously to examine them, it is proper I should at the same time examine what sense-perception is, and inquire whether from those ideas that are apprehended by this mode of thinking (consciousness), I cannot obtain a certain proof of the existence of corporeal objects.

And, in the first place, I will recall to my mind the things I have hitherto held as true, because perceived by the senses, and the foundations upon which my belief in their truth rested; I will, in the second place, examine the reasons that afterwards constrained me to doubt of them; and, finally, I will consider what of them I ought now to believe.

Firstly, then, I perceived that I had a head, hands, feet, and other members composing that body which I considered as part, or perhaps even as a whole, of myself. I perceived further, that that body was placed among many others, by which it was capable of being affected in diverse ways, both beneficial and hurtful; and what was beneficial I remarked by a certain sensation of pleasure, and what was hurtful by a sensation of pain. And, besides this pleasure and pain, I was likewise conscious of hunger, thirst, and other appetites, as well as certain corporeal inclinations towards joy, sadness, anger, and similar passions. And, out of myself, besides the extension, figure, and motions of bodies, I likewise perceived in them hardness, heat, and the other tactile qualities, and, in addition, light, colours, odours, tastes, and sounds, the variety of which gave me the means of distinguishing the sky, the earth, the sea, and generally all the other bodies, from one another. And certainly, considering the ideas of all these qualities, which were presented to my mind, and which alone I properly and immediately perceived, it was not without reason that I thought I perceived certain objects wholly different from my thought, namely, bodies from which those ideas proceeded; for I was conscious that the ideas were presented to me without my consent being required, so that I could not perceive any object, however desirous I might be, unless it were present to the organ of sense; and it was wholly out of my power not to perceive it when it was thus present. And because the ideas I perceived by the senses were much more lively and clear, and even, in their own way, more distinct than any of those I could of myself frame by meditation, or which I found impressed on my memory, it seemed that they could not have proceeded from myself, and must therefore have been caused in me by some other objects; and as of those objects I had no knowledge beyond what the ideas themselves gave me, nothing was so likely to occur to my mind as the supposition that the objects were similar to the ideas which they caused. And because I recollected also that I had formerly trusted to the senses, rather than to reason, and that the ideas which I myself formed were not so clear as those I perceived by sense, and that they were even for the most part composed of parts of the latter, I was readily persuaded that I had no idea in my intellect which had not formerly passed through the senses. Nor was I altogether wrong in likewise believing that that body which, by a special right, I called my own, pertained to me more properly and strictly than any of the others; for in truth, I could never be separated from it as from other bodies: I felt in it and on account of it all my appetites and affections, and in fine I was affected in its parts by pain and the titillation of pleasure, and not in the parts of the other bodies that were separated from it. But when I inquired into the reason why, from this I know not what sensation of pain, sadness of mind should follow, and why from the sensation of pleasure joy should arise, or why this indescribable twitching of the stomach, which I call hunger, should put me in mind of taking food, and the parchedness of the throat of drink, and so in other cases, I was unable to give any explanation, unless that I was so taught by nature; for there is assuredly no affinity, at least none that I am able to comprehend, between this irritation of the stomach and the desire of food, any more than between the perception of an object that causes pain and the consciousness of sadness which springs from the perception. And in the same way it seemed to me that all the other judgments I had formed regarding the objects of sense, were dictates of nature; because I remarked that those judgments were formed in me, before I had leisure to weigh and consider the reasons that might constrain me to form them.

But, afterwards, a wide experience by degrees sapped the faith I had reposed in my senses; for I frequently observed that towers, which at a distance seemed round, appeared square when more closely viewed, and that colossal figures, raised on the summits of these towers, looked like small statues, when viewed from the bottom of them; and, in other instances without number, I also discovered error in judgments founded on the external senses; and not only in those founded on the external, but even in those that rested on the internal senses; for is there aught more internal than pain? and yet I have sometimes been informed by parties whose arm or leg had been amputated, that they still occasionally seemed to feel pain in that part of the body which they had lost,—a circumstance that led me to think that I could not be quite certain even that any one of my members was affected when I felt pain in it. And to these grounds of doubt I shortly afterwards also added two others of very wide generality: the first of them was that I believed I never perceived anything when awake which I could not occasionally think I also perceived when asleep, and as I do not believe that the ideas I seem to perceive in my sleep proceed from objects external to me, I did not any more observe any ground for believing this of such as I seem to perceive when awake; the second was that since I was as yet ignorant of the author of my being, or at least supposed myself to be so, I saw nothing to prevent my having been so constituted by nature as that I should be deceived even in matters that appeared to me to possess the greatest truth. And, with respect to the grounds on which I had before been persuaded of the existence of sensible objects, I had no great difficulty in finding suitable answers to them; for as nature seemed to incline me to many things from which reason made me averse, I thought that I ought not to confide much in its teachings. And although the perceptions of the senses were not dependent on my will, I did not think that I ought on that ground to conclude that they proceeded from things different from myself, since perhaps there might be found in me some faculty, though hitherto unknown to me, which produced them.

But now that I begin to know myself better, and to discover more clearly the author of my being, I do not, indeed, think that I ought rashly to admit all which the senses seem to teach, nor, on the other hand, is it my conviction that I ought to doubt in general of their teachings.

And, firstly, because I know that all which I clearly and distinctly conceive can be produced by God exactly as I conceive it, it is sufficient that I am able clearly and distinctly to conceive one thing apart from another, in order to be certain that the one is different from the other, seeing they may at least be made to exist separately, by the omnipotence of God; and it matters not by what power this separation is made, in order to be compelled to judge them different; and, therefore, merely because I know with certitude that I exist, and because, in the meantime, I do not observe that aught necessarily belongs to my nature or essence beyond my being a thinking thing, I rightly conclude that my essence consists only in my being a thinking thing, [or a substance whose whole essence or nature is merely thinking]. And although

I may, or rather, as I will shortly say, although I certainly do possess a body with which I am very closely conjoined; nevertheless, because, on the one hand, I have a clear and distinct idea of myself, in as far as I am only a thinking and unextended thing, and as, on the other hand, I possess a distinct idea of body, in as far as it is only an extended and unthinking thing, it is certain that I, [that is, my mind, by which I am what I am], is entirely and truly distinct from my body, and may exist without it.

Moreover, I find in myself diverse faculties of thinking that have each their special mode: for example, I find I possess the faculties of imagining and perceiving, without which I can indeed clearly and distinctly conceive myself as entire, but I cannot reciprocally conceive them without conceiving myself, that is to say, without an intelligent substance in which they reside, for [in the notion we have of them, or to use the terms of the schools] in their formal concept, they comprise some sort of intellection; whence I perceive that they are distinct from myself as modes are from things. I remark likewise certain other faculties, as the power of changing place, of assuming diverse figures, and the like, that cannot be conceived and cannot therefore exist, any more than the preceding, apart from a substance in which they inhere. It is very evident, however, that these faculties, if they really exist, must belong to some corporeal or extended substance, since in their clear and distinct concept there is contained some sort of extension, but no intellection at all. Farther, I cannot doubt but that there is in me a certain passive faculty of perception, that is, of receiving and taking knowledge of the ideas of sensible things; but this would be useless to me, if there did not also exist in me, or in some other thing, another active faculty capable of forming and producing those ideas. But this active faculty cannot be in me [in as far as I am but a thinking thing], seeing that it does not presuppose thought, and also that those ideas are frequently produced in my mind without my contributing to it in any way, and even frequently contrary to my will. This faculty must therefore exist in some substance different from me, in which all the objective reality of the ideas that are produced by this faculty, is contained formally or eminently, as I before remarked; and this substance is either a body, that is to say, a corporeal nature in which is contained formally [and in effect] all that is objectively [and by representation] in those ideas; or it is God himself, or some other creature, of a rank superior to body, in which the same is contained eminently. But as God is no deceiver, it is manifest that he does not of himself and immediately communicate those ideas to me, nor even by the intervention of any creature in which their objective reality is not formally, but only eminently, contained. For as he has given me no faculty whereby I can discover this to be the case, but, on the contrary, a very strong inclination to believe that those ideas arise from corporeal objects, I do not see how he could be vindicated from the charge of deceit, if in truth they proceeded from any other source, or were produced by other causes than corporeal things: and accordingly it must be concluded, that corporeal objects exist. Nevertheless they are not perhaps exactly such as we perceive by the senses, for their comprehension by the senses is, in many instances, very obscure and confused; but it is at least necessary to admit that all which I clearly and distinctly conceive as in them, that is, generally speaking, all that is comprehended in the object of speculative geometry, really exists external to me.

But with respect to other things which are either only particular, as, for example, that the sun is of such a size and figure, etc., or are conceived with less clearness and distinctness, as light, sound, pain, and the like, although they are highly dubious and uncertain, nevertheless on the ground alone that God is no deceiver, and that consequently he has permitted no falsity in my opinions which he has not likewise given me a faculty of correcting, I think I may with safety conclude that I possess in myself the means of arriving at the truth. And, in the first place, it cannot be doubted that in each of the dictates of nature there is some truth: for by nature, considered in general, I now understand nothing more than God himself, or the order and disposition established by God in created things; and by my nature in particular I understand the assemblage of all that God has given me.

But there is nothing which that nature teaches me more expressly [or more sensibly] than that I have a body which is ill affected when I feel pain, and stands in need of food and drink when I experience the sensations of hunger and thirst, etc. And therefore I ought not to doubt but that there is some truth in these informations.

Nature likewise teaches me by these sensations of pain, hunger, thirst, etc., that I am not only lodged in my body as a pilot in a vessel, but that I am besides so intimately conjoined, and as it were intermixed with it, that my mind and body compose a certain unity. For if this were not the case, I should not feel pain when my body is hurt, seeing I am merely a thinking thing, but should perceive the wound by the understanding alone, just as a pilot perceives by sight when any part of his vessel is damaged; and when my body has need of food or drink, I should have a clear knowledge of this, and not be made aware of it by the confused sensations of hunger and thirst: for, in truth, all these sensations of hunger, thirst, pain, etc., are nothing more than certain confused modes of thinking, arising from the union and apparent fusion of mind and body.

Besides this, nature teaches me that my own body is surrounded by many other bodies, some of which I have to seek after, and others to shun. And indeed, as I perceive different sorts of colours, sounds, odours, tastes, heat, hardness, etc., I safely conclude that there are in the bodies from which the diverse perceptions of the senses proceed, certain varieties corresponding to them, although, perhaps, not in reality like them; and since, among these diverse perceptions of the senses, some are agreeable, and others disagreeable, there can be no doubt that my body, or rather my entire self, in as far as I am composed of body and mind, may be variously affected, both beneficially and hurtfully, by surrounding bodies.

But there are many other beliefs which, though seemingly the teaching of nature, are not in reality so, but which obtained a place in my mind through a habit of judging inconsiderately of things. It may thus easily happen that such judgments shall contain error: thus, for example, the opinion I have that all space in which there is nothing to affect [or make an impression on] my senses is void; that in a hot body there is something in every respect similar to the idea of heat in my mind; that in a white or green body there is the same whiteness or greenness which I perceive; that in a bitter or sweet body there is the same taste, and so in other instances; that the stars, towers, and all distant bodies, are of the same size and figure as they appear to our eyes, etc. But that I may avoid everything like indistinctness of conception, I must accurately define what I properly understand by being taught by nature. For nature is here taken in a narrower sense than when it signifies the sum of all the things which God has given me; seeing that in that meaning the notion comprehends much that belongs only to the mind [to which I am not here to be understood as referring when I use the term nature]; as, for example, the notion I have of the truth, that what is done cannot be undone, and all the other truths I discern by the natural light [without the aid of the body]; and seeing that it comprehends likewise much besides that belongs only to body, and is not here any more contained under the name nature, as the quality of heaviness, and the like, of which I do not speak,—the term being reserved exclusively to designate the things which God has given to me as a being composed of mind and body. But nature, taking the term in the sense explained, teaches me to shun what causes in me the sensation of pain, and to pursue what affords me the sensation of pleasure, and other things of this sort; but I do not discover that it teaches me, in addition to this, from these diverse perceptions of the senses, to draw any conclusions respecting external objects without a previous [careful and mature] consideration of them by the mind; for it is, as appears to me, the office of the mind alone, and not of the composite whole of mind and body, to discern the truth in those matters. Thus, although the impression a star makes on my eye is not larger than that from the flame of a candle, I do not, nevertheless, experience any real or positive impulse determining me to believe that the star is not greater than the flame; the true account of the matter being merely that I have so judged from my youth without any rational ground. And, though on approaching the fire I feel heat, and even pain on approaching it too closely, I have, however, from this no ground for holding that something resembling the heat I feel is in the fire, any more than that there is something similar to the pain; all that I have ground for believing is, that there is something in it, whatever it may be, which excites in me those sensations of heat or pain. So also, although there are spaces in which I find nothing to excite and affect my senses, I must not therefore conclude that those spaces contain in them no body; for I see that in this, as in many other similar matters, I have been accustomed to pervert the order of nature, because these perceptions of the senses, although given me by nature merely to signify to my mind what things are beneficial and hurtful to the composite whole of which it is a part, and being sufficiently clear and distinct for that purpose, are nevertheless used by me as infallible rules by which to determine immediately the essence of the bodies that exist out of me, of which they can of course afford me only the most obscure and confused knowledge.

But I have already sufficiently considered how it happens that, notwithstanding the supreme goodness of God, there is falsity in my judgments. A difficulty, however, here presents itself, respecting the things which I am taught by nature must be pursued or avoided, and also respecting the internal sensations in which I seem to have occasionally detected error, [and thus to be directly deceived by nature]: thus, for example, I may be so deceived by the agreeable taste of some viand with which poison has been mixed, as to be induced to take the poison. In this case, however, nature may be excused, for it simply leads me to desire the viand for its agreeable taste, and not the poison, which is unknown to it; and thus we can infer nothing from this circumstance beyond that our nature is not omniscient; at which there is assuredly no ground for surprise, since, man being of a finite nature, his knowledge must likewise be of limited perfection. But we also not unfrequently err in that to which we are directly impelled by nature, as is the case with invalids who desire drink or food that would be hurtful to them. It will here, perhaps, be alleged that the reason why such persons are deceived is that their nature is corrupted; but this leaves the difficulty untouched, for a sick man is not less really the creature of God than a man who is in full heath; and therefore it is as repugnant to the goodness of God that the nature of the former should be deceitful as it is for that of the latter to be so. And, as a clock, composed of wheels and counter weights, observes not the less accurately all the laws of nature when it is ill made, and points out the hours incorrectly, than when it satisfies the desire of the maker in every respect; so likewise if the body of man be considered as a kind of machine, so made up and composed of bones, nerves, muscles, veins, blood, and skin, that although there were in it no mind, it would still exhibit the same motions which it at present manifests involuntarily, and therefore without the aid of the mind, [and simply by the dispositions of its organs], I easily discern that it would also be as natural for such a body, supposing it dropsical, for example, to experience the parchedness of the throat that is usually accompanied in the mind by the sensation of thirst, and to be disposed by this parchedness to move its nerves and its other parts in the way required for drinking, and thus increase its malady and do itself harm, as it is natural for it, when it is not indisposed to be stimulated to drink for its good by a similar cause; and although looking to the use for which a clock was destined by its maker, I may say that it is deflected from its proper nature when it incorrectly indicates the hours, and on the same principle, considering the machine of the human body as having been formed by God for the sake of the motions which it usually manifests, although I may likewise have ground for thinking that it does not follow the order of its nature when the throat is parched and drink does not tend to its preservation, nevertheless I yet plainly discern that this latter acceptation of the term nature is very different from the other; for this is nothing more than a certain denomination, depending entirely on my thought, and hence called extrinsic, by which I compare a sick man and an imperfectly constructed clock with the idea I have of a man in good health and a well made clock; while by the other acceptation of nature is understood something which is truly found in things, and therefore possessed of some truth.

But certainly, although in respect of a dropsical body, it is only by way of exterior denomination that we say its nature is corrupted, when, without requiring drink, the throat is parched; yet, in respect of the composite whole, that is, of the mind in its union with the body, it is not a pure denomination, but really an error of nature, for it to feel thirst when drink would be hurtful to it: and, accordingly, it still remains to be considered why it is that the goodness of God does not prevent the nature of man thus taken from being fallacious.

To commence this examination accordingly, I here remark, in the first place, that there is a vast difference between mind and body, in respect that body, from its nature, is always divisible, and that mind is entirely indivisible. For in truth, when I consider the mind, that is, when I consider myself in so far only as I am a thinking thing, I can distinguish in myself no parts, but I very clearly discern that I am somewhat absolutely one and entire; and although the whole mind seems to be united to the whole body, yet, when a foot, an arm, or any other part is cut off, I am conscious that nothing has been taken from my mind; nor can the faculties of willing, perceiving, conceiving, etc., properly be called its parts, for it is the same mind that is exercised [all entire] in willing, in perceiving, and in conceiving, etc. But quite the opposite holds in corporeal or extended things; for I cannot imagine any one of them [how small soever it may be], which I cannot easily sunder in thought, and which, therefore, I do not know to be divisible. This would be sufficient to teach me that the mind or soul of man is entirely different from the body, if I had not already been apprised of it on other grounds.

I remark, in the next place, that the mind does not immediately receive the impression from all the parts of the body, but only from the brain, or perhaps even from one small part of it, viz., that in which the common sense (*sensus communis*) is said to be, which as often as it is affected in the same way, gives rise to the same perception in the mind, although meanwhile the other parts of the body may be diversely disposed, as is proved by innumerable experiments, which it is unnecessary here to enumerate.

I remark, besides, that the nature of body is such that none of its parts can be moved by another part a little removed from the other, which cannot likewise be moved in the same way by any one of the parts that lie between those two, although the most remote part does not act at all. As, for example, in the cord A, B, C, D, [which is in tension], if its last part D, be pulled, the first part A, will not be moved in a different way than it would be were one of the intermediate parts B or C to be pulled, and the last part D meanwhile to remain fixed. And in the same way, when I feel pain in the foot, the science of physics teaches me that this sensation is experienced by means of the nerves dispersed over the foot, which, extending like cords from it to the brain, when they are contracted in the foot, contract at the same time the inmost parts of the brain in which they have their origin, and excite in these parts a certain motion appointed by nature to cause in the mind a sensation of pain, as if existing in the foot: but as these nerves must pass through the tibia, the leg, the loins, the back, and neck, in order to reach the brain, it may happen that although their extremities in the foot are not affected, but only certain of their parts that pass through the loins or neck, the same movements, nevertheless, are excited in the brain by this motion as would have been caused there by a hurt received in the foot, and hence the mind will necessarily feel pain in the foot, just as if it had been hurt; and the same is true of all the other perceptions of our senses.

I remark, finally, that as each of the movements that are made in the part of the brain by which the mind is immediately affected, impresses it with but a single sensation, the most likely supposition in the circumstances is, that this movement causes the mind to experience, among all the sensations which it is capable of impressing upon it, that one which is the best fitted, and generally the most useful for the preservation of the human body when it is in full health. But experience shows us that all the perceptions which nature has given us are of such a kind as I have mentioned; and accordingly, there is nothing found in them that does not manifest the power and goodness of God. Thus, for example, when the nerves of the foot are violently or more than usually shaken, the motion passing through the medulla of the spine to the innermost parts of the brain affords a sign to the mind on which it experiences a sensation, viz., of pain, as if it were in the foot, by which the mind is admonished and excited to do its utmost to remove the cause of it as dangerous and hurtful to the foot. It is true that God could have so constituted the nature of man as that the same motion in the brain would have informed the mind of something altogether different: the motion might, for example, have been the occasion on which the mind became conscious of itself, in so far as it is in the brain, or in so far as it is in some place intermediate between the foot and the brain, or, finally, the occasion on which it perceived some other object quite different, whatever that might be; but nothing of all this would have so well contributed to the preservation of the body as that which the mind actually feels. In the same way, when we stand in need of drink, there arises from this want a certain parchedness in the throat that moves its nerves, and by means of them the internal parts of the brain; and this movement affects the mind with the sensation of thirst, because there is nothing on that occasion which is more useful for us than to be made aware that we have need of drink for the preservation of our health; and so in other instances.

Whence it is quite manifest that, notwithstanding the sovereign goodness of God, the nature of man, in so far as it is composed of mind and body, cannot but be sometimes fallacious. For, if there is any cause which excites, not in the foot, but in some one of the parts of the nerves that stretch from the foot to the brain, or even in the brain itself, the same movement that is ordinarily created when the foot is ill affected, pain will be felt, as it were, in the foot, and the sense will thus be naturally deceived; for as the same movement in the brain can but impress the mind with the same sensation, and as this sensation is much more frequently excited by a cause which hurts the foot than by one acting in a different quarter, it is reasonable that it should lead the mind to feel pain in the foot rather than in any other part of the body. And if it sometimes happens that the parchedness of the throat does not arise, as is usual, from drink being necessary for the health of the body, but from quite the opposite cause, as is the case with the dropsical, yet it is much better that it should be deceitful in that instance, than if, on the contrary, it were continually fallacious when the body is well-disposed; and the same holds true in other cases.

And certainly this consideration is of great service, not only in enabling me to recognize the errors to which my nature is liable, but likewise in rendering it more easy to avoid or correct them: for, knowing that all my senses more usually indicate to me what is true than what is false, in matters relating to the advantage of the body, and being able almost always to make use of more than a single sense in examining the same object, and besides this, being able to use my memory in connecting present with past knowledge, and my understanding which has already discovered all the causes of my errors, I ought no longer to fear that falsity may be met with in what is daily presented to me by the senses. And I ought to reject all the doubts of those bygone days, as hyperbolical and ridiculous, especially the general uncertainty respecting sleep, which I could not distinguish from the waking state: for I now find a very marked difference between the two states, in respect that our memory can never connect our dreams with each other and with the course of life, in the way it is in the habit of doing with events that occur when we are awake. And, in truth, if some one, when I am awake, appeared to me all of a sudden and as suddenly disappeared, as do the images I see in sleep, so that I could not observe either whence he came or whither he went, I should not without reason esteem it either a spectre or phantom formed in my brain, rather than a real man. But when I perceive objects with regard to which I can distinctly determine both the place whence they come, and that in which they are, and the time at which they appear to me, and when, without interruption, I can connect the perception I have of them with the whole of the other parts of my life, I am perfectly sure that what I thus perceive occurs while I am awake and not during sleep. And I ought not in the least degree to doubt of the truth of those presentations, if, after having called together all my senses, my memory, and my understanding for the purpose of examining them, no deliverance is given by any one of these faculties which is repugnant to that of any other: for since God is no deceiver, it necessarily follows that I am not herein deceived. But because the necessities of action frequently oblige us to come to a determination before we have had leisure for so careful an examination, it must be confessed that the life of man is frequently obnoxious to error with respect to individual objects; and we must, in conclusion, acknowledge the weakness of our nature.

From the Reply to the Second Objections

¶ Reasons which Establish the Existence of God, and the Distinction between the Mind and Body of Man, Disposed in Geometrical Order

Definitions

I. By the term *thought,* I comprehend all that is in us, so that we are immediately conscious of it. Thus, all the operations of the will, intellect, imagination, and senses, are thoughts. But I have used the word *immediately* expressly to exclude whatever follows or depends upon our thoughts; for example, voluntary motion has, in truth, thought for its source (principle), but yet it is not itself thought. [Thus, walking is not a thought, but the perception of knowledge we have of our walking is.]

II. By the word *idea* I understand that form of any thought, by the immediate perception of which I am conscious of that same thought; so that I can express nothing in words, when I understand what I say, without making it certain, by this alone, that I possess the idea of the thing that is signified by these words. And thus I give the appellation idea not to the images alone that are depicted in the phantasy; on the contrary, I do not here apply this name to them, in so far as they are in the corporeal phantasy, that is to say, in so far as they are depicted in certain parts of the brain, but only in so far as they inform the mind itself, when turned towards that part of the brain.

III. By the *objective reality of an idea* I understand the entity or being of the thing represented by the idea, in so far as this entity is in the idea; and, in the same manner, it may be called either an objective perfection, or objective artifice, etc. For all that we conceive to be in the objects of the ideas is objectively [or by representation] in the ideas themselves.

IV. The same things are said to be *formally* in the objects of the ideas when they are in them such as we conceive them; and they are said to be in the objects *eminently* when they are not indeed such as we conceive them, but are so great that they can supply this defect by their excellence.

V. Everything in which there immediately resides, as in a subject, or by which there exists any object we perceive, that is, any property, or quality, or attribute of which we have in us a real idea, is called *substance*. For we have no other idea of substance, accurately taken, except that it is a thing in which exists formally or eminently this property or quality which we perceive, or which is objectively in some one of our ideas, since we are taught by the natural light that nothing can have no real attribute.

VI. The substance in which thought immediately resides is here called *mind*. I here speak, however, of *mens* rather than of *anima*, for the latter is equivocal, being frequently applied to denote a corporeal object.

VII. The substance which is the immediate subject of local extension, and of the accidents that presuppose this extension, as figure, situation, local motion, etc., is called *body*. But whether the substance which is called mind be the same with that which is called body, or whether they are two diverse substances, is a question to be hereafter considered.

VIII. The substance which we understand to be supremely perfect, and in which we conceive nothing that involves any defect, or limitation of perfection, is called *God*.

IX. When we say that some attribute is contained in the nature or concept of a thing, this is the same as if we said that the attribute is true of the thing, or that it may be affirmed of the thing itself.

X. Two substances are said to be really distinct, when each of them may exist without the other.

Postulates

1st. I request that my readers consider how feeble are the reasons that have hitherto led them to repose faith in their senses, and how uncertain are all the judgments which they afterwards founded on them; and that they will revolve this consideration in their mind so long and so frequently, that, in fine, they may acquire the habit of no longer trusting so confidently in their senses; for I hold that this is necessary to render one capable of apprehending metaphysical truths.

2d. That they consider their own mind, and all those of its attributes of which they shall find they cannot doubt, though they may have supposed that all they ever received by the senses was entirely false, and that they do not leave off considering it until they have acquired the habit of conceiving it distinctly, and of believing that it is more easy to know than any corporeal object.

3d. That they diligently examine such propositions as are self-evident, which they will find within themselves, as the following:—That the same thing cannot at once be and not be; that nothing cannot be the efficient cause of anything, and the like;—and thus exercise that clearness of understanding that has been given them by nature, but which the perceptions of the senses are wont greatly to disturb and obscure—exercise it, I say, pure and delivered from the objects of sense; for in this way the truth of the following axioms will appear very evident to them.

4th. That they examine the ideas of those natures which contain in them an assemblage of several attributes, such as the nature of the triangle, that of the square, or of some other figure; as also the nature of mind, the nature of body, and above all that of God, or of a being supremely perfect. And I request them to observe that it may with truth be affirmed that all these things are in objects, which we clearly conceive to be contained in them: for example, because that, in the nature of the rectilineal triangle, this property is found contained—viz., that its three angles are equal to two right angles, and that in the nature of body or of an extended thing, divisibility is comprised (for we do not conceive any extended thing so small that we cannot divide it, at least in thought)—it is true that the three angles of a rectilineal triangle are equal to two right angles, and that all body is divisible.

5th. That they dwell much and long on the contemplation of the supremely perfect Being, and, among other things, consider that in the ideas of all other natures, possible existence is indeed contained, but that in the idea of God is contained not only possible but absolutely necessary existence. For, from this alone, and without any reasoning, they will discover that God exists: and it will be no less evident in itself than that two is an equal and three an unequal number, with other truths of this sort. For there are certain truths that are thus manifest to some without proof, which are not comprehended by others without a process of reasoning.

6th. That carefully considering all the examples of clear and distinct perception, and all of obscure and confused, of which I spoke in my Meditations, they accustom themselves to distinguish things that are clearly known from those that are obscure, for this is better learnt by example than by rules; and I think that I have there opened up, or at least in some degree touched upon, all examples of this kind.

7th. That readers adverting to the circumstance that they never discovered any falsity in things which they clearly conceived, and that, on the contrary, they never found, unless by chance, any truth in things which they conceived but obscurely, consider it to be wholly irrational, if, on account only of certain prejudices of the senses, or hypotheses which contain what is unknown, they call in doubt what is clearly and distinctly conceived by the pure understanding; for they will thus readily admit the following axioms to be true and indubitable, though I confess that several of them might have been much better unfolded, and ought rather to have been proposed as theorems than as axioms, if I had desired to be more exact.

Axioms or Common Notions

I. Nothing exists of which it cannot be inquired what is the cause of its existing; for this can even be asked respecting God; not that there is need of any cause for his existence, but because the very immensity of his nature is the cause or reason why there is no need of any cause of his existence.

II. The present time is not dependent on that which immediately preceded it; for this reason, there is not need of a less cause for conserving a thing than for at first producing it.

III. Any thing or any perfection of a thing actually existent cannot have *nothing,* or a thing non-existent, for the cause of its existence.

IV. All the reality or perfection which is in a thing is found formally or eminently in its first and total cause.

V. Whence it follows likewise, that the objective reality of our ideas requires a cause in which this same reality is contained, not simply objectively, but formally or eminently. And it is to be observed that this axiom must of necessity be admitted, as upon it alone depends the knowledge of all things, whether sensible or insensible. For whence do we know, for example, that the sky exists? Is it because we see it? But this vision does not affect the mind unless in so far as it is an idea, and an idea inhering in the mind itself, and not an image depicted on the phantasy; and, by reason of this idea, we cannot judge that the sky exists unless we suppose that every idea must have a cause of its objective reality which is really existent; and this cause we judge to be the sky itself, and so in the other instances.

VI. There are diverse degrees of reality, that is, of entity [or perfection]: for substance has more reality than accident or mode, and infinite substance than finite; it is for this reason also that there is more objective reality in the idea of substance than in that of accident, and in the idea of infinite than in the idea of finite substance.

VII. The will of a thinking being is carried voluntarily and freely, for that is of the essence of will, but nevertheless infallibly, to the good that is clearly known to it; and, therefore, if it discover any perfections which it does not possess, it will instantly confer them on itself if they are in its power; [for it will perceive that to possess them is a greater good than to want them].

VIII. That which can accomplish the greater or more difficult, can also accomplish the less or the more easy.

IX. It is a greater and more difficult thing to create or conserve a substance than to create or conserve its attributes or properties; but this creation of a thing is not greater or more difficult than its conservation, as has been already said.

X. In the idea or concept of a thing existence is contained, because we are unable to conceive anything unless under the form of a thing which exists; but with this difference that, in the concept of a limited thing, possible or contingent existence is alone contained, and in the concept of a being sovereignly perfect, perfect and necessary existence is comprised.

Proposition I

The existence of God is known from the consideration of his nature alone.

Demonstration

To say that an attribute is contained in the nature or in the concept of a thing, is the same as to say that this attribute is true of this thing, and that it may be affirmed to be in it. (Definition IX.)

But necessary existence is contained in the nature or in the concept of God (by Axiom X).

Hence it may with truth be said that necessary existence is in God, or that God exists.

And this syllogism is the same as that of which I made use in my reply to the sixth article of these objections; and its conclusion may be known without proof by those who are free from all prejudice, as has been said in Postulate V. But because it is not so easy to reach so great perspicacity of mind, we shall essay to establish the same thing by other modes.

Proposition II

The existence of God is demonstrated, *a posteriori,* from this alone, that his idea is in us.

Demonstration

The objective reality of each of our ideas requires a cause in which this same reality is contained, not simply objectively, but formally or eminently (by Axiom V).

But we have in us the idea of God (by Definitions II and VIII), and of this idea the objective reality is not contained in us, either formally or eminently (by Axiom VI), nor can it be contained in any other except in God himself (by Definition VIII).

Therefore this idea of God which is in us demands God for its cause, and consequently God exists (by Axiom III).

Proposition III

The existence of God is also demonstrated from this, that we ourselves, who possess the idea of him, exist.

Demonstration

If I possessed the power of conserving myself, I should likewise have the power of conferring, *a fortiori,* on myself, all the perfections that are awanting to me (by Axiom VIII and IX), for these perfections are only attributes of substance whereas I myself am a substance.

But I have not the power of conferring on myself these perfections, for otherwise I should already possess them (by Axiom VII).

Hence, I have not the power of self-conservation.

Further, I cannot exist without being conserved, so long as I exist, either by myself, supposing I possess the power, or by another who has this power (by Axioms I and II).

But I exist, and yet I have not the power of self-conservation, as I have recently proved. Hence I am conserved by another.

Further, that by which I am conserved has in itself formally or eminently all that is in me (by Axiom IV).

But I have in me the perception of many perfections that are awanting to me, and that also of the idea of God (by Definitions II and VIII). Hence the perception of these same perfections is in him by whom I am conserved.

Finally, that same being by whom I am conserved cannot have the perception of any perfections that are awanting to him, that is to say, which he has not in himself formally or eminently (by Axiom VII); for having the power of conserving me, as has been recently said, he should have, *a fortiori,* the power of conferring these perfections on himself, if they were awanting to him (by Axioms VIII and IX).

But he has the perception of all the perfections which I discover to be wanting to me, and which I conceive can be in God alone, as I recently proved:

Hence he has all these in himself, formally or eminently, and thus he is God.

Corollary

God has created the sky and the earth and all that is therein contained; and besides this he can make all the things which we clearly conceive in the manner in which we conceive them.

Demonstration

All these things clearly follow from the preceding proposition. For in it we have proved the existence of God, from its being necessary that some one should exist in whom are contained formally or eminently all the perfections of which there is in us any idea.

But we have in us the idea of a power so great, that by the being alone in whom it resides, the sky and the earth, etc., must have been created, and also that by the same being all the other things which we conceive as possible can be produced.

Hence, in proving the existence of God, we have also proved with it all these things.

Proposition IV

The mind and body are really distinct.

Demonstration

All that we clearly conceive can be made by God in the manner in which we conceive it (by foregoing Corollary).

But we clearly conceive mind, that is, a substance which thinks, without body, that is to say, without an extended substance (by Postulate II); and, on the other hand, we as clearly conceive body without mind (as every one admits).

Hence, at least, by the omnipotence of God, the mind can exist without the body, and the body without the mind.

Now, substances which can exist independently of each other, are really distinct (by Definition X).

But the mind and the body are substances (by Definitions V, VI, and VII), which can exist independently of each other, as I have recently proved:

Hence the mind and the body are really distinct.

And it must be observed that I have here made use of the omnipotence of God in order to found my proof on it, not that there is need of any extraordinary power in order to separate the mind from the body, but for this reason, that, as I have treated of God only in the foregoing propositions, I could not draw my proof from any other source than from him: and it matters very little by what power two things are separated in order to discover that they are really distinct.

XI

HOBBES

THOMAS HOBBES (1588-1679) was born at Malmesbury, England, just as the Spanish Armada was approaching. He studied at Oxford and then became tutor to the young Earl of Devonshire. He traveled widely, worked on a translation of the Greek historian, Thucydides, and studied geometry and optics. From 1634-1637, he lived in Paris, was part of Mersenne's circle, and began writing. From 1640 to 1651, he was in exile in Paris for his political views, and, during this period, he wrote his objections to Descartes (1640-1641), *De Cive* (1642), and the *Leviathan* (from which the following selections are taken). He returned to England in 1651 under Cromwell and was later reluctantly accepted by Charles II (whose tutor he had been in France). He was engaged in political, religious, mathematical, and philosophical polemics until the end of his life.

Leviathan

PART 1—OF MAN

Chapter I.—OF SENSE

Concerning the thoughts of man, I will consider them first singly and afterwards in train or dependence upon one another. Singly, they are every one a *representation* or *appearance* of some quality or other accident of a body without us which is commonly called an *object*. Which object works on the eyes, ears, and other parts of a man's body, and by diversity of working produces diversity of appearances.

The original of them all is that which we call SENSE, for there is no conception in a man's mind which has not at first, totally or by parts, been begotten upon the organs of sense. The rest are derived from that original.

To know the natural cause of sense is not very necessary to the business now in hand, and I have elsewhere written of the same at large. Nevertheless, to fill each part of my present method, I will briefly deliver the same in this place.

The cause of sense is the external body or object which presses the organ proper to each sense, either immediately as in the taste and touch, or mediately as in seeing, hearing, and smelling; which pressure, by the mediation of the nerves and other strings and membranes of the body continued inward to the brain and heart, causes there a resistance or counter-pressure or endeavor of the heart to deliver itself, which endeavor, because *outward*, seems to be some matter without. And this *seeming* or *fancy* is that which men call *sense*, and consists, as to the eye, in a *light* or *color figured;* to the ear, in a *sound;* to the nostril, in an *odor;* to the tongue and palate, in a *savor;* and to the rest of the body, in *heat, cold, hardness, softness,* and such other qualities as we discern by *feeling*. All which qualities, called *sensible,* are in the object that causes them but so many several motions of the matter by which it presses our organs diversely. Neither in us that are pressed are they anything else but divers motions, for motion produces nothing but motion. But their appearance to us is fancy, the same waking that dreaming. And as pressing, rubbing, or striking the eye makes us fancy a light, and pressing the ear produces a din, so do the bodies also we see or hear produce the same by their strong, though unobserved, action. For if those colors and sounds were in the bodies or objects that cause them, they could not be severed from them as by glasses, and in echoes by reflection, we see they are, where we know the thing we see is in one place, the appearance in another. And though at some certain distance the real and very object seem invested with the fancy it begets in us, yet still the object is one thing, the image or fancy is another. So that sense, in all cases, is nothing else but original fancy, caused, as I have said, by the pressure—that is, by the motion—of external things upon our eyes, ears, and other organs thereunto ordained.

But the philosophy schools through all the universities of Christendom, grounded upon certain texts of Aristotle, teach another doctrine, and say, for the cause of *vision,* that the thing seen sends forth on every side a *visible species*—in English, a *visible show, apparition,* or *aspect,* or *a being seen*—the receiving whereof into the eye is *seeing*. And for the cause of *hearing,* that the thing heard sends forth an *audible species*—that is, an *audible aspect* or *audible being seen*—which, entering at the ear, makes *hearing*. Nay, for the cause of *understanding* also they say the thing understood sends forth an *intelligible species* —that is, an *intelligible being seen*—which, coming into the understanding, makes us understand. I say not this as disproving the use of universities; but because I am to speak hereafter of their office in a commonwealth, I must let you see on all occasions by the way what things would be amended in them, among which the frequency of insignificant speech is one.

Chapter II.—OF IMAGINATION

That when a thing lies still, unless somewhat else stir it, it will lie still forever is a truth that no man doubts of. But that when a thing is in motion it will eternally be in motion unless somewhat else stay it, though the reason be the same—namely, that nothing can change itself

–is not so easily assented to. For men measure not only other men but all other things by themselves, and, because they find themselves subject after motion to pain and lassitude, think everything else grows weary of motion and seeks repose of its own accord, little considering whether it be not some other motion wherein that desire of rest they find in themselves consists. From hence it is that the schools say heavy bodies fall downward out of an appetite to rest and to conserve their nature in that place which is most proper for them, ascribing appetite and knowledge of what is good for their conservation, which is more than man has, to things inanimate, absurdly.

When a body is once in motion, it moves, unless something else hinder it, eternally; and whatsoever hinders it cannot in an instant, but in time and by degrees, quite extinguish it; and as we see in the water, though the wind cease, the waves give not over rolling for a long time after, so also it happens in that motion which is made in the internal parts of a man then when he sees, dreams, etc. For after the object is removed or the eye shut, we still retain an image of the thing seen, though more obscure than when we see it. And this is it the Latins call *imagination* from the image made in seeing, and apply the same, though improperly, to all the other senses. But the Greeks call it *fancy,* which signifies *appearance* and is as proper to one sense as to another. IMAGINATION, therefore, is nothing but *decaying sense* and is found in men and many other living creatures as well sleeping as waking.

The decay of sense in men waking is not the decay of the motion made in sense but an obscuring of it in such manner as the light of the sun obscures the light of the stars, which stars do no less exercise their virtue by which they are visible in the day than in the night. But because among many strokes which our eyes, ears, and other organs receive from external bodies the predominant only is sensible, therefore, the light of the sun being predominant, we are not affected with the action of the stars. And any object being removed from our eyes, though the impression it made in us remain, yet other objects more present succeeding and working on us, the imagination of the past is obscured and made weak, as the voice of a man is in the noise of the day. From whence it follows that the longer the time is after the sight or sense of any object, the weaker is the imagination. For the continual change of man's body destroys in time the parts which in sense were moved, so that distance of time and of place has one and the same effect in us. For as at a great distance of place that which we look at appears dim and without distinction of the smaller parts, and as voices grow weak and inarticulate, so also, after great distance of time, our imagination of the past is weak and we lose, for example, of cities we have seen many particular streets, and of actions many particular circumstances. This *decaying sense,* when we would express the thing itself—I mean *fancy* itself—we call *imagination,* as I said before; but when we would express the decay and signify that the sense is fading, old, and past, it is called *memory.* So that imagination and memory are but one thing, which for divers considerations has divers names.

Much memory, or memory of many things, is called *experience.* Again, imagination being only of those things which have been formerly perceived by sense, either all at once or by parts at several times, the former, which is the imagining the whole object as it was presented to the sense, is *simple* imagination, as when one imagines a man or horse which he has seen before. The other is *compounded,* as when, from the sight of a man at one time and of a horse at another, we conceive in our mind a centaur. So when a man compounds the image of his own person with the image of the actions of another man, as when a man imagines himself a Hercules or an Alexander—which happens often to them that are much taken with reading of romances—it is a compound imagination and properly but a fiction of the mind. There be also other imaginations that rise in men, though waking, from the great impression made in sense: as from gazing upon the sun, the impression leaves an image of the sun before our eyes a long time after; and from being long and vehemently attent upon geometrical figures, a man shall in the dark, though awake, have the images of lines and angles before his eyes; which kind of fancy has no particular name, as being a thing that does not commonly fall into men's discourse.

The imaginations of them that sleep are those we call *dreams.* And these also, as all other imaginations, have been before, either totally or by parcels, in the sense. And because in sense the brain and nerves, which are the necessary organs of sense, are so benumbed in sleep as not easily to be moved by the action of external objects, there can happen in sleep no imagination and therefore no dream but what proceeds from the agitation of the inward parts of man's body; which inward parts, for the connection they have with the brain and other organs, when they be distempered do keep the same in motion; whereby the imaginations there formerly made appear as if a man were waking, saving that the organs of sense being now benumbed so as there is no new object which can master and obscure them with a more vigorous impression, a dream must needs be more clear, in this silence of sense, than our waking thoughts. And hence it comes to pass that it is a hard matter, and by many thought impossible, to distinguish exactly between sense and dreaming. For my part, when I consider that in dreams I do not often nor constantly think of the same persons, places, objects, and actions that I do waking, nor remember so long a train of coherent thoughts dreaming as at other times; and because waking I often observe the absurdity of dreams, but never dream of the absurdities of my waking thoughts—I am well satisfied that, being awake, I know I dream not, though when I dream I think myself awake.

And seeing dreams are caused by the distemper of some of the inward parts of the body, divers distempers must needs cause different dreams. And hence it is that lying cold breeds dreams of fear and raises the thought and image of some fearful object, the motion from the brain to the inner parts and from the inner parts to the brain being reciprocal; and that as anger causes heat in some parts of the body when we are awake, so when we sleep the overheating of the same parts causes anger and raises up in the brain the imagination of an enemy. In the same manner as natural kindness, when we are awake, causes desire, and desire makes heat in certain other parts of the body, so also too much heat in those parts while we sleep raises in the brain an imagination of some kindness shown. In sum, our dreams are the reverse of our waking imaginations, the motion when we are awake beginning at one end and when we dream at another. The most difficult discerning of a man's dream from his waking thoughts is then when by some accident we observe not that we have slept, which is easy to happen to a man full of fearful thoughts and whose conscience is much troubled and that sleeps without the circumstances of going to bed or putting off his clothes, as one that nods in a chair. For he that takes pains and industriously lays himself to sleep, in case any uncouth and exorbitant fancy come unto him, cannot easily think it other than a dream. . . .

From this ignorance of how to distinguish dreams and other strong fancies from vision and sense did arise the greatest part of the religion of the gentiles in time past that worshiped satyrs, fauns, nymphs, and the like, and nowadays the opinion that rude people have of fairies, ghosts, and goblins and of the power of witches. For as for witches, I think not that their witchcraft is any real power, but yet that they are justly punished for the false belief they have that they can do such mischief joined with their purpose to do it if they can, their trade being nearer to a new religion than to a craft or science. And for fairies and walking ghosts, the opinion of them has, I think, been on purpose either taught or not confuted to keep in credit the use of exorcism, of crosses, of holy water, and other such inventions of ghostly men. Nevertheless, there is no doubt but God can make unnatural apparitions; but that he does it so often as men need to fear such things more than they fear the stay or change of the course of nature, which he also can stay and change, is no point of Christian faith. But evil men, under pretext that God can do anything, are so bold as to say anything when it serves their turn, though they think it untrue; it is the part of a wise man to believe them no farther than right reason makes that which they say appear credible. If this superstitious fear of spirits were taken away, and with it prognostics from dreams, false prophecies, and many other things depending thereon by which crafty, ambitious persons abuse the simple people, men would be much more fitted than they are for civil obedience.

And this ought to be the work of the schools, but they rather nourish such doctrine. For, not knowing what imagination or the senses are, what they receive they teach: some saying that imaginations rise of themselves and have no cause, others that they rise most commonly from the will and that good thoughts are blown (inspired) into a man by God and evil thoughts by the devil, or that good thoughts are poured (infused) into a man by God and evil ones by the devil. Some say the senses receive the species of things and deliver them to the common sense, and the common sense delivers them over to the fancy, and the fancy to the memory, and the memory to the judgment, like handing of things from one to another, with many words making nothing understood.

The imagination that is raised in man, or any other creature endowed with the faculty of imagining, by words or other voluntary signs is that we generally call *understanding* and is common to man and beast. For a dog by custom will understand the call or the rating of his master, and so will many other beasts. That understanding which is peculiar to man is the understanding not only his will but his conceptions and thoughts by the sequel and contexture of the names of things into affirmations, negations, and other forms of speech; and of this kind of understanding I shall speak hereafter.

Chapter III.—OF THE CONSEQUENCE OR TRAIN OF IMAGINATIONS

By *consequence* or TRAIN of thoughts, I understand that succession of one thought to another which is called, to distinguish it from discourse in words, *mental discourse.*

When a man thinks on anything whatsoever, his next thought after is not altogether so casual as it seems to be. Not every thought to every thought succeeds indifferently. But as we have no imagination whereof we have not formerly had sense, in whole or in parts, so we have no transition from one imagination to another whereof we never had the like before in our senses. The reason whereof is this. All fancies are motions within us, relics of those made in the sense; and those motions that immediately succeed one another in the sense continue also together after sense; insomuch as the former coming again to take place and be predominant, the latter follows by coherence of the matter moved, in such manner as water upon a plane table is drawn which way any one part of it is guided by the finger. But because in sense to one and the same thing perceived sometimes one thing, sometimes another succeeds, it comes to pass in time that in the imagining of anything there is no certainty what we shall imagine next; only this is certain: it shall be something that succeeded the same before at one time or another.

This train of thoughts, or mental discourse, is of two sorts. The first is *unguided,* without design and inconstant, wherein there is no passionate thought to govern and direct those that follow to itself as the end and scope of some desire or other passion—in which case the thoughts are said to wander, and seem impertinent one to another as in a dream. Such are commonly the thoughts of men that are not only without company but also without care of anything, though even then their thoughts are as busy as at other times but without harmony—as the sound which a lute out of tune would yield to any man, or in tune to one that could not play. And yet in this wild ranging of the mind, a man may ofttimes perceive the way of it and the dependence of one thought upon another. For in a discourse of our present civil war, what could seem more impertinent than to ask, as one did, what was the value of a Roman penny? Yet the coherence to me was manifest enough. For the thought of the war introduced the thought of the delivering up the king to his enemies; the thought of that brought in the thought of the delivering up of Christ; and that again the thought of the thirty pence, which was the price of that treason; and thence easily followed that malicious question—and all this in a moment of time, for thought is quick.

The second is more constant, as being *regulated* by some desire and design. For the impression made by such things as we desire or fear is strong and permanent, or, if it cease for a time, of quick return; so strong it is sometimes as to hinder and break our sleep. From desire arises the thought of some means we have seen produce the like of that which we aim at; and from the thought of that, the thought of means to that mean; and so continually till we come to some beginning within our own power. And because the end, by the greatness of the impression, comes often to mind, in case our thoughts begin to wander they are quickly again reduced into the way; which, observed by one of the seven wise men, made him give men this precept, which is now worn out: *Respice finem* [consider the end]—that is to say, in all your actions look often upon what you would have as the thing that directs all your thoughts in the way to attain it.

The train of regulated thoughts is of two kinds: one, when of an effect imagined we seek the causes or means that produce it, and this is common to man and beast. The other is when, imagining anything whatsoever, we seek all the possible effects that can by it be produced —that is to say, we imagine what we can do with it when we have it. Of which I have not at any time seen any sign but in man only, for this is a curiosity hardly incident to the nature of any living creature that has no other passion but sensual, such as are hunger, thirst, lust, and anger. In sum, the discourse of the mind, when it is governed by design, is nothing but *seeking* or the faculty of invention . . . a hunting out of the causes of some effect, present or past, or of the effects of some present or pase cause. Sometimes as man seeks what he has lost; and from that place and time wherein he misses it his mind runs back, from place to place and time to time, to find where and when he had it —that is to say, to find some certain and limited time and place in which to begin a method of seeking. Again, from thence his thoughts run over the same places and times to find what action or other occasion might make him lose it. This we call *remembrance* or calling to mind; . . . as it were a *re-conning* of our former actions.

Sometimes a man knows a place determinate, within the compass whereof he is to seek; and then his thoughts run over all the parts thereof, in the same manner as one would sweep a room to find a jewel, or as a spaniel ranges the field till he find a scent, or as a man should run over the alphabet to start a rhyme. Sometimes a man desires to know the event of an action; and then he thinks of some like action past and the events thereof one after another, supposing like events will follow like actions. As he that foresees what will become of a criminal re-cons what he has seen follow on the like crime before, having this order of thoughts: the crime, the officer, the prison, the judge, and the gallows. Which kind of thoughts is called *foresight,* and *prudence* or *providence,* and sometimes *wisdom,* though such conjecture, through the difficulty of observing all circumstances, be very fallacious. But this is certain: by how much one man has more experience of things past than another, by so much also he is more prudent, and his expectations the seldomer fail him. The *present* only has a being in nature; things *past* have a being in the memory only; but things *to come* have no being at all, the *future* being but a fiction of the mind applying the sequels of actions past to the actions that are present, which with most certainty is done by him that has most experience, but not with certainty enough. And though it be called prudence when the event answers our expectation, yet in its own nature it is but presumption. For the foresight of things to come, which is providence, belongs only to him by whose will they are to come. From him only, and supernaturally, proceeds prophecy. The best prophet naturally is the best guesser, and the best guesser he that is most versed and studied in the matters he guesses at, for he has most *signs* to guess by.

A *sign* is the evident antecedent of the consequent, and, contrarily, the consequent of the antecedent when the like consequences have been observed before; and the oftener they have been observed, the less uncertain is the sign. And therefore he that has most experience in any kind of business has most signs whereby to guess at the future time and consequently is the most prudent; and so much more prudent than he that is new in that kind of business as not to be equaled by any advantage of natural and extemporary wit—though perhaps many young men think the contrary.

Nevertheless it is not prudence that distinguishes man from beast. There be beasts that at a year old observe more, and pursue that which is for their good more prudently, than a child can do at ten.

As prudence is a *presumption* of the *future,* contracted from the *experience* of time *past,* so there is a presumption of things past taken from other things, not future but past also. For he that has seen by what courses and degrees a flourishing state has first come into civil war and then to ruin, upon the sight of the ruins of any other state will guess the like war and the like courses have been there also. But this conjecture has the same uncertainty almost with the conjecture of the future, both being grounded only upon experience.

There is no other act of man's mind that I can remember, naturally planted in him, so as to need no other thing to the exercise of it but to be born a man and live with the use of his five senses. Those other faculties of which I shall speak by and by, and which seem proper to man only, are acquired and increased by study and industry, and of most men learned by instruction and discipline, and proceed all from the invention of words and speech. For besides sense and thoughts and the train of thoughts, the mind of man has no other motion; though by the help of speech and method the same faculties may be improved to such a height as to distinguish men from all other living creatures.

Whatsoever we imagine is *finite*. Therefore there is no idea or conception of anything we call *infinite*. No man can have in his mind an image of infinite magnitude nor conceive infinite swiftness, infinite time, or infinite force, or infinite power. When we say anything is infinite, we signify only that we are not able to conceive the ends and bounds of the things named, having no conception of the thing but of our own inability. And therefore the name of God is used, not to make us conceive him—for he is incomprehensible, and his greatness and power are unconceivable—but that we may honor him. Also because whatsoever, as I said before, we conceive has been perceived first by sense, either all at once or by parts, a man can have no thought representing anything not subject to sense. No man, therefore, can conceive anything but he must conceive it in some place and endowed with some determinate magnitude and which may be divided into parts, nor that anything is all in this place and all in another place at the same time, nor that two or more things can be in one and the same place at once; for none of these things ever have nor can be incident to sense, but are absurd speeches taken upon credit, without any signification at all, from deceived philosophers and deceived or deceiving Schoolmen.

Chapter IV.—OF SPEECH

The invention of *printing,* though ingenious, compared with the invention of *letters* is no great matter. But who was the first that found the use of letters is not known. He that first brought them into Greece, men say, was Cadmus, the son of Agenor, king of Phoenicia. A profitable invention for continuing the memory of time past and the conjunction of mankind, dispersed into so many and distant regions of the earth; and withal difficult, as proceeding from a watchful observation of the divers motions of the tongue, palate, lips, and other organs of speech, whereby to make as many differences of characters to remember them. But the most noble and profitable invention of all other was that of SPEECH, consisting of *names* or *appellations* and their connection, whereby men register their thoughts, recall them when they are past, and also declare them one to another for mutual utility and conversation; without which there had been among men neither commonwealth nor society nor contract nor peace, no more than among lions, bears, and wolves. The first author of *speech* was God himself, that instructed Adam how to name such creatures as he presented to his sight, for the Scripture goes no further in this matter. But this was sufficient to direct him to add more names as the experience and use of the creatures should give him occasion, and to join them in such manner by degrees as to make himself understood; and so by succession of time so much language might be gotten as he had found use for, though not so copious as an orator or philosopher has need of, for I do not find anything in the Scripture out of which, directly or by consequence, can be gathered that Adam was taught the names of all figures, numbers, measures, colors, sounds, fancies, relations–much less the names of words and speech, as *general, special, affirmative, negative, interrogative, optative, infinitive,* all which are useful, and least of all of *entity, intentionality, quiddity,* and other insignificant words of the school.

But all this language gotten and augmented by Adam and his posterity was again lost at the Tower of Babel, when, by the hand of God, every man was stricken for his rebellion with an oblivion of his former language. And being hereby forced to disperse themselves into several parts of the world, it must needs be that the diversity of tongues that now is proceeded by degrees from them in such manner as need, the mother of all inventions, taught them, and in tract of time grew everywhere more copious.

The general use of speech is to transfer our mental discourse into verbal, or the train of our thoughts into a train of words; and that for two commodities, whereof one is the registering of the consequences of our thoughts, which, being apt to slip out of our memory and put us to a new labor, may again be recalled by such words as they were marked by. So that the first use of names is to serve for *marks* or *notes* of remembrance. Another is when many use the same words to signify, by their connection and order, one to another, what they conceive or think of each matter, and also what they desire, fear, or have any other passion for. And for this use they are called *signs*. Special uses of speech are these: First, to register what by cogitation we find to be the cause of anything, present or past, and what we find things present or past may produce or effect—which, in sum, is acquiring of arts. Secondly, to show to others that knowledge which we have attained —which is to counsel and teach one another. Thirdly, to make known to others our wills and purposes, that we may have the mutual help of one another. Fourthly, to please and delight ourselves and others by playing with our words, for pleasure or ornament, innocently.

To these uses there are also four correspondent abuses. First, when men register their thoughts wrong by the inconstancy of the signification of their words, by which they register for their conception that which they never conceived, and so deceive themselves. Secondly, when they use words metaphorically—that is, in other senses than that they are ordained for—and thereby deceive others. Thirdly, by words when they declare that to be their will which is not. Fourthly, when they use them to grieve one another, for, seeing nature has armed living creatures, some with teeth, some with horns, and some with hands, to grieve an enemy, it is but an abuse of speech to grieve him with the tongue, unless it be one whom we are obliged to govern, and then it is not to grieve but to correct and amend.

The manner how speech serves to the remembrance of the consequence of causes and effects consists in the imposing of *names* and the *connection* of them.

Of names, some are *proper* and singular to one only thing, as *Peter, John, this man, this tree;* and some are *common* to many things, *man, horse, tree,* every of which, though but one name, is nevertheless the name of divers particular things, in respect of all which together it is called a *universal,* there being nothing in the world universal but names, for the things named are every one of them individual and singular.

One universal name is imposed on many things for their similitude in some quality or other accident; and whereas a proper name brings to mind one thing only, universals recall any one of those many.

And of names universal, some are of more and some of less extent, the larger comprehending the less large; and some again of equal extent, comprehending each other reciprocally. As for example: the name *body* is of larger signification than the word *man* and comprehends it; and the names *man* and *rational* are of equal extent, comprehending mutually one another. But here we must take notice that by a name is not always understood, as in grammar, one only word, but sometimes by circumlocution many words together. For all these words, *he that in his actions observes the laws of his country,* make but one name, equivalent to this one word—*just.*

By this imposition of names, some of larger, some of stricter signification, we turn the reckoning of the consequences of things imagined in the mind into a reckoning of the consequences of appellations. For example: a man that has no use of speech at all, such as is born and remains perfectly deaf and dumb, if he set before his eyes a triangle and by it two right angles such as are the corners of a square figure, he may, by meditation, compare and find that the three angles of that triangle are equal to those two right angles that stand by it. But if another triangle be shown him, different in shape from the former, he cannot know, without a new labor, whether the three angles of that also be equal to the same. But he that has the use of words, when he observes that such equality was consequent, not to the length of the sides nor to any other particular thing in his triangle, but only to this, that the sides were straight and the angles three, and that that was all for which he named it a triangle, will boldly conclude universally that such equality of angles is in all triangles whatsoever, and register his invention in these general terms: *every triangle has its three angles equal to two right angles.* And thus the consequence found in one particular comes to be registered and remembered as a universal rule and discharges our mental reckoning of time and place, and delivers us from all labor of the mind saving the first, and makes that which was found true *here* and *now* to be true in *all times* and *places.*

But the use of words in registering our thoughts is in nothing so evident as in numbering. A natural fool that could never learn by heart the order of numeral words, as *one, two,* and *three,* may observe every stroke of the clock, and nod to it, or say *one, one, one,* but can never know what hour it strikes. And it seems there was a time when those names of number were not in use, and men were fain to apply their fingers of one or both hands to those things they desired to keep account of; and that thence it proceeded that now our numeral words are but ten in any nation, and in some but five, and then they begin again. And he that can tell ten, if he recite them out of order will lose himself and not know when he has done. Much less will he be able to add and subtract and perform all other operations of arithmetic. So that without words there is no possibility of reckoning of numbers, much less of magnitudes, of swiftness, of force, and other things the reckonings whereof are necessary to the being or well-being of mankind.

When two names are joined together into a consequence or affirmation, as thus: *a man is a living creature,* or thus: *if he be a man, he is a living creature,* if the latter name, *living creature,* signify all that the former name *man* signifies, then the affirmation or consequence is *true;* otherwise *false.* For *true* and *false* are attributes of speech, not of things. And where speech is not, there is neither *truth* nor *falsehood; error* there may be, as when we expect that which shall not be or suspect what has not been, but in neither case can a man be charged with untruth.

Seeing then that truth consists in the right ordering of names in our affirmations, a man that seeks precise truth had need to remember what every name he uses stands for and to place it accordingly, or else he will find himself entangled in words as a bird in lime twigs, the more he struggles the more belimed. And therefore in geometry, which is the only science that it has pleased God hitherto to bestow on mankind, men begin at settling the significations of their words, which settling of significations they call *definitions* and place them in the beginning of their reckoning.

By this it appears how necessary it is for any man that aspires to true knowledge to examine the definitions of former authors, and either to correct them where they are negligently set down or to make them himself. For the errors of definitions multiply themselves according as the reckoning proceeds, and lead men into absurdities which at last they see but cannot avoid without reckoning anew from the beginning, in which lies the foundation of their errors. From whence it happens that they which trust to books do as they that cast up many little sums into a greater, without considering whether those little sums were rightly cast up or not; and at last finding the error visible, and not mistrusting their first grounds, know not which way to clear themselves, but spend time in fluttering over their books as birds that, entering by the chimney and finding themselves enclosed in a chamber, flutter at the false light of a glass window for want of wit to consider which way they came in. So that in the right definition of names lies the first use of speech, which is the acquisition of science; and in wrong or no definitions lies the first abuse, from which proceed all false and senseless tenets which make those men that take their instruction from the authority of books, and not from their own meditation, to be as much below the condition of ignorant men as men endowed with true science are above it. For between true science and erroneous doctrines, ignorance is in the middle. Natural sense and imagination are not subject to absurdity. Nature itself cannot err; and as men abound in copiousness of language, so they become more wise or more mad than ordinary. Nor is it possible without letters for any man to become either excellently wise or, unless his memory be hurt by disease or ill constitution of organs, excellently foolish. For words are wise men's counters, they do but reckon by them; but they are the money of fools that value them by the authority of an Aristotle, a Cicero, or a Thomas, or any other doctor whatsoever, if but a man.

Subject to names is whatsoever can enter into or be considered in an account, and be added one to another to make a sum, or subtracted one from another and leave a remainder. The Latins called accounts of money *rationes,* and accounting *ratiocinatio;* and that which we in bills or books of account call *items,* they call *nomina*—that is, *names;* and thence it seems to proceed that they extended the word *ratio* to the faculty of reckoning in all other things. The Greeks have but one word, *logos,* for both *speech* and *reason*—not that they thought there was no speech without reason, but no reasoning without speech—and the act of reasoning they called *syllogism,* which signifies summing up of the consequences of one saying to another. And because the same thing may enter into account for divers accidents, their names are, to show that diversity, diversely wrested and diversified. This diversity of names may be reduced to four general heads.

First, a thing may enter into account for *matter* or *body,* as *living, sensible, rational, hot, cold, moved, quiet,* with all which names the word *matter* or *body* is understood, all such being names of matter.

Secondly, it may enter into account or be considered for some accident or quality which we conceive to be in it, as for *being moved,* for *being so long,* for *being hot,* etc.; and then, of the name of the thing itself, by a little change or wresting, we make a name for that accident which we consider; and for *living* put into the account *life;* for *moved, motion;* for *hot, heat;* for *long, length,* and the like; and all such names are the names of the accidents and properties by which one matter and body is distinguished from another. These are called *names abstract,* because severed, not from matter, but from the account of matter.

Thirdly, we bring into account the properties of our own bodies, whereby we make such distinction as, when anything is seen by us, we reckon not the thing itself but the sight, the color, the idea of it in the fancy; and when anything is heard, we reckon it not, but the hearing or sound only, which is our fancy or conception of it by the ear; and such are names of fancies.

Fourthly, we bring into account, consider, and give names to *names* themselves, and to *speeches,* for *general, universal, special, equivocal* are names of names. And *affirmation, interrogation, commandment, narration, syllogism, sermon, oration,* and many other such are names of speeches. And this is all the variety of names *positive,* which are put to mark somewhat which is in nature or may be feigned by the mind of man: as bodies that are or may be conceived to be; or, of bodies, the properties that are or may be feigned to be; or words and speech.

There be also other names, called *negative,* which are notes to signify that a word is not the name of the thing in question, as these words: *nothing, no man, infinite, indocible, three want four,* and the like, which are nevertheless of use in reckoning or in correcting of reckoning, and call to mind our past cogitations, though they be not names of anything because they make us refuse to admit of names not rightly used.

All other names are but insignificant sounds, and those of two sorts. One, when they are new and yet their meaning not explained by definition, whereof there have been abundance coined by Schoolmen and puzzled philosophers.

Another, when men make a name of two names whose significations are contradictory and inconsistent, as this name: an *incorporeal body* or, which is all one, an *incorporeal substance,* and a great number more. For whensoever any affirmation is false, the two names of which it is composed, put together and made one, signify nothing at all. For example, if it be a false affirmation to say *a quadrangle is round,* the word *round quadrangle* signifies nothing but is a mere sound. So likewise, if it be false to say that virtue can be poured, or blown up and down, the words *inpoured virtue, inblown virtue* are as absurd and insignificant as a *round quadrangle.* And therefore you shall hardly meet with a senseless and insignificant word that is not made up of some Latin or Greek names. . . .

When a man, upon the hearing of any speech, has those thoughts which the words of that speech and their connection were ordained and constituted to signify, then he is said to understand it, *understanding* being nothing else but conception caused by speech. And therefore if speech be peculiar to man, as for aught I know it is, then is understanding peculiar to him also. And therefore of absurd and false affirmations, in case they be universal, there can be no understanding, though many think they understand them when they do but repeat the words softly or con them in their mind.

What kinds of speeches signify the appetites, aversions, and passions of man's mind, and of their use and abuse, I shall speak when I have spoken of the passions.

The names of such things as affect us—that is, which please and displease us—because all men be not alike affected with the same thing nor the same man at all times, are in the common discourses of men of *inconstant* signification. For seeing all names are imposed to signify our conceptions, and all our affections are but conceptions, when we conceive the same things differently we can hardly avoid different naming of them. For though the nature of that we conceive be the same, yet the diversity of our reception of it, in respect of different constitutions of body and prejudices of opinion, gives everything a tincture of our different passions. And therefore in reasoning a man must take heed of words which, besides the signification of what we imagine of their nature, have a signification also of the nature, disposition, and interest of the speaker: such as are the names of virtues and vices, for one man calls *wisdom* what another calls *fear,* and one *cruelty* what another *justice,* one *prodigality* what another *magnanimity,* and one *gravity* what another *stupidity,* etc. And therefore such names can never be true grounds of any ratiocination. No more can metaphors and tropes of speech; but these are less dangerous, because they profess their inconstancy, which the other do not.

Chapter V.—OF REASON AND SCIENCE

When a man *reasons,* he does nothing else but conceive a sum total from *addition* of parcels, or conceive a remainder from *subtraction* of one sum from another; which, if it be done by words, is conceiving of the consequence of the names of all the parts to the name of the whole, or from the names of the whole and one part to the name of the other part. And though in some things, as in numbers, besides adding and subtracting men name other operations, as *multiplying* and *dividing,* yet they are the same; for multiplication is but adding together of things equal, and division but subtracting of one thing as often as we can. These operations are not incident to numbers only, but to all manner of things that can be added together and taken one out of another. For as arithmeticians teach to add and subtract in *numbers,* so the geometricians teach the same in *lines, figures* solid and superficial, *angles, proportions, times,* degrees of *swiftness, force, power,* and the like; the logicians teach the same in *consequences of words,* adding together two *names* to make an *affirmation,* and two *affirmations* to make a *syllogism,* and *many syllogisms* to make a *demonstration;* and from the *sum* or *conclusion* of a *syllogism* they subtract one *proposition* to find the other. Writers of politics add together *pactions* to find men's *duties,* and lawyers *laws* and *facts* to find what is *right* and *wrong* in the actions of private men. In sum, in what matter soever there is place for *addition* and *subtraction,* there also is place for *reason;* and where these have no place, there *reason* has nothing at all to do.

Out of all which we may define—that is to say, determine—what that is which is meant by this word *reason* when we reckon it among the faculties of the mind. For REASON, in this sense, is nothing but *reckoning*—that is, adding and subtracting—of the consequences of general names agreed upon for the *marking* and *signifying* of our thoughts; I say *marking* them when we reckon by ourselves, and *signifying* when we demonstrate or approve our reckonings to other men.

And as in arithmetic unpracticed men must, and professors themselves may often, err and cast up false, so also in any other subject of reasoning the ablest, most attentive, and most practiced men may deceive themselves and infer false conclusions; not but that reason itself is always right reason, as well as arithmetic is a certain and infallible art, but no one man's reason, nor the reason of any one number of men, makes the certainty, no more than an account is therefore well cast up because a great many men have unanimously approved it. And therefore as when there is a controversy in an account the parties must by their own accord set up, for right reason, the reason of some arbitrator or judge, to whose sentence they will both stand, or their controversy must either come to blows or be undecided for want of a right reason constituted by nature, so is it also in all debates of what kind soever. And when men that think themselves wiser than all others clamor and demand right reason for judge, yet seek no more but that things should be determined by no other men's reason but their own, it is as intolerable in the society of men as it is in play after trump is turned to use for trump on every occasion that suit whereof they have most in their hand. For they do nothing else that will have every of their passions, as it comes to bear sway in them, to be taken for right reason, and that in their own controversies, betraying their want of right reason by the claim they lay to it.

The use and end of reason is not the finding of the sum and truth of one or a few consequences remote from the first definitions and settled significations of names, but to begin at these and proceed from one consequence to another. For there can be no certainty of the last conclusion without a certainty of all those affirmations and negations on which it was grounded and inferred. As when a master of a family, in taking an account, casts up the sums of all the bills of expense into one sum, and not regarding how each bill is summed up by those that give them in account nor what it is he pays for, he advantages himself no more than if he allowed the account in gross, trusting to every of the accountants' skill and honesty; so also in reasoning of all other things he that takes up conclusions on the trust of authors, and does not fetch them from the first items in every reckoning, which are the significations of names settled by definitions, loses his labor; and does not know anything, but only believes.

When a man reckons without the use of words, which may be done in particular things, as when upon the sight of any one thing we conjecture what was likely to have preceded or is likely to follow upon it, if that which he thought likely to follow follows not, or that which he thought likely to have preceded it has not preceded it, this is called *error,* to which even the most prudent men are subject. But when we reason in words of general signification and fall upon a general inference which is false, though it be commonly called *error,* it is indeed an *absurdity* or senseless speech. For error is but a deception in presuming that somewhat is past or to come of which, though it were not past, or not to come, yet there was no impossibility discoverable. But when we make a general assertion, unless it be a true one, the possibility of it is inconceivable. And words whereby we conceive nothing but the sound are those we call *absurd, insignificant,* and *nonsense.* And therefore if a man should talk to me of a *round quadrangle,* or *accidents of bread in cheese,* or *immaterial substances,* or of *a free subject, a free will,* or any *free* but free from being hindered by opposition, I should not say he were in an error but that his words were without meaning—that is to say, absurd.

I have said before, in the second chapter, that a man did excel all other animals in this faculty: that when he conceived anything whatsoever, he was apt to inquire the consequences of it and what effects he could do with it. And now I add this other degree of the same excellence: that he can by words reduce the consequences he finds to general rules, called *theorems* or *aphorisms*—that is, he can reason or reckon not only in number but in all other things whereof one may be added unto or subtracted from another.

But this privilege is allayed by another, and that is, by the privilege of absurdity, to which no living creature is subject but man only. And of men, those are of all most subject to it that profess philosophy. For it is most true that Cicero says of them somewhere that there can be nothing so absurd but may be found in the books of philosophers. And the reason is manifest. For there is not one of them that begins his ratiocination from the definitions or explications of the names they are to use, which is a method that has been used only in geometry, whose conclusions have thereby been made indisputable.

1. The first cause of absurd conclusions I ascribe to the want of method in that they begin not their ratiocination from definitions—that is, from settled significations of their words—as if they could cast account without knowing the value of the numeral words *one, two,* and *three.*

And whereas all bodies enter into account upon divers considerations, which I have mentioned in the precedent chapter, these considerations being diversely named, divers absurdities proceed from the confusion and unfit connection of their names into assertions. And therefore,

2. The second cause of absurd assertions I ascribe to the giving of names of *bodies* to *accidents,* or of *accidents* to *bodies:* as they do that say *faith is infused* or *inspired* when nothing can be *poured* or *breathed* into anything, but body; and that *extension* is *body;* that *phantasms* are *spirits,* etc.

3. The third I ascribe to the giving of the names of the *accidents* of *bodies without us* to the *accidents* of our *own bodies:* as they do that say the *color is in the body, the sound is in the air,* etc.

4. The fourth, to the giving of the names of *bodies* to *names* or *speeches:* as they do that say that *there be things universal,* that a *living creature is genus* or *a general thing,* etc.

5. The fifth, to the giving of the names of *accidents* to *names* and *speeches:* as they do that say *the nature of a thing is its definition, a man's command is his will,* and the like.

6. The sixth, to the use of metaphors, tropes, and other rhetorical figures instead of words proper. For though it be lawful to say, for example, in common speech *the way goes or leads hither or thither,*

the proverb says this or that, whereas ways cannot go nor proverbs speak, yet in reckoning and seeking of truth such speeches are not to be admitted.

7. The seventh, to names that signify nothing but are taken up and learned by rote from the schools: as *hypostatical, transubstantiate, consubstantiate, eternal-now,* and the like canting of Schoolmen.

To him that can avoid these things it is not easy to fall into any absurdity, unless it be by the length of an account, wherein he may perhaps forget what went before. For all men by nature reason alike and well when they have good principles. For who is so stupid as both to mistake in geometry and also to persist in it when another detects his error to him?

By this it appears that reason is not, as sense and memory, born with us, nor gotten by experience only, as prudence is, but attained by industry: first in apt imposing of names, and secondly by getting a good and orderly method in proceeding from the elements, which are names, to assertions made by connection of one of them to another, and so to syllogisms, which are the connections of one assertion to another, till we come to a knowledge of all the consequences of names appertaining to the subject in hand; and that is it men call SCIENCE. And whereas sense and memory are but knowledge of fact, which is a thing past and irrevocable, *science* is the knowledge of consequences and dependence of one fact upon another, by which out of that we can presently do we know how to do something else when we will, or the like another time; because when we see how anything comes about, upon what causes and by what manner, when the like causes come into our power we see how to make it produce the like effects.

Children, therefore, are not endowed with reason at all till they have attained the use of speech, but are called reasonable creatures for the possibility apparent of having the use of reason in time to come. And the most part of men, though they have the use of reasoning a little way, as in numbering to some degree, yet it serves them to little use in common life, in which they govern themselves, some better, some worse, according to their differences of experience, quickness of memory, and inclinations to several ends, but specially according to good or evil fortune and the errors of one another. For as for *science* or certain rules of their actions, they are so far from it that they know not what it is. Geometry they have thought conjuring; but for other sciences, they who have not been taught the beginnings and some progress in them, that they may see how they be acquired and generated, are in this point like children that, having no thought of generation, are made believe by the women that their brothers and sisters are not born but found in the garden.

But yet they that have no *science* are in better and nobler condition with their natural prudence than men that, by misreasoning or by trusting them that reason wrong, fall upon false and absurd general rules. For ignorance of causes and of rules does not set men so far out of their way as relying on false rules and taking for causes of what they aspire to those that are not so, but rather causes of the contrary.

To conclude, the light of human minds is perspicuous words, but by exact definitions first snuffed and purged from ambiguity; *reason* is the *pace;* increase of *science,* the *way;* and the benefit of mankind, the *end*. And on the contrary, metaphors and senseless and ambiguous words are like *ignes fatui;* and reasoning upon them is wandering among innumerable absurdities; and their end, contention and sedition, or contempt.

As much experience is *prudence,* so is much science *sapience*. For though we usually have one name of wisdom for them both, yet the Latins did always distinguish between *prudentia* and *sapientia,* ascribing the former to experience, the latter to science. But to make their difference appear more clearly, let us suppose one man endowed with an excellent natural use and dexterity in handling his arms, and another to have added to that dexterity an acquired science of where he can offend or be offended by his adversary in every possible posture or guard; the ability of the former would be to the ability of the latter as prudence to sapience: both useful, but the latter infallible. But they that, trusting only to the authority of books, follow the blind blindly are like him that, trusting to the false rules of a master of fence, ventures presumptuously upon an adversary that either kills or disgraces him.

The signs of science are some certain and infallible, some uncertain. Certain, when he that pretends the science of anything can teach the same—that is to say, demonstrate the truth thereof perspicuously to another; uncertain, when only some particular events answer to his pretense, and upon many occasions prove so as he says they must. Signs of prudence are all uncertain, because to observe by experience and remember all circumstances that may alter the success is impossible. But in any business whereof a man has not infallible science to proceed by, to forsake his own natural judgment and be guided by general sentences read in authors and subject to many exceptions is a sign of folly and generally scorned by the name of pedantry. And even of those men themselves that in councils of the commonwealth love to show their reading of politics and history, very few do it in their domestic affairs where their particular interest is concerned, having prudence enough for their private affairs; but in public they study more the reputation of their own wit than the success of another's business.

Chapter VI.—OF THE INTERIOR BEGINNINGS OF VOLUNTARY MOTIONS COMMONLY CALLED THE PASSIONS, AND THE SPEECHES BY WHICH THEY ARE EXPRESSED

There be in animals two sorts of *motions* peculiar to them: one called *vital*, begun in generation and continued without interruption through their whole life—such as are the *course* of the *blood*, the *pulse*, the *breathing*, the *concoction*, *nutrition*, *excretion*, etc.—to which motions there needs no help of imagination; the other is *animal motion*, otherwise called *voluntary motion*—as to *go*, to *speak*, to *move* any of our limbs in such manner as is first fancied in our minds. That sense is motion in the organs and interior parts of man's body caused by the action of the things we see, hear, etc., and that fancy is but the relics of the same motion remaining after sense, has been already said in the first and second chapters. And because *going*, *speaking*, and the like voluntary motions depend always upon a precedent thought of *whither*, *which way*, and *what*, it is evident that the imagination is the first internal beginning of all voluntary motion. And although unstudied men do not conceive any motion at all to be there where the thing moved is invisible or the space it is moved in is, for the shortness of it, insensible, yet that does not hinder but that such motions are. For let a space be never so little, that which is moved over a greater space, whereof that little one is part, must first be moved over that. These small beginnings of motion within the body of man, before they appear in walking, speaking, striking, and other visible actions, are commonly called ENDEAVOR.

This endeavor, when it is toward something which causes it, is called APPETITE or DESIRE, the latter being the general name and the other oftentimes restrained to signify the desire of food, namely *hunger* and *thirst*. And when the endeavor is fromward something, it is generally called AVERSION. These words, *appetite* and *aversion*, we have from the Latins; and they both of them signify the motions, one of approaching, the other of retiring. . . . For nature itself does often press upon men those truths which afterwards, when they look for somewhat beyond nature, they stumble at. For the Schools find in mere appetite to go or move no actual motion at all; but because some motion they must acknowledge, they call it metaphorical motion, which is but an absurd speech, for though words may be called metaphorical, bodies and motions cannot.

That which men desire they are also said to LOVE, and to HATE those things for which they have aversion. So that desire and love are the same thing, save that by desire we always signify the absence of the object, by love most commonly the presence of the same. So also by aversion we signify the absence, and by hate the presence of the object.

Of appetites and aversions, some are born with men, as appetite of food, appetite of excretion, and exoneration, which may also and more properly be called aversions from somewhat they feel in their bodies; and some other appetites, not many. The rest, which are appetites of particular things, proceed from experience and trial of their effects upon themselves or other men. For of things we know not at all, or believe not to be, we can have no further desire than to taste and try. But aversion we have for things, not only which we know have hurt us, but also that we do not know whether they will hurt us or not.

Those things which we neither desire nor hate we are said to *contemn*, CONTEMPT being nothing else but an immobility or contumacy of the heart in resisting the action of certain things; and proceeding from that the heart is already moved otherwise by other more potent objects or from want of experience of them.

And because the constitution of a man's body is in continual mutation, it is impossible that all the same things should always cause in him the same appetites and aversions; much less can all men consent in the desire of almost any one and the same object.

But whatsoever is the object of any man's appetite or desire, that is it which he for his part calls *good;* and the object of his hate and aversion, *evil;* and of his contempt, *vile* and *inconsiderable*. For these words of good, evil, and contemptible are ever used with relation to the person that uses them, there being nothing simply and absolutely so, nor any common rule of good and evil to be taken from the nature of the objects themselves—but from the person of the man, where there is no commonwealth, or, in a commonwealth, from the person that represents it, or from an arbitrator or judge whom men disagreeing shall by consent set up and make his sentence the rule thereof. . . .

As in sense that which is really within us is, as I have said before, only motion caused by the action of external objects, but in appearance to the sight light and color, to the ear sound, to the nostril odor, etc., so when the action of the same object is continued from the eyes, ears, and other organs to the heart, the real effect there is nothing but motion or endeavor, which consists in appetite or aversion to or from the object moving. But the appearance or sense of that motion is that we either call *delight* or *trouble of mind*. . . .

Pleasure, therefore, or *delight* is the appearance or sense of good; and *molestation* or *displeasure* the appearance or sense of evil. And consequently all appetite, desire, and love is accompanied with some delight more or less, and all hatred and aversion with more or less displeasure and offense. . . .

Fear of power invisible, feigned by the mind or imagined from tales publicly allowed, RELIGION; not allowed, SUPERSTITION. And when the power imagined is truly such as we imagine, TRUE RELIGION.

Fear without the apprehension of why or what, PANIC TERROR, called so from the fables that make Pan the author of them; whereas in truth there is always in him that so fears, first, some apprehension of the cause, though the rest run away by example, everyone supposing his fellow to know why. And therefore this passion happens to none but in a throng or multitude of people. . . .

When in the mind of man appetites and aversions, hopes and fears concerning one and the same thing arise alternately, and divers good and evil consequences of the doing or omitting the thing propounded come successively into our thoughts, so that sometimes we have an appetite to it, sometimes an aversion from it, sometimes hope to be able to do it, sometimes despair or fear to attempt it—the whole sum of desires, aversions, hopes, and fears continued till the thing be either done or thought impossible is that we call DELIBERATION.

Therefore of things past there is no *deliberation*, because manifestly impossible to be changed; nor of things known to be impossible, or thought so, because men know or think such deliberation vain. But of things impossible which we think possible, we may deliberate, not knowing it is in vain. And it is called *deliberation* because it is a putting an end to the *liberty* we had of doing or omitting according to our own appetite or aversion.

This alternate succession of appetites, aversions, hopes, and fears is no less in other living creatures than in man, and therefore beasts also deliberate.

Every *deliberation* is then said to *end* when that whereof they deliberate is either done or thought impossible, because till then we retain the liberty of doing or omitting according to our appetite or aversion.

In *deliberation,* the last appetite or aversion immediately adhering to the action or to the omission thereof is that we call the WILL—the act, not the faculty, of *willing*. And beasts that have *deliberation* must necessarily also have *will*. The definition of the *will* given commonly by the Schools, that it is a *rational appetite,* is not good. For if it were, then could there be no voluntary act against reason. For a *voluntary act* is that which proceeds from the *will,* and no other. But if instead of a rational appetite we shall say an appetite resulting from a precedent deliberation, then the definition is the same that I have given here. *Will,* therefore, *is the last appetite in deliberating*. And though we say in common discourse a man had a will once to do a thing that nevertheless he forbore to do, yet that is properly but an inclination which makes no action voluntary, because the action depends not of it but of the last inclination or appetite. For if the intervenient appetites make any action voluntary, then by the same reason all intervenient aversions should make the same action involuntary; and so one and the same action should be both voluntary and involuntary.

By this it is manifest that not only actions that have their beginning from covetousness, ambition, lust, or other appetites to the thing propounded, but also those that have their beginning from aversion or fear of those consequences that follow the omission, are *voluntary actions*. . . .

And because in deliberation the appetites and aversions are raised by foresight of the good and evil consequences and sequels of the action whereof we deliberate, the good or evil effect thereof depends on the foresight of a long chain of consequences, of which very seldom any man is able to see to the end. But for so far as a man sees, if the good in those consequences be greater than the evil, the whole chain is that which writers call *apparent* or *seeming good*. And contrarily, when the evil exceeds the good the whole is *apparent* or *seeming evil,* so that he who has by experience or reason the greatest and surest prospect of consequences deliberates best himself and is able when he will to give the best counsel unto others.

Continual success in obtaining those things which a man from time to time desires—that is to say, continual prospering—is that men call FELICITY; I mean the felicity of this life. For there is no such thing as perpetual tranquillity of mind while we live here, because life itself it but motion and can never be without desire, nor without fear, no more than without sense. What kind of felicity God has ordained to them that devoutly honor him, a man shall no sooner know than enjoy, being joys that now are as incomprehensible as the word of Schoolmen, *beatifical vision,* is unintelligible. . . .

Chapter VII.—OF THE ENDS OR RESOLUTIONS OF DISCOURSE

Of all *discourse* governed by desire of knowledge there is at last an *end,* either by attaining or by giving over. And in the chain of discourse, wheresoever it be interrupted, there is an end for that time.

If the discourse be merely mental, it consists of thoughts that the thing will be and will not be, or that it has been and has not been, alternately. So that wheresoever you break off the chain of a man's discourse, you leave him in a presumption of *it will be* or *it will not be,* or *it has been* or *has not been.* All which is *opinion.* And that which is alternate appetite, in deliberating concerning good and evil, the same is alternate opinion in the inquiry of the truth of *past* and *future.* And as the last appetite in deliberation is called the *will,* so the last opinion in search of the truth of past and future is called the JUDGMENT or *resolute* and *final sentence* of him that *discourses.* And as the whole chain of appetites alternate in the question of good or bad is called *deliberation,* so the whole chain of opinions alternate in the question of true or false is called DOUBT.

No discourse whatsoever can end in absolute knowledge of fact, past or to come. For as for the knowledge of fact, it is originally sense, and ever after memory. And for the knowledge of consequence, which I have said before is called science, it is not absolute but conditional. No man can know by discourse that this or that is, has been, or will be, which is to know absolutely, but only that if this be, that is; if this has been, that has been; if this shall be, that shall be—which is to know conditionally, and that not the consequence of one thing to another, but of one name of a thing to another name of the same thing.

And therefore when the discourse is put into speech and begins with the definitions of words, and proceeds by connection of the same into general affirmations, and of these again into syllogisms, the end or last sum is called the conclusion; and the thought of the mind by it signified is that conditional knowledge, or knowledge of the consequence of words, which is commonly called SCIENCE. But if the first ground of such discourse be not definitions, or if the definitions be not rightly joined together into syllogisms, then the end or conclusion is again OPINION, namely of the truth of somewhat said, though sometimes in absurd and senseless words without possibility of being understood. When two or more men know of one and the same fact, they are said to be CONSCIOUS of it one to another, which is as much as to know it together. And because such are fittest witnesses of the facts of one another or of a third, it was and ever will be reputed a very evil act for any man to speak against his *conscience,* or to corrupt or force another so to do, insomuch that the plea of conscience has been always hearkened unto very diligently in all times. Afterwards, men made use of the same word metaphorically for the knowledge of their own secret facts and secret thoughts; and therefore it is rhetorically said that the conscience is a thousand witnesses. And last of all, men vehemently in love with their own new opinions, though never so absurd, and obstinately bent to maintain them, gave those their opinions also that reverenced name of conscience, as if they would have it seem unlawful to change or speak against them, and so pretend to know they are true when they know at most but that they think so.

When a man's discourse begins not at definitions, it begins either at some other contemplation of his own—and then it is still called opinion—or it begins at some saying of another, of whose ability to know the truth and of whose honesty in not deceiving he doubts not; and then the discourse is not so much concerning the thing as the person, and the resolution is called BELIEF and FAITH: *faith in* the man, *belief* both *of* the man and *of* the truth of what he says. So that in belief are two opinions: one of the saying of the man, the other of his virtue. To *have faith in,* or *trust to,* or *believe a man* signify the same thing—namely, an opinion of the veracity of the man—but to *believe what is said* signifies only an opinion of the truth of the saying. But we are to observe that this phrase, *I believe in,* . . . [is] never used but in the writings of divines. Instead . . . in other writings are put *I believe him, I trust him, I have faith in him, I rely on him;* . . . and that this singularity of the ecclesiastic use of the word has raised many disputes about the right object of the Christian faith.

But by *believing in,* as it is in the creed, is meant, not trust in the person, but confession and acknowledgment of the doctrine. For not only Christians, but all manner of men do so believe in God as to hold all for truth they hear him say, whether they understand it or not, which is all the faith and trust can possibly be had in any person whatsoever; but they do not all believe the doctrine of the creed.

From whence we may infer that when we believe any saying, whatsoever it be, to be true from arguments taken, not from the thing itself or from the principles of natural reason, but from the authority and good opinion we have of him that has said it, then is the speaker or person we believe in or trust in, and whose word we take, the object of our faith; and the honor done in believing is done to him only. And consequently, when we believe that the Scriptures are the word of God, having no immediate revelation from God himself, our belief, faith, and trust is in the Church, whose word we take and acquiesce therein. And they that believe that which a prophet relates unto them in the name of God take the word of the prophet, do honor to him, and in him trust and believe touching the truth of what he relates, whether he be a true or a false prophet. And so it is also with all other history. For if I should not believe all that is written by historians of the glorious acts of Alexander or Caesar, I do not think the ghost of Alexander or Caesar had any just cause to be offended, or anybody else but the historian. If Livy say the gods made once a cow speak and we believe it not, we distrust not God therein but Livy. So that it is evident that whatsoever we believe upon no other reason than what is drawn from authority of men only and their writings, whether they be sent from God or not, is faith in men only. . . .

XII

PASCAL

Blaise Pascal (1623-1662), born in Clermont-Ferrand and raised in Paris, was the son of a prominent man who was closely associated with many of the leading scientists of the day. Young Pascal was a mathematical prodigy, completing a work on conic sections at sixteen and inventing an arithmetical machine when nineteen. During 1644-1646, he studied and wrote on the nature of the vacuum. In 1648, he performed the crucial experiment with the barometer, having it carried up Le Puy-de Dome. Besides his mathematical and scientific work, Pascal and his family became involved in the Jansenist movement, an austere, Augustinian form of Catholicism. After a mystical experience in Paris, he became completely dedicated to Jansenism, frequently staying at its monastery at Port-Royal from 1655 onwards. There he wrote much of his *Provincial Letters,* attacking Jesuit moral theories, and his *Pensées* (from which the selections below are taken), a defense of Christianity. The *Pensées* were incomplete when Pascal died and consist of various discussions and comments on philosophy, science, religion, morality, and so forth. The translation is by W. F. Trotter.

Pensées

195[1]

Before entering into the proofs of the Christian religion, I find it necessary to point out the sinfulness of those men who live in indifference to the search for truth in a matter which is so important to them, and which touches them so nearly.

Of all their errors, this doubtless is the one which most convicts them of foolishness and blindness, and in which it is easiest to confound them by the first glimmerings of common sense, and by natural feelings.

For it is not to be doubted that the duration of this life is but a moment; that the state of death is eternal, whatever may be its nature; and that thus all our actions and thoughts must take such different directions according to the state of that eternity, that it is impossible to take one step with sense and judgment, unless we regulate our course by the truth of that point which ought to be our ultimate end.

There is nothing clearer than this; and thus, according to the principles of reason, the conduct of men is wholly unreasonable, if they do not take another course.

On this point, therefore, we condemn those who live without thought of the ultimate end of life, who let themselves be guided by their own inclinations and their own pleasures without reflection and without concern, and, as if they could annihilate eternity by turning away their thought from it, think only of making themselves happy for the moment.

Yet this eternity exists, and death, which must open into it, and threatens them every hour, must in a little time infallibly put them under the dreadful necessity of being either annihilated or unhappy for ever, without knowing which of these eternities is for ever prepared for them.

This is a doubt of terrible consequence. They are in peril of eternal

1. The numbering is according to the Brunschvicg edition.

woe; and thereupon, as if the matter were not worth the trouble, they neglect to inquire whether this is one of those opinions which people receive with too credulous a facility, or one of those which, obscure in themselves, have a very firm, though hidden, foundation. Thus they know not whether there be truth or falsity in the matter, nor whether there be strength or weakness in the proofs. They have them before their eyes; they refuse to look at them; and in that ignorance they choose all that is necessary to fall into this misfortune if it exists, to await death to make trial of it, yet to be very content in this state, to make profession of it, and indeed to boast of it. Can we think seriously on the importance of this subject without being horrified at conduct so extravagant?

This resting in ignorance is a monstrous thing, and they who pass their life in it must be made to feel its extravagance and stupidity, by having it shown to them, so that they may be confounded by the sight of their folly. For this is how men reason, when they choose to live in such ignorance of what they are, and, without seeking enlightenment. "I know not," they say. . . .

199

Let us imagine a number of men in chains, and all condemned to death, where some are killed each day in the sight of the others, and those who remain see their own fate in that of their fellows, and wait their turn, looking at each other sorrowfully and without hope. It is an image of the condition of men.

200

A man in a dungeon, ignorant whether his sentence be pronounced, and having only one hour to learn it, but this hour enough, if he know that it is pronounced, to obtain its repeal, would act unnaturally in spending that hour, not in ascertaining his sentence, but in playing piquet. So it is against nature that man, etc. It is making heavy the hand of God.

Thus not only the zeal of those who seek Him proves God, but also the blindness of those who seek Him not. . . .

222

Atheists.—What reason have they for saying that we cannot rise from the dead? What is more difficult, to be born or to rise again; that what has never been should be, or that what has been should be again? Is it more difficult to come into existence that to return to it? Habit makes the one appear easy to us; want of habit makes the other impossible. A popular way of thinking!

Why cannot a virgin bear a child? Does a hen not lay eggs without a cock? What distinguishes these outwardly from others? And who has told us that the hen may not form the germ as well as the cock? . . .

225

Atheism shows strength of mind, but only to a certain degree. . . .

233

Infinite–nothing.–Our soul is cast into a body, where it finds number, time, dimension. Thereupon it reasons, and calls this nature, necessity, and can believe nothing else.

Unity joined to infinity adds nothing to it, no more than one foot to an infinite measure. The finite is annihilated in the presence of the infinite, and becomes a pure nothing. So our spirit before God, so our justice before divine justice. There is not so great a disproportion between our justice and that of God, as between unity and infinity.

The justice of God must be vast like His compassion. Now justice to the outcast is less vast, and ought less to offend our feelings than mercy towards the elect.

We know that there is an infinite, and are ignorant of its nature. As we know it to be false that numbers are finite, it is therefore true that there is an infinity in number. But we do not know what it is. It is false that it is even, it is false that it is odd; for the addition of a unit can make no change in its nature. Yet it is a number, and every number is odd or even (this is certainly true of every finite number). So we may well know that there is a God without knowing what He is. Is there not one substantial truth, seeing there are so many things which are not the truth itself?

We know then the existence and nature of the finite, because we also are finite and have extension. We know the existence of the infinite, and are ignorant of its nature, because it has extension like us, but not limits like us. But we know neither the existence nor the nature of God, because He has neither extension nor limits.

But by faith we know His existence; in glory we shall know His nature. Now, I have already shown that we may well know the existence of a thing, without knowing its nature.

Let us now speak according to natural lights.

If there is a God, He is infinitely incomprehensible, since, having neither parts nor limits, He has no affinity to us. We are then incapable of knowing either what He is or if He is. This being so, who will dare to undertake the decision of the question? Not we, who have no affinity to Him.

Who then will blame Christians for not being able to give a reason for their belief, since they profess a religion for which they cannot give a reason? They declare, in expounding it to the world, that it is a foolishness, *stultitiam;* and then you complain that they do not prove it! If they proved it, they would not keep their word; it is in lacking proofs, that they are not lacking in sense. "Yes, but although this excuses those who offer it as such, and takes away from them the blame of putting it forward without reason, it does not excuse those who receive it." Let us then examine this point, and say, "God is, or He is not." But to which side shall we incline? Reason can decide nothing here. There is an infinite chaos which separated us. A game is being played at the extremity of this infinite distance where heads or tails will turn up. What will you wager? According to reason, you can do neither the one thing nor the other; according to reason, you can defend neither of the propositions.

Do not then reprove for error those who have made a choice; for you know nothing about it. "No, but I blame them for having made, not this choice, but a choice; for again both he who chooses heads and he who chooses tails are equally at fault, they are both in the wrong. The true course is not to wager at all."

Yes; but you must wager. It is not optional. You are embarked. Which will you choose then? Let us see. Since you must choose, let us see which interests you least. You have two things to lose, the true and the good; and two things to stake, your reason and your will, your knowledge and your happiness; and your nature has two things to shun, error and misery. Your reason is no more shocked in choosing one rather than the other, since you must of necessity choose. This is one point settled. But your happiness? Let us weigh the gain and the loss in wagering that God is. Let us estimate these two chances. If you gain, you gain all; if you lose, you lose nothing. Wager, then, without hesitation that He is.—"That is very fine. Yes, I must wager; but I may perhaps wager too much."—Let us see. Since there is an equal risk of gain and of loss, if you had only to gain two lives, instead of one, you might still wager. But if there were three lives to gain, you would have to play (since you are under the necessity of playing), and you would be imprudent, when you are forced to play, not to chance your life to gain three at a game where there is an equal risk of loss and gain. But there is an eternity of life and happiness. And this being so, if there were an infinity of chances, of which one only would be for you, you would still be right in wagering one to win two, and you would act stupidly, being obliged to play, by refusing to stake one life against three at a game in which out of an infinity of chances there is one for you, if there were an infinity of an infinitely happy life to gain. But there is here an infinity of an infinitely happy life to gain, a chance of gain against a finite number of chances of loss, and what you stake is finite. It is all divided; wherever the infinite is and there is not an infinity of chances of loss against that of gain, there is no time to hesitate, you must give all. And thus, when one is forced to play, he must renounce reason to preserve his life, rather than risk it for infinite gain, as likely to happen as the loss of nothingness.

For it is no use to say it is uncertain if we will gain, and it is certain that we risk, and that the infinite distance between the *certainty* of what is staked and the *uncertainty* of what will be gained, equals the finite good which is certainly staked against the uncertain infinite. It is not so, as every player stakes a certainty to gain an uncertainty, and yet he stakes a finite certainty to gain a finite uncertainty, without transgressing against reason. There is not an infinite distance between the certainty staked and the uncertainty of the gain; that is untrue. In truth, there is an infinity between the certainty of gain and the certainty of loss. But the uncertainty of the gain is proportioned to the certainty of the stake according to the proportion of the chances of gain and loss. Hence it comes that, if there are as many risks on one side as on the other, the course is to play even; and then the certainty of the stake is equal to the uncertainty of the gain, so far is it from fact that there is an infinite distance between them. And so our proposition is of infinite force, when there is the finite to stake in a game where there are equal risks of gain and of loss, and the infinite to gain. This is demonstrable; and if men are capable of any truths, this is one.

"I confess it, I admit it. But, still, is there no means of seeing the faces of the cards?"—Yes, Scripture and the rest, etc. "Yes, but I have my hands tied and my mouth closed; I am forced to wager, and am not free. I am not released, and am so made that I cannot believe. What, then, would you have me do?"

True. But at least learn your inability to believe, since reason brings you to this, and yet you cannot believe. Endeavour then to convince yourself, not by increase of proofs of God, but by the abatement of your passions. You would like to attain faith, and do not know the way; you would like to cure yourself of unbelief, and ask the remedy for it. Learn of those who have been found like you, and who now stake all their possessions. These are people who know the way which you would follow, and who are cured of an ill of which you would be cured. Follow the way by which they began; by acting as if they believed, taking the holy water, having masses said, etc. Even this will naturally make you believe, and deaden your acuteness.—"But this is what I am afraid of."—And why? What have you to lose?

But to show you that this leads you there, it is this which will lessen the passions, which are your stumbling-blocks.

The end of this discourse.—Now, what harm will befall you in taking this side? You will be faithful, honest, humble, grateful, generous, a sincere friend, truthful. Certainly you will not have those poisonous pleasures, glory and luxury; but will you not have others? I will tell you that you will thereby gain in this life, and that, at each step you take on this road, you will see so great certainty of gain, so much nothingness in what you risk, that you will at last recognise that you have wagered for something certain and infinite, for which you have given nothing.

"Ah! This discourse transports me, charms me," etc.

If this discourse pleases you and seems impressive, know that it is made by a man who has knelt, both before and after it, in prayer to that Being, infinite and without parts, before whom he lays all he has, for you also to lay before Him all you have for your own good and for His glory, that so strength may be given to lowliness.

234

If we must not act save on a certainty, we ought not to act on religion, for it is not certain. But how many things we do on an uncertainty, sea voyages, battles! I say then we must do nothing at all, for nothing is certain, and that there is more certainty in religion than there is as to whether we may see to-morrow; for it is not certain that we may see to-morrow, and it is certainly possible that we may not see it. We cannot say as much about religion. It is not certain that it is; but who will venture to say that it is certainly possible that it is not? Now when we work for to-morrow, and so on an uncertainty, we act reasonably; for we ought to work for an uncertainty according to the doctrine of chance which was demonstrated above.

Saint Augustine has seen that we work for an uncertainty, on sea, in battle, etc. But he has not seen the doctrine of chance which proves that we should do so. Montaigne has seen that we are shocked at a fool, and that habit is all-powerful; but he has not seen the reason of this effect.

All these persons have seen the effects, but they have not seen the causes. They are, in comparison with those who have discovered the causes, as those who have only eyes are in comparison with those who have intellect. For the effects are perceptible by sense, and the causes are visible only to the intellect. And although these effects are seen by the mind, this mind is, in comparison with the mind which sees the causes, as the bodily senses are in comparison with the intellect. . . .

268

Submission.—We must know where to doubt, where to feel certain, where to submit. He who does not do so, understands not the force of reason. There are some who offend against these three rules, either by affirming everything as demonstrative, from want of knowing what demonstration is; or by doubting everything, from want of knowing where to submit; or by submitting in everything, from want of knowing where they must judge.

269

Submission is the use of reason in which consists true Christianity. . . .

272

There is nothing so conformable to reason as this disavowal of reason.

273

If we submit everything to reason, our religion will have no mysterious and supernatural element. If we offend the principles of reason, our religion will be absurd and ridiculous. . . .

277

The heart has its reasons, which reason does not know. We feel it in a thousand things. I say that the heart naturally loves the Universal Being, and also itself naturally, according as it gives itself to them; and it hardens itself against one or the other at its will. You have rejected the one, and kept the other. Is it by reason that you love yourself? . . .

282

We know truth, not only by the reason, but also by the heart, and it is in this last way that we know first principles; and reason, which has no part in it, tries in vain to impugn them. The sceptics, who have only this for their object, labour to no purpose. We know that we do not dream, and however impossible it is for us to prove it by reason, this inability demonstrates only the weakness of our reason, but not, as they affirm, the uncertainty of all our knowledge. For the knowledge of first principles, as space, time, motion, number, is as sure as any of those which we get from reasoning. And reason must trust these intuitions of the heart, and must base them on every argument. (We have intuitive knowledge of the tri-dimensional nature of space, and of the infinity of number, and reason then shows that there are no two square numbers one of which is double of the other. Principles are intuited, propositions are inferred, all with certainty, though in different ways.) And it is as useless and absurd for reason to demand from the heart proofs of her first principles, before admitting them, as it would be for the heart to demand from reason an intuition of all demonstrated propositions before accepting them.

This inability ought, then, to serve only to humble reason, which would judge all, but not to impugn our certainty, as if only reason were capable of instructing us. Would to God, on the contrary, that we had never need of it, and that we knew everything by instinct and intuition! But nature has refused us this boon. On the contrary, she has given us but very little knowledge of this kind; and all the rest can be acquired only by reasoning.

Therefore, those to whom God has imparted religion by intuition are very fortunate, and justly convinced. But to those who do not have it, we can give it only by reasoning, waiting for God to give them spiritual insight, without which faith is only human, and useless for salvation. . . .

374

What astonishes me most is to see that all the world is not astonished at its own weakness. Men act seriously, and each follows his own mode of life, not because it is in fact good to follow since it is the custom, but as if each man knew certainly where reason and justice are. They find themselves continually deceived, and by a comical humility think it is their own fault, and not that of the art which they claim always to possess. But it is well there are so many such people in the world, who are not sceptics for the glory of scepticism, in order to show that man is quite capable of the most extravagant opinions, since he is capable of believing that he is not in a state of natural and inevitable weakness, but, on the contrary, of natural wisdom.

Nothing fortifies scepticism more than that there are some who are not sceptics; if all were so, they would be wrong. . . .

387

[It may be that there are true demonstrations; but this is not certain. Thus, this proves nothing else but that it is not certain that all is uncertain, to the glory of scepticism. . . .][2]

394

All the principles of sceptics, stoics, atheists, etc., are true. But their conclusions are false, because the opposite principles are also true.

395

Instinct, reason.—We have an incapacity of proof, insurmountable by all dogmatism. We have an idea of truth, invincible to all scepticism. . . .

414

Men are so necessarily mad, that not to be mad would amount to another form of madness. . . .

422

It is good to be tired and wearied by the vain search after the true good, that we may stretch out our arms to the Redeemer. . . .

432

Scepticism is true; for, after all, men before Jesus Christ did not know where they were, nor whether they were great or small. And those who have said the one or the other, knew nothing abóut it, and guessed without reason and by chance. They also erred always in excluding the one or the other.

Quod ergo ignorantes, quaeritis, religio annuntiat vobis. . . .

434

The chief arguments of the sceptics—I pass over the lesser ones—are that we have no certainty of the truth of these principles apart from faith and revelation, except in so far as we naturally perceive

2. Brackets indicate passages Pascal crossed out or erased in his manuscript.

them in ourselves. Now this natural intuition is not a convincing proof of their truth; since, having no certainty, apart from faith, whether man was created by a good God, or by a wicked demon, or by chance, it is doubtful whether these principles given to us are true, or false, or uncertain, according to our origin. Again, no person is certain, apart from faith, whether he is awake or sleeps, seeing that during sleep we believe that we are awake as firmly as we do when we *are* awake; we believe that we see space, figure, and motion; we are aware of the passage of time, we measure it, and in fact we act as if we were awake. So that half of our life being passed in sleep, we have on our own admission no idea of truth, whatever we may imagine. As all our intuitions are then illusions, who knows whether the other half of our life, in which we think we are awake, is not another sleep a little different from the former, from which we awake when we suppose ourselves asleep?

[And who doubts that, if we dreamt in company, and the dreams chanced to agree, which is common enough, and if we were always alone when awake, we should believe that matters were reversed? In short, as we often dream that we dream, heaping dream upon dream, may it not be that this half of our life, wherein we think ourselves awake, is itself only a dream on which the others are grafted, from which we wake at death, during which we have as few principles of truth and good as during natural sleep, these different thoughts which disturb us being perhaps only illusions like the flight of time and the vain fancies of our dreams?]

These are the chief arguments on one side and the other.

I omit minor ones, such as the sceptical talk against the impressions of custom, education, manners, country, and the like. Though these influence the majority of common folk, who dogmatise only on shallow foundations, they are upset by the least breath of the sceptics. We have only to see their books if we are not sufficiently convinced of this, and we shall very quickly become so, perhaps too much.

I notice the only strong point of the dogmatists, namely, that, speaking in good faith and sincerely, we cannot doubt natural principles. Against this the sceptics set up in one word the uncertainty of our origin, which includes that of our nature. The dogmatists have been trying to answer this objection ever since the world began.

So there is open war among men, in which each must take a part, and side either with dogmatism or scepticism. For he who thinks to remain neutral is above all a sceptic. This neutrality is the essence of the sect; he who is not against them is essentially for them. [In this appears their advantage.] They are not for themselves; they are neutral, indifferent, in suspense as to all things, even themselves being no exception.

What then shall man do in this state? Shall he doubt everything? Shall he doubt whether he is awake, whether he is being pinched, or whether he is being burned? Shall he doubt whether he doubts? Shall he doubt whether he exists? We cannot go so far as that; and I lay it down as a fact that there never has been a real complete sceptic. Nature sustains our feeble reason, and prevents it raving to this extent.

Shall he then say, on the contrary, that he certainly possesses truth —he who, when pressed ever so little, can show no title to it, and is forced to let go his hold?

What a chimera then is man! What a novelty! What a monster, what a chaos, what a contradiction, what a prodigy! Judge of all things, imbecile worm of the earth; depositary of truth, a sink of uncertainty and error; the pride and refuse of the universe!

Who will unravel this tangle? Nature confutes the sceptics, and reason confutes the dogmatists. What then will you become, O men! who try to find out by your natural reason what is your true condition? You cannot avoid one of these sects, nor adhere to one of them.

Know then, proud man, what a paradox you are to yourself. Humble yourself, weak reason; be silent, foolish nature; learn that man infinitely transcends man, and learn from your Master your true condition, of which you are ignorant. Hear God.

For in fact, if man had never been corrupt, he would enjoy in his innocence both truth and happiness with assurance; and if man had always been corrupt, he would have no idea of truth or bliss. But, wretched as we are, and more so than if there were no greatness in our condition, we have an idea of happiness, and cannot reach it. We perceive an image of truth, and possess only a lie. Incapable of absolute ignorance and of certain knowledge, we have thus been manifestly in a degree of perfection from which we have unhappily fallen.

It is, however, an astonishing thing that the mystery furthest removed from our knowledge, namely, that of the transmission of sin, should be a fact without which we can have no knowledge of ourselves. For it is beyond doubt that there is nothing which more shocks our reason than to say that the sin of the first man has rendered guilty those, who, being so removed from this source, seem incapable of participation in it. This transmission does not only seem to us impossible, it seems also very unjust. For what is more contrary to the rules of our miserable justice than to damn eternally an infant incapable of will, for a sin wherein he seems to have so little a share, that it was committed six thousand years before he was in existence? Certainly nothing offends us more rudely than this doctrine; and yet, without this mystery, the most incomprehensible of all, we are incomprehensible to ourselves. The knot of our condition takes its twists and turns in this abyss, so that man is more inconceivable without this mystery than this mystery is inconceivable to man.

[Whence it seems that God, willing to render the difficulty of our existence unintelligible to ourselves, has concealed the knot so high, or, better speaking, so low, that we are quite incapable of reaching it; so that it is not by the proud exertions of our reason, but by the simple submissions of reason, that we can truly know ourselves.

These foundations, solidly established on the inviolable authority of religion, make us know that there are two truths of faith equally certain: the one, that man, in the state of creation, or in that of grace, is raised above all nature, made like unto God and sharing in His divinity; the other, that in the state of corruption and sin, he is fallen from this state and made like unto the beasts. . . .

XIII

SPINOZA

Baruch (Benedict) Spinoza (1632-1677) was born and grew up in the Spanish- and Portuguese-Jewish community of Amsterdam. Originally the star student of its Hebrew school, he developed heretical ideas, and was expelled in 1656. He moved away, living quietly earning his living grinding lenses, studying philosophy, science, and theology, and corresponding with leading thinkers all over the world. His *Tractatus-Theologico-Politicus,* published in 1670, was apparently a revised version of his lost, original reply to the Amsterdam Synagogue. The *Ethics,* the full version of his metaphysical system, was only published after his death, but had circulated in manuscript versions earlier. This translation is by R. H. M. Elwes.

Theologico-Political Treatise

PREFACE

Men would never be superstitious, if they could govern all their circumstances by set rules, or if they were always favoured by fortune: but being frequently driven into straits where rules are useless, and being often kept fluctuating pitiably between hope and fear by the uncertainty of fortune's greedily coveted favours, they are consequently, for the most part, very prone to credulity. The human mind is readily swayed this way or that in times of doubt, especially when hope and fear are struggling for the mastery, though usually it is boastful, over-confident, and vain.

This as a general fact I suppose everyone knows, though few, I believe, know their own nature; no one can have lived in the world without observing that most people, when in prosperity, are so over-brimming with wisdom (however inexperienced they may be), that they take every offer of advice as a personal insult, whereas in adversity they know not where to turn, but beg and pray for counsel from every passer-by. No plan is then too futile, too absurd, or too fatuous for their adoption; the most frivolous causes will raise them to hope, or plunge them into despair—if anything happens during their fright which reminds them of some past good or ill, they think it portends a happy or unhappy issue, and therefore (though it may have proved abortive a hundred times before) style it a lucky or unlucky omen. Anything which excites their astonishment they believe to be a portent signifying the anger of the gods or of the Supreme Being, and, mistaking superstition for religion, account it impious not to avert the evil with prayer and sacrifice. Signs and wonders of this sort they conjure up perpetually, till one might think Nature as mad as themselves, they interpret her so fantastically.

Thus it is brought prominently before us, that superstition's chief victims are those persons who greedily covet temporal advantages;

they it is, who (especially when they are in danger, and cannot help themselves) are wont with prayers and womanish tears to implore help from God: upbraiding Reason as blind, because she cannot show a sure path to the shadows they pursue, and rejecting human wisdom as vain; but believing the phantoms of imagination, dreams, and other childish absurdities, to be the very oracles of Heaven. As though God had turned away from the wise, and written His decrees, not in the mind of man but in the entrails of beasts, or left them to be proclaimed by the inspiration and instinct of fools, madmen, and birds. Such is the unreason to which terror can drive mankind!

Superstition, then, is engendered, preserved, and fostered by fear. . . .

The origin of superstition above given affords us a clear reason for the fact, that it comes to all men naturally, though some refer its rise to a dim notion of God, universal to mankind, and also tends to show, that it is no less inconsistent and variable than other mental hallucinations and emotional impulses, and further that it can only be maintained by hope, hatred, anger, and deceit; since it springs, not from reason, but solely from the more powerful phases of emotion. Furthermore, we may readily understand how difficult it is, to maintain on the same course men prone to every form of credulity. For, as the mass of mankind remains always at about the same pitch of misery, it never assents long to any one remedy, but is always best pleased by a novelty which has not yet proved illusive.

This element of inconsistency has been the cause of many terrible wars and revolutions. . . . Immense pains have therefore been taken to counteract this evil by investing religion, whether true or false, with such pomp and ceremony, that it may rise superior to every shock, and be always observed with studious reverence by the whole people—a system which has been brought to great perfection by the Turks, for they consider even controversy impious, and so clog men's minds with dogmatic formulas, that they leave no room for sound reason, not even enough to doubt with. . . .

Now, seeing that we have the rare happiness of living in a republic, where everyone's judgment is free and unshackled, where each may worship God as his conscience dictates, and where freedom is esteemed before all things dear and precious, I have believed that I should be undertaking no ungrateful or unprofitable task, in demonstrating that not only can such freedom be granted without prejudice to the public peace, but also, that without such freedom, piety cannot flourish nor the public peace be secure.

Such is the chief conclusion I seek to establish in this treatise; but, in order to reach it, I must first point out the misconceptions which, like scars of our former bondage, still disfigure our notion of religion, and must expose the false views about the civil authority which many have most impudently advocated, endeavouring to turn the mind of the people, still prone to heathen superstition, away from its legitimate rulers, and so bring us again into slavery. . . .

I have often wondered, that persons who make a boast of professing the Christian religion, namely, love, joy, peace, temperance, and charity to all men, should quarrel with such rancorous animosity, and display daily towards one another such bitter hatred, that this, rather than the virtues they claim, is the readiest criterion of their faith. Matters have long since come to such a pass, that one can only pronounce a man Christian, Turk, Jew, or Heathen, by his general appearance and attire, by his frequenting this or that place of worship, or employing the phraseology of a particular sect—as for manner of life, it is in all cases the same. Inquiry into the cause of this anomaly leads me unhesitatingly to ascribe it to the fact, that the ministries of the Church are regarded by the masses merely as dignities, her offices as posts of emolument—in short, popular religion may be summed up as respect for ecclesiastics. The spread of this misconception inflamed every worthless fellow with an intense desire to enter holy orders, and thus the love of diffusing God's religion degenerated into sordid avarice and ambition. Every church became a theatre, where orators, instead of church teachers, harangued, caring not to instruct the people, but striving to attract admiration, to bring opponents to public scorn, and to preach only novelties and paradoxes, such as would tickle the ears of their congregation. This state of things necessarily stirred up an amount of controversy, envy, and hatred, which no lapse of time could appease; so that we can scarcely wonder that of the old religion nothing survives but its outward forms (even these, in the mouth of the multitude, seem rather adulation than adoration of the Deity), and that faith has become a mere compound of credulity and prejudices—aye, prejudices too, which degrade man from rational being to beast, which completely stifle the power of judgment between true and false, which seem, in fact, carefully fostered for the purpose of extinguishing the last spark of reason! Piety, great God! and religion are become a tissue of ridiculous mysteries; men, who flatly despise reason, who reject and turn away from understanding as naturally corrupt, these, I say, these of all men, are thought, O lie most horrible! to possess light from on High. Verily, if they had but one spark of light from on High, they would not insolently rave, but would learn to worship God more wisely, and would be as marked among their fellows for mercy as they now are for malice; if they were concerned for their opponents' souls, instead of for their own reputations, they would no longer fiercely persecute, but rather be filled with pity and compassion.

Furthermore, if any Divine light were in them, it would appear from their doctrine. I grant that they are never tired of professing their wonder at the profound mysteries of Holy Writ; still I cannot discover that they teach anything but speculations of Platonists and Aristotelians, to which (in order to save their credit for Christianity) they have made Holy Writ conform; not content to rave with the Greeks themselves, they want to make the prophets rave also; showing conclusively, that never even in sleep have they caught a glimpse of Scripture's Divine nature. The very vehemence of their admiration for the mysteries plainly attests, that their belief in the Bible is a formal assent rather than a living faith: and the fact is made still more apparent by their laying down beforehand, as a foundation for the study and true interpretation of Scripture, the principle that it is in every passage true and divine. Such a doctrine should be reached only after strict scrutiny and thorough comprehension of the Sacred Books (which would teach it much better, for they stand in need of no human fictions), and not be set up on the threshold, as it were, of inquiry.

As I pondered over the facts that the light of reason is not only despised, but by many even execrated as a source of impiety, that human commentaries are accepted as divine records, and that credulity is extolled as faith; as I marked the fierce controversies of philosophers raging in Church and State, the source of bitter hatred and dissension, the ready instruments of sedition and other ills innumerable, I determined to examine the Bible afresh in a careful, impartial, and unfettered spirit, making no assumptions concerning it, and attributing to it no doctrines, which I do not find clearly therein set down. With these precautions I constructed a method of Scriptural interpretation, and thus equipped proceeded to inquire—What is prophecy? in what sense did God reveal Himself to the prophets, and why were these particular men chosen by Him? Was it on account of the sublimity of their thoughts about the Deity and nature, or was it solely on account of their piety? These questions being answered, I was easily able to conclude, that the authority of the prophets has weight only in matters of morality, and that their speculative doctrines affect us little. . . .

Having thus laid bare the bases of belief, I draw the conclusion that Revelation has obedience for its sole object, and therefore, in purpose no less than in foundation and method, stands entirely aloof from ordinary knowledge; each has its separate province, neither can be called the handmaid of the other.

Furthermore, as men's habits of mind differ, so that some more readily embrace one form of faith, some another, for what moves one to pray may move another only to scoff, I conclude, in accordance with what has gone before, that everyone should be free to choose for himself the foundations of his creed, and that faith should be judged only by its fruits; each would then obey God freely with his whole heart, while nothing would be publicly honoured save justice and charity. . . .

Chapter IV.—OF THE DIVINE LAW

. . . Law, then, being a plan of living which men have for a certain object laid down for themselves or others, may, as it seems, be divided into human law and Divine law.

By human law I mean a plan of living which serves only to render life and the state secure.

By Divine law I mean that which only regards the highest good, in other words, the true knowledge of God and love.

I call this law Divine because of the nature of the highest good, which I will here shortly explain as clearly as I can.

Inasmuch as the intellect is the best part of our being, it is evident that we should make every effort to perfect it as far as possible if we desire to search for what is really profitable to us. For in intellectual perfection the highest good should consist. Now, since all our knowledge, and the certainty which removes every doubt, depend solely on the knowledge of God;—firstly, because without God nothing can exist or be conceived; secondly, because so long as we have no clear and distinct idea of God we may remain in universal doubt—it follows that our highest good and perfection also depend solely on the knowledge of God. Further, since without God nothing can exist or be conceived, it is evident that all natural phenomena involve and express the conception of God as far as their essence and perfection extend, so that we have greater and more perfect knowledge of God in proportion to our knowledge of natural phenomena: conversely (since the knowledge of an effect through its cause is the same thing as the knowledge of a particular property of a cause) the greater our knowledge of natural phenomena, the more perfect is our knowledge of the essence of God (which is the cause of all things). So, then, our highest good not only depends on the knowledge of God, but wholly consists therein; and it further follows that man is perfect or the reverse in proportion to the nature and perfection of the object of his special desire, hence the most perfect and the chief sharer in the highest blessedness is he who prizes above all else, and takes especial delight in, the intellectual knowledge of God, the most perfect Being.

Hither, then, our highest good and our highest blessedness aim—namely, to the knowledge and love of God; therefore the means demanded by this aim of all human actions, that is, by God in so far as the idea of Him is in us, may be called the commands of God, because they proceed, as it were, from God Himself, inasmuch as He exists in our minds, and the plan of life which has regard to this aim may be fitly called the law of God.

The nature of the means, and the plan of life which this aim demands, how the foundations of the best states follow its lines, and how men's life is conducted, are questions pertaining to general ethics. Here I only proceed to treat of the Divine law in a particular application.

As the love of God is man's highest happiness and blessedness, and the ultimate end and aim of all human actions, it follows that he alone lives by the Divine law who loves God not from fear of punishment, or from love of any other object, such as sensual pleasure, fame, or the like; but solely because he has knowledge of God, or is convinced that the knowledge and love of God is the highest good. The sum and chief precept, then, of the Divine law is to love God as the highest good, namely, as we have said, not from fear of any pains and penalties, or from the love of any other object in which we desire to take pleasure. The idea of God lays down the rule that God is our highest good—in other words, that the knowledge and love of God is the ultimate aim to which all our actions should be directed. The worldling cannot understand these things, they appear foolishness to him, because he has too meagre a knowledge of God, and also because in this highest good he can discover nothing which he can handle or eat, or which affects the fleshly appetites wherein he chiefly delights, for it consists solely in thought and the pure reason. They, on the other hand, who know that they possess no greater gift than intellect and sound reason, will doubtless accept what I have said without question.

We have now explained that wherein the Divine law chiefly consists, and what are human laws, namely, all those which have a different aim unless they have been ratified by revelation, for in this respect also things are referred to God (as we have shown above) and in this sense the law of Moses, although it was not universal, but entirely adapted to the disposition and particular preservation of a single people, may yet be called a law of God or Divine law, inasmuch as we believe that it was ratified by prophetic insight. If we consider the nature of natural Divine law as we have just explained it, we shall see

I. That it is universal or common to all men, for we have deduced it from universal human nature.

II. That it does not depend on the truth of any historical narrative whatsoever, for inasmuch as this natural Divine law is comprehended solely by the consideration of human nature, it is plain that we can conceive it as existing as well in Adam as in any other man, as well in a man living among his fellows, as in a man who lives by himself.

The truth of a historical narrative, however assured, cannot give us the knowledge nor consequently the love of God, for love of God springs from knowledge of Him, and knowledge of Him should be derived from general ideas, in themselves certain and known, so that the truth of a historical narrative is very far from being a necessary requisite for our attaining our highest good.

Still, though the truth of histories cannot give us the knowledge and love of God, I do not deny that reading them is very useful with a view to life in the world, for the more we have observed and known of men's customs and circumstances, which are best revealed by their actions, the more warily we shall be able to order our lives among them, and so far as reason dictates to adapt our actions to their dispositions.

III. We see that this natural Divine law does not demand the performance of ceremonies—that is, actions in themselves indifferent, which are called good from the fact of their institution, or actions symbolizing something profitable for salvation, or (if one prefers this definition) actions of which the meaning surpasses human understanding. The natural light of reason does not demand anything which it is itself unable to supply, but only such as it can very clearly show to be good, or a means to our blessedness. Such things as are good simply because they have been commanded or instituted, or as being symbols of something good, are mere shadows which cannot be reckoned among actions that are the offspring, as it were, or fruit of a sound mind and of intellect. There is no need for me to go into this now in more detail. . . .

Chapter VI.—OF MIRACLES

As men are accustomed to call Divine the knowledge which transcends human understanding, so also do they style Divine, or the work of God, anything of which the cause is not generally known: for the masses think that the power and providence of God are most clearly displayed by events that are extraordinary and contrary to the conception they have formed of nature, especially if such events bring them any profit or convenience: they think that the clearest possible proof of God's existence is afforded when nature, as they suppose, breaks her accustomed order, and consequently they believe that those who explain or endeavour to understand phenomena or miracles through their natural causes are doing away with God and His providence. They suppose, forsooth, that God is inactive so long as nature works in her accustomed order, and *vice versâ,* that the power of nature and natural causes are idle so long as God is acting: thus they imagine two powers distinct one from the other, the power of God and the power of nature, though the latter is in a sense determined by God, or (as most people believe now) created by Him. What they mean by either, and what they understand by God and nature they do not know, except that they imagine the power of God to be like that of some royal potentate, and nature's power to consist in force and energy.

The masses then style unusual phenomena "miracles," and partly from piety, partly for the sake of opposing the students of science, prefer to remain in ignorance of natural causes, and only to hear of those things which they know least, and consequently admire most. In fact, the common people can only adore God, and refer all things to His power by removing natural causes, and conceiving things happening out of their due course, and only admires the power of God when the power of nature is conceived of as in subjection to it.

This idea seems to have taken its rise among the early Jews who saw the Gentiles round them worshipping visible gods such as the sun, the moon, the earth, water, air, &c., and in order to inspire the conviction that such divinities were weak and inconstant, or changeable, told how they themselves were under the sway of an invisible God, and narrated their miracles, trying further to show that the God whom they worshipped arranged the whole of nature for their sole benefit: this idea was so pleasing to humanity that men go on to this day imagining miracles, so that they may believe themselves God's favourites, and the final cause for which God created and directs all things.

What pretension will not people in their folly advance! They have no single sound idea concerning either God or nature, they confound God's decrees with human decrees, they conceive nature as so limited that they believe man to be its chief part! I have spent enough space in setting forth these common ideas and prejudices concerning nature and miracles, but in order to afford a regular demonstration I will show—

I. That nature cannot be contravened, but that she preserves a fixed and immutable order, and at the same time I will explain what is meant by a miracle.

II. That God's nature and existence, and consequently His providence cannot be known from miracles, but that they can all be much better perceived from the fixed and immutable order of nature.

III. That by the decrees and volitions, and consequently the providence of God, Scripture (as I will prove by Scriptural examples) means nothing but nature's order following necessarily from her eternal laws.

IV. Lastly, I will treat of the method of interpreting Scriptural miracles, and the chief points to be noted concerning the narratives of them. . . .

Our first point is easily proved from what we showed in Chap. IV. about Divine law—namely, that all that God wishes or determines involves eternal necessity and truth, for we demonstrated that God's understanding is identical with His will, and that it is the same thing to say that God wills a thing, as to say that He understands it; hence, as it follows necessarily from the Divine nature and perfection that God understands a thing as it is, it follows no less necessarily that He wills it as it is. Now, as nothing is necessarily true save only by Divine decree, it is plain that the universal laws of nature are decrees of God following from the necessity and perfection of the Divine nature. Hence, any event happening in nature which contravened nature's universal laws, would necessarily also contravene the Divine decree, nature, and understanding; or if anyone asserted that God acts in contravention to the laws of nature, he, *ipso facto,* would be compelled to assert that God acted against His own nature—an evident absurdity. One might easily show from the same premises that the power and efficiency of nature are in themselves the Divine power and efficiency, and that the Divine power is the very essence of God, but this I gladly pass over for the present.

Nothing, then, comes to pass in nature[1] in contravention to her universal laws, nay, everything agrees with them and follows from them, for whatsoever comes to pass, comes to pass by the will and eternal decree of God; that is, as we have just pointed out, whatever comes to pass, comes to pass according to laws and rules which involve eternal necessity and truth; nature, therefore, always observes laws and rules which involve eternal necessity and truth, although they may not all be known to us, and therefore she keeps a fixed and immutable order. Nor is there any sound reason for limiting the power and efficacy of nature, and asserting that her laws are fit for certain purposes, but not for all; for as the efficacy and power of nature, are the very efficacy and power of God, and as the laws and rules of nature are the decrees of God, it is in every way to be believed that the power of nature is infinite, and that her laws are broad enough to embrace everything conceived by the Divine intellect; the only alternative is to assert that God has created nature so weak, and has ordained for her laws so barren, that He is repeatedly compelled to come afresh to her aid if He wishes that she should be preserved, and that things should happen as He desires: a conclusion, in my opinion, very far removed from reason. Further, as nothing happens in nature which does not follow from her laws, and as her laws embrace everything conceived by the Divine intellect, and lastly, as nature preserves a fixed and immutable order; it most clearly follows that miracles are only intelligible as in relation to human opinions, and merely mean events of which the natural cause cannot be explained by a reference to any ordinary occurrence, either by us, or at any rate, by the writer and narrator of the miracle.

We may, in fact, say that a miracle is an event of which the causes cannot be explained by the natural reason through a reference to ascertained workings of nature; but since miracles were wrought according to the understanding of the masses, who are wholly ignorant of the workings of nature, it is certain that the ancients took for a miracle whatever they could not explain by the method adopted by the unlearned in such cases, namely, an appeal to the memory, a re-

1. N.B. I do not mean here by "nature," merely matter and its modifications, but infinite other things besides matter.

calling of something similar, which is ordinarily regarded without wonder; for most people think they sufficiently understand a thing when they have ceased to wonder at it. The ancients, then, and indeed most men up to the present day, had no other criterion for a miracle; hence we cannot doubt that many things are narrated in Scripture as miracles of which the causes could easily be explained by reference to ascertained workings of nature. . . .

It is now time to pass on to the second point, and show that we cannot gain an understanding of God's essence, existence, or providence by means of miracles, but that these truths are much better perceived through the fixed and immutable order of nature.

I thus proceed with the demonstration. As God's existence is not self-evident,[2] it must necessarily be inferred from ideas so firmly and incontrovertibly true, that no power can be postulated or conceived sufficient to impugn them. They ought certainly so to appear to us when we infer from them God's existence, if we wish to place our conclusion beyond the reach of doubt; for if we could conceive that such ideas could be impugned by any power whatsoever, we should doubt of their truth, we should doubt of our conclusion, namely, of God's existence, and should never be able to be certain of anything. Further, we know that nothing either agrees with or is contrary to nature, unless it agrees with or is contrary to these primary ideas; wherefore if we would conceive that anything could be done in nature by any power whatsoever which would be contrary to the laws of nature, it would also be contrary to our primary ideas, and we should have either to reject it as absurd, or else to cast doubt (as just shown) on our primary ideas, and consequently on the existence of God, and on everything howsoever perceived. Therefore miracles, in the sense of events contrary to the laws of nature, so far from demonstrating to us the existence of God, would, on the contrary, lead us to doubt it, where, otherwise,

---

2. We doubt of the existence of God, and consequently of all else, so long as we have no clear and distinct idea of God, but only a confused one. For as he who knows not rightly the nature of a triangle, knows not that its three angles are equal to two right angles, so he who conceives the Divine nature confusedly, does not see that it pertains to the nature of God to exist. Now, to conceive the nature of God clearly and distinctly, it is necessary to pay attention to a certain number of very simple notions, called general notions, and by their help to associate the conceptions which we form of the attributes of the Divine nature. It then, for the first time, becomes clear to us, that God exists necessarily, that He is omnipresent, and that all our conceptions involve in themselves the nature of God and are conceived through it. Lastly, we see that all our adequate ideas are true. . . .

we might have been absolutely certain of it, as knowing that nature follows a fixed and immutable order.

Let us take miracle as meaning that which cannot be explained through natural causes. This may be interpreted in two senses: either as that which has natural causes, but cannot be examined by the human intellect; or as that which has no cause save God and God's will. But as all things which come to pass through natural causes, come to pass also solely through the will and power of God, it comes to this, that a miracle, whether it has natural causes or not, is a result which cannot be explained by its cause, that is a phenomenon which surpasses human understanding; but from such a phenomenon, and certainly from a result surpassing our understanding, we can gain no knowledge. For whatsoever we understand clearly and distinctly should be plain to us either in itself or by means of something else clearly and distinctly understood; wherefore from a miracle or a phenomenon which we cannot understand, we can gain no knowledge of God's essence, or existence, or indeed anything about God or nature; whereas when we know that all things are ordained and ratified by God, that the operations of nature follow from the essence of God, and that the laws of nature are eternal decrees and volitions of God, we must perforce conclude that our knowledge of God and of God's will increases in proportion to our knowledge and clear understanding of nature, as we see how she depends on her primal cause, and how she works according to eternal law. Wherefore so far as our understanding goes, those phenomena which we clearly and distinctly understand have much better right to be called works of God, and to be referred to the will of God than those about which we are entirely ignorant, although they appeal powerfully to the imagination, and compel men's admiration.

It is only phenomena that we clearly and distinctly understand, which heighten our knowledge of God, and most clearly indicate His will and decrees. Plainly, they are but triflers who, when they cannot explain a thing, run back to the will of God; this is, truly, a ridiculous way of expressing ignorance. Again, even supposing that some conclusion could be drawn from miracles, we could not possibly infer from them the existence of God: for a miracle being an event under limitations is the expression of a fixed and limited power; therefore we could not possibly infer from an effect of this kind the existence of a cause whose power is infinite, but at the utmost only of a cause whose power is greater than that of the said effect. I say at the utmost, for a phenomenon may be the result of many concurrent causes, and its power may be less than the power of the sum of such causes, but far greater than that of any one of them taken individually. On the other hand, the laws of nature, as we have shown, extend over infinity, and are conceived by us as, after a fashion, eternal, and nature works in accordance with them in a fixed and immutable order; therefore, such laws indicate to us in a certain degree the infinity, the eternity, and the immutability of God.

We may conclude, then, that we cannot gain knowledge of the existence and providence of God by means of miracles, but that we can far better infer them from the fixed and immutable order of nature. By miracle, I here mean an event which surpasses, or is thought to surpass, human comprehension: for in so far as it is supposed to destroy or interrupt the order of nature or her laws, it not only can give us no knowledge of God, but, contrariwise, takes away that which we naturally have, and makes us doubt of God and everything else.

Neither do I recognize any difference between an event against the laws of nature and an event beyond the laws of nature (that is, according to some, an event which does not contravene nature, though she is inadequate to produce or effect it)—for a miracle is wrought in, and not beyond nature, though it may be said in itself to be above nature, and, therefore, must necessarily interrupt the order of nature, which otherwise we conceive of as fixed and unchangeable, according to God's decrees. If, therefore, anything should come to pass in nature which does not follow from her laws, it would also be in contravention to the order which God has established in nature for ever through universal natural laws: it would, therefore, be in contravention to God's nature and laws, and, consequently, belief in it would throw doubt upon everything, and lead to Atheism. . . .

Chapter XV.—THEOLOGY IS SHOWN NOT TO BE SUBSERVIENT TO REASON, NOR REASON TO THEOLOGY: A DEFINITION OF THE REASON WHICH ENABLES US TO ACCEPT THE AUTHORITY OF THE BIBLE

Those who know not that philosophy and reason are distinct, dispute whether Scripture should be made subservient to reason, or reason to Scripture: that is, whether the meaning of Scripture should be made to agree with reason; or whether reason should be made to agree with Scripture: the latter position is assumed by the sceptics who deny the certitude of reason, the former by the dogmatists. Both parties are, as I have shown, utterly in the wrong, for either doctrine would require us to tamper with reason or with Scripture.

We have shown that Scripture does not teach philosophy, but merely obedience, and that all it contains has been adapted to the understanding and established opinions of the multitude. Those, therefore, who wish to adapt it to philosophy, must needs ascribe to the prophets many ideas which they never even dreamed of, and give an extremely forced interpretation to their words: those on the other hand, who would make reason and philosophy subservient to theology, will be forced to accept as Divine utterances the prejudices of the ancient Jews, and to fill and confuse their mind therewith. In short, one party will run wild with the aid of reason, and the other will run wild without the aid of reason. . . .

The sphere of reason is, as we have said, truth and wisdom; the sphere of theology is piety and obedience. The power of reason does not extend so far as to determine for us that men may be blessed through simple obedience, without understanding. Theology tells us nothing else, enjoins on us no command save obedience, and has neither the will nor the power to oppose reason: she defines the dogmas of faith . . . only in so far as they may be necessary for obedience, and leaves reason to determine their precise truth: for reason is the light of the mind, and without her all things are dreams and phantoms. . . .

We ought not to be hindered if we find that our investigation of the meaning of Scripture thus conducted shows us that it is here and there repugnant to reason; for whatever we may find of this sort in the Bible, which men may be in ignorance of, without injury to their charity, has, we may be sure, no bearing on theology or the Word of God, and may, therefore, without blame, be viewed by everyone as he pleases.

To sum up, we may draw the absolute conclusion that the Bible must not be accommodated to reason, nor reason to the Bible.

Now, inasmuch as the basis of theology—the doctrine that man may be saved by obedience alone—cannot be proved by reason whether it be true or false, we may be asked, Why, then, should we believe it? If we do so without the aid of reason, we accept it blindly, and act foolishly and injudiciously; if, on the other hand, we settle that it can be proved by reason, theology becomes a part of philosophy, and inseparable therefrom. But I make answer that I have absolutely established that this basis of theology cannot be investigated by the natural light of reason, or, at any rate, that no one ever has proved it by such means, and, therefore, revelation was necessary. We should, however, make use of our reason, in order to grasp with moral certainty what is revealed—I say, with moral certainty, for we cannot hope to attain greater certainty than the prophets: yet their certainty was only moral. . . .

I admit that those who believe that theology and philosophy are mutually contradictory, and that therefore either one or the other must be thrust from its throne—I admit, I say, that such persons are not unreasonable in attempting to put theology on a firm basis, and to demonstrate its truth mathematically. Who, unless he were desperate or mad, would wish to bid an incontinent farewell to reason, or to despise the arts and sciences, or to deny reason's certitude? But, in the meanwhile, we cannot wholly absolve them from blame, inasmuch as they invoke the aid of reason for her own defeat, and attempt infallibly to prove her fallible. While they are trying to prove mathematically the authority and truth of theology, and to take away the authority of natural reason, they are in reality only bringing theology under reason's dominion, and proving that her authority has no weight unless natural reason be at the back of it.

If they boast that they themselves assent because of the inward testimony of the Holy Spirit, and that they only invoke the aid of reason because of unbelievers, in order to convince them, not even so can this meet with our approval, for we can easily show that they have spoken either from emotion or vain-glory. . . . No spirit gives testimony concerning the certitude of matters within the sphere of speculation, save only reason, who is mistress, as we have shown, of the whole realm of truth. If then they assert that they possess this Spirit which makes them certain of truth, they speak falsely, and according to the prejudices of the emotions, or else they are in great dread lest they should be vanquished by philosophers and exposed to public ridicule, and therefore they flee, as it were, to the altar; but their refuge is vain, for what altar will shelter a man who has outraged reason? . . .

The Ethics

Part I.—CONCERNING GOD

¶ Definitions

I. By that which is *self-caused,* I mean that of which the essence involves existence, or that of which the nature is only conceivable as existent.

II. A thing is called *finite after its kind,* when it can be limited by another thing of the same nature; for instance, a body is called finite because we always conceive another greater body. So, also, a thought is limited by another thought, but a body is not limited by thought, nor a thought by body.

III. By *substance,* I mean that which is in itself, and is conceived through itself: in other words, that of which a conception can be formed independently of any other conception.

IV. By *attribute,* I mean that which the intellect perceives as constituting the essence of substance.

V. By *mode,* I mean the modifications of substance, or that which exists in, and is conceived through, something other than itself.

VI. By *God,* I mean a being absolutely infinite—that is, a substance consisting in infinite attributes, of which each expresses eternal and infinite essentiality.

Explanation.—I say absolutely infinite, not infinite after its kind: for, of a thing infinite only after its kind, infinite attributes may be denied; but that which is absolutely infinite, contains in its essence whatever expresses reality, and involves no negation.

VII. That thing is called free, which exists solely by the necessity of its own nature, and of which the action is determined by itself alone. On the other hand, that thing is necessary, or rather constrained, which is determined by something external to itself to a fixed and definite method of existence or action.

VIII. By *eternity,* I mean existence itself, in so far as it is conceived necessarily to follow solely from the definition of that which is eternal.

Explanation.—Existence of this kind is conceived as an eternal truth, like the essence of a thing, and, therefore, cannot be explained by means of continuance or time, though continuance may be conceived without a beginning or end.

¶ Axioms

I. Everything which exists, exists either in itself or in something else.

II. That which cannot be conceived through anything else must be conceived through itself.

III. From a given definite cause an effect necessarily follows; and, on the other hand, if no definite cause be granted, it is impossible that an effect can follow.

IV. The knowledge of an effect depends on and involves the knowledge of a cause.

V. Things which have nothing in common cannot be understood, the one by means of the other; the conception of one does not involve the conception of the other.

VI. A true idea must correspond with its ideate or object.

VII. If a thing can be conceived as non-existing, its essence does not involve existence.

¶ Propositions

Prop. I. *Substance is by nature prior to its modifications.*

Proof.—This is clear from Deff. iii. and v.

Prop. II. *Two substances, whose attributes are different, have nothing in common.*

Proof.—Also evident from Def. iii. For each must exist in itself, and be conceived through itself; in other words, the conception of one does not imply the conception of the other.

Prop. III. *Things which have nothing in common cannot be one the cause of the other.*

Proof.—If they have nothing in common, it follows that one cannot be apprehended by means of the other (Ax. v.), and, therefore, one cannot be the cause of the other (Ax. iv.). *Q.E.D.*

Prop. IV. *Two or more distinct things are distinguished one from the other, either by the difference of the attributes of the substances, or by the difference of their modifications.*

Proof.—Everything which exists, exists either in itself or in something else (Ax. i.),—that is (by Deff. iii. and v.), nothing is granted in addition to the understanding, except substance and its modifications. Nothing is, therefore, given besides the understanding, by which several things may be distinguished one from the other, except the substances, or, in other words (see Ax. iv.), their attributes and modifications. *Q.E.D.*

PROP. V. *There cannot exist in the universe two or more substances having the same nature or attribute.*

Proof.—If several distinct substances be granted, they must be distinguished one from the other, either by the difference of their attributes, or by the difference of their modifications (Prop. iv.). If only by the difference of their attributes, it will be granted that there cannot be more than one with an identical attribute. If by the difference of their modifications—as substance is naturally prior to its modifications (Prop. i.),—it follows that setting the modifications aside, and considering substance in itself, that is truly, (Deff. iii. and vi.), there cannot be conceived one substance different from another,—that is (by Prop. iv.), there cannot be granted several substances, but one substance only. *Q.E.D.*

PROP. VI. *One substance cannot be produced by another substance.*

Proof.—It is impossible that there should be in the universe two substances with an identical attribute, *i.e.* which have anything common to them both (Prop. ii.), and, therefore (Prop. iii.), one cannot be the cause of another, neither can one be produced by the other. *Q.E.D.*

Corollary.—Hence it follows that a substance cannot be produced by anything external to itself. For in the universe nothing is granted, save substances and their modifications (as appears from Ax. i. and Deff. iii. and v.). Now (by the last Prop.) substance cannot be produced by another substance, therefore it cannot be produced by anything external to itself. *Q.E.D.* This is shown still more readily by the absurdity of the contradictory. For, if substance be produced by an external cause, the knowledge of it would depend on the knowledge of its cause (Ax. iv.), and (by Def. iii.) it would itself not be substance.

PROP. VII. *Existence belongs to the nature of substance.*

Proof.—Substance cannot be produced by anything external (Corollary, Prop. vi.), it must, therefore, be its own cause—that is, its essence necessarily involves existence, or existence belongs to its nature.

PROP. VIII. *Every substance is necessarily infinite.*

Proof.—There can only be one substance with an identical attribute, and existence follows from its nature (Prop. vii.); its nature, therefore, involves existence, either as finite or infinite. It does not exist as finite, for (by Def. ii.) it would then be limited by something else of the same kind, which would also necessarily exist (Prop. vii.); and there would be two substances with an identical attribute, which is absurd (Prop. v.). It therefore exists as infinite. *Q.E.D.* . . .

Note II.—No doubt it will be difficult for those who think about things loosely, and have not been accustomed to know them by their primary causes, to comprehend the demonstration of Prop. vii.: for such persons make no distinction between the modifications of substances and the substances themselves, and are ignorant of the manner in which things are produced; hence they attribute to substances the beginning which they observe in natural objects. Those who are ignorant of true causes, make complete confusion—think that trees might talk just as well as men—that men might be formed from stones as well as from seed; and imagine that any form might be changed into any other. So, also, those who confuse the two natures, divine and human, readily attribute human passions to the deity, especially so long as they do not know how passions originate in the mind. But, if people would consider the nature of substance, they would have no doubt about the truth of Prop. vii. In fact, this proposition would be a universal axiom, and accounted a truism. For, by substance, would be understood that which is in itself, and is conceived through itself—that is, something of which the conception requires not the conception of anything else; whereas modifications exist in something external to themselves, and a conception of them is formed by means of a conception of the thing in which they exist. Therefore, we may have true ideas of non-existent modifications; for, although they may have no *actual* existence apart from the conceiving intellect, yet their essence is so involved in something external to themselves that they may through it be conceived. Whereas the only truth substances can have, external to the intellect, must consist in their existence, because they are conceived through themselves. Therefore, for a person to say that he has a clear and distinct—that is, a true—idea of a substance, but that he is not sure whether such substance exists, would be the same as if he said that he had a true idea, but was not sure whether or no it was false (a little consideration will make this plain); or if anyone affirmed that substance is created, it would be the same as saying that a false idea was true—in short, the height of absurdity.

It must, then, necessarily be admitted that the existence of substance as its essence is an eternal truth. And we can hence conclude by another process of reasoning—that there is but one such substance. I think that this may profitably be done at once; and, in order to proceed regularly with the demonstration, we must premise:—

1. The true definition of a thing neither involves nor expresses anything beyond the nature of the thing defined. From this it follows that—

2. No definition implies or expresses a certain number of individuals, inasmuch as it expresses nothing beyond the nature of the thing defined. For instance, the definition of a triangle expresses nothing beyond the actual nature of a triangle: it does not imply any fixed number of triangles.

3. There is necessarily for each individual existent thing a cause why it should exist.

4. This cause of existence must either be contained in the nature and definition of the thing defined, or must be postulated apart from such definition.

It therefore follows that, if a given number of individual things exist in nature, there must be some cause for the existence of exactly that number, neither more nor less. For example, if twenty men exist in the universe (for simplicity's sake, I will suppose them existing simultaneously, and to have had no predecessors), and we want to account for the existence of these twenty men, it will not be enough to show the cause of human existence in general; we must also show why there are exactly twenty men, neither more nor less: for a cause must be assigned for the existence of each individual. Now this cause cannot be contained in the actual nature of man, for the true definition of man does not involve any consideration of the number twenty. Consequently, the cause for the existence of these twenty men, and, consequently, of each of them, must necessarily be sought externally to each individual. Hence we may lay down the absolute rule, that everything which may consist of several individuals must have an external cause. And, as it has been shown already that existence appertains to the nature of substance, existence must necessarily be included in its definition; and from its definition alone existence must be deducible. But from its definition (as we have shown, Notes ii., iii.), we cannot infer the existence of several substances; therefore it follows that there is only one substance of the same nature. *Q.E.D.*

PROP. IX. *The more reality or being a thing has the greater the number of its attributes* (Def. iv.).

Prop. X. *Each particular attribute of the one substance must be conceived through itself.*

Proof.—An attribute is that which the intellect perceives of substance, as constituting its essence (Def. iv.), and, therefore, must be conceived through itself (Def. iii.). *Q.E.D.*

Note.—It is thus evident that, though two attributes are, in fact, conceived as distinct—that is, one without the help of the other—yet we cannot, therefore, conclude that they constitute two entities, or two different substances. For it is the nature of substance that each of its attributes is conceived through itself, inasmuch as all the attributes it has have always existed simultaneously in it, and none could be produced by any other; but each expresses the reality or being of substance. It is, then, far from an absurdity to ascribe several attributes to one substance: for nothing in nature is more clear than that each and every entity must be conceived under some attribute, and that its reality or being is in proportion to the number of its attributes expressing necessity or eternity and infinity. Consequently it is abundantly clear, that an absolutely infinite being must necessarily be defined as consisting in infinite attributes, each of which expresses a certain eternal and infinite essence.

If anyone now ask, by what sign shall he be able to distinguish different substances, let him read the following propositions, which show that there is but one substance in the universe, and that it is absolutely infinite, wherefore such a sign would be sought for in vain.

Prop. XI. *God, or substance, consisting of infinite attributes, of which each expresses eternal and infinite essentiality, necessarily exists.*

Proof.—If this be denied, conceive, if possible, that God does not exist: then his essence does not involve existence. But this (by Prop. vii.) is absurd. Therefore God necessarily exists.

Another proof.—Of everything whatsoever a cause or reason must be assigned, either for its existence, or for its non-existence—*e.g.* if a triangle exist, a reason or cause must be granted for its existence; if, on the contrary, it does not exist, a cause must also be granted, which prevents it from existing, or annuls its existence. This reason or cause must either be contained in the nature of the thing in question, or be external to it. For instance, the reason for the non-existence of a square circle is indicated in its nature, namely, because it would involve a contradiction. On the other hand, the existence of substance follows also solely from its nature, inasmuch as its nature involves existence. (See Prop. vii.)

But the reason for the existence of a triangle or a circle does not follow from the nature of those figures, but from the order of universal nature in extension. From the latter it must follow, either that a triangle necessarily exists, or that it is impossible that it should exist. So much is self-evident. It follows therefrom that a thing necessarily exists, if no cause or reason be granted which prevents its existence.

If, then, no cause or reason can be given, which prevents the existence of God, or which destroys his existence, we must certainly conclude that he necessarily does exist. If such a reason or cause should be given, it must either be drawn from the very nature of God, or be external to him—that is, drawn from another substance of another nature. For if it were of the same nature, God, by that very fact, would be admitted to exist. But substance of another nature could have nothing in common with God (by Prop. ii.), and therefore would be unable either to cause or to destroy his existence.

As, then, a reason or cause which would annul the divine existence cannot be drawn from anything external to the divine nature, such cause must perforce, if God does not exist, be drawn from God's own nature, which would involve a contradiction. To make such an affirmation about a being absolutely infinite and supremely perfect, is absurd; therefore, neither in the nature of God, nor externally to his nature, can a cause or reason be assigned which would annul his existence. Therefore, God necessarily exists. *Q.E.D.*

Another proof.—The potentiality of non-existence is a negation of power, and contrariwise the potentiality of existence is a power, as is obvious. If, then, that which necessarily exists is nothing but finite beings, such finite beings are more powerful than a being absolutely infinite, which is obviously absurd; therefore, either nothing exists, or else a being absolutely infinite necessarily exists also. Now we exist either in ourselves, or in something else which necessarily exists (see Axiom i. and Prop. vii.). Therefore a being absolutely infinite—in other words, God (Def. vi.)—necessarily exists. *Q.E.D.*

Note.—In this last proof, I have purposely shown God's existence *à posteriori,* so that the proof might be more easily followed, not because, from the same premises, God's existence does not follow *à priori.* For, as the potentiality of existence is a power, it follows that, in proportion as reality increases in the nature of a thing, so also will it increase its strength for existence. Therefore a being absolutely infinite, such as God, has from himself an absolutely infinite power of existence, and hence he does absolutely exist. Perhaps there will be many who will be unable to see the force of this proof, inasmuch as they are accustomed only to consider those things which flow from external causes. Of such things, they see that those which quickly come to pass—that is, quickly come into existence—quickly also disappear; whereas they regard as more difficult of accomplishment—that is, not so easily brought into existence—those things which they conceive as more complicated.

However, to do away with this misconception, I need not here show the measure of truth in the proverb, "What comes quickly, goes quickly," nor discuss whether, from the point of view of universal nature, all things are equally easy, or otherwise: I need only remark, that I am not here speaking of things, which come to pass through causes external to themselves, but only of substances which (by Prop. vi.) cannot be produced by any external cause. Things which are produced by external causes, whether they consist of many parts or few, owe whatsoever perfection or reality they possess solely to the efficacy of their external cause, and therefore their existence arises solely from the perfection of their external cause, not from their own. Contrariwise, whatsoever perfection is possessed by substance is due to no external cause; wherefore the existence of substance must arise solely from its own nature, which is nothing else but its essence. Thus, the perfection of a thing does not annul its existence, but, on the contrary, asserts it. Imperfection, on the other hand, does annul it; therefore we cannot be more certain of the existence of anything, than of the existence of a being absolutely infinite or perfect—that is, of God. For inasmuch as his essence excludes all imperfection, and involves absolute perfection, all cause for doubt concerning his existence is done away, and the utmost certainty on the question is given. This, I think, will be evident to every moderately attentive reader.

PROP. XII. *No attribute of substance can be conceived from which it would follow that substance can be divided.*

Proof.—The parts into which substance as thus conceived would be divided, either will retain the nature of substance, or they will not. If the former, then (by Prop. viii.) each part will necessarily be infinite, and (by Prop. vi.) self-caused, and (by Prop. v.) will perforce consist of a different attribute, so that, in that case, several substances could be formed out of one substance, which (by Prop. vi.) is absurd. Moreover, the parts (by Prop. ii.) would have nothing in common with their whole, and the whole (by Def. iv. and Prop. x.) could both exist and be conceived without its parts, which everyone will admit to be absurd. If we adopt the second alternative—namely, that the parts will not retain the nature of substance—then, if the whole substance were divided into equal parts, it would lose the nature of substance, and would cease to exist, which (by Prop. vii.) is absurd.

Prop. XIII. *Substance absolutely infinite is indivisible.*

Proof.—If it could be divided, the parts into which it was divided would either retain the nature of absolutely infinite substance, or they would not. If the former, we should have several substances of the same nature, which (by Prop. v.) is absurd. If the latter, then (by Prop. vii.) substance absolutely infinite could cease to exist, which (by Prop. xi.) is also absurd.

Corollary.—It follows, that no substance, and consequently no extended substance, in so far as it is substance, is divisible.

Note.—The indivisibility of substance may be more easily understood as follows. The nature of substance can only be conceived as infinite, and by a part of substance, nothing else can be understood than finite substance, which (by Prop. viii.) involves a manifest contradiction.

Prop. XIV. *Besides God no substance can be granted or conceived.*

Proof.—As God is a being absolutely infinite, of whom no attribute that expresses the essence of substance can be denied (by Def. vi.), and he necessarily exists (by Prop. xi.); if any substance besides God were granted, it would have to be explained by some attribute of God, and thus two substances with the same attribute would exist, which (by Prop. v.) is absurd; therefore, besides God no substance can be granted, or, consequently, be conceived. If it could be conceived, it would necessarily have to be conceived as existent; but this (by the first part of this proof) is absurd. Therefore, besides God no substance can be granted or conceived. *Q.E.D.*

Corollary I.—Clearly, therefore: 1. God is one, that is (by Def. vi.) only one substance can be granted in the universe, and that substance is absolutely infinite, as we have already indicated (in the note to Prop. x.).

Corollary II.—It follows: 2. That extension and thought are either attributes of God or (by Ax. i.) accidents (*affectiones*) of the attributes of God.

Prop. XV. *Whatsoever is, is in God, and without God nothing can be, or be conceived.*

Proof.—Besides God, no substance is granted or can be conceived (by Prop. xiv.), that is (by Def. iii.) nothing which is in itself and is conceived through itself. But modes (by Def. v.) can neither be, nor be conceived without substance; wherefore they can only be in the divine nature, and can only through it be conceived. But substances and modes form the sum total of existence (by Ax. i.), therefore, without God nothing can be, or be conceived. *Q.E.D.*

Note.—Some assert that God, like a man, consists of body and mind, and is susceptible of passions. How far such persons have strayed from the truth is sufficiently evident from what has been said. But these I pass over. For all who have in anywise reflected on the divine nature deny that God has a body. Of this they find excellent proof in the fact that we understand by body a definite quantity, so long, so broad, so deep, bounded by a certain shape, and it is the height of absurdity to predicate such a thing of God, a being absolutely infinite. But meanwhile by the other reasons with which they try to prove their point, they show that they think corporeal or extended substance wholly apart from the divine nature, and say it was created by God. Wherefrom the divine nature can have been created, they are wholly ignorant; thus they clearly show, that they do not know the meannig of their own words. I myself have proved sufficiently clearly, at any rate in my own judgment (Coroll. Prop. vi., and Note 2, Prop. viii.), that no substance can be produced or created by anything other than itself. Further, I showed (in Prop. xiv.), that besides God no substance can be granted or conceived. Hence we drew the conclusion that extended substance is one of the infinite attributes of God. . . .

Prop. XVI. *From the necessity of the divine nature must follow an infinite number of things in infinite ways—that is, all things which can fall within the sphere of infinite intellect. . . .*

Corollary I.—Hence it follows, that God is the efficient cause of all that can fall within the sphere of an infinite intellect.

Corollary II.—It also follows that God is a cause in himself, and not through an accident of his nature.

Corollary III.—It follows, thirdly, that God is the absolutely first cause.

Prop. XVII. *God acts solely by the laws of his own nature, and is not constrained by anyone.*

Proof.—We have just shown (in Prop. xvi.), that solely from the necessity of the divine nature, or, what is the same thing, solely from the laws of his nature, an infinite number of things absolutely follow in an infinite number of ways; and we proved (in Prop. xv.), that without God nothing can be nor be conceived; but that all things are in God. Wherefore nothing can exist outside himself, whereby he can be conditioned or constrained to act. Wherefore God acts solely by the laws of his own nature, and is not constrained by anyone. *Q.E.D.*

Corollary I.—It follows: 1. That there can be no cause which, either extrinsically or intrinsically, besides the perfection of his own nature, moves God to act.

Corollary II.—It follows: 2. That God is the sole free cause. For God alone exists by the sole necessity of his nature (by Prop. xi. and Prop. xiv., Coroll. i.), and acts by the sole necessity of his nature, wherefore God is (by Def. vii.) the sole free cause. *Q.E.D.*

Note.—Others think that God is a free cause, because he can, as they think, bring it about, that those things which we have said follow from his nature—that is, which are in his power, should not come to pass, or should not be produced by him. But this is the same as if they said, that God could bring it about, that it should not follow from the nature of a triangle, that its three interior angles should not be equal to two right angles; or that from a given cause no effect should follow, which is absurd.

Moreover, I will show below, without the aid of this proposition, that neither intellect nor will appertain to God's nature. . . .

PROP. XX. *The existence of God and his essence are one and the same.* . . .

PROP. XXI. *All things which follow from the absolute nature of any attribute of God must always exist and be infinite, or, in other words, are eternal and infinite through the said attribute.* . . .

PROP. XXIII. *Every mode, which exists both necessarily and as infinite, must necessarily follow either from the absolute nature of some attribute of God, or from an attribute modified by an attribute modified by a modification which exists necessarily, and as infinite.* . . .

PROP. XXIV. *The essence of things produced by God does not involve existence.*

Proof.—This proposition is evident from Def. i. For that of which the nature (considered in itself) involves existence is self-caused, and exists by the sole necessity of its own nature. . . .

PROP. XXV. *God is the efficient cause not only of the existence of things, but also of their essence.*

Proof.—If this be denied, then God is not the cause of the essence of things; and therefore the essence of things can (by Ax. iv.) be conceived, without God. This (by Prop. xv.) is absurd. Therefore, God is the cause of the essence of things. *Q.E.D.* . . .

Corollary.—Individual things are nothing but modifications of the attributes of God, or modes by which the attributes of God are expressed in a fixed and definite manner. The proof appears from Prop. xv. and Def. v.

PROP. XXIX. *Nothing in the universe is contingent, but all things are conditioned to exist and operate in a particular manner by the necessity of the divine nature. . . .*

Note.—Before going any further, I wish here to explain, what we should understand by nature viewed as active (*natura naturans*), and nature viewed as passive (*natura naturata*). I say to explain, or rather call attention to it, for I think that, from what has been said, it is sufficiently clear, that by nature viewed as active we should understand that which is in itself, and is conceived through itself, or those attributes of substance, which express eternal and infinite essence, in other words (Prop. xiv., Coroll. i., and Prop. xvii., Coroll. ii.) God, in so far as he is considered as a free cause.

By nature viewed as passive I understand all that which follows from the necessity of the nature of God, or of any of the attributes of God, that is, all the modes of the attributes of God, in so far as they are considered as things which are in God, and which without God cannot exist or be conceived. . . .

PROP. XXXIII. *Things could not have been brought into being by God in any manner or in any order different from that which has in fact obtained.*

Proof.—All things necessarily follow from the nature of God (Prop. xvi.), and by the nature of God are conditioned to exist and act in a particular way (Prop. xxix.). If things, therefore, could have been of a different nature, or have been conditioned to act in a different way, so that the order of nature would have been different, God's nature would also have been able to be different from what it now is; and therefore (by Prop. xi.) that different nature also would have perforce existed, and consequently there would have been able to be two or more Gods. This (by Prop. xiv., Coroll. i.) is absurd. Therefore things could not have been brought into being by God in any other manner, &c. *Q.E.D.* . . .

¶ APPENDIX

In the foregoing I have explained the nature and properties of God. I have shown that he necessarily exists, that he is one: that he is, and acts solely by the necessity of his own nature; that he is the free cause of all things, and how he is so; that all things are in God, and so depend on him, that without him they could neither exist nor be conceived; lastly, that all things are predetermined by God, not through his free will or absolute fiat, but from the very nature of

God or infinite power. I have further, where occasion offered, taken care to remove the prejudices, which might impede the comprehension of my demonstrations. Yet there still remain misconceptions not a few, which might and may prove very grave hindrances to the understanding of the concatenation of things, as I have explained it above. I have therefore thought it worth while to bring these misconceptions before the bar of reason.

All such opinions spring from the notion commonly entertained, that all things in nature act as men themselves act, namely, with an end in view. It is accepted as certain, that God himself directs all things to a definite goal (for it is said that God made all things for man, and man that he might worship him). I will, therefore, consider this opinion, asking first, why it obtains general credence, and why all men are naturally so prone to adopt it? secondly, I will point out its falsity; and, lastly, I will show how it has given rise to prejudices about good and bad, right and wrong, praise and blame, order and confusion, beauty and ugliness, and the like. However, this is not the place to deduce these misconceptions from the nature of the human mind: it will be sufficient here, if I assume as a starting point, what ought to be universally admitted, namely, that all men are born ignorant of the causes of things, that all have the desire to seek for what is useful to them, and that they are conscious of such desire. Herefrom it follows, first, that men think themselves free inasmuch as they are conscious of their volitions and desires, and never even dream, in their ignorance, of the causes which have disposed them so to wish and desire. Secondly, that men do all things for an end, namely, for that which is useful to them, and which they seek. Thus it comes to pass that they only look for a knowledge of the final causes of events, and when these are learned, they are content, as having no cause for further doubt. If they cannot learn such causes from external sources, they are compelled to turn to considering themselves, and reflecting what end would have induced them personally to bring about the given event, and thus they necessarily judge other natures by their own. Further, as they find in themselves and outside themselves many means which assist them not a little in their search for what is useful, for instance, eyes for seeing, teeth for chewing, herbs and animals for yielding food, the sun for giving light, the sea for breeding fish, &c., they come to look on the whole of nature as a means for obtaining such conveniences. Now as they are aware, that they found these conveniences and did not make them, they think they have cause for believing, that some other being has made them for their use. As they look upon things as means, they cannot believe them to be self-created; but, judging from the means which they are accustomed to prepare for themselves, they are bound to believe in some ruler or rulers of the universe endowed with human freedom, who have arranged and adapted everything for human use. They are bound to estimate the nature of such rulers (having no information on the subject) in accordance with their own nature, and therefore they assert that the gods ordained everything for the use of man, in order to bind man to themselves and obtain from him the highest honour. Hence also it follows, that everyone thought out for himself, according to his abilities, a different way of worshipping God, so that God might love him more than his fellows, and direct the whole course of nature for the satisfaction of his blind cupidity and insatiable avarice. Thus the prejudice developed into superstition, and took deep root in the human mind; and for this reason everyone strove most zealously to understand and explain the final causes of things; but in their endeavour to show that nature does nothing in vain, *i.e.*, nothing which is useless to man, they only seem to have demonstrated that nature, the gods, and men are all mad together. Consider, I pray you, the result: among the many helps of nature they were bound to find some hindrances, such as storms, earthquakes, diseases, &c.: so they declared that such things happen, because the gods are angry at some wrong done them by men, or at some fault committed in their worship. Experience day by day protested and showed by infinite examples, that good and evil fortunes fall to the lot of pious and impious alike; still they would not abandon their inveterate prejudice, for it was more easy for them to class such contradictions among other unknown things of whose use they were ignorant, and thus to retain their actual and innate condition of ignorance, than to destroy the whole fabric of their reasoning and start afresh. They therefore laid down as an axiom, that God's judgments far transcend human understanding. Such a doctrine might well have suffered to conceal the truth from the human race for all eternity, if mathematics had not furnished another standard of verity in considering solely the essence and properties of figures without regard to their final causes. There are other reasons (which I need not mention here) besides mathematics, which might have caused men's minds to be directed to these general prejudices, and have led them to the knowledge of the truth.

I have now sufficiently explained my first point. There is no need to show at length, that nature has no particular goal in view, and that final causes are mere human figments. This, I think, is already evident enough, both from the causes and foundations on which I have shown such prejudice to be based, and also from Prop. xvi., and the Corollary of Prop. xxxii., and, in fact, all those propositions in which I have shown, that everything in nature proceeds from a sort of necessity, and with the utmost perfection. However, I will add a few remarks, in order to overthrow this doctrine of a final cause utterly. That which is really a cause it considers as an effect, and *vice versâ*: it makes that which is by nature first to be last, and that which is highest and most perfect to be most imperfect. Passing over the questions of cause and priority as self-evident, it is plain from Props. xxi., xxii., xxiii. that that effect is most perfect which is produced immediately by God; the effect which requires for its production several intermediate causes is, in that respect, more imperfect. But if those things which were made immediately by God were made to enable him to attain his end, then the things which come after, for the sake of which the first were made, are necessarily the most excellent of all.

Further, this doctrine does away with the perfection of God: for, if God acts for an object, he necessarily desires something which he lacks. Certainly, theologians and metaphysicians draw a distinction between the object of want and the object of assimilation; still they confess that God made all things for the sake of himself, not for the sake of creation. They are unable to point to anything prior to creation, except God himself, as an object for which God should act, and are therefore driven to admit (as they clearly must), that God lacked those things for whose attainment he created means, and further that he desired them.

We must not omit to notice that the followers of this doctrine, anxious to display their talent in assigning final causes, have imported a new method of argument in proof of their theory—namely, a reduction, not to the impossible, but to ignorance; thus showing that they have no other method of exhibiting their doctrine. For example, if a stone falls from a roof on to someone's head, and kills him, they will demonstrate by their new method, that the stone fell in order to kill the man; for, if it had not by God's will fallen with that object, how could so many circumstances (and there are often many concurrent circumstances) have all happened together by chance? Perhaps you will answer that the event is due to the facts that the wind was blowing, and the man was walking that way. "But why," they will insist, "was the wind blowing, and why was the man at that very time walking that way?" If you again answer, that the wind had then sprung up because the sea had begun to be agitated the day before, the weather being previously calm, and that the man had been invited by a friend, they will again insist: "But why was the sea agitated, and why was the man invited at that time?" So they will pursue their questions from cause to cause, till at last you take refuge in the will of God—in other words, the sanctuary of ignorance. So, again, when they survey the frame of the human body, they are amazed; and being ignorant of the causes of so great a work of art, conclude that it has been fashioned, not mechanically, but by divine and supernatural skill, and has been so put together that one part shall not hurt another.

Hence anyone who seeks for the true causes of miracles, and strives to understand natural phenomena as an intelligent being, and not to gaze at them like a fool, is set down and denounced as a impious heretic by those, whom the masses adore as the interpreters of nature and the gods. Such persons know that, with the removal of ignorance, the wonder which forms their only available means for proving and preserving their authority would vanish also. But I now quit this subject, and pass on to my third point.

After men persuaded themselves, that everything which is created is created for their sake, they were bound to consider as the chief quality in everything that which is most useful to themselves, and to account those things the best of all which have the most beneficial effect on mankind. Further, they were bound to form abstract notions for the explanation of the nature of things, such as *goodness, badness, order, confusion, warmth, cold, beauty, deformity,* and so on; and from the belief that they are free agents arose the further notions *praise* and *blame, sin* and *merit.*

I will speak of these latter hereafter, when I treat of human nature; the former I will briefly explain here.

Everything which conduces to health and the worship of God they have called *good,* everything which hinders these objects they have styled *bad;* and inasmuch as those who do not understand the nature of things do not verify phenomena in any way, but merely imagine them after a fashion, and mistake their imagination for understanding, such persons firmly believe that there is an *order* in things, being really ignorant both of things and their own nature. When phenomena are of such a kind, that the impression they make on our senses requires little effort of imagination, and can consequently be easily remembered, we say that they are *well-ordered;* if the contrary, that they are *ill-ordered* or *confused.* Further, as things which are easily imagined are more pleasing to us, men prefer order to confusion—as though there were any order in nature, except in relation to our imagination—and say that God has created all things in order; thus, without knowing it, attributing imagination to God, unless, indeed, they would have it that God foresaw human imagination, and arranged everything, so that it should be most easily imagined. If this be their theory, they would not, perhaps, be daunted by the fact that we find an infinite number of phenomena, far surpassing our imagination, and very many others which confound its weakness. But enough has been said on this subject. The other abstract notions are nothing but modes of imagining, in which the imagination is differently affected, though they are considered by the ignorant as the chief attributes of things, inasmuch as they believe that everything was created for the sake of themselves; and, according as they are affected by it, style it good or bad, healthy or rotten and corrupt. For instance, if the motion which objects we see communicate to our nerves be conducive to health, the objects causing it are styled *beautiful;* if a contrary motion be excited, they are styled *ugly*.

Things which are perceived through our sense of smell are styled fragrant or fetid; if through our taste, sweet or bitter, full-flavoured or insipid; if through our touch, hard or soft, rough or smooth, &c.

Whatsoever affects our ears is said to give rise to noise, sound, or harmony. In this last case, there are men lunatic enough to believe, that even God himself takes pleasure in harmony; and philosophers are not lacking who have persuaded themselves, that the motion of the heavenly bodies gives rise to harmony—all of which instances sufficiently show that everyone judges of things according to the state of his brain, or rather mistakes for things the forms of his imagination. We need no longer wonder that there have arisen all the controversies we have witnessed, and finally scepticism: for, although human bodies in many respects agree, yet in very many others they differ; so that what seems good to one seems bad to another; what seems well ordered to one seems confused to another; what is pleasing to one displeases another, and so on. I need not further enumerate, because this is not the place to treat the subject at length, and also because the fact is sufficiently well known. It is commonly said: "So many men, so many minds; everyone is wise in his own way; brains differ as completely as palates." All of which proverbs show, that men judge of things according to their mental disposition, and rather imagine than understand: for, if they understood phenomena, they would, as mathematics attest, be convinced, if not attracted, by what I have urged.

We have now perceived, that all the explanations commonly given of nature are mere modes of imagining, and do not indicate the true nature of anything, but only the constitution of the imagination; and, although they have names, as though they were entities, existing externally to the imagination, I call them entities imaginary rather than real; and, therefore, all arguments against us drawn from such abstractions are easily rebutted.

Many argue in this way. If all things follow from a necessity of the absolutely perfect nature of God, why are there so many imperfections in nature? such, for instance, as things corrupt to the point of putridity, loathsome deformity, confusion, evil, sin, &c. But these reasoners are, as I have said, easily confuted, for the perfection of things is to be reckoned only from their own nature and power; things are not more or less perfect, according as they delight or offend human senses, or according as they are serviceable or repugnant to mankind. To those who ask why God did not so create all men, that they should be governed only by reason, I give no answer but this: because matter was not lacking to him for the creation of every degree of perfection from highest to lowest; or, more strictly, because the laws of his nature are so vast, as to suffice for the production of everything conceivable by an infinite intelligence, as I have shown in Prop. xvi.

Such are the misconceptions I have undertaken to note; if there are any more of the same sort, everyone may easily dissipate them for himself with the aid of a little reflection.

Part II.—OF THE NATURE AND ORIGIN OF THE MIND

¶ Preface

I now pass on to explaining the results, which must necessarily follow from the essence of God, or of the eternal and infinite being; not, indeed, all of them (for we proved in Part i., Prop. xvi., that an infinite number must follow in an infinite number of ways), but only those which are able to lead us, as it were by the hand, to the knowledge of the human mind and its highest blessedness.

¶ Definitions

I. By *body* I mean a mode which expresses in a certain determinate manner the essence of God, in so far as he is considered as an extended thing. (See Pt. i., Prop. xxv. Coroll.)

II. I consider as belonging to the essence of a thing that, which being given, the thing is necessarily given also, and, which being removed, the thing is necessarily removed also; in other words, that without which the thing, and which itself without the thing, can neither be nor be conceived.

III. By *idea,* I mean the mental conception which is formed by the mind as a thinking thing.

Explanation.—I say *conception* rather than perception, because the word perception seems to imply that the mind is passive in respect to the object; whereas conception seems to express an activity of the mind.

IV. By *an adequate idea,* I mean an idea which, in so far as it is considered in itself, without relation to the object, has all the properties or intrinsic marks of a true idea.

Explanation.—I say *intrinsic,* in order to exclude that mark which is extrinsic, namely, the agreement between the idea and its object (*ideatum*).

V. *Duration* is the indefinite continuance of existing.

Explanation.—I say *indefinite,* because it cannot be determined through the existence itself of the existing thing, or by its efficient cause, which necessarily gives the existence of the thing, but does not take it away.

VI. *Reality* and *perfection* I use as synonymous terms.

VII. By *particular things,* I mean things which are finite and have a conditioned existence; but if several individual things concur in one action, so as to be all simultaneously the effect of one cause, I consider them all, so far, as one particular thing. . . .

¶ Propositions

Prop. I. *Thought is an attribute of God, or God is a thinking thing. . . .*

Prop. II. *Extension is an attribute of God, or God is an extended thing. . . .*

Prop. III. *In God there is necessarily the idea not only of his essence, but also of all things which necessarily follow from his essence. . . .*

Prop. IV. *The idea of God, from which an infinite number of things follow in infinite ways, can only be one. . . .*

Prop. VII. *The order and connection of ideas is the same as the order and connection of things.*

Proof.—This proposition is evident from Part i., Ax. iv. For the idea of everything that is caused depends on a knowledge of the cause, whereof it is an effect.

Corollary.—Hence God's power of thinking is equal to his realized power of action—that is, whatsoever follows from the infinite nature of God in the world of extension (*formaliter*), follows without exception in the same order and connection from the idea of God in the world of thought (*objective*).

Note.—Before going any further, I wish to recall to mind what has been pointed out above—namely, that whatsoever can be perceived by the infinite intellect as constituting the essence of substance, belongs altogether only to one substance: consequently, substance thinking and substance extended are one and the same substance, comprehended now through one attribute, now through the other. So, also, a mode of extension and the idea of that mode are one and the same thing, though expressed in two ways. This truth seems to have been dimly recognized by those Jews who maintained that God, God's intellect, and the things understood by God are identical. For instance, a circle existing in nature, and the idea of a circle existing, which is also in God, are one and the same thing displayed through different attributes. Thus, whether we conceive nature under the attribute of extension, or under the attribute of thought, or under any other attribute, we shall find the same order, or one and the same chain of causes—that is, the same things following in either case.

I said that God is the cause of an idea—for instance, of the idea of a circle,—in so far as he is a thinking thing; and of a circle, in so far as he is an extended thing, simply because the actual being of the idea of a circle can only be perceived as a proximate cause through another mode of thinking, and that again through another, and so on to infinity; so that, so long as we consider things as modes of thinking, we must explain the order of the whole of nature, or the whole chain of causes, through the attribute of thought only. And, in so far as we consider things as modes of extension, we must explain the order of the whole of nature through the attribute of extension only; and so on, in the case of other attributes. Wherefore of things as they are in themselves God is really the cause, inasmuch as he consists of infinite attributes. I cannot for the present explain my meaning more clearly. . . .

PROP. XXXI. *We can only have a very inadequate knowledge of the duration of particular things external to ourselves. . . .*

Corollary.—Hence it follows that all particular things are contingent and perishable. For we can have no adequate idea of their duration (by the last Prop.), and this is what we must understand by the contingency and perishableness of things. (I. xxxiii., Note i.) For (I. xxix.), except in this sense, nothing is contingent.

Prop. XXXII. *All ideas, in so far as they are referred to God, are true. . . .*

Prop. XXXIII. *There is nothing positive in ideas, which causes them to be called false.*

Proof.—If this be denied, conceive, if possible, a positive mode of thinking, which should constitute the distinctive quality of falsehood. Such a mode of thinking cannot be in God (II. xxxii.); external to God it cannot be or be conceived (I. xv.). Therefore there is nothing positive in ideas which causes them to be called false. *Q.E.D.*

Prop. XXXIV. *Every idea, which in us is absolute or adequate and perfect, is true.*

Proof.—When we say that an idea in us is adequate and perfect, we say, in other words (II. xi. Coroll.), that the idea is adequate and perfect in God, in so far as he constitutes the essence of our mind; consequently (II. xxxii.), we say that such an idea is true. *Q.E.D.*

Prop. XXXV. *Falsity consists in the privation of knowledge, which inadequate, fragmentary, or confused ideas involve.*

Proof.—There is nothing positive in ideas, which causes them to be called false (II. xxxiii); but falsity cannot consist in simple privation (for minds, not bodies, are said to err and to be mistaken), neither can it consist in absolute ignorance, for ignorance and error are not identical; wherefore it consists in the privation of knowledge, which inadequate, fragmentary, or confused ideas involve. *Q.E.D.*

Note.—In the note to II. xvii. I explained how error consists in the privation of knowledge, but in order to throw more light on the subject I will give an example. For instance, men are mistaken in thinking themselves free; their opinion is made up of consciousness of their own actions, and ignorance of the causes by which they are conditioned. Their idea of freedom, therefore, is simply their ignorance of any cause for their actions. As for their saying that human actions depend on the will, this is a mere phrase without any idea to correspond thereto. What the will is, and how it moves the body, they none of them know; those who boast of such knowledge, and feign dwellings and habitations for the soul, are wont to provoke either laughter or disgust. So, again, when we look at the sun, we imagine that it is distant from us about two hundred feet; this error does not lie solely in this fancy, but in the fact that, while we thus imagine, we do not know the sun's true distance or the cause of the fancy. For although we afterwards learn, that the sun is distant from us more than six hundred of the earth's diameters, we none the less shall fancy it to be near; for we do not imagine the sun as near us, because we are ignorant of its true distance, but because the modification of our body involves the essence of the sun, in so far as our said body is affected thereby. . . .

PROP. XL. *Whatsoever ideas in the mind follow from ideas which are therein adequate, are also themselves adequate.*

Proof.—This proposition is self-evident. For when we say that an idea in the human mind follows from ideas which are therein adequate, we say, in other words (II. xi. Coroll.), that an idea is in the divine intellect, whereof God is the cause, not in so far as he is infinite, nor in so far as he is affected by the ideas of very many particular things, but only in so far as he constitutes the essence of the human mind. . . .

Note II.—From all that has been said above it is clear, that we, in many cases, perceive and form our general notions:—(1.) From particular things represented to our intellect fragmentarily, confusedly, and without order through our senses (II. xxix. Coroll.); I have settled to call such perceptions by the name of knowledge from the mere suggestions of experience. (2.) From symbols, *e.g.*, from the fact of having read or heard certain words we remember things and for certain ideas concerning them, similar to those through which we imagine things (II. xviii. note). I shall call both these ways of regarding things *knowledge of the first kind, opinion,* or *imagination.* (3.) From the fact that we have notions common to all men, and adequate ideas of the properties of things (II. xxxviii. Coroll., xxxix. and Coroll. and xl.); this I call *reason* and *knowledge of the second kind.* Besides these two kinds of knowledge, there is, as I will hereafter show, a third kind of knowledge, which we will call intuition. This kind of knowledge proceeds from an adequate idea of the absolute essence of certain attributes of God to the adequate knowledge of the essence of things. I will illustrate all three kinds of knowledge by a single example. Three numbers are given for finding a fourth, which shall be to the third as the second is to the first. Tradesmen without hesitation multiply the second by the third, and divide the product by the first; either because they have not forgotten the rule which they received from a master without any proof, or because they have often made trial of it with simple numbers, or by virtue of the proof of the nineteenth proposition of the seventh book of Euclid, namely, in virtue of the general property of proportionals.

But with very simple numbers there is no need of this. For instance, one, two, three, being given, everyone can see that the fourth proportional is six; and this is much clearer, because we infer the fourth number from an intuitive grasping of the ratio, which the first bears to the second.

PROP. XLI. *Knowledge of the first kind is the only source of falsity, knowledge of the second and third kinds is necessarily true.*

Proof.—To knowledge of the first kind we have (in the foregoing note) assigned all those ideas, which are inadequate and confused; therefore this kind of knowledge is the only source of falsity (II. xxxv.). Furthermore, we assigned to the second and third kinds of knowledge those ideas which are adequate; therefore these kinds are necessarily true (II. xxxiv.). *Q.E.D.*

PROP. XLII. *Knowledge of the second and third kinds, not knowledge of the first kind, teaches us to distinguish the true from the false.*

Proof.—This proposition is self-evident. He, who knows how to distinguish between true and false, must have an adequate idea of true and false. That is (II. xl., note ii.), he must know the true and the false by the second or third kind of knowledge.

PROP. XLIII. *He, who has a true idea, simultaneously knows that he has a true idea, and cannot doubt of the truth of the thing perceived.*

Proof.—A true idea in us is an idea which is adequate in God, in so far as he is displayed through the nature of the human mind (II. xi. Coroll.). Let us suppose that there is in God, in so far as he is displayed through the human mind, an adequate idea, A. The idea of this idea must also necessarily be in God, and be referred to him in the same way as the idea A (by II. xx., whereof the proof is of universal application). But the idea A is supposed to be referred to God, in so far as he is displayed through the human mind; therefore, the idea of the idea A must be referred to God in the same manner; that is (by II. xi. Coroll.), the adequate idea of the idea A will be in the mind, which has the adequate idea A; therefore he, who has an adequate idea or knows a thing truly (II. xxxiv.), must at the same time have an adequate idea or true knowledge of his knowledge; that is, obviously, he must be assured. *Q.E.D.* . . .

PROP. XLIV. *It is not in the nature of reason to regard things as contingent, but as necessary.*

Proof.—It is in the nature of reason to perceive things truly (II. xli.), namely (I. Ax. vi.), as they are in themselves—that is (I. xxix.), not as contingent, but as necessary. *Q.E.D.*

Corollary I.—Hence it follows, that it is only through our imagination that we consider things, whether in respect to the future or the past, as contingent. . . .

Corollary II.—It is in the nature of reason to perceive things under a certain form of eternity (*sub quâdam aeternitatis specie*). . . .

PROP. XLV. *Every idea of every body, or of every particular thing actually existing, necessarily involves the eternal and infinite essence of God. . . .*

PROP. XLVII. *The human mind has an adequate knowledge of the eternal and infinite essence of God. . . .*

Note.—Hence we see, that the infinite essence and the eternity of God are known to all. Now as all things are in God, and are conceived through God, we can from this knowledge infer many things, which we may adequately know, and we may form that third kind of knowledge of which we spoke in the note to II. xl., and of the excellence and use of which we shall have occasion to speak in Part V. Men have not so clear a knowledge of God as they have of general notions, because they are unable to imagine God as they do bodies, and also because they have associated the name God with images of things that they are in the habit of seeing, as indeed they can hardly avoid doing, being, as they are, men, and continually affected by external bodies. Many errors, in truth, can be traced to this head, namely, that we do not apply names to things rightly. For instance, when a man says that the lines drawn from the center of a circle to its circumference are not equal, he then, at all events, assuredly attaches a meaning to the word circle different from that assigned by mathematicians. So again, when men make mistakes in calculation, they have one set of figures in their mind, and another on the paper. If we could see into their minds, they do not make a mistake; they seem to do so, because we think, that they have the same numbers in their mind as they have on the paper. If this were not so, we should not believe them to be in error, any more than I thought that a man was in error, whom I lately heard exclaiming that his entrance hall had flown into a neighbour's hen, for his meaning seemed to me sufficiently clear. Very many controversies have arisen from the fact, that men do not rightly explain their meaning, or do not rightly interpret the meaning of others. For, as a matter of fact, as they flatly contradict themselves, they assume now one side, now another, of the argument, so as to oppose the opinions, which they consider mistaken and absurd in their opponents.

Part III.—ON THE ORIGIN AND NATURE OF THE EMOTIONS

Most writers on the emotions and on human conduct seem to be treating rather of matters outside nature than of natural phenomena following nature's general laws. They appear to conceive man to be situated in nature as a kingdom within a kingdom: for they believe that he disturbs rather than follows nature's order, that he has absolute control over his actions, and that he is determined solely by himself. They attribute human infirmities and fickleness, not to the power of nature in general, but to some mysterious flaw in the nature of man, which accordingly they bemoan, deride, despise, or, as usually happens, abuse: he, who succeeds in hitting off the weakness of the human mind more eloquently or more acutely than his fellows, is looked upon as a seer. Still there has been no lack of very excellent men (to whose toil and industry I confess myself much indebted), who have written many noteworthy things concerning the right way of life, and have given much sage advice to mankind. But no one, so far as I know, has defined the nature and strength of the emotions, and the power of the mind against them for their restraint.

I do not forget, that the illustrious Descartes, though he believed, that the mind has absolute power over its actions, strove to explain human emotions by their primary causes, and, at the same time, to point out a way, by which the mind might attain to absolute dominion over them. However, in my opinion, he accomplishes nothing beyond a display of the acuteness of his own great intellect, as I will show in the proper place. For the present I wish to revert to those, who would rather abuse or deride human emotions than understand them. Such persons will, doubtless think it strange that I should attempt to treat of human vice and folly geometrically, and should wish to set forth with rigid reasoning those matters which they cry out against as repugnant to reason, frivolous, absurd, and dreadful. However, such is my plan. Nothing comes to pass in nature, which can be set down to a flaw therein; for nature is always the same, and everywhere one and the same in her efficacy and power of action; that is, nature's laws and ordinances, whereby all things come to pass and change from one form to another, are everywhere and always the same; so that there should be one and the same method of understanding the nature of all things whatsoever, namely, through nature's universal laws and rules. Thus the passions of hatred, anger, envy, and so on, considered in themselves, follow from this same necessity and efficacy of nature; they answer to certain definite causes, through which they are understood, and possess certain properties as worthy of being known as the properties of anything else, whereof the contemplation in itself affords us delight. I shall, therefore, treat of the nature and strength of the emotions according to the same method, as I employed heretofore in my investigations concerning God and the mind. I shall consider human actions and desires in exactly the same manner, as though I were concerned with lines, planes, and solids. . . .

Part IV.—OF HUMAN BONDAGE, OR THE STRENGTH OF THE EMOTIONS

¶ Preface

Human infirmity in moderating and checking the emotions I name bondage: for, when a man is a prey to his emotions, he is not his own master, but lies at the mercy of fortune: so much so, that he is often compelled, while seeing that which is better for him, to follow that which is worse. Why this is so, and what is good or evil in the emotions, I propose to show in this part of my treatise. But, before I begin, it would be well to make a few prefatory observations on perfection and imperfection, good and evil.

When a man has purposed to make a given thing, and has brought it to perfection, his work will be pronounced perfect, not only by himself, but by everyone who rightly knows, or thinks that he knows, the intention and aim of its author. For instance, suppose anyone sees a work (which I assume to be not yet completed), and knows that the aim of the author of that work is to build a house, he will call the work imperfect; he will, on the other hand, call it perfect, as soon as he sees that it is carried through to the end, which its author had purposed for it. But if a man sees a work, the like whereof he has never seen before, and if he knows not the intention of the artificer, he plainly cannot know, whether that work be perfect or imperfect. Such seems to be the primary meaning of these terms.

But, after men began to form general ideas, to think out types of houses, buildings, towers, &c., and to prefer certain types to others, it came about, that each man called perfect that which he saw agree with the general idea he had formed of the thing in question, and called imperfect that which he saw agree less with his own preconceived type, even though it had evidently been completed in accordance with the idea of its artificer. This seems to be the only reason for calling natural phenomena, which, indeed, are not made with human hands, perfect or imperfect: for men are wont to form general ideas of things natural, no less than of things artificial, and such ideas they hold as types, believing that Nature (who they think does nothing without an object) has them in view, and has set them as types before herself. Therefore, when they behold something in Nature, which does not wholly conform to the preconceived type which they have formed of the thing in question, they say that Nature has fallen short or has blundered, and has left her work incomplete. Thus we see that men are wont to style natural phenomena perfect or imperfect rather from their own prejudices, than from true knowledge of what they pronounce upon.

Now we showed in the Appendix to Part I., that Nature does not work with an end in view. For the eternal and infinite Being, which we call God or Nature, acts by the same necessity as that whereby it exists. For we have shown, that by the same necessity of its nature, whereby it exists, it likewise works (I. xvi.). The reason or cause why God or Nature exists, and the reason why he acts, are one and the same. Therefore, as he does not exist for the sake of an end, so neither does he act for the sake of an end; of his existence and of his action there is neither origin nor end. Wherefore, a cause which is called final is nothing else but human desire, in so far as it is considered as the origin or cause of anything. For example, when we say that to be inhabited is the final cause of this or that house, we mean nothing more than that a man, conceiving the conveniences of household life, had a desire to build a house. Wherefore, the being inhabited, in so far as it is regarded as a final cause, is nothing else but this particular desire, which is really the efficient cause; it is regarded as the primary cause, because men are generally ignorant of the causes of their desires. They are, as I have often said already, conscious of their own actions and appetites, but ignorant of the causes whereby they are determined to any particular desire. Therefore, the common saying that Nature sometimes falls short, or blunders, and produces things which are imperfect, I set down among the glosses treated of in the Appendix to Part I. Perfection and imperfection, then, are in reality merely modes of thinking, or notions which we form from a comparison among one another of individuals of the same species; hence I said above (II. Def. vi.), that by reality and perfection I mean the same thing. For we are wont to refer all the individual things in nature to one genus, which is called the highest genus, namely, to the category of Being, whereto absolutely all individuals in nature belong. Thus, in so far as we refer the individuals in nature to this category, and comparing them one with another, find that some possess more of being or reality than others, we, to this extent, say that some are more perfect than others. Again, in so far as we attribute to them anything implying negation—as term, end, infirmity, etc.,—we, to this extent, call them imperfect, because they do not affect our mind so much as the things which we call perfect, not because they have any intrinsic deficiency, or because Nature has blundered. For nothing lies within the scope of a thing's nature, save that which follows from the necessity of the nature of its efficient cause, and whatsoever follows from the necessity of the nature of its efficient cause necessarily comes to pass.

As for the terms *good* and *bad,* they indicate no positive quality in things regarded in themselves, but are merely modes of thinking, or notions which we form from the comparison of things one with another. Thus one and the same thing can be at the same time good, bad, and indifferent. For instance, music is good for him that is melancholy, bad for him that mourns; for him that is deaf, it is neither good nor bad.

Nevertheless, though this be so, the terms should still be retained. For, inasmuch as we desire to form an idea of man as a type of human nature which we may hold in view, it will be useful for us to retain the terms in question, in the sense I have indicated.

In what follows, then, I shall mean by "good" that which we certainly know to be a means of approaching more nearly to the type of human nature, which we have set before ourselves; by "bad," that which we certainly know to be a hindrance to us in approaching the said type. Again, we shall say that men are more perfect, or more imperfect, in proportion as they approach more or less nearly to the said type. For it must be specially remarked that, when I say that a man passes from a lesser to a greater perfection, or *vice versâ,* I do not mean that he is changed from one essence or reality to another; for instance, a horse would be as completely destroyed by being changed into a man, as by being changed into an insect. What I mean is, that we conceive the thing's power of action, in so far as this is understood by its nature, to be increased or diminished. Lastly, by perfection in general I shall, as I have said, mean reality—in other words, each thing's essence, in so far as it exists, and operates in a particular manner, and without paying any regard to its duration. For no given thing can be said to be more perfect, because it has passed a longer time in existence. The duration of things cannot be determined by their essence, for the essence of things involves no fixed and definite period of existence; but everything, whether it be more perfect or less perfect, will always be able to persist in existence with the same force wherewith it began to exist; wherefore, in this respect, all things are equal.

Part V.—OF THE POWER OF THE UNDERSTANDING, OR HUMAN FREEDOM

¶ Preface

At length I pass to the remaining portion of my Ethics, which is concerned with the way leading to freedom. I shall therefore treat therein of the power of the reason, showing how far the reason can control the emotions, and what is the nature of Mental Freedom or Blessedness; we shall then be able to see, how much more powerful the wise man is than the ignorant. It is no part of my design to point out the method and means whereby the understanding may be perfected, nor to show the skill whereby the body may be so tended, as to be capable of the due performance of its functions. The latter question lies in the province of Medicine, the former in the province of Logic. Here, therefore, I repeat, I shall treat only of the power of the mind, or of reason; and I shall mainly show the extent and nature of its dominion over the emotions, for their control and moderation. That we do not possess absolute dominion over them, I have already shown. Yet the Stoics have thought, that the emotions depended absolutely on our will, and that we could absolutely govern them. But these philosophers were compelled, by the protest of experience, not from their own principles, to confess, that no slight practice and zeal is needed to control and moderate them: and this someone endeavoured to illustrate by the example (if I remember rightly) of two dogs, the one a house-dog and the other a hunting-dog. For by long training it could be brought about, that the house-dog should become accustomed to hunt, and the hunting-dog to cease from running after hares. To this opinion Descartes not a little inclines. For he maintained, that the soul or mind is specially united to a particular part of the brain, namely, to that part called the pineal gland, by the aid of which the mind is enabled to feel all the movements which are set going in the body, and also external objects, and which the mind by a simple act of volition can put in motion in various ways. He asserted, that this gland is so suspended in the midst of the brain, that it could be moved by the slightest motion of the animal spirits: further, that this gland is suspended in the midst of the brain in as many different manners, as the animal spirits can impinge thereon; and, again, that as many different marks are impressed on the said gland, as there are different external objects which impel the animal spirits towards it; whence it follows, that if the will of the soul suspends the gland in a position, wherein it has already been suspended once before by the animal spirits driven in one way or another, the gland in its turn reacts on the said spirits, driving and determining them to the condition wherein they were, when repulsed before by a similar position of the gland. He further asserted, that every act of mental volition is united in nature to a certain given motion of the gland. For instance, whenever anyone desires to look at a remote object, the act of volition causes the pupil of the eye to dilate, whereas, if the person in question had only thought of the dilatation of the pupil, the mere wish to dilate it would not have brought about the result, inasmuch as the motion of the gland, which serves to impel the animal spirits towards the optic nerve in a way which would dilate or contract the pupil, is not associated in nature with the wish to dilate or contract the pupil, but with the wish to look at remote or very near objects. Lastly, he maintained that, although every motion of the aforesaid gland seems to have been united by nature to one particular thought out of the whole number of our thoughts from the very beginning of our life, yet it can nevertheless become through habituation associated with other thoughts; this he endeavours to prove in the *Passions de l'âme,* I. 50. He thence concludes, that there is no soul so weak, that it cannot, under proper direction, acquire absolute power over its passions. For passions as defined by him are "perceptions, or feelings, or disturbances of the soul, which are referred to the soul as species, and which (mark the expression) are produced, preserved, and strengthened through some movement of the spirits." (*Passions de l'âme,* I. 27.) But, seeing that we can join any motion of the gland, or consequently of the spirits, to any volition, the determination of the will depends entirely on our own powers; if, therefore, we determine our will with sure and firm decisions in the direction to which we wish our actions to tend, and associate the motions of the passions which we wish to acquire with the said decisions, we shall acquire an absolute dominion over our passions. Such is the doctrine of this illustrious philosopher (in so far as I gather it from his own words); it is one which, had it been less ingenious, I could hardly believe to have proceeded from so great a man. Indeed, I am lost in wonder, that a philosopher, who had stoutly asserted, that he would draw no conclusions which do not follow from self-evident premisses, and would affirm nothing which he did not clearly and distinctly perceive, and who had so often taken to task the scholastics for wishing to explain obscurities through occult qualities, could maintain a hypothesis, besides which occult qualities are commonplace. What does he understand, I ask, by the union of the mind and the body? What clear and distinct conception has he got of thought in most intimate union with a certain particle of extended matter? Truly I should like him to explain this union through its proximate cause. But he had so distinct a conception of mind being distinct from body, that he could not assign any particular cause of the union between the two, or of the mind itself, but was obliged to have recourse to the cause of the whole universe, that is to God. Further, I should much like to know, what degree of motion the mind can impart to this pineal gland, and with what force can it hold it suspended? For I am in ignorance, whether this gland can be agitated more slowly or more quickly by the mind than by the animal spirits, and whether the motions of the passions, which we have closely united with firm decisions, cannot be again disjoined therefrom by physical causes; in which case it would follow that, although the mind firmly intended to face a given danger, and had united to this decison the motions of boldness, yet at the sight of the danger the gland might become suspended in a way, which would preclude the mind thinking of anything except running away. In truth, as there is no common standard of volition and motion, so is there no comparison possible between the powers of the mind and the power or strength of the body; consequently the strength of one cannot in any wise be determined by the strength of the other. We may also add, that there is no gland discoverable in the midst of the brain, so placed that it can thus easily be set in motion in so many ways, and also that all the nerves are not prolonged so far as the cavities of the brain. Lastly, I omit all the assertions which he makes concerning the will and its freedom, inasmuch as I have abundantly proved that his premisses are false. Therefore, since the power of the mind, as I have shown above, is defined by the understanding only, we shall determine solely by the knowledge of the mind the remedies against the emotions, which I believe all have had experience of, but do not accurately observe or distinctly see, and from the same basis we shall deduce all those conclusions, which have regard to the mind's blessedness. . . .

PROP. XLII. *Blessedness is not the reward of virtue, but virtue itself; neither do we rejoice therein, because we control our lusts, but, contrariwise, because we rejoice therein, we are able to control our lusts. . . .*

Note.—I have thus completed all I wished to set forth touching the mind's power over the emotions and the mind's freedom. Whence it appears, how potent is the wise man, and how much he surpasses the ignorant man, who is driven only by his lusts. For the ignorant man is not only distracted in various ways by external causes without ever gaining the true acquiescence of his spirit, but moreover lives, as it were unwitting of himself, and of God, and of things, and as soon as he ceases to suffer, ceases also to be.

Whereas the wise man, in so far as he is regarded as such, is scarcely at all disturbed in spirit, but, being conscious of himself, and of God, and of things, by a certain eternal necessity, never ceases to be, but always possesses true acquiescence of his spirit.

If the way which I have pointed out as leading to this result seems exceedingly hard, it may nevertheless be discovered. Needs must it be hard, since it is so seldom found. How would it be possible, if salvation were ready to our hand, and could without great labour be found, that it should be by almost all men neglected? But all things excellent are as difficult as they are rare.

XIV

MALEBRANCHE

Nicolas Malebranche (1638-1715), a cripple, was educated at home, then trained in Aristotelianism, and finally studied theology at the Sorbonne. At twenty-two, disappointed with what he had been taught, he joined the pious Oratory, founded by Cardinal Bérulle, to study church history, Hebrew, and biblical criticism. The Oratory was of Augustinian orientation, and some of its members were interested in Cartesianism. Malebranche undertook a systematic study of mathematics and Descartes' writings. During 1674-1675, he first published his views in his *The Search After Truth,* which was widely read and criticized. The *Dialogues on Metaphysics and on Religion* (1688) (from which the selections that follow are taken) represent a more literary and definitive statement of his views. His rationalism was attacked by Arnauld, Leibniz, Locke, and others, and some of his works were put on the Index (for his views about Grace). He greatly influenced Berkeley and Hume in the next century. The translation is by Morris Ginsberg.

Dialogues on Metaphysics and on Religion

FIRST DIALOGUE

. . . THEODORE. Draw the curtain. This bright light will inconvenience us a little and perhaps give too much lustre to certain objects. That is all right. Be seated. Reject, Aristes, all that has come into your mind by means of the senses. Silence your imagination. Let all things in you be in perfect silence. Forget also, if you can, that you have a body, and think only of what I am going to tell you. In a word, be attentive, and do not find fault with my preamble. Your attention is all I ask of you. Without this effort or this struggle of the mind against the impressions of sense, we can make no conquest in the realm of truth.

ARISTES. I believe so, too, Theodore. Speak, but permit me to stop you when I cannot follow you.

THEODORE. That is quite right. Listen.

I. Nothing or Non-being has no qualities. I think, therefore I am.[1] But what am I, I that think during the time that I am thinking? Am I a body, a mind, a man? As yet I know nothing of all this. I know only that during the time in which I think I am something that thinks. Now let us see. Can a body think? Can a piece of extension whether of length, width or depth, reason, desire, feel? No, beyond a doubt, for all the modifications of such an extension consist only in certain relations of distance; and it is obvious that such relations are not perceptions, reasonings, pleasures, desires, feelings, in a word, thoughts. This "I" that thinks, then, my own substance, is not a body, since my perceptions, which certainly belong to me, are entirely different things from these relations of distance.

1. St. Augustine, *City of God,* Bk. XI, chap. xxvi.

Aristes. It is clear to me that modifications of extension can only be relations of distance, and that, therefore, extension cannot know, will or feel. But perhaps my body is something else besides extension. For, it seems to me, it is my finger that feels the pain of a prick, my heart which desires, my brain which reasons. The inner feeling I have of all that goes on within me teaches me what I am saying to you. Prove to me that my body is nothing but extension, and I will admit that my mind, or that in me which thinks, wills and reasons, is not material or corporeal.

II. Theodore. What, Aristes! Do you believe that your body consists of some substance other than extension? Do you not understand that it suffices alone to have extension to form out of it a brain, a heart, arms, hands, all the veins, the arteries, the nerves, and whatever else the body is composed of? If God were to destroy the extension of your body would you still have a brain, veins, arteries, etc.? Do you believe, then, that a body can be reduced to a mathematical point? That God can form all that there is in the universe out of the extension of a grain of sand, I do not doubt. But, assuredly, when there is no extension (I say *no* extension), there is no corporeal substance. . . .

All that is or has being can either be conceived by itself, or it cannot. There is no middle course, for these two propositions are contradictories. Now, all that can be conceived by itself and without the thought of anything else, all, I say, that can be conceived by itself as existing independently of every other thing, and without the idea which we have of it representing any other thing, is assuredly a being or a substance, and all that cannot be conceived by itself and without the thought of anything else is a mode of Being or a modification of Substance.

For example. We cannot think of roundness without thinking of extension. Roundness, then, is not a being or substance, but a mode of being. We can think of extension without thinking of any other thing in particular. Therefore, extension is not a mode of being. It is itself a being. Since the modification of a substance is only the substance itself determined in a particular way, it is evident that the idea of a modification necessarily involves the idea of the substance of which it is a modification. Again, since a substance is that which subsists by itself, the idea of a substance does not necessarily involve the idea of any other being. We have no other way of distinguishing substances or beings, modifications or modes of being, than by the different ways in which we think of them. Now, consider. Is it not true that you can think of extension without thinking of any other thing? Is it not true that you can become aware of extension by itself? Extension, therefore, is a substance and not a mode of substance. Accordingly, extension and matter are one and the same substance. But I can think of thought, desires, pleasures, without thinking of extension, and even if I suppose that there is no extension. Hence all these are not modes of extension, but modes of a substance which thinks, which feels, which desires, and which is quite different from extension.

All the modifications of extension consist in nothing but relations of distance. But it is evident that my pleasures, my desires, my thoughts, are not relations of distance. All relations of distance can be compared, measured, determined, in an exact manner by the principles of geometry, but we cannot compare or measure our perceptions or our feelings in this way. Therefore, my soul is not material. It is not a modification of my body. It is a substance which thinks and which has no resemblance to the extended substance of which my body is made up.

ARISTES. That seems to me demonstrated. But what conclusions can you draw from it?

III. THEODORE. I can deduce an infinite number of truths from it. For the distinction of body and soul is the basis of the main tenets of philosophy, and among others of the immortality of the soul. For, let me say this in passing, if the soul is a substance distinguished from the body, it is clear that, even if death were to annihilate our body (which it does not do), it would not follow from that that our soul was also annihilated. . . .

IV. THEODORE. I think of a quantity of things, of a number, a circle, a house, of such and such beings, of Being. Therefore, all these *are* at least during the time in which I am thinking of them. Surely, when I think of a circle, of a number, of Being or the Infinite, of a certain being, I am aware of these realities. For if the circle of which I am aware were nothing, in thinking of it I should be thinking of nothing. But the circle of which I am thinking has properties which no other figure has. Hence this circle exists during the time in which I am thinking of it, since nothing or non-entity has no properties, and one non-entity cannot be different from any other non-entity.

ARISTES. What, Theodore! Do you mean to say that whatever you may choose to think of exists? Does your mind give being to this cabinet, this bureau, this chair, because you think of them?

THEODORE. Not so fast. I am saying that all that I think of *is* or, if you like, exists. The cabinet, the bureau, these chairs which I see, all these *are* at least during the time in which I see them. But you are mixing up what I see with a piece of furniture that I do not see. There is a greater difference between the bureau that I see and that which you believe you see than there is between your mind and your body.

ARISTES. I understand you partly, Theodore, and I am sorry for having interrupted you. I am convinced that all that we see, and all that we think of, has some reality. You are not talking of objects, but of the ideas of objects. Yes, no doubt, the ideas which we have of objects exist during the time in which they are present to the mind. But I thought you were speaking of the objects themselves.

V. THEODORE. *Of the objects themselves,* why, we have not got to them! I am trying to think the matter out in the proper order. Many more principles than you may suppose are necessary to prove what no one doubts. For where are the people who doubt whether they have bodies, whether they are walking on this earth, whether they are living in a material world? But you will know soon what few people understand well, namely, that if our body moves about in a corporeal world, our mind, on the other hand, transports us incessantly into a world of intelligence which touches it, and which thereby becomes accessible to the senses. Since men attach no value to the ideas which they have of things, they give to the created world more reality than it has. They do not doubt the existence of objects, and they attribute to them many qualities which they have not. Yet they do not think of the reality of their ideas. This is so because they listen to their senses and do not consult inner truth. For, once again, it is much easier to prove the reality of ideas, or, if I may use your terms, the reality of this other world filled with the beauties of intelligence than to prove the existence of the material world. My reasons are as follows. Ideas have an eternal and necessary existence, but the corporeal world exists only because it has pleased God to create it. So, in order to see the intelligible world, it is sufficient to consult reason which contains the ideas, or the eternal and necessary intelligible essences, and this can be accomplished by all minds that are rational or are united to the infinite Reason. But in order to see the material world, or rather to judge that this world exists, since that world is invisible in itself, it is necessary that God should reveal it to us, for we cannot see His arbitrary volitions in the necessary Reason. Now God reveals the existence of His creations in two ways, by the authority of the sacred writings and by means of the senses. . . .

SECOND DIALOGUE

. . . ARISTES. Here, then, is the argument in simple and non-figurative language:

Infinite intelligible extension is not a modification of my mind. It is immutable, eternal, necessary. I cannot doubt its reality or immensity. But nothing that is immutable, eternal, necessary, and, above all, infinite is a created thing, nor can it belong to a created thing. Hence it belongs to the Creator and can be only in God. Hence there is a God, and a Reason, a God in whom there is the archetype which I contemplate of the created world which I inhabit—a God in whom there is that Reason which illumines me by means of the purely intellectual ideas which it furnishes in abundance to my mind and to the minds of all men. For I am sure that all men are united with the same Reason as I am, and since I am certain that they see or can see what I see when I enter into myself and when I discover therein the truth or necessary relations which are contained in the intelligible substance of the universal Reason which dwells in me, or rather in which all intelligences dwell.

II. THEODORE. You have not been led astray, my dear Aristes. You have followed reason, and it has led you to Him who engendered it out of His own substance and who possesses it throughout all eternity. But do not imagine that it has disclosed to you the nature of that supreme Being to whom it has led you. When you contemplate intelligible extension you only see as yet the archetype of the material world which we inhabit and that of an infinity of other possible worlds. You do in truth see the divine Substance, for it alone is visible, it alone can illumine the mind. Yet you do not see it in itself or as it really is. You only see it in its relation to material creations, you only see it so far as they participate in it, or in so far as it is representative of them. Consequently it is not, strictly speaking, God Himself that you see, but only the matter which He can produce.

You certainly see, by means of the infinite intelligible extension, *that* God is. For He alone can possess all that you see, since nothing finite can contain an infinite reality. But you do not see *what* God is. For there is no limit to the Divine perfections, and that which you see when you think of immense spaces is lacking in an infinity of perfections. I say "that which you see," not the substance which represents to you what you see. For this substance, which you do not see in itself, has infinite perfections.

Assuredly, the substance which contains this intelligible extension is all-powerful. It is infinitely wise. It includes an infinity of perfections and realities. It includes, for example, an infinity of intelligible numbers. But the intelligible extension has nothing in common with all these things. There is no wisdom, power or unity in all this extension which you contemplate. For you know that all numbers are commensurable among themselves, since they have unity for a common measure. If, then, the parts of extension divided and subdivided by the mind can be reduced to unity, they will always be commensurable amongst themselves by this unity, which as you know is certainly not the case. Thus the divine Substance in that simplicity to which we cannot attain contains an infinity of quite different intelligible perfections by means of which God illumines us without allowing Himself to be seen as He is, or in His individual and absolute reality, but merely in His reality which is general and relative to possible created beings. Nevertheless, try to follow me. I will try to lead you as near as possible to the Divine.

III. The infinite intelligible extension is only the archetype of an infinity of possible worlds similar to our own. By means of it I only see certain determinate beings—material things. When I think of this extension I do not see the divine Substance, except in so far as it is representative of bodies and is participated in by them. But now, when I think of Being, and not of determinate beings, when I think of *the* Infinite, and not of such and such an infinite, it is certain, in the first place, that I do not see such a vast reality in the modifications of my mind. For if I cannot find in these modifications sufficient reality to enable me to represent to myself an infinity in extension, a fortiori I cannot find in it sufficient reality for representing to myself what is infinite in every way. Thus, it is only God, the Infinite, the Unlimited, it is only the Infinite infinitely infinite who can comprise the infinitely infinite reality which I see when I think of Being, and not of such and such beings or of such and such infinities.

IV. In the second place, it is certain that the idea of Being, of reality, of unlimited perfection, or of the infinite in every way, is not the divine substance in so far as it is representative of such and such a created thing or is participated in by such and such a created thing. For every created thing is necessarily a definite being. It is a contradiction that God should make or create a Being in general or one Infinite in every way which should not be God Himself, or should not be equal to His own principle. . . . Here it is in two words. The idea of Being without restrictions, of the infinite, of the general, is not the idea of created things, or of the essences of created things, but the idea which represents the Divine or the essence of the Divine. All particular beings participate in Being, but no particular being can equal it. Being comprises all things, but all beings created or possible, in all their manifold variety, cannot exhaust the immense extension of Being.

ARISTES. It seems to me, I can see your meaning. You define God as He defined Himself in speaking to Moses, "God is that which is."[2] Intelligible extension is the idea or archetype of bodies. But the being without restrictions, in a word, Being, is the idea of God; it is that which represents Him to our minds as we see Him in this life.

V. THEODORE. Very good. But above all you must note that God or the Infinite is not visible by an idea representative of Him. The Infinite is its own idea. It has no Archetype. It can be known, but it cannot be constructed. Only created things, only determinate beings, can be constructed, or can be visible through ideas which represent them even before they are produced. We can see a circle, a house, a sun, though they may not actually exist. For all that is finite can be seen in the Infinite, which comprises all intelligible ideas of the finite. The Infinite, on the other hand, can be seen only in itself, for nothing finite can represent the Infinite. If we think of God, it follows that He exists. A finite being, though known, may not exist. We can see its essence without its existence, its idea without itself. But we cannot see the essence of the Infinite without its existence, or the idea of Being without Being. For Being can have no idea representative of it. There is no archetype which could comprise all its intelligible reality. The Infinite is its own archetype, and contains within itself the archetype of all beings.

Thus, you see that the proposition, "there is a God," is in itself the clearest of all existential propositions, and that it is even as certain as the proposition, "I think, therefore I am." You see, moreover, what is meant by God, for God, Being, and the Infinite, are one and the same.

VI. But, once more, make no mistake about this matter. You see only confusedly and as from a distance what God is. You do not see Him as He is, because, though you see the Infinite or Being without

2. Exod. 3:14.

restriction, you only see it in a very imperfect manner. You do not see it as a single being. You see a multiplicity of created things in the infinity of uncreated Being, but you do not see its unity distinctly. For you cannot see it so much in its absolute reality as in the reality which attaches to it in its relation to possible created things, the number of which it could increase indefinitely without their ever equalling the reality which represents them. You see it as the universal Reason which illumines all intelligences according to the measure of light necessary for their guidance, and for revealing as much of His perfections as can be shared in by limited beings. But you do not discover the property which is essential to the Infinite, that, namely, of being at the same time one and many, composed, so to speak, of an infinity of different perfections, and yet so simple that in it each perfection comprises all the others without any real distinction.

God does not communicate His substance to any of His creatures; He only communicates to them His perfections; not as they are in His substance, but in so far as His substance is representative of them, and in accordance with the limitations bound up with the nature of created things. Intelligible extension, for instance, represents bodies; it is their archetype or their idea. But, although this extension occupies no place, bodies are and must be locally extended because of the limitations essential to all finite created things, and because no finite created thing can have this property or character, incomprehensible to the human mind, of being at the same time one thing and all things, of being at the same time perfectly simple and yet in possession of all sorts of perfections.

Thus, intelligible extension represents infinite spaces, but it does not fill any; and although it fills, so to speak, all minds and discloses itself to them, it follows in no way that our mind is spatial. If our mind could only see infinite spaces through local conjunction with locally extended spaces, then, in order to see infinite spaces, it would itself have to be infinitely extended.

The divine Substance is everywhere, without being extended locally. It has no limits. It is not contained in the universe. But it is not this Substance as expanded everywhere that we see when we think of spaces. For were this the case our mind, being finite, would never be able to think of infinite spaces. Yet the intelligible extension, which we see in the divine Substance which comprises it, is this Substance only in so far as it is representative of material beings and participated in by them. This is all I can tell you. . . .

THIRD DIALOGUE

. . . Theodore. The idea or archetype of extension is eternal, necessary. We see this idea, as I have already proved to you, and God sees it also, for there is nothing in Him which He does not discover. We see it, I say, clearly and distinctly, without thinking of anything else. We can think of it in itself, or rather we cannot think of it as a modification of some other thing, for it contains no necessary relation to other ideas. But, God can create that which He sees and which He causes us to see in His light clearly and distinctly. He can create whatever is not self-contradictory, for He is all-powerful. Hence He can make extension all by itself. This extension will, then, be a being or a substance, and the idea which we have of it will represent its nature. If we suppose further that God has created this extension, it will follow that there will be matter. For what kind of being would this extension be? Now, I believe that you see that this matter is not capable of thinking, feeling, or reasoning.

Aristes. I admit that, since our ideas are necessary and eternal and the same as God consults, it follows, that if He acts at all, He will take that which these ideas represent, and that we are not mistaken when we attribute to matter only that which we see in its archetype. Yet perhaps we do not see this archetype in its entirety. Since modes of extension can only be spatial relations, it follows that extension is not capable of thought. I agree. But the subject or bearer of extension, that something which is perhaps contained in the archetype of matter and which is to us unknown, that may very well be able to think.

XII. Theodore. This unknown something will be able to do a good many other things; it will be able to do whatsoever you choose to ascribe to it without anyone being able to dispute your assertions. It may have thousands upon thousands of faculties, virtues, admirable qualities. It may be able to act on your soul, enlighten it, render it happy and unhappy. In a word, it will have as many powers, and if you press the point as many divinities, as there are different bodies. For, indeed, how do I know that this other thing, which you take to be the essence of matter, will not have all the properties which it may please you to ascribe to it, since I have no knowledge of it whatever?

Thus you see, perhaps, that in order to know the works of God, it is necessary to consult the ideas which He gives us of them, those ideas which are clear and in accordance with which He has formed them; and that we run a great risk, if we follow another course. For if we consult our senses, if we blindly yield to their testimony, they will persuade us that there are at least certain bodies, the power and intelligence of which are marvellous. Our senses tell us that fire diffuses heat and light. They persuade us that animals and plants work for the preservation of their life and of their species, with a kind of intelligence. Yet we see that these faculties are something other than figures and movements. We judge, then, on the ground of the confused and obscure deliverances of our senses, that there must be in bodies something other than extension, since modes of extension can only be motions and figures. But let us attentively consult reason. Let us linger over the clear idea which we have of body. Let us not confuse it with our being, and we shall find perhaps that we attribute to such bodies qualities and properties which they do not possess and which belong to us alone.

It may be, you argue, that we do not see the archetype or idea of matter in its entirety. If that were so, we ought only to attribute to it what our idea of it represents to us, for we cannot ascribe to anything that which we do not know. Assuredly, if unbelivers think that they are permitted to reason about chimeras of which they have no idea whatever, they must allow that we can reason about things by the ideas which we have of them. But, in order to remove everything which may be the cause of stumbling or of their gaining confidence in their strange errors, note once more, that we can think of extension without thinking of any other thing; for it is here that the principle lies. Hence, God could make extension without making anything else. This extension would then exist without the unknown something which they attribute to matter. This extension would then be a substance and not a modification of substance. And this is what, for several reasons, I believe we ought to call body or matter; not only because we cannot think of modifications without thinking of the entities of which they are the modifications, or because there is no other way of distinguishing entities from their modes than by ascertaining whether we can think of the former without thinking of the latter, but also because by means of extension alone and the properties ascribed to it by everybody we can explain sufficiently all the natural effects; I mean that we observe no effect of matter the natural cause of which cannot be found in the idea of extension.

Aristes. What you are saying now appears to me convincing. I understand better than I did that, in order to know the works of God, it is necessary to consult attentively the ideas which He possesses in His wisdom and to silence our senses and above all our imagination. Yet this way of discovering truth is so hard and difficult that there is hardly anybody who follows it. To see that the sun is brilliant with light we need only open our eyes. To ascertain whether sound is in the air, it is sufficient to make a noise. Nothing is easier. But the mind is overstrained when attending to ideas which do not strike the senses. One soon gets tired: I know this from experience. Happy you who can meditate on metaphysical matters! . . .

. . . I understand clearly that sound is not propagated in the air, and that a string cannot produce it. The reasons which you have just given me are to me convincing. For, in short, neither sound nor the power to produce it is contained in the idea of matter, since the modifications of body consist in nothing but spatial relations. That is sufficient for me. Nevertheless, here is another proof which occurs to me and which is convincing. In a fever which I had some time ago I heard the incessant howling of an animal which without a doubt did not howl, seeing that it was dead. I believe also that in sleep it happens to you as well as to me that one hears a concert, or at least the sound of a trumpet or drum, though everything may be in a deep silence. Being ill, then, I heard yells and howlings, for I remember to this day that they caused me much pain. But these unpleasant sounds were not in the air, although I heard them therein, just as I hear therein the sounds which this instrument makes. Thus, in spite of the fact that we hear sounds as though they were propagated in the air, it does not follow from this fact that they are really there. They exist really only in the soul, for they are only sensations which affect it, only modifications which belong to it. Nay, I go even further. For all that you have just told me induces me to believe that there is nothing in the objects of our senses resembling the sensations which we have of them. These objects stand in a certain relation to their ideas, but it seems to me that they stand in no relation to our sensations. Bodies are nothing but extension capable of motion and of various figures. This becomes clear when we consult the ideas which represent them.

THEODORE. Bodies, you say, have nothing that resembles the sensations which we have, and in order to know their properties we must consult not our senses, but the clear idea of extension which represents their nature. . . .

FOURTH DIALOGUE

. . . ARISTES. I, therefore, silenced them [the senses], being quite determined no longer to judge of the works of God on the basis of their testimony, but rather on that of the ideas which represent those works and in accordance with which they were formed.

It was in following this principle that I realised that light is neither in the sun nor in the air where we see it; that colours are not on the surface of bodies; that the sun could perhaps set in motion the fine particles of the air, and these latter could communicate the same impression of movement to the optic nerve, and thence to that part of the brain where the soul resides, and that these small bodies in movement when encountering solid objects might be reflected differently according to the diversity in the surfaces which were causing them to rebound. So much for their boasted light and variety of colours.

VI. I have understood likewise that the heat which I feel is not in the fire, nor the cold in the ice, nor even pain in my own body, in which I have often felt it so cruelly acute. Neither is sweetness in the sugar, nor bitterness in the aloes, nor acidity in sour grapes, nor sourness in vinegar, nor that sweetness and strength in wine which deceives and stupefies so many drunkards. I see all this, by the same reason which enables me to see that sound must be regarded as not in the air and that there is an infinite difference between the vibrations of strings and the sounds which they yield, between the proportions of their vibrations and the variety of the consonances.

. . . But I cannot conceal from you a difficulty which, despite all my efforts, I was unable to surmount. I follow, for instance, without misgiving, the action of the sun through all the space which separates it from me. For, granted that there is no empty space, I can understand that the sun can make no impression in the places it occupies without the impression being transmitted to the place which I occupy or to my eyes, and by my eyes to my brain. But, in following the clear idea of movement, I could not understand whence there came to me the sensation of light. I see quite well that the movement of the optic nerve is alone sufficient to produce the sensation in me. For, pressing the corner of my eye with my finger on a spot behind which I know the optic nerve is located, I saw a bright light in a place otherwise dark on the side opposite to that on which my eye was pressed. Yet this change from movement to light seemed to me then and seems to me still altogether incomprehensible. What a strange metamorphosis, from a pressure on the eye to a brilliant light! And this is all the more astounding because I do not see this radiance of light in my soul of which it is the modification, nor in my brain, where the disturbance ends, nor in the eye where the pressure takes place, nor on the side on which I press my eye, but in the air—in the air which surely is incapable of such a modification, and on the side opposite to the eye which I press. What a marvellous thing!

VII. At first I thought that my soul, on being warned of the disturbance that had taken place in my body, was the cause of the sensations which it had of the things around it. But a little reflection undeceived me. For it is not true, it seems to me, that the soul knows anything of the disturbance caused by the sun in the fibres of the brain. I saw light before I knew of this disturbance. For children who do not even know that they have a brain are struck by the brilliance of light just as much as philosophers are. Again, what relation is there between the vibrations of a corporeal thing and the different sensations which follow such vibrations? How can I see light in bodies if it is a modification of my soul, how see it in bodies around me, if the disturbance takes place in my body alone? I press the corner of my eye on the right side, why do I see the light on the left side, notwithstanding the fact that I am well aware that it is not on that side that I am pressing?

From all this, and from a number of other things which it would take me too long to tell you, I concluded that the sensations were in myself, that I was in no wise their cause, and that if corporeal things were capable of acting on me and of making themselves felt in the way I feel them, it would be necessary that they should be of a nature more excellent than my body, endowed with a terrible power, and some of them even with a wisdom truly marvellous, always uniform in their behaviour, always effective in their action, always incomprehensible in the astounding results of their power. All this appeared to me tremendous and terrible to think of, though my senses encouraged the madness and quite accommodated themselves to it. But, Theodore, will you kindly clear this matter up for me?

THEODORE. There is no time to resolve your difficulties unless you desire that we should leave the general truths of metaphysics and enter upon an explanation of the principles of physics and of the laws of the conjunction of soul and body. . . .

VIII. . . . Listen, then; but remember to meditate upon what I have already told you. When we seek to find the reason of certain effects, and in following the chain of causes and effects arrive at last at a general cause or at a cause that we can quite well see has no relation to the effect which it produces or rather appears to produce, then instead of being satisfied with chimeras, we ought to have recourse to the author of the laws of nature. For example, if you were to ask me what is the cause of the pain which one feels when one is pricked, I should be wrong to tell you forthwith that it is one of the laws of the author of nature that a prick should be followed by pain. I ought to tell you that the prick cannot separate the fibres of my flesh without disturbing the nerves which propagate stimulation to the brain, and without disturbing the brain itself. But if you wish to know how it is that when a certain part of my brain is disturbed in a given way, I feel the pain of a prick, this question concerns a general effect; and, as one cannot by tracing the matter further, find a natural or particular cause, one must have recourse to a general cause. For this amounts to a question as to who is the author of the general laws of the conjunction of soul and body. Now, since admittedly, there can be no relation or necessary connection between a disturbance in the brain and certain sensations, it is evident that we must have recourse to a power which is not to be met with in either of these entities. It is not sufficient to say that as the prick wounds the body, the soul must be warned of the fact by pain, so that it may go to its assistance. For this would be to substitute a final for an efficient cause, and the difficulty would remain; for we should still have to ascertain the cause which brings it about, that, on the occasion of the body being wounded, the soul suffers in consequence, and experiences a particular kind of pain for a particular kind of wound.

IX. Further, to say, with certain philosophers, that the soul is the cause of the pain, because the pain is but the sadness which the soul feels when there takes place in the body which it loves some disturbance of which it is warned by the difficulty which it has in the exercise of its functions, is to neglect the inner feeling which we experience of what takes place in us. For every one feels unmistakably, when he is being bled, for example, or when he burns himself, that he is not the cause of the pain. He feels it against his own will, and he cannot doubt that it comes to him from an external cause. Again, the soul does not feel pain and a particular kind of pain because it has learnt that a disturbance is taking place in the brain, and a particular kind of disturbance. Nothing is more certain than this. Finally, pain and sadness are entirely different. Pain precedes the awareness of the evil, sadness follows it. . . . Pain, then, is entirely different from sadness. Moreover, I think that the soul is not the cause of its sadness; and that the thought which we have of the loss of some good only produces this feeling in us in consequence of the natural and necessary movement which God unceasingly impresses upon us for our welfare. But let us return to the difficulties which you have regarding the action and the qualities of light.

X. Firstly, there is no metamorphosis. The disturbance that takes place in the brain cannot change into light or into colours. For as modifications of bodies are nothing but these bodies themselves determined in a particular manner, they cannot be transformed into modifications of mind. That is evident.

Secondly, you press the corner of your eye and you have a certain sensation. That is so because He who alone can act upon minds has established certain laws owing to which body and soul operate and suffer in reciprocal determination.

Thirdly, when you press your eye you have a sensation of light, though there is present no luminous body, because it is by a pressure similar to that which your finger exerts upon your eye, and from there on your brain, that bodies which we call luminous operate upon those around them, and through the latter upon our eyes and our brains. All this takes place in consequence of natural laws. For it is one of the laws of the conjunction of soul and body in accordance with which God acts incessantly upon those two substances, that a particular pressure or a particular disturbance should be followed by a particular sensation.

Fourthly, you see the light which is a modification of your mind and which, therefore, can exist in it alone; for there is a contradiction in the thought of a modification of a being existing where that being is not. You see it, I say, in the vast spaces which your mind does not fill, for the mind does not occupy space. Those spaces which you see are only intelligible spaces which do not occupy any place. For the spaces which you see are quite different from the material spaces which you survey. One must not confuse the ideas of things with the things themselves. Remember, that we do not see bodies in themselves, and that it is only through their ideas that they are visible. Often we can see what does not actually exist, a proof positive that those things which we see are intelligible and quite different from those which we look at.

Fifthly and lastly, you see the light not on the side on which you press your eye but on the opposite side, because, the nerve being constructed and adapted to receive impressions from luminous bodies through the pupil of the eye and not otherwise, the pressure of your finger on the left produces the same effect on your eye as a luminous body on the right whose rays were to pass the pupil and the transparent part of the eye would produce. For in pressing the eye from without you are pressing the optic nerve from within against what is called the vitreous humour, which in turn offers some resistance. Thus, God makes you experience the light on the side on which you see it because He always follows the laws which He has established in order to keep His procedure perfectly uniform; God never performs miracles; He never acts according to particular volitions against His own laws, for the order does not demand or permit it. His action always bears the character of His attributes. It continues always the same, if what He owes to his immutability is of no smaller importance than what He owes to any other of His perfections. . . .

XI. There is no necessary relation between the two substances of which we are composed. The modifications of our bodies cannot, by their own activity, change those of our minds. Nevertheless, the modifications of a certain part of the brain which I will not further determine are always followed by modifications or feelings of our soul; and this solely in consequence of the continual exercise of the laws of the union of these two substances,—that is to say, to speak more clearly, in consequence of the constant and ever effective will of the author of our being. There is no relation of causality between a body and a mind. What am I saying? That there is no relation between a mind and a body. I am saying more. There is no real relation between one body and another, between one mind and another. In a word, no created thing can act upon another by an activity which is its own. This I will prove to you presently. But, at least, it is evident that a body, that extension, a purely passive substance, cannot operate by its own activity upon a mind, upon a being of another nature and infinitely more excellent than it. Thus, it is clear that, in the union of soul and body, there is no other bond than the efficacy of divine and immutable decrees, an efficacy never without its effects. God has then willed, and wills without ceasing, that the various disturbances of the brain shall always be followed by the various thoughts of the mind with which it is in union. And it is this constant and efficient will of the Creator which causes the union of these two substances. For there is no other nature, I mean no other natural laws, than the efficient volitions of the Omnipotent.

XII. Do not ask, Aristes, why God wills to unite minds to bodies. The fact is unquestionable, but the principal reasons for it hitherto have remained unknown to philosophy, and perhaps even religion does not teach us. There is, however, one reason which it may be well to offer to you. God apparently desired to give us, in respect to His Son, a victim which we could offer to Him. He desired to give us an opportunity of meriting by a kind of sacrifice and annihilation of self the possession of eternal happiness. This, assuredly, seems just and in conformity with the order of things. Now we are on our trial in our body. It is through it, as occasional cause, that we receive from God thousands upon thousands of different feelings which through the grace of Jesus Christ constitute the occasion of our merits.

SIXTH DIALOGUE

. . . III. THEODORE. There are only three kinds of being of which we have any knowledge and with which we can have any connection: God or the infinitely perfect Being, who is the principle or cause of all things; minds which we know only by the inner feeling which we have of our own nature; bodies of the existence of which we are assured by the revelation which we have of them. For what we call a man is but a complex. . . .

ARISTES. Gently, Theodore. I know that there is a God or an infinitely perfect Being.[3] For if I think of Him, and certainly I do think of Him, it follows that He exists, since nothing finite can represent the Infinite. I know likewise that minds exist, granted that there are beings who resemble myself, for I cannot doubt but that I think and I know that whatever thinks is other than extension or matter.[4] You have demonstrated all this. But what do you mean when you say that we are assured of the existence of bodies by the revelation which we have of them? What! Do we not see them, do we not feel them? We have no need of a revelation to teach us that we have a body; when we are pricked, we feel it quite sufficiently.

THEODORE. Yes, no doubt we feel it. But the feeling of pain which we have is a kind of revelation. This expression is a striking one. But it is precisely for that reason that I make use of it. For you always forget that it is God alone who produces in your soul all those different feelings which it experiences, on the occasion of the changes which take place in your body, in consequence of the general laws of the conjunction of the two natures of which man is constituted; laws which are nothing but the efficient and constant volitions of the Creator, as I shall explain in the sequel. The point through which our hand is pricked does not cause the pain through the hole which it makes in the body. Neither is it the soul which produces this uncomfortable feel-

3. Dialogue II.
4. Dialogue I.

ing, since it suffers the pain despite itself. It is produced assuredly by a superior power. It is God Himself, who through the feelings with which He affects us reveals to us all that takes place outside us, I mean in our body and in the bodies of our environment. Remember, please, what I have already said so many times.

IV. ARISTES. I was wrong, Theodore. But what you are telling me has suggested to my mind a very strange thought. I hardly dare to submit it to you, for I fear you will look upon me as a dreamer. I am beginning now to doubt whether there are any bodies. My reason is that the revelation which God gives us of their existence is not certain. For, after all, it is certain that we frequently see bodies which really do not exist, as for example during sleep, or when a fever causes an excitement in the brain. If God, in consequence of the general laws, as you call them, can sometimes give us deceptive sensations, if He can reveal false things to us through our senses, why should He not do so always, and how can we distinguish what is true from what is false in the obscure and confused testimony of our senses? It seems to me that I had better prudently reserve my judgment with regard to the existence of bodies. I will ask you kindly to give me an exact demonstration of it.

THEODORE. An exact demonstration! That is a little too much, Aristes. It seems to me, on the contrary, that I have an exact demonstration of the impossibility of such a demonstration. But keep up your courage, do not despair. Proofs are not lacking which are sufficient to dispel your doubt. And I am glad that such a doubt occurred to you. For, after all, to doubt the existence of bodies on the strength of reasons which show that one cannot doubt the existence of God or the incorporeal nature of the soul is some proof that one has put oneself above all prejudices, and instead of subjecting reason to the senses as most men do, one has recognised the right which it has to pronounce judgment authoritatively. That it is impossible to give an exact demonstration of the existence of bodies I can prove conclusively, unless I am much mistaken, thus:—

V. The notion of the infinitely perfect Being involves no necessary relation to any created thing. God is perfectly self-sufficient. Matter is, therefore, no necessary emanation from the Divinity. At least—and this is sufficient for the present purpose—it is not evident that it is such a necessary emanation. Now, one can give no exact demonstration of a truth unless one can show that it is necessarily connected with its principle, unless one can show that there is a necessary relation involved in the ideas which are being compared. Hence it is not possible to demonstrate rigorously that bodies exist.

In fact, the existence of bodies is arbitrary. If any exist, it is because God has willed to create them. Now, it is not the same in the case of the volition to create the world as it is in the case of that to punish sins, reward good deeds, exact from all of us love and fear, and the like. These latter volitions of God and a thousand other similar ones are necessarily contained in the divine Reason, in that substantial Law which is the inviolable rule of the will of the infinitely perfect Being and generally of all intelligent minds. The will to create corporeal things, on the other hand, is not necessarily involved in the notion of the infinitely perfect Being, the Being that is perfectly self-sufficient. Far from being so, this notion seems to exclude such a volition from God. There is, then, no other way than revelation to assure us that God has willed to create corporeal things, admitting at the same time, what you do not doubt, that they are not visible in themselves, that they cannot act upon the mind nor represent themselves to it, and that our mind itself can know them only through the ideas which represent them, and feel them only through the modifications or sensations of which they can be the cause only in consequence of the arbitrary laws of the conjunction of the soul and the body. . . .

SEVENTH DIALOGUE

. . . X. THEODORE. The act of creation never ceases, the conservation of created things being on the part of God merely a continuous creation, merely an act of volition which persists and operates without ceasing. Now, God cannot conceive and hence cannot will that a body should be nowhere, or that it should stand to other bodies in no relation of distance. God cannot will that this chair should exist and by this act of will create and preserve it, unless He places it here or there or elsewhere. Hence, there is a contradiction in saying that one body can move another. I go further. There is a contradiction in saying that you can move your chair. Nay, more, there is a contradiction in maintaining that all the angels and demons together can move a bit of straw. The proof of this is clear. No power, however vast it may be imagined to be, can surpass or even equal the power of God. Now, there is a contradiction in saying that God could will that this chair should be, unless He at the same time wills that it should be somewhere and unless He places it there by the efficacy of His will, unless He keeps it there, creates it there. It follows that no power can transport it whither God does not transport it, nor fix or keep it where God does not fix or keep it, if it is God alone who adapts the efficacy of His actions to the ineffective actions of His creations. This it is necessary to explain to you in order to harmonize reason with experience and in order to make you understand the greatest, most fruitful and necessary of all principles, namely, that God communicates His power to created beings only because He has made their modifications the occasional causes of the effects which He produces in Himself—occasional causes, I say, which determine the activity of His volitions in consequence of the general laws which He has prescribed to Himself, in order to make His mode of operation bear the character of His attributes and to display in His work that uniformity of action which is necessary in order to link together the parts which compose it and to save it from the irregularity and confusion of a kind of chaos wherein minds could never understand anything. . . .

XI. THEODORE. Let us suppose, then, Aristes, that God wills that there shall be a certain body upon this floor, say a ball; forthwith this is accomplished. Nothing is more movable than a sphere upon a plane, but all the powers imaginable could not disturb it so long as God does not intervene; for, once again, so long as God wills to create or keep this ball at the point A, or at any other point you please, and of necessity He must place it somewhere, no force could make it leave that point. Do not forget this; it is the basal principle.

ARISTES. I hold it in mind, this principle. The Creator alone can be the mover, only He who gives being to bodies can put them in the places which they occupy.

THEODORE. Very well. The moving force of a body is, therefore, nothing but the activity of God's will which conserves it successively in different places. This being granted, let us suppose that this ball is set in motion, and that in the line of its motion it meets with another ball at rest. Experience teaches us that this other ball will move without fail, and according to a certain velocity always exactly observed. Now, it is not the first ball which sets the second in motion. This is clear from our principle, for a body cannot move another without communicating to it its moving force. But the moving force of a body in motion is nothing but the will of the Creator who keeps it successively in different places. It is not a quality which belongs to the body itself. Nothing belongs to it but its own modifications; and modifications are inseparable from substances. Hence bodies cannot move one another, and their encounter or shock is merely an occasional cause for the distribution of their movement. . . . God always moves or tends to move bodies in a straight line, because this line is the simplest and the shortest. When bodies meet, He changes the direction of their movement as little as possible, and I believe that He never changes the quantity of the moving force which animates matter. Upon these principles are founded the general laws of the communication of movements in accordance with which God acts incessantly. This is not the time to prove my contention, because it is sufficient for the present that you should know that bodies can neither set themselves in motion nor any bodies which they meet,—facts which our reasoning has just shown, and that there are certain laws in accordance with which God moves them unfailingly—a fact which experience teaches us.

ARISTES. This seems to me incontestable. But what do you think of this, Theotimus? You never contradict Theodore.

XII. THEOTIMUS. I have been convinced of these truths for a long time. But since you wish me to contest Theodore's opinion, I ask you to solve a little difficulty. Here it is. I quite understand that a body cannot of itself set itself in motion; but supposing it to be once moved, I maintain that it can set another body in motion, as a cause between which and its effect there is a necessary connection. For let us suppose that God had not yet established laws for the communication of motion, there would then in that case be no occasional causes. This being so, let the body A be set in motion, and in following the line of its motion let it slip on the body B, which I suppose to be concave and as the mould of the body A. What will happen? Decide.

ARISTES. What will happen? Nothing, for when there is no cause there can be no effect.

THEOTIMUS. What? Nothing? Something new must take place, for the body B will either be moved in consequence of the shock, or it will not be moved.

ARISTES. It will not be.

THEOTIMUS. So far, so good. But, Aristes, what becomes of the body A when it meets B? Either it will rebound or not. If it rebounds, we have a new effect of which B is the cause. If not, the matter is worse still, for we have then a force which is destroyed, or at least which does not act. The shock of bodies, then, is not an occasional cause, but a very real and veritable cause, since there is a necessary connection between the shock and such effect as you choose. Thus . . .

ARISTES. Wait a moment, Theotimus. What is it you are proving? That bodies being impenetrable, it follows necessarily that at the moment of the shock God determines to make a choice with regard to what you have just put before me. That is all. I am not alarmed. You do not prove at all that a body in motion can by virtue of something which belongs to it move whatever it encounters. If God had not as yet established the laws for the communication of motion, the nature of bodies, their impenetrability, would constrain Him to make such laws as He deemed fit, and He would determine Himself in accordance with those laws which are the simplest, if these latter were sufficient for the execution of the works which He willed to form out of matter. But it is clear that impenetrability has no efficacy of its own, and that it can only give God, who deals with things in accordance with their nature, an occasion for varying or diversifying His activity without changing anything in His mode of operation.

. . . Matter is essentially movable. It has, by its nature, a passive capacity for movement. But it has no active capacity; it is actually moved only by the continual action of the Creator. Thus, no body can disturb another body by any activity which belongs to its own nature. If bodies had in themselves the force to set themselves in motion, the strongest would subvert those which they encountered, as efficient causes; but being moved only by another force, their contact or encounter is only an occasional cause which, because of their impenetrability, constrains the mover or Creator to distribute His action. And because God is bound to act in a simple and uniform way, He had to make general laws and the simplest possible ones, in order that when a change is necessary He should change as little as is possible, and in order that by the same mode of operation He should produce an infinity of different effects. It is thus, Theotimus, that I understand these matters.

THEOTIMUS. You understand them very well.

XIII. THEODORE. Perfectly well. We are, accordingly, agreed upon the principle. Let us pursue it a little further. You cannot, then, Aristes, of yourself move your arm or alter your position, situation, posture, do to other men good or evil, or effect the least change in the world. You find yourself in the world, without any power, immovable as a rock, stupid, so to speak, as a log of wood. Let your soul be united to your body as closely as you please, let there come about a union between it and all the bodies of your environment. What advantage would you derive from this imaginary union? What would you do in order merely to move the tip of your finger, or to utter even a monosyllable? Alas! unless God came to your aid, your efforts would be vain, the desires which you formed impotent; for just think, do you know what is necessary for the pronunciation of your best friend's name, or for bending or holding up that particular finger which you use most? But let us suppose that you know quite well what no one knows, about which even some scientists are not agreed, namely, that the arm can be moved only by means of the animal spirits, which flowing along the nerves to the muscles make them contract and draw towards themselves the bones to which they are attached. Let us suppose that you are acquainted with the anatomy and the action of your mechanism as well as a clockmaker is acquainted with his handiwork. But, at any rate, remember the principle that no one but the Creator of bodies can be their mover. This principle is sufficient to bind, indeed to annihilate, all your boasted faculties; for, after all, the animal spirits are bodies, however small they may be. They are, indeed, nothing but the subtlest parts of the blood and the humours. God alone, then, is able to move these small bodies. He alone knows how to make them flow from the brain along the nerves, from the nerves through the muscles, from one muscle to its antagonist—all of which is necessary for the movement of our limbs. It follows that, notwithstanding the conjunction of soul and body in whatever way it may please you to imagine it, you would be dead and inert if it were not for the fact that God wills to adapt his volitions to yours—His volitions, which are always effective, to your desires, which are always impotent. This then, my dear Aristes, is the solution of the mystery. All creatures are united to God alone in an immediate union. They depend essentially and directly upon Him. Being all alike equally impotent, they cannot be in reciprocal dependence upon one another. One may, indeed, say that they are united to one another and that they depend upon one another. I grant this, provided it is not understood in the ordinary and vulgar sense of the term, provided that one agrees that they are so only in consequence of the immutable and ever effective will of the Creator, only in consequence of the general laws which He has established, and by means of which He regulates the ordinary course of His providence. God has willed that my arm shall be set in motion at the instant that I will it myself (given the necessary conditions). His will is efficacious, His will is immutable, it alone is the source of my power and faculties. He has willed that I should experience certain feelings, certain emotoins, whenever there are present in my brain certain traces, or whenever a certain disturbance takes place therein. In a word, He has willed—He wills incessantly—that the modifications of the mind and those of the body shall be reciprocal. This is the conjunction and the natural dependence of the two parts of which we are constituted. It is but the mutual and reciprocal dependence of our modifications based on the unshakable foundation of the divine decrees—decrees which through their efficacy endow me with the power which I have over my body, and through it over certain other bodies—decrees which through their immutability unite me with my body, and through it to my friends, my possessions, my whole environment. I derive nothing whatever from my own nature, nothing from the nature imagined by the philosophers—all comes from God and His decrees. God has linked together all His works, though He has not on that account produced in them entities charged with the function of union. He has subordinated them to one another without endowing them with active qualities. The latter are but the vain pretensions of human pride, the chimerical productions of the philosophers' ignorance. Men's senses being affected by the presence of obects, their minds being moved by the inner feeling which they have of their own movements, they have not recognised the invisible operations of the Creator, the uniformity of His mode of action, the fruitfulness of His laws, the ever-present efficacy of His volitions, the infinite wisdom of His providence. Do not say any more, my dear Aristes, that your soul is united to your body more intimately than to anything else; since its immediate union is with God alone, since the divine decrees are the indissoluble bonds of union between the various parts of the universe and of the marvellous network of all the subordinate causes.

XIV. Aristes. Ah, Theodore, how clear, how sound and how Christian your principles are! Moreover, how estimable and affecting! I am deeply moved by them. What! It is then God Himself who is present in the midst of us, not as a mere spectator nor as an observer of our good and bad actions, but as the principle of our society, the bond of our friendship, the soul, so to speak, of the intercourse and communication which we have with one another. I can speak to you only through the efficacy of His powers, touch you or disturb you only by means of the movement which He communicates to me. . . . Ah, Theodore and Theotimus, God alone is the bond of our society. May He be its *end,* since He is its originating cause! Let us not abuse His power. Unhappy they who make use of it for their criminal passions! Nothing is more sacred than power, nothing more divine. It is a kind of sacrilege to make a profane use of it; now I see that to do this would mean to make the just avenger of crimes assist in iniquity. Of ourselves we can do nothing, hence of ourselves we ought to will nothing. We can act only through the efficacy of the divine power, hence we ought to will nothing except in accordance with the divine law. Nothing is more evident than these truths.

THEODORE. These are excellent conclusions.

XV. THEOTIMUS. They are wonderful principles for ethics. But let us return to metaphysics. Our soul is not united to our body in the ordinary sense of these terms. It is immediately and directly united to God alone. It is through the efficacy of His action alone that the three of us are here together; nay, more, that we all share the same opinion, are penetrated by the same truth, animated, it seems to me, by the same spirit, kindled with the same enthusiasm. God joins us together by means of the body, in consequence of the laws of the communication of movements. He affects us with the same feelings in consequence of the laws of the conjunction of body and soul. But, Aristes, how comes it about that we are so strongly united in mind? Theodore utters some words unto your ears. These are but the air struck by the organs of the voice. God transforms, so to speak, this air into words, into various sounds. He makes you understand these various sounds through the modifications by which you are affected. But where do you get the sense of the words from? Who is it that discloses to you and to myself the same truth as Theodore is contemplating? If the air which He forces back when speaking does not contain the sounds you hear, assuredly it will not contain the truths which you understand.

ARISTES. I follow you, Theotimus. We are united in mind because all of us are united to the universal Reason which illumines all intelligences. I am wiser than you think. Theodore has already led me to the point to which you wish to conduct me. He has convinced me that there is nothing visible, nothing which can act upon the mind and reveal itself thereto, but the substance of Reason, which is not only efficacious but also intelligent. Yes, nothing that is created can be the immediate object of our knowledge. We see things in this material world, wherein our bodies dwell, only because our mind through its attention lives in another world, only because it contemplates the beauties of the archetypal and intelligible world which Reason contains. . . .

XV

LEIBNIZ

GOTTFRIED WILHELM VON LEIBNIZ (1646-1716) was born in Leipzig and studied there and at Jena and Altorf. He then became a diplomat for the Elector of Mainz and traveled to Paris, where he lived for a few years and met with leading scientists and philosophers, to London, where he was made a member of the Royal Society, and to Holland, where he met with Spinoza. He next became a functionary at Hanover and later lived in the court of Queen Sophie Charlotte of Prussia in Berlin. He was interested in almost all fields of study and made great contributions in mathematics (discovering the calculus independently of Newton), logic, physics, law, linguistics, history, and so forth. He corresponded widely and developed his philosophical views mainly in answer to other thinkers; he published his results mainly as articles. He left an enormous number of unpublished papers, still being edited, in which many of his most advanced ideas appear. The selections below are from his letters and articles—some in answer to the skeptics Simon Foucher and Pierre Bayle, his unpublished papers, and from his massive reply to Bayle's views on the problem of evil, *The Theodicy* (1710). The translation is by Leroy E. Loemker, Philip P. Wiener, and Austin Farrar. Other selections, concerned with his replies to Locke and Newton, appear in *Eighteenth-Century Philosophy,* in this series.

Letter to Simon Foucher (1675)

I agree with you that it is important once and for all to examine all our presuppositions in order to establish something sound. For I hold that it is only when we can prove everything we assert that we understand perfectly the thing being considered. I know that such studies are not very popular, but I also know that to take the pains to understand matters to their roots is not very popular. As I see it, your purpose is to examine those truths which affirm that there is something outside of us. You seem to be most fair in this, for thus you will grant us all hypothetical truths which affirm, not that something does exist outside of us, but only what would happen if anything existed there. So we at once save arithmetic, geometry, and a large number of propositions in metaphysics, physics, and morals, whose convenient expression depends on arbitrarily chosen definitions, and whose truth depends on those axioms which I am wont to call identical; such, for example, as that two contradictories cannot exist and that at any given time a thing is as it is; that it is, for example, equal to itself, as great as itself, similar to itself, etc.

But, although you do not enter explicitly into an examination of hypothetical propositions, I am still of the opinion that this should be done and that we should admit none without having entirely demonstrated and resolved it into identities.

It is the truths which deal with what is in fact outside of us which are the primary subject of your investigations. Now in the first place, we cannot deny that the very truth of hypothetical propositions themselves is something outside of us and independent of us. For all hypothetical propositions assert what would be or would not be, if something or its contrary were posited; consequently, they assume two things at the same time which agree with each other, or the possibility or impossibility, necessity or indifference, of something. But this possibility, impossibility, or necessity (for the necessity of one thing is the impossibility of its contrary) is not a chimera which we create, since all that we do consists in recognizing them, in spite of ourselves and in a constant manner. So, of all the things which actually are, the possibility or impossibility of being is itself the first. But this possibility and this necessity form or compose what are called the essences or natures and the truths which are usually called eternal. And we are right in calling them this, for there is nothing so eternal as what is necessary. Thus the nature of the circle with its properties is something which exists and is eternal, that is, there is some constant cause outside of us which makes everyone who thinks carefully about a circle discover the same thing, not merely in the sense that their thoughts agree with each other, for this could be attributed solely to the nature of the human mind, but also in the sense that phenomena or experiences confirm them when some appearance of a circle strikes our senses. These phenomena necessarily have some cause outside of us.

But, although the existence of necessities comes before all others in itself and in the order of nature, I nevertheless agree that it is not first in the order of our knowledge. For you see that, in order to prove its existence, I have taken for granted that we think and that we have sensations. So there are two absolute general truths; truths, that is, which tell of the actual existence of things. One is that we think; the other, that there is a great variety in our thoughts. From the former it follows that we are; from the latter, that there is something other than us, that is to say, something other than that which thinks, which is the cause of the variety of our experiences. Now one of these truths is just as incontestable and as independent as the other, and, having stressed only the former in the order of his meditations, Descartes failed to attain the perfection to which he had aspired. If he had followed with exactness what I call a *filum meditandi,* I believe that he would really have achieved the *first philosophy*. But not even the greatest genius can force things; we must of necessity enter through the openings which nature has made, in order to avoid being lost. What is more, one man alone cannot do everything all at once, and for myself, when I think of all that Descartes has said that is excellent and original, I am more amazed at what he has done than at some things which he failed to do. I admit that I have not yet been able to read his writings with all the care that I had intended to give them, and, as my friends know, it happened that I read most of the other modern philosophers before I read him. Bacon and Gassendi were the first to fall into my hands. Their familiar and easy style was better adapted to a man who wanted to read everything. It is true that I have often glanced through Galileo and Descartes, but since I have only recently become a geometrician, I was soon repelled by their style of writing, which requires deep meditation. Personally, though I have always loved to think by myself, I have always found it hard to read books which one cannot understand without much meditation, for in following one's own thoughts one follows a certain natural inclination and so gains profit with pleasure. One is violently disturbed, in contrast, when compelled to follow the thoughts of someone else. I always liked books which contained some good thoughts, but which I could run through without stopping, for they aroused ideas in me which I could follow up in my own fancy and pursue as far as I pleased. This also prevented me from reading the books on geometry carefully; I freely admit that I have not yet been able to make myself read Euclid in any other way than one usually reads history. I have learned from experience that this method is good in general, yet I have recognized nevertheless that there are authors for whom one must make an exception, such as Plato and Aristotle among ancient philosophers, and Galileo and Descartes among our own. Yet what I know of the metaphysical and physical meditations of Descartes has come almost entirely from the reading of a number of books written in a more popular style which report his opinions. And perhaps I have not as yet understood him well. To the extent that I have read him over myself, however, it seems to me that I have at least been able to discover what he has not done or tried to do, and, among other things, this is to analyze all our assumptions. This is why I am inclined to applaud all who examine even the smallest truth to the end, for I know that it is much to understand something perfectly, no matter how small or easy it may seem. One can go very far in this way and, finally, establish the art of discovery, which depends on knowledge of the simplest things, but on a distinct and perfect knowledge of them. It is for this reason that I have found no fault with the plan of De Roberval, who tried to demonstrate everything in geometry, even some of the axioms. I grant that we should not enforce such exactness upon others, but I believe that it is good to demand it of ourselves.

But I return to these truths which are primary with respect to ourselves, and first to those which assert that there is something outside of us; namely, that we think and that there is a great variety in our thoughts. This variety cannot come from that which thinks, since one thing by itself cannot be the cause of the changes occurring in it. For everything remains in the state in which it is, unless there is something which changes it. And since it has not been determined by itself to undergo certain changes rather than others, we cannot begin to attribute any variety to it without saying something which admittedly has no reason, which is absurd. Even if we tried to say that our thoughts have no beginning, we should be obliged to assert that each of us has existed from all eternity; yet we should not escape the difficulty, for we should always have to admit that there is no reason for this variety which would have existed from all eternity in our thoughts, since there is nothing in us which determines us to one variety rather than another. Thus there is some cause outside of us for the variety of our thoughts. And since we agree that there are some subordinate causes of this variety which themselves still need a cause, we have established particular beings or substances to whom we ascribe some action, that is, from whose change we think that some change follows in us. So we make great strides toward fabricating what we call matter and body.

But at this point you are right in stopping us for a while and renewing the criticisms of the ancient Academy. For at bottom all our experiences assure us of only two things: first, that there is a connection among our appearances which provides the means to predict future appearances successfully; and, second, that this connection must have a constant cause. But it does not follow strictly from this that matter or bodies exist but only that there is something which give us appearances in a good sequence. For if some invisible power were to take pleasure in giving us dreams that are well tied into our preceding life and in conformity with each other, could we distinguish them from reality before we had awakened? Now, what prevents the course of our life from being one long well-ordered dream, about which we could be undeceived in a moment? Nor do I see that such a power would be imperfect just on this ground, as Descartes asserts, to say nothing of the fact that its imperfection is not involved in the present question. For it might be a kind of subordinate power, or a demon who for some unknown reason could interfere with our affairs and who would have at least as much power over us as that caliph had over the man whom he caused to be carried, drunk, into his palace, and let taste of the paradise of Mohammed after he was awakened; after which he was once more made drunk and returned in that condition to the place where he had been found. When this man came to himself, he naturally interpreted this experience, which seemed inconsistent with the course of his life, as a vision, and spread among the people maxims and revelations which he believed he had learned in his pretended paradise; this was precisely what the caliph wished. Since reality has thus passed for a vision, what is to prevent a vision from passing for reality? The more consistency we see in what happens to us, it is true, the more our belief is confirmed that what appears to us is reality. But it is also true that, the more closely we examine our appearances, the better ordered we find them, as microscopes and other means of observation have shown. This permanent consistency gives us great assurance, but, after all, it will be only moral until somebody discovers a priori the origin of the world which we see and pursues the question of why things are as they appear back to its foundations in essence. For when this is done, he will have demonstrated that what appears to us is reality and that it is impossible for us ever to be deceived in it. But I believe that this would very nearly approach the beatific vision and that it is difficult to aspire to this in our present state. Yet we do learn therefrom how confused the knowledge which we commonly have of the body and matter must be, since we believe we are certain that they exist, but eventually find that we could be mistaken. This confirms Mr. Descartes's excellent thought concerning the proof of the difference between body and soul, since one can doubt the one without being able to question the other. For even if there were only appearances or dreams, we should be nonetheless certain of the existence of that which thinks, as Descartes has very well said. I may add that one could still demonstrate the existence of God by ways different from those of Descartes but, I believe, leading farther. For we have no need to assume a being who guarantees us against being deceived, since it lies in our power to undeceive ourselves about many things, at least about the most important ones.

I wish, Sir, that your meditations on this matter may have all the success you desire; but, to accomplish this, it is well to proceed in order and to establish your propositions. This is the way to gain ground and make sure progress. I believe you would oblige the public also by conveying to it, from time to time, selections from the Academy and especially from Plato, for I know that there are things in them more beautiful and substantial than is usually thought.

On True Method in Philosophy and Theology (c. 1686)

As I turned in my zeal for knowledge from the serious study of Holy Scripture and of divine and human law to the mathematical sciences, and was soon delighted by the thoroughly luminous teachings of the latter, I came near to remaining caught on siren cliffs. For some wonderful theorems were revealed to me to which others were opposed; I saw the road open then to more and greater things and many a structure which had arisen quietly in my mind at play, appeared to me also to bear promise of fruit. With what joy a beautiful theorem fills one can be judged only by those who are able to comprehend such inner *harmony* with a purified mind. Meanwhile the memory of the diviner science afflicted my soul and I deplored the fact that that science should forego a comparable clarity and order. I saw how the most distinguished men, Saint Thomas and Saint Bonaventura and William Durand and Gregory of Rimini and many other authors of former times, have offered not a few theorems of marvelous subtlety to First Philosophy which might have been demonstrated with the utmost rigor. I recognized how Natural Theology, which had been most gloriously created by these men, had been submerged in a barbaric darkness, and through a confused use of words floundered between doubtful distinctions, and so I often actually played the mathematician in theology, incited by the novelty of the rôle; I set up definitions and tried to deduce from them certain elements which were not inferior to those of Euclid in clarity but far exceeded them in the magnitude of their consequences. For I reflected as follows: Geometry clarifies configurations and motions; as a result we have discovered the geography of lands and the course of the stars, and machines have been made which overcome great burdens, whence civilization and the difference between civilized and barbaric peoples. But the science which distinguishes the just man from the unjust, and through which the secrets of the mind are explained and the path to happiness is paved, is neglected. We have demonstrations about the circle, but only conjectures about the soul; the laws of motion are presented with mathematical rigor, but nobody applies a comparable diligence to research on the secrets of thinking. The source of human misery lies in the fact that man devotes more thought to everything but the highest good in life, like the negligent merchant who sleeps at the beginning and with the growth of his account-book eschews order and clarity, and is then unable to put together all the entries of receipts and disbursements from the beginning. Whence we have the clandestine atheism planted in men, the fear of death, doubts about the nature of the soul, the weakest or at least, vacillating pronouncements about God, and the fact that many men are honest by habit or necessity rather than by virtue of their judgment.

I saw that certain philosophers could not have kept their excessive promises because they have written with prepossessed minds or have preached mathematical rigor but have themselves practised otherwise and taken to light, popular ways of speaking, obtaining applause rather than assent. For—just to give one example—if the very distinguished René Descartes had only once of his own free will converted his meditations into propositions and his discourses into demonstrations, he would have himself seen the large number of flaws in them. This resulted, under pressure from his friends rather than from his own conviction, in his dressing up his proof of God's existence in a mathematical garb. For if I should assume that he himself had taken it for a proof, I should be doing his genius an injury.

Many think that mathematical rigor has no place ouside of the sciences ordinarily called mathematical. But they overlook the fact that to write mathematically is the same as what the logicians call reasoning according to form, and that a single definition can take the place of the captious distinctions on which so much time is wasted. For the Scholastics labored under only one vice, that is, with all the order they sufficiently showed for the most part, and, so to speak, in mathematical ratiocination, they left the use of their words in uncertainty. Whence instead of one definition arose many, instead of one irrefragable proof arose many arguments pro and con; their dogmas of God and their often admirable reflections could easily be purged or clarified by a mathematically schooled mind.

I thought such a task all the more useful because I saw dangerous expressions slipping into men's souls; they are a sort of mathematical larva from which arises a false philosophy, and with that the whole of scholastic doctrine would be rejected.

For how many at most are there of those who, educated in the custom of the present century, really regard these trivialities, as the scholastic doctrines are called, worth reading? I congratulate myself for my youthful days when I had the opportunity to learn these studies also, before my mind was imbued with mathematical studies, and I thus acquired the habit of attending patiently to other studies. There are historical periods for these studies; there was a time when scholastic theology alone obtained the principal part, but today it is scarcely kept alive anywheres but in religious orders and convents. With the glowing light of the humanistic studies we find a contrary extreme emphasis, and there is as much of a tumult made over a syllable of Plautus and Apuleius as there used to be over universals and moral distinctions.

Now that we are cured of this malady, we face a greater danger. We have grown into manhood and with the maturing of judgment have discarded all our juvenile clothes in the same way as though the world grown out of barbarism had taken on wisdom with the years. We have known how long it took for mankind to acquire an interest in learning to know nature and to establish the laws of space and motion through which our powers are enhanced. But just as man in a free republic works mostly for others and little for himself, so we gather by successful investigations into the hereafter only the material from which, after many centuries, the edifice of truth will be erected. And I see that great men who in their youth pursued the study of mathematics and the humanities, and later on did experiments on nature or went into the business of the world, with the advent of age return to the advancement of the sciences and of the mind with which they associate their own happiness. It is a wise saying of that distinguished man Francis Bacon: a little philosophy "inclineth man's mind to atheism, but depth in philosophy bringeth men's minds about to religion." I say the same to our century; the value of a religious philosophy will be recognized by those who return to it, and mathematical studies will be used partly as an example of more rigorous judgment, partly for the knowledge of harmony and of the idea of beauty, experiments on nature will lead to admiration for the author of nature, who has expressed an image of the ideal world in the sensible one, so that all studies finally will lead to happiness.

For the most part we hail those minds who blandish the novelty of their philosophy by dressing it up in mathematical attire at the expense of divine truth. It is an indubitable fact, and one recognized also by Aristotle, that everything in nature is derived from size, figure, and motion. The theory of size and figure has been developed in a preeminent way; the innermost nature of motion is not yet patent due to the neglect of First Philosophy from which its laws are derived. For it is the task of Metaphysics to treat of continuous temporal modifications in the universe, since motion is only one kind of modification. In so far as the nature of motion is not understood, important philosophers having attributed the essence of matter only to extension, there has resulted a notion of bodies, previously unheard of, which fails to do justice to either the phenomena of nature or the mysteries of faith. For it can be demonstrated that extension without the addition of other qualities is not capable of either action or its passive reception; that everything becomes fluid in the most extreme way, that is, becomes vacuous; that then the cohesion of bodies and what is felt as solid in them cannot be explained, and that, therefore, the laws of motion are thereby constituted contrary to experience. All of which appears illustrated plainly in the principles of Descartes, since he makes motion purely relative and has thought up a kind of body which is in no way different from the void, and he has derived the cohesion and solidity of bodies from mere rest, because on his view bodies must come to rest immediately after they have come in contact with each other, since there can be no forces to separate them. Furthermore, he has laid down laws about motion and the impact of bodies which the most exact experiments have made obsolete. He has also artfully evaded the mysteries of faith by claiming to pursue philosophy rather than theology, as though philosophy were incompatible with religion, or as though a religion can be true which opposes truths demonstrated elsewhere. Once when he had to discuss the Holy Eucharist, he substituted for real species only apparent ones, and thus revived a doctrine rejected by a universal consensus of theologians. But this would mean little, if his philosophy could allow bodies to exist in several places at once. For if body and space are one and the same, how can we avoid the consequence that in different spaces or places there must be different bodies? Those who in forming a theory of corporeal nature add to extension a certain resistance or impenetrability (or, as they call it, antitype *αντιτυπια*) or bulk—as Gassendi and other scholars have done—have indeed philosophized correctly but they have not gotten rid of the difficulties. For what is needed to analyze the idea of body is some positive notion, which impenetrability does not have, since it is not yet proven that the penetration of bodies is not present in nature: condensation provides an argument (many think it results from penetration), although another explanation for it can be recognized. Finally, the absolute impenetrability of bodies contradicts both the teachings of our faith and the doctrine of *πολυτοπια* (being in several places at the same time), and it is just as difficult to see how a body can be in several places as several bodies in the same place.

What must we then add to extension in order to complete the concept of body? Nothing except what the senses themselves testify to. They inform us at once of three things: first, that we observe, and that we observe bodies, and that what we observe is a variety of things, composite or extended. Consequently, action has to be added to the notion of extension or variety. Therefore *body is extended activity* (*agens extensum*), and a substance may be said to be extended if we hold that every substance is active and every active thing is called a substance. Now we can show from the inner truths of metaphysics that what is not active is nothing, for there is no such thing as a mere potentiality to act without any initial action. The force of a taut bow is in no wise a small one; only we say it is not yet in action. In any case, it is already present before the shooting of the bow, for the bow tugs with an effort, and every effort is an activity. Moreover, there are certainly *many* and *important* things to be said of the nature of effort (*conatus*) and of the principle of activity, or as the Scholastics called them, substantial forms, things which also illuminate Natural Theology and the mysteries of faith and dispel the darkness due to the obscurantist objections of philosophers.

The result is that not only souls but all substances can be said to exist in a place only through the operations of their active principle; that souls cannot be destroyed by any power of body and that all forces act for the highest mind whose will is the final reason for all things, the cause being the universal harmony; that God as creator can unite the body to the soul; that, in fact, every finite soul is embodied, even the angels are not excepted (in which true philosophy is in agreement with the teachings of the Church Fathers); and finally, that neither πολυτοπια (the same body in several places) nor μετουσιαμον (several bodies in the same place) contains anything contradictory. For we can find something wonderful in the fact that the consubstantiation of bodies becomes resolved in transubstantiation. On the other hand, whoever says that the body is contained in the bread, does not realize that he is asserting the destruction of the substance of the bread and still leaving its properties intact—all such fallacies can be avoided once the true and inevitable concept of substance is understood. Of what great significance these theorems are for the firm foundation of religious faith and for peace among the Churches, the understanding will appreciate.

On Some Philosophical Axioms and Mathematical Fictions

From a Letter to Canon Foucher, "Journal des Savans" (1692)

I share your thought that it would be good to seek proofs for all the important truths that can be proved. But that should not prevent us from going ahead with particular problems while we are expecting to establish first principles. That is how geometers proceed with them. However, I should like very much to have your opinion in explanation of this, for fear that those who do not understand it sufficiently may not improperly imagine that Academicians are opposed to the progress of the sciences.

Mr. Descartes does not seem to me to have taken pains to establish his axioms firmly, despite the fact that he for one began with that reasonable doubt which you Academicians first professed to introduce.

Moreover we know that *Proclus* and even *Apollonius* had already envisaged a plan for working on the proof of axioms. But those who like to go into scientific detail scorn abstract and general inquiries, and those who work on fundamental principles rarely go into particulars. For my part, I have an equally high regard for both general and particular investigations.

My axiom that nature never acts by a leap has a great use in Physics. It destroys atoms, small lapses of motion, globules of the second element, and other similar chimeras. It rectifies the laws of motion. Sir, lay aside your fears about the tortoise that the Pyrrhonian sceptics have made to move as fast as Achilles. You are right in saying that *all magnitudes may be infinitely subdivided. There is none so small in which we cannot conceive an inexhaustible infinity of subdivisions.* But I see no harm in that or any necessity to exhaust them. A space infinitely divisible is traversed in a time also infinitely divisible. I conceive no physical indivisibles short of a miracle, and I believe nature can reduce bodies to the smallness Geometry can consider.

Mr. Ozanam will, I hope, not be put out by my not having given him my first insight into the quadrature of the circle about which he and I had spoken, and I would have sent him my demonstration of it if he had asked me for it. He will also acknowledge that I am the first to have shown him the employment of local (geometrical) equations for constructions; he was delighted with it, and has made very fine use of it, as I see in his Dictionary. It is true that this use of local equations is not an invention of mine. I had learned it from Mr. Slusius.

Some time ago I had an insight profitable to Mr. Ozanam; namely, a plan for drawing up certain analytical or specious (algebraic) tables based on combinations. If this were done, it would be a wonderful aid to Analysis and Geometry, and the rest of mathematics; it would push Analysis to a perfection beyond its present limits. It would serve advanced geometry as much as the old table of sines serves trigonometry. And as Mr. Ozanam is one of the most facile men in the world when it comes to the ordinary algebraic calculations, I had thought that through his means a thing as useful as that could be accomplished.

The reason why I left behind me in Florence an essay on a new science of Dynamics is that there was a friend there who promised to straighten it out and put it into shape and even to have it published. It is my fault that it has not appeared for I only had to send him the end. But every time I thought of doing so, a host of new ideas came to me which I have not yet had a chance to digest.

Expressions like "Extremes meet" go a little too far, e.g., when we say that the infinite is a sphere whose center is everywhere and circumference nowhere. Such expressions must not be taken too strictly or literally. Nevertheless, they still have a particular use in discovery, something like that of imaginaries in Algebra. Thus we conceive the parabola as an ellipse with an infinitely distant focus; and in that way we maintain a certain universality in the propositions of conic sections. Calculation leads us sometimes to infinity without thinking about it in advance. It would be possible thus to arrive at a conclusion, at least in the case of a velocity assumed to be infinite, that each point of a circle is in the same place, although, after all, an infinite velocity as well as an infinite circle are impossible. With all that, that infinite circle may still have its use in calculating: for if analysis made me see that the radius of the circle posited in the given plane is infinite, I should conclude that the entire plane of the posited circle is the locus sought. Thus if I did not find what I am looking for, namely, a circle that is posited, I should at least find what I was to seek, namely, that the required locus is the plane, and there is no such circle in this plane. So that *omnia sana sanis* (all is reasonable to the reasonable) still stands, and analysis obtains real uses from imaginary expressions. I have very important examples of this. It is true that from truths we can conclude only truths; but there are certain falsehoods which are useful for finding the truth.

The Horizon of Human Doctrine (After 1690)

The entire body of the sciences may be regarded as an ocean, continuous everywhere and without a break or division, though men conceive parts in it and give them names according to their convenience. And as there are seas which are either unknown or sailed only by a few boats venturing on them by chance, so we may say there are sciences about which something is known only by chance and without a plan. One of them is the art of combinations which for me has as much significance as the science of forms or formulas or else of variations in general; in a word it is the Universal Specious or Characteristic. Such is the science that treats of the same and the diverse; of the similar and the dissimilar; of the absolute and the relational; as the usual Mathematics deals with the one and the many, the large and the small, the whole and the part. We may even say that Logistics or Algebra is subordinate to it in a certain sense, for when we make use of several marks indifferently which at the beginning of a calculation might be exchanged and mutually substituted without harming the reasoning (in this respect the letters of the Alphabet come in handy), and when these letters or marks signify magnitudes or general numbers the result is the Algebra or rather the Specious of Viète. And that is exactly where the advantage of Viète's and Descartes' Algebra over that of the ancients resides: by making use of letters instead of known or unknown numbers we obtain formulas in which there is some connection and order, which gives our mind a means for noticing theorems and general rules. Thus the best advantages of algebra are only samples of the art of characters whose use is not limited to numbers or magnitudes. For if these letters designated points (a common practise actually among Geometers), we could form a certain *calculus* or sort of operation which would be entirely different from Algebra and would continue to enjoy the same advantages as the latter has (about this I shall have more to say another time). When these letters designate terms or notions, as in Aristotle, we obtain that part of logic which treats of the figures and moods. I had figured that out when I first began my studies, when I hazarded publishing a little treatise on the Art of Combinations, which was well received and reprinted [in 1690 at Frankfurt] against my wishes, for having since had many other views on the subject, I could have treated things quite differently. However, I may say in passing that I had since then noticed this general theorem of Logic: that the four figures of syllogisms have each a like number of useful moods; and that in each figure there are six moods. Finally when the letters or other characters designate the actual letters of the Alphabet or of language, then the art of combinations together with the observation of languages yields the Cryptography of deciphering.

I have also remarked that there is a calculus of combinations in which the composite is not a collective but a distributive whole, that is to say, one in which the combined things do not come together except alternatively, and this calculus also has six laws quite different from those of Algebra. Finally, the general Specious takes in a thousand ways of expression, and Algebra contains only one. Now without entering into the particular discussion of the laws which diversify the Specious, we can combine it with Arithmetic by calculating the *number of possible variations* which the general marks may receive. These variations may be taken in different ways; in the writings we form by using letters of the alphabet there is variety as much with respect to the letters as to their arrangement, and intervals or separations (for we do not write everything without stop, but we leave some separation among the words). Now since all human knowledge can be expressed by the letters of the Alphabet, and since we may say that whoever understands the use of the alphabet knows everything, it follows that we can calculate the number of truths which men are able to express, and that we can determine the size of a work which would contain all possible human knowledge, in which there would be everything which could ever be known, written, or discovered; and even more than that, for it would contain not only the true but also the false propositions which we can assert, and even expressions which signify nothing. This inquiry helps us understand better how little man is in comparison with infinite substance, since the number of all the truths which all men together can know is quite mediocre, even if there were an infinity of men who for all eternity should exalt themselves in the advancement of the sciences, assuming all the time that human nature is no more perfect than it is now, for we are not considering here life in the hereafter when the human soul will be elevated to a more sublime state. This paradox differs quite in magnitude from the one Archimedes proposed to the courtesans of King Hero by showing them that the number of grains of sand which would fill not only the whole globe of the earth but also the space of a good part of the universe extending from here to the stars, is quite a small number and easy to write. For this number is almost nothing in comparison with the number of truths, since there is no grain of sand without its particular shape and which could not furnish a great number of truths, not to mention truths drawn from other things. It does not, however, follow that, if the world and mankind should last long enough, we should not be able to discover any but truths already known, for mankind could be content with a certain small number of truths during a whole eternity which would be only a part of those it is capable of attaining and thus would always leave something behind. But assuming man always goes forward as long as he can, though perhaps slowly and steadily making progress all the time, in the end everything must be exhausted, and a Novel cannot be written which has not already been written, nor a new dream be possible. Thus it would remain necessarily true that literally nothing will be said any longer which has not already been said. For we shall say what has been said or else, if we want to continue to say new things, we shall exhaust what remains to be said, since that is finite, as we shall demonstrate by and by. It is a question then of giving a number greater than the number of everything which can be said or asserted; that is what we are going to do. . . .[1]

On Wisdom (c. 1693)

Wisdom is a perfect knowledge of the principles of all the sciences and of the art of applying them. By *principles* I mean all the fundamental truths which suffice to enable us to derive any conclusions we may need, by dint of some exertion and some little application; in sum, that which serves the mind to regulate manners, to make an honest living, and everywhere (even if one were surrounded by barbarians), to preserve one's health, to perfect one's self in any sort of things we may need, and finally, to provide for the conveniences of living. The art of applying these principles to situations includes in it the art of judging well or reasoning, the art of discovering unknown truths, and finally, the art of recalling what one knows on the instant and whenever needed.

The *art of reasoning well* consists of the following maxims:

1. We must never recognize as true anything but what is manifestly indubitable. That is why it will be well in beginning these inquiries to imagine ourselves interested in supporting the contrary in order to see if such incitement might not stimulate us to see whether we can find something solid to be said in its favor. For we must avoid prejudices and attribute to things only what they include. But we must also never be dogmatic.

2. When there does not seem to be any means of arriving at such an assurance, we must be content with probability while waiting for greater light. But we must distinguish degrees of probabilities, and we must

1. The paper breaks off here, but, in at least one other fragment, Leibniz calculates the number of all the statements which can be made by starting with an alphabet of twenty-four letters, and reaches a number of the order of one followed by seventy-three trillion zeros; cf. L. Couturat, *Opuscules et fragments inédits de Leibniz* [Paris, 1903], p. 96, and also footnote 3 in which Couturat refers to another fragment in which Leibniz maintains the contrary view that the number of terms and consequently of primary propositions is infinite. Archimedes' Sand-Reckoner showed how to express a number as high as one followed by eighty thousand zeros.

remember that whatever we derive from a merely probable principle will retain the imperfection of its source, especially when we must assume several probabilities in order to arrive at that conclusion, for again, the latter becomes less sure than each probability serving as its ground.

3. To derive one truth from another we must keep uninterruptedly to a certain chain. For as we may be sure that a chain will hold when we are sure that each separate ring is of sound material, and that it clasps the two neighboring rings, namely, the one before and the one after it, so likewise, we may be sure of the accuracy of the reasoning when the matter is sound, that is to say, when it contains nothing doubtful, and when the form consists of a perpetual linking of truths with no gaps. For example, A is B and B is C and C is D, therefore A is D. Such a connecting chain will teach us never to put into the conclusion more than there was in the premises.

The *art of discovery* consists of the following maxims:

1. In order to become acquainted with a thing we must consider all of its prerequisites, that is, everything which suffices to distinguish it from any other thing. This is what is called definition, nature, essential property.

2. After we have found a means of distinguishing it from every other thing, we must apply this same rule to the consideration of each condition or prerequisite entering into this means, and consider all the prerequisites of each prerequisite. And that is what I call *true analysis,* or distribution of the difficulty into several parts.

3. When we have pushed the analysis to the end, that is, when we have considered the prerequisites entering into the consideration of the proposed thing, and even the prerequisites of the prerequisites, and finally have come to considering a few natures understood only by themselves without prerequisites and needing nothing outside themselves to be conceived, then we have arrived at a *perfect knowledge* of the proposed thing.

4. When the thing merits it, we must try to have this perfect knowledge present in our mind all at once, and that is done by repeating the analysis several times until it seems to us that we see it as a complete whole in a single act of the mind. And to obtain that result we must observe some gradation in the repetition.

5. The mark of perfect knowledge is that nothing appears in the thing under consideration which cannot be accounted for, and that nothing is encountered whose occurrence cannot be predicted in advance. It is very difficult to complete an analysis of things, but it is not

so difficult to complete the analysis we need to make of things. Because the analysis of a truth is completed when we have found the demonstration of the proposition. Most often the beginning of the analysis of the thing suffices for the analysis or perfect acquaintance of the truth of the thing with which we are acquainted.

6. We must always begin our inquiries with the easiest things, like the most general and simplest things, i.e., those on which it is easy to make experiments and to account for, like numbers, lines, motions.

7. We must ascend in order, both by going from easy to difficult things and by trying to discover some progression in the order of our thoughts for the sake of having nature itself as a guide and guarantee.

8. We must try to omit nothing in all of our distributions or enumerations. And that is why dichotomies with opposite members are very good.

9. The fruit of several analyses of different particular matters will be the catalogue of simple thoughts, or those which are not very far from being simple.

10. Having the catalogue of simple thoughts, we shall be ready to begin again *a priori* to explain the origin of things starting from their source in a perfect order and from a combination or synthesis which is absolutely complete. And that is all our soul can do in its present state.

The *art of recalling what one knows on the instant and whenever needed* consists of the following observations:

1. We must accustom ourselves to having presence of mind, that is, to be able to think in a disturbance, on the spur of the occasion and in danger, as well as in our study. That is why we must test ourselves on occasions and we must even seek such occasions with this precaution, however, that we do not expose ourselves to irreparable harm. In the meantime it is good to try ourselves out on occasions where the danger is imaginary or small, for example, in games, lectures, conversations, exercises, and humorous stories.

2. We must get used to making enumerations. That is why it is good to practise reporting all the possible cases of the problem under consideration, all the possible species of a kind, all the conveniences or inconveniences of a means, all the possible means for arriving at some end.

3. We must accustom ourselves to making distinctions, namely, given two or more very similar things, to find immediately all their differences.

4. We must accustom ourselves to analogies, namely, given two or more very different things, to find their similarities.

5. We must be able to relate immediately things which resemble

strongly the given thing or differ very much from it. For example, when people deny me some general maxim, it is good if I can bring in some examples immediately. And when another person brings up some maxim against me, it is good if I can mention a counter instance; when a story is told me, it is good if I can immediately relate a similar story.

6. When there are truths or familiar facts in which the natural connection of the subject with its predicate is not known to us, as happens with matters of fact and truths of experience, we must use a few artifices in order to retain them, as, for example, concerning the specific properties of simple things in natural, civil, or ecclesiastical history, in geography, customs, laws, canons, languages. I see nothing so good for retaining such things as humorous verses and sometimes diagrams; item, hypotheses concocted to explain them in imitation of natural things (like a suitable true or false etymology for languages—*Regula Mundi* by imagining certain orders of providence for history).

7. Finally, it is good to make a written inventory of things known by acquaintance which are most useful, with an index or alphabetical table. And we should draw up, finally, a portable manual of what is most necessary and most usual.

New System of Nature and of the Communication of Substances, as Well as of the Union of Soul and Body

"Journal des Savans" (June 27, 1695)

1. Several years ago I conceived this system and communicated with some learned men about it, especially with one of the greatest theologians and philosophers of our time [Mons. Arnauld] who, having learnt some of my thoughts through a person of the highest quality, had found them quite paradoxical. But after receiving my elucidations, he changed his attitude in the most generous and edifying way in the world; and having approved a part of my propositions, he withdrew his censure regarding the rest of them with which he had still remained in disagreement. Since then I have on occasions continued my meditations in order to give the public only well examined opinions, and I

have tried thus to satisfy objections made against my Essays on Dynamics (*Act. Erudit.*, April 1695) connected with this one. Now, at last, since important persons have desired to see my thoughts elucidated more, I have hazarded these meditations, though they are in no way popular nor appropriately served to any kind of mind. I have brought myself to do it mainly in order to profit by the judgments of those who are enlightened in these matters; for it would be too embarrassing to seek and summon in particular all those who would be disposed to give me instructions, which I shall always be very glad to receive, provided the love of truth appears in them rather than a passion for prejudiced opinions.

2. Although I am one of those who have worked hard on mathematics, I have not ceased meditating on philosophy since my youth, for it always seemed to me there was a means to establish in philosophy something solid through clear demonstrations. I had penetrated far into the land of the scholastics when mathematics and the modern authors made me emerge from it while I was still young. I was charmed by their beautiful ways of explaining Nature mechanically, and I despised with reason the method of those who use only forms or faculties from which nothing is learnt. But since, having tried to lay the foundations of the very principles of mechanics in order to give a rational account of the laws of nature known to us by experiment, I realized that the sole consideration of an extended mass did not suffice, and that we must again employ the notion of force which is very intelligible despite its springing from metaphysics. It seemed to me also that the opinion of those who transform or degrade animals into pure machines, though a possible one apparently, is against appearances, and even against the order of things.

3. In the beginning when I had freed myself from the yoke of Aristotle, I had taken to the void and the atoms, for they best fill the imagination; but on recovering from that, after many reflections, I realized that it is impossible to find the principles of *a true unity* in matter alone or in that which is only passive, since everything in it is only a collection or mass of parts to infinity. Now multitude can only get its reality from *true unities* which come from elsewhere and are quite different from points (it is known that the continuum cannot be composed of points). Therefore to find these *real unities* I was compelled to have recourse to a formal atom, since a material being cannot be both material and perfectly indivisible or endowed with a true unity. It was necessary, hence, to recall and, so to speak, rehabilitate the *substantial forms* so decried today, but in a way which would make

them intelligible and which would separate the use we should make of them from the abuse that has been made of them. I thence found that their nature consists in force, and that from that there ensues something analogous to feeling and appetite; and that accordingly they must be conceived in imitation of the idea we have of Souls. But as the soul should never be used to explain any detail of the economy of the animal's body, I judged likewise that these forms must not be used to explain the particular problems of nature though they are necessary to establish true general prinicples. Aristotle calls them *first Entelechies*. I call them perhaps more intelligibly, *primitive Forces* which do not contain only the *act* or the complement of possibility, but further an *original activity*.

4. I saw that these forms and these souls should be indivisible, as our mind is, remembering indeed that that was the thought of Saint Thomas regarding the souls of animals. But this truth renewed the great difficulties of the origin and duration of souls and forms. For every substance, being a true unity and not capable of beginning or ceasing to exist without a miracle, it follows that they can only begin by creation and end only by annihilation. Thus, except the souls that God wishes still to create expressly, I was obliged to recognize that it is necessary that the forms constitutive of substances should have been created with the world and that they should subsist forever. Thus a few scholastics like Albert the Great and John Bacon had glimpsed a part of the truth about their origin. And that should not appear extraordinary, since we are only giving to forms the duration which the Gassendists give to their atoms.

5. I judged, however, that we must not be indifferent to the different grades of minds or reasonable souls, the higher orders being incomparably more perfect than those forms buried in matter, being like little Gods by contrast with the latter, and are made in the image of God, having in them some ray of the light of Divinity. That is why God governs minds as a Prince governs his subjects, and even as a father cares for his children, whereas he disposes of other substances as an engineer manipulates his machines. Thus minds have particular laws which put them above the revolutions of matter; and we may say that everything else is made only for them, these very revolutions being accommodated for the happiness of the good and the punishment of the wicked.

6. Nevertheless, giving back to ordinary forms or *material* souls that duration which must be attributed to them in the place of what had been attributed to atoms, might arouse the suspicion that they go

from one body to another, which would be *metempsychosis,* almost as some philosophers have believed in the propagation of motion and that of species. But this is a piece of imagination far removed from the nature of things. There is no such passage; and this is where the 'metamorphoses' of Messrs. Swammerdam, Malpighi, and Leeuwenhoeck, who are excellent observers in our day, have come to my aid, and have made me admit more confidently that the animal as every other organized substance has no beginning, though we think so, and that its apparent generation is only a development and a kind of augmentation. Thus I have noticed that the author of the *Recherche de la vérité* [Malebranche], Mr. Regis, Mr. Hartsoeker, and other able men, have not been very far from having this thought.

7. But there still remained the biggest question, what becomes of these souls or forms after the death of the animal or the destruction of the individual with organized substance? And that is a most embarrassing problem; in so far as it scarcely seems reasonable for souls to remain uselessly in a chaos of confused matter. That made me finally judge that there was only one single reasonable line to take, and that is the conservation not only of the soul but also of the animal itself and its organic machine even though the destruction of the gross parts may have reduced it to a smallness which is as much beyond our senses as it was before being born. Thus nobody can really observe the true time of death; the latter may pass a long time for a simple suspension of noticeable actions, and at bottom is never anything else in simple animals: witness the resuscitations of drowned flies buried under pulverized chalk, and several other similar examples which make us sufficiently aware that there would be many other resuscitations, and even more than that, if men were able to restore the machine. And there is some evidence apparently that something of that sort was discussed by the great Democritus, atomist that he was, though Pliny makes fun of him. It is, hence, natural that the animal having always been alive and organized (as some persons of great penetration are beginning to recognize), he remains so always. And since there is no first birth nor entirely new generation of the animal, it follows that there will not be any final extinction, nor any complete death taken in a strict metaphysical sense. Consequently, instead of the transmigration of souls, there is only a transformation of the same animal, according to the different ways the organs are unfolded and more or less developed.

8. However, reasonable souls follow much higher laws and are

exempt from anything which might make them lose the quality of being citizens of the society of spirits. God has so well seen to it that no changes of matter can make them lose the moral qualities of their personality. And we may say that everything tends to the perfection, not solely of the universe in general, but also of those creatures in particular who are destined to such a degree of happiness that the Universe finds itself interested by virtue of the divine goodness which is communicated to each one as much as the sovereign Wisdom may permit.

9. Concerning the ordinary course of animals and other corporeal substances whose complete extinction has been accepted until now, and whose changes depend on mechanical rather than on moral laws, I noticed with pleasure that the ancient author of the book *On Diet,* attributed to Hippocrates, had glimpsed something of the truth when he said explicitly that animals are not born and do not die, and that the things believed to begin and to perish only appear and disappear. That is the thought also of Parmenides and of Melissus, according to Aristotle. For these ancients were more solid than people believe.

10. I am the most readily disposed person in the world to do justice to the moderns; however, I find they have carried reform too far. Among other things, they confuse natural with artificial things for lack of insufficiently broad ideas about the majesty of nature. They conceive the difference existing between her machines and ours to be only one of size, Nature's being larger. This view has recently led a very able man (Fontenelle), the author of *Entretiens sur la pluralité des mondes* (*Dialogues on the Plurality of Worlds*), to say that on looking closely at Nature, we find her less admirable than we had thought, and more like the shop of a working man. I believe that that view does not give us a worthy enough idea of her. Only in my system is one able to realize at last the true and immense distance between the smallest productions and mechanisms of divine wisdom and the greatest masterpieces of art of a limited mind, this difference being not simply one of degree but of very kind. We must then know that Nature's machines have a truly infinite number of organs, and are so well supplied and resistant to all accidents that it is impossible to destroy them. A natural machine still remains a machine in its least parts, and furthermore, it remains forever the same machine that it has been, being only transformed by the different habits it takes on, at one time expansive, at another restrictive and concentrated, when believed to be lost.

11. Besides, by means of the soul or form, there is a true unity which answers to what is called the Ego in us. This cannot take place in the machines of art, nor in the simple mass of matter no matter how organized it is. Matter can only be considered like an army or herd, or like a pond full of fish, or like a watch made up of springs and wheels. However, if there were no true substantial unities, there would be nothing substantial or real in the collection. That was what forced Mr. Cordemoi to abandon Descartes and embrace the Democritean doctrine of atoms in order to find a true unity. But *material atoms* are contrary to reason, apart from the fact that they are still composed of parts, since the invincible attachment of one part to the other (if one could conceive or suppose it with reason) would not destroy their multitude. There are only *substantial atoms,* that is to say, real unities, absolutely destitute of parts, which are the sources of actions; they are the first absolute principles of the composition of things, and like the last elements of the analysis of substances. They might be called *metaphysical points:* they have *something vital* and a kind of perception; *mathematical points* are their *point of view* for expressing the Universe. But when corporeal substances are close together, all their organs together make only one *physical point* relatively to us. Thus physical points are indivisible only in appearance; mathematical points are exact, but they are only modalities; only metaphysical or substantial points (constituted by forms or souls) are exact *and* real; without them there would be nothing real, since without true unities there would be no multitude.

12. After establishing these things, I thought I had arrived in port; but when I began to meditate on the union of the soul with the body, I was cast back, as it were, into the open sea. For I found no way of explaining how the body causes something to happen in the soul, or *vice versa;* nor how a substance can communicate with another created substance. Descartes had given up the game on that point, so far as we can know from his writings; but his disciples seeing that the common opinion is inconceivable judged that we feel the qualities of bodies because God causes thoughts to arise in the soul on the occasion of the movements of matter, and when our soul wishes in its turn to move the body they judged that it is God who moves it for the soul. And as the communication of the movements appeared to them inconceivable again, they believed that God gives movement to a body on the occasion of the movement of another body. That is what they call the *System of Occasional Causes,* which has been made very fashionable through

the beautiful reflections of the author of the *Recherche de la vérité*.

13. It must be admitted that by noting what cannot be the case concerning the soul and body, the Cartesians have at least penetrated to the difficulty, but it has not been alleviated by simply describing what in fact happens. In strict metaphysical language, there is very truly no real influence of one created substance on another, all things with all their realities being continually produced by the power of God; but in order to solve problems it is not enough to employ the general cause and to invoke what is called *Deus ex machinâ*. For when that is done without any other explanation drawn from the order of secondary causes, recourse is being taken to miracle, properly speaking. In philosophy we must try to give reasons by showing in what way things are brought about by divine wisdom in conformity with the notion of the subject under investigation.

14. Therefore, though I was obliged to agree that it is impossible for the soul, or any other true substance, to receive any influence from the outside except through divine omnipotence, I was gradually led to a thought which surprised me but seems to me inevitable and indeed has very great advantages and a very considerable attraction. That is, we must say that God has from the first created the soul or any other real unity in such a way that everything arises in it from its own internal nature through a perfect *spontaneity* relatively to itself, and yet with a perfect *conformity* to external things. Thus our internal thoughts, that is, those in the soul itself and not in the brain nor in the subtle parts of the body (which are only phenomena following on external beings, or else, true appearances, like well ordered dreams), these perceptions internal to the soul itself, must happen to it through its own original constitution, that is to say, through its representative nature (capable of expressing beings outside itself by the mediation of its organs) given to it since its creation and constituting its individual character. And that is what makes each one of these substances represent, each exactly in its own way, the whole universe from a certain point of view. The perceptions or expressions of external things occur in the soul at a fixed moment by virtue of its own laws, as in a world apart and as if there existed nothing but God and itself (to use a manner of speaking employed by a certain person [Mons. Foucher] of great spiritual elevation and famous for his holiness). There will be a perfect harmony among all these substances which produces the same effect that would be noticed if they communicated mutually through that propagation of species or of qualities imagined by the common

run of philosophers. Moreover, the organized mass in which the point of view of the soul lies, is expressed more proximately and finds itself in turn ready to act itself by obeying the laws of the bodily machine at the moment the soul wishes to act, without disturbing the laws of nature, the spirits and blood then having exactly the motions they need to correspond to the soul's passions and perceptions. It is this mutual relationship regulated in advance in each substance of the universe which produces what we call their communication, and which alone causes *the union of soul and body.* . . .

15. This hypothesis is indeed possible. For why could not God first give to substance a nature or internal force which could produce in it, in an orderly way, everything which will happen to it (as in a *spiritual or formal automaton* but *free* in that it has a share of reason), that is, all the appearances or expressions it will have, and that, without the aid of any creature? All the more so since the nature of substance requires necessarily and conceals a progression or change without which it would not have the force to act. And this nature of the soul being representative of the universe in a very exact though more or less distinct manner, the series of representations produced in the soul will correspond naturally to the series of changes in the Universe itself: as, conversely, the body has also been accommodated to the soul in those transactions in which the soul is conceived as acting on external things. This is all the more reasonable in so far as bodies are made only for minds capable of entering into society with God and to appreciate his glory. Thus, as soon as one sees the possibility of this hypothesis of harmonies, it is seen as most reasonable both for giving a marvelous idea of the harmony of the Universe and of the perfection of God's works.

16. There is to be discovered in it also this great advantage that instead of saying that we are free only in appearance in a way sufficient for practical life, as several intelligent persons have believed, we should rather say that we are determined only in appearance but that in strict metaphysical language we are perfectly independent relatively to the influence of all other creatures. This again puts in a marvelous light the immortality of our soul and the constantly uniform conservation of our individuality, perfectly well regulated by its own nature, protected from all external accidents, notwithstanding any appearance to the contrary. Never has a system put our elevation in greater evidence. Every mind being like a world apart, sufficient unto itself, independent of any other creature, containing the infinite, ex-

pressing the universe, is as enduring, as subsistent, and as absolute as the very universe of creatures. Thus one should judge that he ought to behave in the most proper way to contribute to the perfection of the society of all the minds which make their moral union in the City of God. We also have in our system a new and surprisingly clear proof of God's existence. For this perfect harmony of so many substances which have no mutual communication can only come from the common cause.

17. Besides all these advantages recommending this hypothesis, we may say that it is something more than a hypothesis, since it scarcely seems possible to explain the thing in any other intelligible way, and since several big difficulties which have until now worried minds seem to disappear by themselves when we have understood the system. Ordinary ways of speaking are still preserved quite well. For we can say that the substance whose disposition gives a reason for change in an intelligible way (so that we can judge that other substances have been harmonized with it on that point from the beginning, according to the order of God's decree), such a substance may be conceived in that respect as *acting* consequently on the others. Thus the action of one substance on another is not the emission or transplantation of an entity; as is commonly conceived, and cannot be taken reasonably except in the way I have just mentioned. It is true that in matter we conceive very well both emissions and receptions of parts through which many are right in explaining all the phenomena of Physics mechanically; but as the material mass is not a substance itself, it cannot be other than what I have just indicated.

18. These considerations, however metaphysical they may appear, still have a marvelous use in Physics for establishing the laws of motion, as our *Dynamics* will enable us to show. For we can say that in the collision of bodies each one suffers only through its own elasticity, because of the movement already in it. And as to absolute motion, nothing can determine it mathematically, since everything terminates in relations: which makes for the perfect equivalence of hypotheses, e.g., in Astronomy; so that whatever number of bodies we take, we may arbitrarily assign rest or any degree of velocity we choose without being refuted by the phenomena of rectilinear, circular, or composite motion. However, it is reasonable to attribute to bodies true movements following the supposition which gives a reason for phenomena in the most intelligible manner, this denomination of movement being in conformity with the notion of action which we have just established.

Second Explanation of the System of the Communication of Substances

"Histoire des Ouvrages des Savans" (February, 1696)

You do not understand, you say, how I could prove what I have proposed concerning the *Communication* or *Harmony* of two *Substances* as different as the *soul* is from the *body*. It is true that I believe I have found the way, and here is how I intend to satisfy you.

Imagine two clocks or watches in perfect agreement. That can happen in three ways:

(1) The first consists in a mutual influence.

(2) The second is to have a skillful worker continually adjust them and keep them in agreement.

(3) The third is to manufacture these two time-pieces with so much art and accuracy that their agreement is guaranteed thereafter.

Now substitute the *soul* and *body* for these two time-pieces; their agreement can be obtained through one of these three ways. The *way of influence* is that of popular philosophy; but as we cannot conceive of material particles which can pass from one of these substances to another, we must abandon this idea. The way of the *continual* assistance of the Creator is that of the system of occasional causes; but I hold that this introduces *Deus ex machinâ* in a natural and ordinary occurrence where, according to reason, it ought not intervene except as it operates in all other natural things. Thus there remains only my hypothesis, that is, the way of *Harmony*. From the beginning God has made each of these two Substances of such a nature that each by following its own laws, given to it with its being, still agrees with the other, just as though there were a mutual influence or as though God always took a hand in it beyond his general supervision of things. There is nothing further I have to prove, unless you wish to ask that I prove God is skillful enough to use this prearranged scheme, examples of which we see even among men. Now assuming that he can, you do see that this way is most admirable and most worthy of God. You suspected that my explanation would be opposed by the very different idea we have of the mind and body; but you see now that nobody has better established their independence. For while people are compelled to explain the communication of mind and body by a sort of miracle, there is cause for many people to fear that the distinction between soul and body might not be as real as they believe, since they have to go so far in order to maintain it. I shall not be vexed if learned persons sound out the thoughts I have just explained to you.

Theodicy

. . . Now when preparing to justify my system in face of the new difficulties of M. Bayle, I purposed at the same time to communicate to him the ideas which I had had for some time already, on the difficulties put forward by him in opposition to those who endeavour to reconcile reason with faith in regard to the existence of evil. Indeed, there are perhaps few persons who have toiled more than I in this matter. Hardly had I gained some tolerable understanding of Latin writings when I had an opportunity of turning over books in a library. I flitted from book to book, and since subjects for meditation pleased me as much as histories and fables, I was charmed by the work of Laurentius Valla against Boethius and by that of Luther against Erasmus, although I was well aware that they had need of some mitigation. I did not omit books of controversy, and amongst other writings of this nature the records of the Montbéliard Conversation, which had revived the dispute, appeared to me instructive. Nor did I neglect the teachings of our theologians: and the study of their opponents, far from disturbing me, served to strengthen me in the moderate opinions of the Churches of the Augsburg Confession. I had opportunity on my journeys to confer with some excellent men of different parties, for instance with Bishop Peter von Wallenburg, Suffragan of Mainz, with Herr Johann Ludwig Fabricius, premier theologian of Heidelberg, and finally with the celebrated M. Arnauld. To him I even tendered a Latin Dialogue of my own composition upon this subject, about the year 1673, wherein already I laid it down that God, having chosen the most perfect of all possible worlds, had been prompted by his wisdom to permit the evil which was bound up with it, but which still did not prevent this world from being, all things considered, the best that could be chosen. I have also since read many and various good authors on these subjects, and I have endeavoured to make progress in the knowledge that seems to me proper for banishing all that could have obscured the idea of supreme perfection which must be acknowledged in God. I have not neglected to examine the most rigorous authors, who have extended furthest the doctrine of the necessity of things, as for instance Hobbes and Spinoza, of whom the former advocated this absolute necessity not only in his *Physical Elements* and elsewhere, but also in a special book against Bishop Bramhall. And Spinoza insists more or less (like an ancient Peripatetic philosopher named Strato) that all has come from the first cause or from primitive Nature by a blind and geometrical necessity, with complete absence of capacity for choice, for goodness and for understanding in his first source of things.

I have found the means, so it seems to me, of demonstrating the contrary in a way that gives one a clear insight into the inward essence of the matter. For having made new discoveries on the nature of active force and the laws of motion, I have shown that they have no geometrical necessity, as Spinoza appears to have believed they had. Neither, as I have made plain, are they purely arbitrary, even though this be the opinion of M. Bayle and of some modern philosophers: but they are dependent upon the fitness of things as I have already pointed out above, or upon that which I call the 'principle of the best'. Moreover one recognizes therein, as in every other thing, the marks of the first substance, whose productions bear the stamp of a supreme wisdom and make the most perfect of harmonies. I have shown also that this harmony connects both the future with the past and the present with the absent. The first kind of connexion unites times, and the other places. This second connexion is displayed in the union of the soul with the body, and in general in the communication of true substances with one another and with material phenomena. But the first takes place in the preformation of organic bodies, or rather of all bodies, since there is organism everywhere, although all masses do not compose organic bodies. So a pond may very well be full of fish or of other organic bodies, although it is not itself an animal or organic body, but only a mass that contains them. Thus I had endeavoured to build upon such foundations, established in a conclusive manner, a complete body of the main articles of knowledge that reason pure and simple can impart to us, a body whereof all the parts were properly connected and capable of meeting the most important difficulties of the ancients and the moderns. I had also in consequence formed for myself a certain system concerning the freedom of man and the cooperation of God. This system appeared to me to be such as would in no wise offend reason and faith; and I desired to submit it to the scrutiny of M. Bayle, as well as of those who are in controversy with him. Now he has departed from us, and such a loss is no small one, a writer whose learning and acumen few have equalled. But since the subject is under consideration and men of talent are still occupied with it, while the public also follows it attentively, I take this to be a fitting moment for the publication of certain of my ideas. . . .

7. *God is the first reason of things:* for such things as are bounded, as all that which we see and experience, are contingent and have nothing in them to render their existence necessary, it being plain that time, space and matter, united and uniform in themselves and indifferent to everything, might have received entirely other motions and shapes, and in another order. Therefore one must seek the reason for the existence of the world, which is the whole assemblage of *contingent* things, and seek it in the substance which carries with it the reason for its existence, and which in consequence is *necessary* and eternal. Moreover, this cause must be intelligent: for this existing world being contingent and an infinity of other worlds being equally possible, and holding, so to say, equal claim to existence with it, the cause of the world must needs have had regard or reference to all these possible worlds in order to fix upon one of them. This regard or relation of an existent substance to simple possibilities can be nothing other than the *understanding* which has the ideas of them, while to fix upon one of them can be nothing other than the act of the *will* which chooses. It is the *power* of this substance that renders its will efficacious. Power relates to *being,* wisdom or understanding to *truth,* and will to *good.* And this intelligent cause ought to be infinite in all ways, and absolutely perfect in *power,* in *wisdom* and in *goodness,* since it relates to all that which is possible. Furthermore, since all is connected together, there is no ground for admitting more than *one.* Its understanding is the source of *essences,* and its will is the origin of *existences.* There in few words is the proof of one only God with his perfections, and through him of the origin of things.

8. Now this supreme wisdom, united to a goodness that is no less infinite, cannot but have chosen the best. For as a lesser evil is a kind of good, even so a lesser good is a kind of evil if it stands in the way of a greater good; and there would be something to correct in the actions of God if it were possible to do better. As in mathematics, when there is no maximum nor minimum, in short nothing distinguished, everything is done equally, or when that is not possible nothing at all is done: so it may be said likewise in respect of perfect wisdom, which is no less orderly than mathematics, that if there were not the best (*optimum*) among all possible worlds, God would not have produced any. I call 'World' the whole succession and the whole agglomeration

of all existent things, lest it be said that several worlds could have existed in different times and different places. For they must needs be reckoned all together as one world or, if you will, as one Universe. And even though one should fill all times and all places, it still remains true that one might have filled them in innumerable ways, and that there is an infinitude of possible worlds among which God must needs have chosen the best, since he does nothing without acting in accordance with supreme reason.

9. Some adversary not being able to answer this argument will perchance answer the conclusion by a counter-argument, saying that the world could have been without sin and without sufferings; but I deny that then it would have been *better*. For it must be known that all things are *connected* in each one of the possible worlds: the universe, whatever it may be, is all of one piece, like an ocean: the least movement extends its effect there to any distance whatsoever, even though this effect become less perceptible in proportion to the distance. Therein God has ordered all things beforehand once for all, having foreseen prayers, good and bad actions, and all the rest; and each thing *as an idea* has contributed, before its existence, to the resolution that has been made upon the existence of all things; so that nothing can be changed in the universe (any more than in a number) save its essence or, if you will, save its *numerical individuality*. Thus, if the smallest evil that comes to pass in the world were missing in it, it would no longer be this world; which, with nothing omitted and all allowance made, was found the best by the Creator who chose it. . . .

20. But it is necessary also to meet the more speculative and metaphysical difficulties which have been mentioned, and which concern the cause of evil. The question is asked first of all, whence does evil come? *Si Deus est, unde malum? Si non est, unde bonus?* The ancients attributed the cause of evil to *matter,* which they believed uncreated and independent of God: but we, who derive all being from God, where shall we find the source of evil? The answer is, that it must be sought in the ideal nature of the creature, in so far as this nature is contained in the eternal verities which are in the understanding of God, independently of his will. For we must consider that there is an *original imperfection in the creature* before sin, because the creature is limited in its essence; whence ensues that it cannot know all, and that it can deceive itself and commit other errors. Plato said in *Timaeus* that the world originated in Understanding united to Necessity. Others have united God and Nature. This can be given a reasonable meaning. God

will be the Understanding; and the Necessity, that is, the essential nature of things, will be the object of the understanding, in so far as this object consists in the eternal verities. But this object is inward and abides in the divine understanding. And therein is found not only the primitive form of good, but also the origin of evil: the Region of the Eternal Verities must be substituted for matter when we are concerned with seeking out the source of things.

This region is the ideal cause of evil (as it were) as well as of good: but, properly speaking, the formal character of evil has no *efficient* cause, for it consists in privation, as we shall see, namely, in that which the efficient cause does not bring about. That is why the Schoolmen are wont to call the cause of evil *deficient*.

21. Evil may be taken metaphysically, physically and morally. *Metaphysical evil* consists in mere imperfection, *physical evil* in suffering, and *moral evil* in sin. Now although physical evil and moral evil be not necessary, it is enough that by virtue of the eternal verities they be possible. And as this vast Region of Verities contains all possibilities it is necessary that there be an infinitude of possible worlds, that evil enter into divers of them, and that even the best of all contain a measure thereof. Thus has God been induced to permit evil.

22. But someone will say to me: why speak you to us of 'permitting'? Is it not God that doeth the evil and that willeth it? Here it will be necessary to explain what 'permission' is, so that it may be seen how this term is not employed without reason. But before that one must explain the nature of will, which has its own degrees. Taking it in the general sense, one may say that *will* consists in the inclination to do something in proportion to the good it contains. This will is called *antecedent* when it is detached, and considers each good separately in the capacity of a good. In this sense it may be said that God tends to all good, as good, *ad perfectionem simpliciter simplicem,* to speak like the Schoolmen, and that by an antecedent will. He is earnestly disposed to sanctify and to save all men, to exclude sin, and to prevent damnation. It may even be said that this will is efficacious *of itself* (*per se*), that is, in such sort that the effect would ensue if there were not some stronger reason to present it: for this will does not pass into final exercise (*ad summum conatum*), else it would never fail to produce its full effect, God being the master of all things. Success entire and infallible belongs only to the *consequent will,* as it is called. This it is which is complete; and in regard to it this rule obtains, that one never fails to do what one wills, when one has the power. Now this consequent will, final and decisive, results from the conflict of all the

antecedent wills, of those which tend towards good, even as of those which repel evil; and from the concurrence of all these particular wills comes the total will. So in mechanics compound movement results from all the tendencies that concur in one and the same moving body, and satisfies each one equally, in so far as it is possible to do all at one time. It is as if the moving body took equal account of these tendencies, as I once showed in one of the Paris Journals (7 Sept. 1693), when giving the general law of the compositions of movement. In this sense also it may be said that the antecedent will is efficacious in a sense and even effective with success.

23. Thence it follows that God wills *antecedently* the good and *consequently* the best. And as for evil, God wills moral evil not at all, and physical evil or suffering he does not will absolutely. Thus it is that there is no absolute predestination to damnation; and one may say of physical evil, that God wills it often as a penalty owing to guilt, and often also as a means to an end, that is, to prevent greater evils or to obtain greater good. The penalty serves also for amendment and example. Evil often serves to make us savour good the more; sometimes too it contributes to a greater perfection in him who suffers it, as the seed that one sows is subject to a kind of corruption before it can germinate: this is a beautiful similitude, which Jesus Christ himself used.

24. Concerning sin or moral evil, although it happens very often that it may serve as a means of obtaining good or of preventing another evil, it is not this that renders it a sufficient object of the divine will or a legitimate object of a created will. It must only be admitted or *permitted* in so far as it is considered to be a certain consequence of an indispensable duty: as for instance if a man who was determined not to permit another's sin were to fail of his own duty, or as if an officer on guard at an important post were to leave it, especially in time of danger, in order to prevent a quarrel in the town between two soldiers of the garrison who wanted to kill each other.

25. The rule which states, *non esse facienda mala, ut eveniant bona,* and which even forbids the permission of a moral evil with the end of obtaining a physical good, far from being violated, is here proved, and its source and its reason are demonstrated. One will not approve the action of a queen who, under the pretext of saving the State, commits or even permits a crime. The crime is certain and the evil for the State is open to question. Moreover, this manner of giving sanction to crimes, if it were accepted, would be worse than a disruption of some one country, which is liable enough to happen in any case, and

would perchance happen all the more by reason of such means chosen to prevent it. But in relation to God nothing is open to question, nothing can be opposed to *the rule of the best,* which suffers neither exception nor dispensation. It is in this sense that God permits sin: for he would fail in what he owes to himself, in what he owes to his wisdom, his goodness, his perfection, if he followed not the grand result of all his tendencies to good, and if he chose not that which is absolutely the best, notwithstanding the evil of guilt, which is involved therein by the supreme necessity of the eternal verities. Hence the conclusion that God wills all good *in himself antecedently,* that he wills the best *consequently* as an *end,* that he wills what is indifferent, and physical evil, sometimes as a *means,* but that he will only permit moral evil as the *sine qua non* or as a hypothetical necessity which connects it with the best. Therefore the *consequent will* of God, which has sin for its object, is only *permissive.*

26. It is again well to consider that moral evil is an evil so great only because it is a source of physical evils, a source existing in one of the most powerful of creatures, who is also most capable of causing those evils. For an evil will is in its department what the evil principle of the Manichaeans would be in the universe; and reason, which is an image of the Divinity, provides for evil souls great means of causing much evil. One single Caligula, one Nero, has caused more evil than an earthquake. An evil man takes pleasure in causing suffering and destruction, and for that there are only too many opportunities. But God being inclined to produce as much good as possible, and having all the knowledge and all the power necessary for that, it is impossible that in him there be fault, or guilt, or sin; and when he permits sin, it is wisdom, it is virtue.

XVI

BAYLE

Pierre Bayle (1647-1706) was a Protestant born in southern France. While studying at the Jesuit college at Toulouse, he converted to Catholicism and then reconverted to Calvinism. As a heretic, he had to flee, and went to Geneva where he completed his studies. He secretly returned to France and became a professor of philosophy at the Protestant Academy of Sedan. In 1681, he had to flee again, because of the persecutions of Louis XIV, and went to Rotterdam where he remained until his death. He taught there for several years and began publishing works critical of superstition and intolerance, whether Catholic or Protestant, while also writing a monthly journal, *The News of the Republic of Letters,* in which he examined works in all intellectual fields. He became engaged in polemics against both orthodox and liberal Protestants and lost his teaching post. He then devoted himself to his major work, the *Historical and Critical Dictionary,* first published in 1697 and greatly enlarged in the 1702 edition. The *Dictionary* was a biographical one, containing brief lives of people (often extremely obscure ones) and long digressive footnotes examining and attacking every possible theory on any possible subject. Leibniz, Malebranche, Locke, Descartes, and so forth, all were targets of Bayle's skeptical onslaught. The *Dictionary* was the major reference work in philosophy well into the eighteenth century and was called "the arsenal of the Enlightenment" by Voltaire. The translation is by Richard H. Popkin.

Historical and Critical Dictionary

PYRRHO

¶ Remark B

. . .

B. (*It is rightly detested in the schools of theology.*) Pyrrhonism is dangerous in relation to this divine science, but it hardly seems so with regard to the natural sciences or to the state. It does not matter much if one says that the mind of man is too limited to discover anything concerning natural truths, concerning the causes producing heat, cold, the tides, and the like. It is enough for us that we employ ourselves in looking for probable hypotheses and collecting data. I am quite sure that there are very few good scientists of this century who are not convinced that nature is an impenetrable abyss and that its springs are known only to Him who made and directs them. Thus, all these philosophers are Academics and Pyrrhonists in this regard. Society has no reason to be afraid of skepticism; for skeptics do not deny that one should conform to the customs of one's country, practice one's moral duties, and act upon matters on the basis of probabilities without waiting for certainty. They could suspend judgment on the question of whether such and such an obligation is naturally and absolutely legitimate; but they did not suspend judgment on the question of whether it ought to be fulfilled on such and such occasions. It is therefore only religion that has anything to fear from Pyrrhonism. Religion ought to be based on certainty. Its aim, its effects, its usages collapse as soon as the firm conviction of its truths is erased from the mind. But this should not be a cause of uneasiness. There never were, and there never will be more than a small number of people who can be fooled by the arguments of the skeptics. The grace of God in the faithful, the force of education in other men, and, even if you wish, ignorance[1] and the natural inclination to reach decisions, all these constitute an impenetrable shield against the arrows of the Pyrrhonists although this sect thinks it is more formidable today than it was in former times. We shall now see what this strange claim is based on.

About two months ago a very able man told me much about a discussion he had attended. Two *abbés,* of whom one knew only his duties and obligations and the other was a good philosopher, got into a fairly heated debate that almost became a full-fledged quarrel. The first had said rather bluntly that he could pardon the pagan philosophers for having drifted into the uncertainty of opinions but that he could not understand how there were still any miserable Pyrrhonists after the arrival of the light of the Gospel. "You are wrong," said the other, "to reason this way. Were Arcesilaus to return to this world, and were he to combat our theologians, he would be a thousand times more formidable than he was against the dogmatists of ancient Greece. Christian theology would furnish him with unanswerable arguments." All those present were much surprised to hear this, and begged the *abbé* to explain himself further, having no doubts that he had advanced a paradox that would only lead to his own confusion. Here is the answer he gave, addressing himself to the first *abbé:* "I will not make use of the advantages the new philosophy has given the Pyrrhonists. One hardly knew the name of Sextus Empiricus in our schools. The methods he had proposed so subtly for bringing about suspense of judgment were not less known than the *Terra Australis,* when Gassendi gave us an abridgement of it, which opened our eyes. Cartesianism put the final touches to this, and now no good philosopher any longer doubts that the skeptics were right to maintain that the qualities of bodies that strike our senses are only appearances. Every one of us can justly say, 'I feel heat in the presence of fire,' but not, 'I know that fire is, in itself, such as it appears to me.' This is the way the ancient Pyrrhonists spoke. Today the new philosophy speaks more positively. Heat, smells, colors, and the like, are not in the objects of our senses. They are modifications of my soul. I know that bodies are not at all as they appear to me. They would have wished to exempt extension and motion, but they could not. For if the objects of our senses appear colored,

1. It is a saying of Simonides that "those people are not clever enough to be deceived by a man like me." Balzac said the same thing about the girls of his village. Agesilaus complained about having to deal with opponents who did not understand enough about war, so that his stratagems were useless; he could not deceive troops who were inexperienced.

hot, cold, odoriferous, and yet they are not so, why can they not appear extended and shaped, in rest and in motion, though they are not so?[2] Still further, sense objects cannot be the cause of my sensations. I could therefore feel heat and cold, see colors and shapes, extension and motion, even though there were no bodies in the universe. I have therefore no good proof of the existence of bodies.[3] The only proof that could be given me of this would be based on the contention that God would be deceiving me if he imprinted in my mind the ideas that I have of bodies without there actually being any.[4] But this proof is very weak; it proves too much. Ever since the beginning of the world, all mankind, except perhaps one out of two hundred millions, has firmly believed that bodies are colored, and this is an error. I ask, does God deceive mankind with regard to colors? If he deceives them about this, what prevents him from so doing with regard to extension? This second deception would not be less innocent, nor less compatible with the nature of a supremely perfect being than the first deception is. If he does not deceive mankind with regard to colors, this is no doubt because he does not irresistibly force them to say, 'These colors exist outside of my mind', but only, 'It seems to me that there are colors there.' The same thing could be said with regard to extension. God does not irresistibly force you to say, 'There is some,' but only to judge that you are aware of it and that it seems to you that there is some. A Cartesian has no more difficulty in suspending judgment on the existence of extension than a peasant has in forbearing affirming that the sun shines, that snow is white, and so on. That is why, if we deceive ourselves in affirming the existence of extension, God would not be the cause, since you grant that he is not the cause of the peasant's errors. These are the advantages that the new philosophers would give to the Pyrrhonists and which I will not use here."

Right afterwards, the philosophical *abbé* declared to the other that if one had any hopes of victory over the skeptics, one would have to prove to them first of all that truth is certainly recognizable by certain marks. These are commonly called the criterion of truth (*criterium*

2. The Abbé Foucher proposed this objection in his *Critique de la recherche de la vérité.* Father Malebranche made no reply to it. He realized how strong it was. See footnote 3, following.

3. Father Malebranche, in *Eclaircissement sur la recherche de la vérité,* shows that "it is extremely difficult to prove that there are bodies and that faith alone can convince us that bodies actually exist."

4. Cf. chap. 28 of Arnauld's *Traité des vrayes et des fausses idées,* where he refutes the above-mentioned *Eclaircissement* of Father Malebranche, by reasons all based on this principle.

veritatis). You could rightly maintain to him that self-evidence (*l'évidence*) is the sure characteristic of truth; for if self-evidence were not, nothing else could be. "So be it," he will say to you. "It is right here that I have been waiting for you. I will make you see that some things you reject as false are as evident as can be. (1) It is evident that things which are not different from a third thing are not different from each other. This is the foundation of all of our reasonings, and it is on this that we base all our syllogisms. And nevertheless, the revelation of the mystery of the Trinity assures us that this axiom is false. Invent as many distinctions as you please, you will never be able to show that this maxim of logic is not denied by this great mystery. (2) It is evident that there is no difference between an individual, a nature, and a person. However, this same mystery has convinced us that persons can be multiplied without the individuals and the natures ceasing to be unique. . . . (4) It is evident that a human body cannot be in several places at the same time and that its head cannot be penetrated with all the rest of its parts into an indivisible point. And nevertheless, the mystery of the Eucharist teaches us that these two things happen every day.[5] From whence it follows that neither you nor I can be certain whether we are distinct from other men, or whether we are at this moment in the seraglio at Constantinople, in Canada, in Japan, and in every city of the world, under different conditions in each place. Since God does nothing in vain, would he create many men when one, created in various places and possessing different qualities according to the places, would suffice? By this doctrine we lose the truths that we found in numbers, for we no longer know how much two and three are. We do not know what constitutes unity or diversity. If we judge that John and Peter are two men, it is only because we see them in different places and because one does not have all the properties of the other. But the basis for this distinction is destroyed by the Eucharist. Perhaps there is only one creature in the whole universe, produced many times in several places and with a diversity of qualities. We make great rules of arithmetic as if there were many distinct things.[6] All is illusory. Not only do we not know if there are

5. Note that it is an *abbé* who is speaking. I am obliged to add this, in the second edition, because several Protestants have been shocked to see the mystery of the Trinity and that of the Incarnation put on the same level as the dogma of the real presence and that of transubstantiation.

6. Note that if a body may be produced in several places, every other being—spirit, place, accident, etc.—may be multiplied in the same manner; and thus there will not be a multitude of beings, but all will be reduced to one sole created being.

two bodies; we do not even know if there is a body and a spirit. For if matter is penetrable, it is clear that extension is only an accident of bodies, and thus that body, according to its essence, is an unextended substance. It can then have all the attributes that we conceive of as belonging to spirit—understanding, will, passions, sensations. Therefore, there is no longer any standard for discerning if a substance is spiritual by nature or if it is corporeal. (5) It is evident that the modes of a substance cannot subsist without that which they modify. Nevertheless, we know by the mystery of transubstantiation that this is false. This confuses all our ideas. There is no longer any means of defining substance; for if the accidents can subsist without any subject, then substance in its turn can subsist dependent on another substance in the way accidents do. Mind could exist in the way bodies do, just as in the Eucharist matter exists in the way minds do. The latter could be impenetrable, just as matter becomes penetrable in the mystery. Now, if in passing from the darkness of paganism to the light of the Gospel, we have learned the falsity of so many self-evident notions and so many certain definitions, what will it be like when we pass from the obscurity of this life to the glory of paradise? Is it not very obvious that we will learn the falsity of thousands of things that now seem incontestable? Let us profit from the temerity with which those who lived before the Gospel tidings affirmed to us as true certain self-evident doctrines whose falsity has been revealed to us by the mysteries of our theology.

"Let us turn to ethics. (1) It is evident that we ought to prevent evil if we can and that we sin if we allow it when we can prevent it. However, our theology shows us that this is false. It teaches us that God does nothing unworthy of his perfections when he permits all the disorders in the world which he could easily have prevented. (2) It is evident that a creature who does not exist cannot be an accomplice in an evil action. (3) And that it is unjust to punish him as an accomplice of that action. Nevertheless, our doctrine of original sin shows us the falsity of these evident truths. (4) It is evident that we ought to prefer what is righteous to what is profitable; and that the more holy a being is, the less it is allowed to prefer what is profitable to what is righteous. Nevertheless, our theologians tell us that God, having to choose between a world perfectly regulated, adorned with every virtue, and a world like ours, where sin and disorder predominate, preferred ours to the other as suiting better the interest of his glory. You are going to tell me that the duties of the creator should not be measured by our standards. But, if you do this, you fall into the nets of your adversaries. This is where they want you. Their major aim is to prove that the absolute nature of things is unknown to us and that we can know them only relatively. We do not know, they say, if sugar is sweet in itself. We know only that it appears sweet when it is placed on our tongues. We do not know if a certain action is righteous in itself and by its nature. We only believe that with regard to such a person, with respect to certain circumstances, it has the appearance of righteousness. But it is something else in other respects and other relations. Behold then what you are exposed to when you say that the ideas we have of justice and righteousness admit of exceptions and are relative. Consider also that the more you elevate the power or right of God not to act according to our ideas, the more you destroy the one means you have left for proving the existence of bodies, namely, that God does not deceive us, and that he would if there were no corporeal world. To show a whole people a sight or spectacle that does not exist outside their minds would be a deception. You might wish to answer that one should distinguish two cases. If a king did it, it would be a deception; but if God does it, it is not; for the obligations of a king and of God are quite different. Besides this, if the exceptions you make to the principles of morality are based on the infinite incomprehensibility of God, then I can never be sure of anything. For I can never be able to comprehend the whole extent of the rights and privileges of God. And now I conclude. If there were a mark or characteristic by which truth could certainly be known, this would be self-evidence. Now, self-evidence is not such a mark since it is compatible with falsities. Therefore, etc."

The *abbé* to whom this long disclosure was directed could hardly forbear interrupting it. He listened to it with pain; and when he saw that no one else was speaking, he flew into a rage against the Pyrrhonists and did not spare the other *abbé* for mentioning the difficulties that he drew from the systems of theology. He was answered modestly that one knew very well that these difficulties were sophisms and trivialities, but that it would be good if those who were so haughty to the skeptics were aware of what the state of things is. "You believed up to now," he was told, "that a Pyrrhonist could not puzzle you. Answer me, therefore; you are forty-five years old; you do not doubt this. And, if you are sure of anything, it is that you are the same person to whom the abbey of ——— was given two years ago. I will show you that you have no good reason at all to be certain of this. I shall argue from the principles of our theology. Your soul has been created. God must therefore renew its existence every moment, for the preservation of creatures is a continual creation. How do you know that this very morning God did not allow that soul, which he continually created from the first moments of your life until now, to fall back into nothingness. How do you know that he has not created another soul with modifications like the ones yours had?[7] This new soul is the one that you have at the moment. Show me what is wrong with my argument and let those present judge the merits of my case." A learned theologian[8] who was present spoke up and acknowledged that once creation was supposed, it was just as easy for God to create a new soul at every moment as it was to reproduce the same soul; but that nevertheless, the ideas of his wisdom, and still more the light that we draw from his Word, are able to give us a legitimate certainty that we have the identical soul today that we had yesterday, the day before that, and so on. He concluded that it was wrong to waste time disputing with the Pyrrhonists or to imagine that their sophisms can be easily eluded by the mere force of reason; that it was necessary above all to make them feel the infirmity of reason so that this feeling might lead them to have recourse to a better guide, which is faith. This is the subject of the following remark.

¶ Remark C

. . . When one is able to comprehend well all the tropes set forth by Sextus Empiricus for suspending judgment, one realizes that this logic is the greatest effort of subtlety that the human mind has been able to accomplish. But, at the same time, one sees that this subtlety is in no way satisfactory. It confounds itself; for if it were solid, it would prove that it is certain that we ought to be in doubt. There would then be some certitude; there would then be a criterion or sure rule of truth. Now this ruins that system, but do not fear that it will come to this, the reasons for doubting being themselves doubtful. We must then doubt if it is necessary to doubt. How great a chaos, and how great a torment for the human mind! It seems therefore that this unfortunate state is the most proper one of all for convincing us that our reason is a path that leads us astray since, when it displays itself with the greatest subtlety, it plunges us into such an abyss. The natural conclusion of this ought to be to renounce this guide and to implore the

7. That is, with the memories he would have reproduced had he continued to create the soul of the *abbé*.

8. [In Bayle's last work, the *Entretiens de Maxime et de Themiste,* it is revealed that this "learned theologian" is none other than Pierre Bayle himself.]

cause of all things to give us a better one. This is a great step toward the Christian religion; for it requires that we look to God for knowledge of what we ought to believe and what we ought to do, and that we enslave our understanding to the obeisance of faith. . . .

ZENO OF ELEA

¶ Remark G

. . . *The modes of suspending judgment employed against the existence of extension.* Add to this that all the means of suspending judgment that overthrow the reality of corporeal qualities also overthrow the reality of extension. Since the same bodies are sweet to some men and bitter to others, one is right in inferring that they are neither sweet nor bitter in themselves and absolutely speaking. The "new" philosophers, although they are not skeptics, have so well understood the bases of suspension of judgment with regard to sounds, smells, heat, cold, hardness, softness, heaviness and lightness, tastes, colors, and the like, that they teach that all these qualities are perceptions of our soul and that they do not exist at all in the objects of our senses. Why should we not say the same thing about extension? If an entity that has no color appears to us, however, with a determinate color with respect to its species, shape, and location, why could not an entity that had no extension be visible to us under an appearance of a determinate, shaped, and located extension of a certain type? And notice carefully that the same body appears to us to be small or large, round or square, according to the place from which it is viewed; and let us have no doubts that a body that seems very small to us appears very large to a fly. It is not then by their own real or absolute extension that bodies present themselves to our minds. We can therefore conclude that they are not extended in themselves. Would you dare to reason in this way today, "Since certain bodies appear sweet to one man, sour to another, bitter to a third, and so on, I ought to affirm that in general they are savory, though I do not know what savor belongs to them absolutely and in themselves"? All the "new" philosophers would hoot at you. Why then would you dare to say, "Since certain bodies appear large to one animal, medium to another, and very small to a third, I ought to affirm that in general they are extended, though I do not know their absolute extension"? . . .

¶ Remark H

H. (*The proofs that reason furnishes us of the existence of matter are not evident enough to furnish a good demonstration on this point.*) There are two philosophical axioms that teach us: the one, that nature does nothing in vain; and the other, that it is useless to do by several methods what may be done by fewer means with the same ease. By these two axioms the Cartesians I am speaking of can maintain that no bodies exist; for whether they exist or not, God is equally able to communicate to us all the thoughts that we have. It is no proof at all that there are bodies to say that our senses assure us of this with the utmost evidence. They deceive us with regard to all of the corporeal qualities, the magnitude, size, and motion of bodies not excepted;[9] and when we believe them about these latter qualities, we are also convinced that there exist outside our souls a great many colors, tastes, and other entities that we call hardness, fluidity, cold, heat, and the like. However it is not true that anything like these exists outside our minds. Why then should we trust our senses with regard to extension? It can very easily be reduced to appearance, just like colors. . . . Thirdly, it is useful to know that a Father of the Oratory, as illustrious for his piety as for his philosophical knowledge, maintained that faith alone can truly convince us of the existence of bodies. Neither the Sorbonne, nor any other tribunal, gave him the least trouble on that account. The Italian inquisitors did not disturb Fardella, who maintained the same thing in a printed work. This ought to show my readers that they must not find it strange that I sometimes point out that, concerning the most mysterious matters in the Gospel, reason gets us nowhere, and thus we ought to be completely satisfied with the light of faith. . . .

MANICHEANS

¶ Remark D

. . . The most certain and the clearest ideas of order teach us that a Being who exists by himself, who is necessary, who is eternal, must be one, infinite, all-powerful, and endowed with every kind of perfection. Thus, by consulting these ideas, one finds that there is nothing

9. See Malebranche.

more absurd than the hypothesis of two principles, eternal and independent of each other, one of which has no goodness and can stop the plans of the other. These are what I call the a priori arguments. They lead us necessarily to reject this hypothesis and to admit only one principle in all things. If this were all that was necessary to determine the goodness of a theory, the trial would be over, to the confusion of Zoroaster and all his followers. But every theory has need of two things in order to be considered a good one: first, its ideas must be distinct; and second, it must account for experience. It is necessary then to see if the phenomena of nature can be easily explained by the hypothesis of a single principle. When the Manicheans tell us that, since many things are observed in the world that are contrary to one another—cold and heat, white and black, light and darkness—therefore there necessarily are two principles, they argue pitifully. The opposition that exists among these entities, fortified as much as one likes by what are called variations, disorders, irregularities of nature, cannot make half an objection against the unity, simplicity, and immutability of God. All these matters are explained either by the various faculties that God has given to bodies, or by the laws of motion he has established, or by the concourse of intelligent occasional causes by which he has been pleased to regulate himself. . . . The heavens and the whole universe declare the glory, the power, and the unity of God. Man alone—this masterpiece of his Creation among the visible things—man alone, I say, furnishes some very great objections against the unity of God. Here is how:

Man is wicked and miserable. Everybody is aware of this from what goes on within himself, and from the commerce he is obliged to carry on with his neighbor. It suffices to have been alive for five or six years to be completely convinced of these two truths. Those who live long and who are much involved in worldly affairs know this still more clearly. Travel gives continual lessons of this. Monuments to human misery and wickedness are found everywhere—prisons, hospitals, gallows, and beggars. Here you see the ruins of a flourishing city; in other places you cannot even find the ruins. . . . Properly speaking, history is nothing but the crimes and misfortunes of the human race. But let us observe that these two evils, the one moral and the other physical, do not encompass all history or all private experience. Both moral good and physical good are found everywhere, some examples of virtue, some examples of happiness; and this is what causes the difficulty. For if all mankind were wicked and miserable, there would be no need to have recourse to the hypothesis of two principles. It is the mixture of happiness and virtue with misery and vice that requires this hypothesis. It is in this that the strength of the sect of Zoroaster lies. . . .

To make people see how difficult it would be to refute this false system, and to make them conclude that it is necessary to have recourse to the light of revelation in order to destroy it, let us suppose here a dispute between Melissus and Zoroaster. They were both pagans and great philosophers. Melissus, who acknowledged only one principle, would say at the outset that his theory agrees admirably with the ideas of order. The necessary Being has no limits. He is therefore infinite and all-powerful, and thus he is one. And it would be both monstrous and inconsistent if he did not have goodness and did have the greatest of all vices—an essential malice. "I confess to you," Zoroaster would answer, "that your ideas are well connected; and I shall willingly acknowledge that in this respect your hypothesis surpasses mine. I will renounce an objection that I could employ, which is that infinity ought to comprehend all that is real, and malice is not less real than goodness.[10] Therefore the universe should require that there be wicked beings and good beings. And since supreme goodness and supreme malice cannot subsist in one subject, it is the case that in the nature of things there must be an essentially good being, and another essentially bad being. I renounce, I say, this objection. I allow you the advantage of being more conformable to the notion of order than I am. But by your hypothesis explain a little to me how it happens that man is wicked and so subject to pain and grief. I defy you to find in your principles the explanation of this phenomenon, as I can find it in mine. I then regain the advantage. You surpass me in the beauty of ideas and in a priori reasons, and I surpass you in the explanation of phenomena and in a posteriori reasons. And since the chief characteristic of a good system is its being capable of accounting for experience, and since the mere incapacity of accounting for it is a proof that a hypothesis is not good, however fine it appears to be in other respects, you must grant that I hit the nail on the head by admitting two principles and that you miss it by admitting only one."

Doubtless we are now at the main point of the whole affair. Here is the great chance for Melissus. . . . Let us continue to listen to Zoroaster.

"If man is the work of a single supremely good, supremely holy, supremely powerful principle, is it possible that he can be exposed to illnesses, to cold, to heat, to hunger, to thirst, to pain, to vexation? Is it

10. That is to say, malicious action. I add this note so that one cannot tell me that evil is only a privation.

possible he should have so many bad inclinations and commit so many crimes? Is it possible that the supreme holiness would produce so criminal a creature? Is it possible that the supreme goodness would produce so unhappy a creature? Would not the supreme power joined to an infinite goodness pour down blessings upon its work and defend it from everything that might annoy or trouble it?" If Melissus consults the ideas of order, he will answer that man was not wicked when God created him. He will say that man received a happy state from God, but not having followed the lights of his conscience, which according to the intention of his author would have conducted him along the virtuous path, he became wicked, and he deserved that the supremely just and supremely good God made him feel the effects of His wrath. Then it is not God who is the cause of moral evil; but he is the cause of physical evil, that is to say, the punishment of moral evil—punishment which, far from being incompatible with the supremely good principle, necessarily flows from one of God's attributes, I mean that of justice, which is no less essential to man than God's goodness. This answer, the most reasonable that Melissus could make, is basically fine and sound. But it can be combatted by arguments which have something in them more specious and dazzling. For Zoroaster would not fail to set forth that, if man were the work of an infinitely good and holy principle, he would have been created not only with no actual evil but also without any inclination to evil, since that inclination is a defect that cannot have such a principle for a cause. It remains then to be said that, when man came from the hands of his creator, he had only the power of self-determination to evil, and that since he determined himself in that way, he is the sole cause of the crime that he committed and the moral evil that was introduced into the universe. But, (1) we have no distinct idea that could make us comprehend how a being not self-existent should, however, be the master of its own actions. Then Zoroaster will say that the free will given to man is not capable of giving him an actual determination since its being is continuously and totally supported by the action of God. (2) He will pose this question, "Did God foresee that man would make bad use of his free will?" If the answer is affirmative he will reply that it appears impossible to foresee what depends entirely on an undetermined cause. "But I will readily agree with you," he will say, "that God foresaw the sin of his creature; and I conclude from this that he would have prevented it; for the ideas of order will not allow that an infinitely good and holy cause that can prevent the introduction of moral evil does not stop it, especially when by permitting it he will find himself obliged to pour down pains and torments upon his own work. If God did not foresee the fall of man, he must at least have judged that it was possible; therefore, since he saw he would be obliged to abandon his paternal goodness if the fall ever did occur, only to make his children miserable by exercising upon them the role of a severe judge, he would have determined man to moral good as he has determined him to physical good. He would not have left in man's soul any power for carrying himself toward sin, just as he did not leave any power for carrying himself toward misery in so far as it was misery. This is where we are led by the clear and distinct ideas of order when we follow, step by step, what an infinitely good principle ought to do. For, if a goodness as limited as that of a human father necessarily requires that he prevent as much as possible the bad use which his children might make of the goods he gives them, much more will an infinite and all-powerful goodness prevent the bad effects of its gifts. Instead of giving them free will, it will determine its creatures to good; or if it gives them free will, it will always efficiently watch over them to prevent their falling into sin." I very well believe that Melissus would not be silenced at this point, but whatever he might answer would be immediately combatted by reasons as plausible as his, and thus the dispute would never terminate. . . .

A thousand great difficulties could be proposed to this philosopher; but as he would still find answers and after that demand that he be given a better hypothesis and claim that he had thoroughly refuted that of Melissus, he would never be led back to the truth. Human reason is too feeble for this. It is a principle of destruction and not of edification. It is only proper for raising doubts, and for turning things on all sides in order to make disputes endless; and I do not think I am mistaken if I say of natural revelation, that is to say, the light of reason, what the theologians say of the Mosaic Dispensation. They say that it was only fit for making man realize his own weakness and the necessity of a redeemer and a law of grace. It was a teacher —these are their terms—to lead us to Jesus Christ. Let us say almost the same thing about reason. It is only fit to make man aware of his own blindness and weakness, and the necessity for another revelation. That is the one of Scripture. It is there that we find the means to refute invincibly the hypothesis of the two principles and all the objections of Zoroaster. There we find the unity of God and his infinite perfections, the fall of the first man, and what follows from it. Let someone tell us with a great apparatus of arguments that it is not possible that moral evil should introduce itself into the world by the work of an infinitely good and holy principle, we will answer that this however is in fact the case, and therefore this is very possible. There is nothing more foolish than to argue against the facts. . . .

THE THIRD CLARIFICATION

. . . Now, of all the philosophers who ought not to be permitted to dispute about the mysteries of Christianity until they have accepted Revelation as the criterion, there are none as unworthy of being heard as the followers of Pyrrhonism; for they are people who profess to acknowledge no certain sign that distinguishes the true from the false; so that if, by chance, they came across the truth, they could never be sure that it was the truth. They are not satisfied with opposing the testimony of the senses, the maxims of morality, the rules of logic, and the axioms of metaphysics; they also try to overthrow the demonstrations of the geometers, and all that the mathematicians can produce of the most evident character. If they stopped at the ten modes or tropes for suspending judgment,[11] and if they had limited themselves to employing them against natural science, they could still be dealt with. But they go much further; they have a kind of weapon that they call the *diallelos*,[12] which they wield at the first instant it is needed. After this is done, it is impossible to withstand them on any subject whatsoever. It is a labyrinth in which the thread of Ariadne cannot be of any help. They lose themselves in their own subtleties; and they are overjoyed at this, since this serves to show more clearly the universality of their hypothesis, that all is uncertain, not even excepting the arguments that attack uncertainty. Their method leads people so far that those who have really seen the consequences of it are forced to admit that they do not know if anything exists.

Theologians should not be ashamed to admit that they cannot enter a contest with such antagonists, and that they do not want to expose the Gospel truths to such an attack. The bark of Jesus Christ is not made for sailing on this stormy sea, but for taking shelter from this tempest in the haven of faith. It has pleased the Father, the Son, and

11. [These are the set of arguments appearing in Sextus Empiricus, *Pyrrhoniarum hypotoposeon* I. 14, dealing mainly with sense data, relativism, and the like.]

12. [This weapon purports to show that the adversary is involved in either circular reasoning or an infinite regress.]

the Holy Ghost, Christians ought to say, to lead us by the path of faith, and not by the path of knowledge or disputation. They are our teachers and our directors. We cannot lose our way with such guides. And reason itself commands us to prefer them to its direction. . . .

. . . One must necessarily choose between philosophy and the Gospel. If you do not want to believe anything but what is evident and in conformity with the common notions, choose philosophy and leave Christianity. If you are willing to believe the incomprehensible mysteries of religion, choose Christianity and leave philosophy. For to have together self-evidence and incomprehensibility is something that cannot be. The combination of these two items is hardly more impossible than the combination of the properties of a square and a circle. A choice must necessarily be made. If the advantages of a round table do not satisfy you, have a square one made; and do not pretend that the same table could furnish you with the advantages of both a round table and a square one. Once again, a true Christian, well versed in the characteristics of supernatural truths and firm on the principles that are peculiar to the Gospel, will only laugh at the subtleties of the philosophers, and especially those of the Pyrrhonists. Faith will place him above the regions where the tempests of disputation reign. He will stand on a peak, from which he will hear below him the thunder of arguments and distinctions; and he will not be disturbed at all by this—a peak, which will be for him the real Olympus of the poets and the real temple of the sages, from which he will see in perfect tranquility the weaknesses of reason and the meanderings of mortals who only follow that guide. Every Christian who allows himself to be disconcerted by the objections of the unbelievers, and to be scandalized by them, has one foot in the same grave as they do. . . .

Nothing is more necessary than faith, and nothing is more important than to make people aware of the price of this theological virtue. Now, what is there that is more suitable for making us aware of this than meditating on the attitude that distinguishes it from the other acts of the understanding? Its essence consists in binding us to the revealed truths by a strong conviction, and in binding us to these solely by the motive of God's authority. Those who believe in the immortality of the soul on the basis of philosophical reasons are orthodox, but so far they have no share in the faith of which we are speaking. They only have a share in it insofar as they believe this doctrine because God has revealed it to us, and they submit humbly to the voice of God everything that philosophy presents to them that is most plausible for convincing them of the mortality of the soul. Thus, the merit of faith becomes greater in proportion as the revealed truth that is its object surpasses all the powers of our mind; for, as the incomprehensibility of this object increases by the greater number of maxims of the natural light that oppose it, we have to sacrifice to God's authority a stronger reluctance of reason; and consequently we show ourselves more submissive to God, and we give him greater signs of our respect than if the item were only moderately difficult to believe. Why was it, I ask you, that the faith of the Father of the faithful [Abraham] was of so great a degree? Is it not because it was he "who against hope believed in hope" (Romans 4:18)? There would not have been very much merit in hoping, on the basis of God's promise, for something that was very probable naturally. The merit therefore consisted in this, that the hope of this promise was opposed by all kinds of appearances. Let us say also that the highest degree of faith is that which embraces on divine testimony truths that are the most opposed to reason.

This view has been set forth in a ridiculous light, coming from the pen of a master. "The devil take me if I believed anything," the Maréchal d'Hocquincourt is made to say, "but since that time I could bear to be crucified for religion. It is not that I see more reason in it than I did before; on the contrary, I see less than ever. But I know not what to say to you, for I would submit to be crucified without knowing why or wherefore." "So much the better, my Lord," replied the father, twanging it very devoutly through the nose, "so much the better; these are not human impulses but are inspired by heaven. Away with reason; this is the true religion, away with reason. What an extraordinary grace, my Lord, has heaven bestowed upon you! 'Be ye as little children.' Children are still in their state of innocence; and why? Because they are not endowed with reason. 'Blessed are the poor in spirit.' They commit no sin, and for this reason, because they are not endowed with reason. 'No reason; I know not why nor wherefore.' Beautiful words! They ought to be written in gold letters. 'It is not that I see more reason in it than I did before; on the contrary, I see less than ever.' This is really altogether divine to those who delight in celestial things. 'Away with reason.' What an extraordinary grace, my Lord, has heaven bestowed upon you."[13] If one gives this passage a more serious and modest air, it will become reasonable. . . .

13. "Conversation between Maréchal d'Hocquincourt and Father Canaye," in *Oeuvres mêlées de St. Evremont,* Vol. IV.

BIBLIOGRAPHY

I. General histories of philosophy covering the sixteenth and seventeenth centuries

George Boas, *Dominant Themes of Modern Philosophy, a History* (New York, 1957); Emile Bréhier, *Histoire de la philosophie* (Paris, 1960), Vol. II, Part I is about the seventeenth century; James D. Collins, *A History of Modern European Philosophy* (Milwaukee, 1961); Frederick C. Copleston, *A History of Philosophy* (Westminster, Md., 1959-1962), Vol. III is on Ockham to Suarez, Vol. IV on Descartes to Leibniz, and Vol. V on Hobbes to Hume; Kuno Fischer, *Geschichte der neueren Philosophie* (Heidelberg, 1897-1904, 10 vols., 3rd ed.), includes volumes on Bacon, Descartes, Spinoza and Leibniz—the first two appeared in English (London, 1857) and (New York, 1887); Harold Hoffding, *A History of Modern Philosophy,* trans. B. E. Meyer (New York, 1950, 2 vols.); D. J. O'Connor, (ed.), *A Critical History of Western Philosophy* (New York, 1964) is a series of essays by leading contemporary philosophers on various historical figures; John Herman Randall, *The Career of Philosophy: from the Middle Ages to the Enlightenment* (New York, 1962); Albert Rivaud, *Histoire de la philosophie,* (Paris, 1960), Vol. III; Gaston Sortais, *La philosophie moderne depuis Bacon jusqu'à Leibniz* (Paris, 1922, 2 vols.)—the two completed volumes deal with Bacon, Gassendi, and Hobbes; Wilhelm Windelband, *History of Philosophy* (New York, 1958), Vol. II.

II. Studies of special problems and topics

Ernst Cassirer, *Das Erkenntnisproblem in der Philosophie und Wissenschaft der neueren Zeit* (Berlin, 1922); James D. Collins, *God in Modern Philosophy* (Chicago, 1959); Paul Dibon, *La philosophie néerlandaise au siècle d'or* (Amsterdam, 1954), covers the period from 1575 to 1650; Paul Hazard, *The European Mind 1680-1715,* trans. J. Lewis May (London, 1964); Arthur O. Lovejoy, *The Great Chain of Being* (Cambridge, Mass., 1948), Ch. IV and V; Richard H. Popkin, "The High Road to Pyrrhonism," *American Philosophical Quarterly,* II (1965) 1-15, on skepticism after

Descartes, and *The History of Scepticism from Erasmus to Descartes* (New York, 1964); Henry G. Van Leeuwen, *The Problem of Certainty in English Thought, 1630-1690* (The Hague, 1963); Richard A. Watson, *The Downfall of Cartesianism* (The Hague, 1965), on Cartesianism from 1675 onward.

III. The history of science in the sixteenth and seventeenth centuries

Edwin A. Burtt, *The Metaphysical Foundations of Modern Physical Science* (New York, 1955); Herbert Butterfield, *The Origins of Modern Science* (New York, 1958, rev. ed.); Alexandre Koyré, *Etudes galiléennes* (Paris, 1939, 3 vols.), and *From the Closed to the Infinite Universe* (New York, 1958); Robert Lenoble, *Mersenne ou la naissance de mécanisme* (Paris, 1943), and *"Les origines de la pensée scientifique moderne,"* in *Encyclopédie de la Pléiade, Histoire de la science*, ed. M. Daumes, pp. 369-534 (Paris, 1957); Edward W. Strong, *Procedures and Metaphysics* (Berkeley, 1936); René Taton, (ed.), *History of Science*, Vol. II: *The Beginnings of Modern Science* (New York, 1964), a translation of a series of important French studies; Richard S. Westfall, *Science and Religion in Seventeenth-Century England* (New Haven, 1958).

IV. The Renaissance

Germán Arciniegas, *Amerigo and The New World,* trans. Harriet de Onís (New York, 1955); Ernst Cassirer, *The Individual and the Cosmos in Renaissance Philosophy,* trans. Mario Domandi (New York, 1963); Ernst Cassirer, Paul O. Kristeller, and John Herman Randall, (eds.), *The Renaissance Philosophy of Man* (Chicago, 1956), translation of Italian Renaissance texts; Américo Castro, *The Structure of Spanish History* (Princeton, 1954); Neil W. Gilbert, *Renaissance Concepts of Method* (New York, 1960); Paul O. Kristeller, *Eight Philosophers of the Italian Renaissance* (Stanford, 1964), and *Renaissance Thought I* and *Renaissance Thought II* (New York, 1961, 1965); Francis A. Yates, *Giordano Bruno and the Heremetic Tradition* (Chicago, 1964).

V. Specific philosophers

Francis Bacon

Francis Bacon, *The Works of Francis Bacon,* eds. J. Spedding, R. L. Ellis, and D. D. Heath, (London 1857-1859, 7 vols.); Fulton H. Anderson, *The Philosophy of Francis Bacon* (Chicago, 1948).

Pierre Bayle

Pierre Bayle, *Dictionaire historique et critique* (Amsterdam, 1740, 5th ed., 4 vols.), of which the last complete English translation was in 1734-1740,

10 vols.; *Oeuvres diverses,* photoreproduction ed. Elisabeth Labrousse (Hildesheim, 1964) contains all of Bayle's works except the *Dictionary* and his letters; and *Selections from the Historical and Critical Dictionary,* trans. Richard H. Popkin (Indianapolis, 1965) contains selections from forty articles and Bayle's clarifications; Paul Dibon (ed.), *Pierre Bayle: Le philosophe de Rotterdam,* (Amsterdam, 1959) contains articles in French and English by several Bayle scholars; Elisabeth Labrousse, *Pierre Bayle* (The Hague, 1963-1964, 2 vols.).

René Descartes

René Descartes, *Oeuvres de Descartes,* eds. C. Adam and P. Tannery (Paris, 1897-1910, 13 vols.) is now being reprinted; *Discours de la méthode,* texte et commentaire par E. Gilson (Paris, 1947) is a detailed commentary providing an analysis of Descartes' thought and its background; *The Philosophical Works of Descartes,* trans. E. S. Haldane and G. T. R. Ross (New York, 1955, 2 vols.) is the most complete set of texts available in English); Henri Gouhier, *La pensée metaphysique de Descartes* (Paris, 1962), and *La pensée religieuse de Descartes* (Paris, 1924); Leon Roth, *Descartes' Discourse on Method* (Oxford, 1948); Gregor Sebba, *Bibliographia Cartesiana: A Critical Guide to the Descartes Literature, 1800-1960* (The Hague, 1964); Norman Kemp Smith, *New Studies in the Philosophy of Descartes* (New York, 1963), and *Studies in the Philosophy of Descartes* (New York, 1962).

Pierre Gassendi

Pierre Gassendi, *Opera omnia,* photoreproduction ed. T. Gregory (Stuttgart, 1964, 6 vols.); *Disquisitio metaphysica,* ed. and trans. (into French) Bernard Rochot (Paris, 1962); and *Dissertationes en forme de paradoxes contre les Aristotéliciens,* ed. and trans. Bernard Rochot (Paris, 1959); Bernard Rochot, *Les travaux de Gassendi sur Epicure et sur l'Atomisme* (Paris, 1944).

Thomas Hobbes

Thomas Hobbes, *The English Works of Thomas Hobbes,* ed. W. Molesworth (Aalen, 1962, 11 vols.), and *Opera philosophica quae latine scripsit omnia,* ed. W. Molesworth (Aalen, 1961, 5 vols.), photoreproductions of 1839-1845 ed.; S. L. Mintz, *The Hunting of Leviathan* (New York, 1962), on the seventeenth century reactions to Hobbes' views. J. W. N. Watkins, *Hobbes's System of Ideas* (New York, 1965).

Gottfried Wilhelm von Leibniz

Gottfried Wilhelm von Leibniz, *Opuscula philosophica selecta,* ed. P. Schrecker (Paris, 1939; French ed., Paris, 1962) contains six of Leibniz' important essays; *Opuscules et fragments inédits de Leibniz,* ed. L. Couturat (Hildesheim, 1961) is a collection of Leibniz' logical papers, photoreproduced from 1903 edition; *Die philosophischen Schriften,* ed. C. Gerhardt (Berlin, 1875-1890; photoreproduction ed., Hildesheim, 1960-1961, 7 vols.);

Philosophical Papers and Letters, trans. L. E. Loemker (Chicago, 1956, 2 vols.); *Sämtliche Schriften und Briefe* (Berlin, 1923) is the Berlin Academy edition that will be the first complete one when finished; and *Selections,* ed. P. P. Wiener (New York, 1951); Yvon Belaval, *Leibniz, critique de Descartes* (Paris, 1960); Herbert W. Carr, *Leibniz* (New York, 1960, reprint of 1929 ed.); Ernst Cassirer, *Leibniz's System in seinen wissenschaftlichen Grundlagen* (Hildesheim 1962, reprint of 1902 ed.); Gottfried Martin, *Leibniz: Logic and Metaphysics,* trans. K. J. Northcott and P. G. Lucas (New York, 1964); Bertrand Russell, *A Critical Exposition of the Philosophy of Leibniz* (London, 1958, 2nd ed.).

Nicolas Malebranche

Nicolas Malebranche, *Oeuvres complètes . . .*, ed. A. Robinet, (Paris, 1958, 20 vols.); *Oeuvres complètes,* ed. D. Roustan and P. Schrecker (Paris, 1938), of which only Vol. I, *De la recherche de la verité,* Livres I et II appeared, with excellent notes; and *Dialogues on Metaphysics and on Religion,* trans. M. Ginsburg (New York, 1923); Ralph W. Church, *A Study in the Philosophy of Malebranche* (London, 1931); Henri Gouhier, *Le philosophie de Malebranche et son expérience religieuse* (Paris, 1948, 2nd ed.); Genevieve Rodis-Lewis, *Nicolas Malebranche* (Paris, 1963); Beatrice Rome, *The Philosophy of Malebranche* (Chicago, 1963).

Michel de Montaigne

Michel de Montaigne, *Les essais de Montaigne,* ed. P. Villey (Paris, 1922, 3 vols.), and *The Complete Works of Montaigne,* trans. Donald M. Frame (Stanford, 1958); Donald M. Frame, *Montaigne's Discovery of Man, The Humanization of a Humanist* (New York, 1955).

Blaise Pascal

Blaise Pascal, *Oeuvres complètes . . .*, ed. L. Brunschvicg, P. Boutroux, F. Gazier (Paris, 1904-1914, 14 vols.), and *Oeuvres complètes,* preface by Henri Gouhier, ed. L. Lafuma (New York, 1963) contains revised text based on Lafuma's studies of the manuscripts.

Baruch Spinoza

Baruch de Spinoza, *Opera,* ed. C. Gebhardt (Heidelberg, 1925, 4 vols.); *The Chief Works of Spinoza,* trans. R. H. M. Elwes (New York, 1951, reprint of 1883 ed., 2 vols.); and *Earlier Philosophical Writings,* trans. F. A. Hayes, intro. D. A. Bidney (Indianapolis, 1963), contains *The Cartesian Principles* and *Thoughts on Metaphysics;* Harold F. Hallett, *Benedict de Spinoza: The Elements of his Philosophy* (London, 1957); Stuart Hampshire, *Spinoza* (Harmondsworth, 1951); Harold H. Joachim, *A Study of the Ethics of Spinoza* (New York, 1964, reprint); I. S. Révah, *Spinoza et le Dr. Juan de Prado* (Paris, 1959); Léon Roth, *Spinoza* (London, 1954), and *Spinoza, Descartes and Maimonides* (New York, 1963); Harry A. Wolfson, *The Philosophy of Spinoza* (New York, 1961.)

INDEX